CHARLES BANKS WILSON

GILCREASE MUSEUM | TULSA, OKLAHOMA

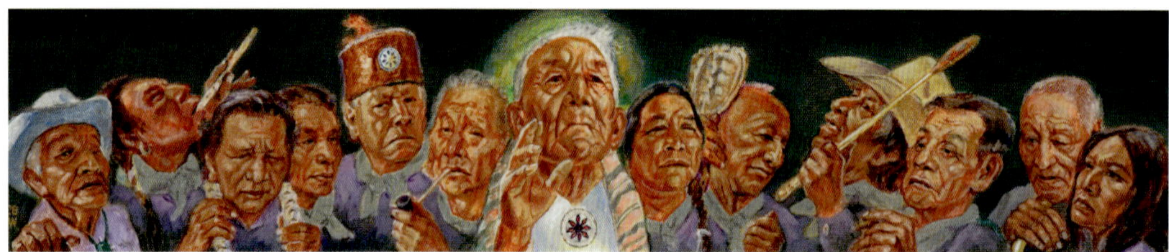

©2007 by Gilcrease Museum. All rights reserved.

GILCREASE MUSEUM

1400 NORTH GILCREASE MUSEUM ROAD

TULSA, OKLAHOMA 74127–2100

International Standard Book Number 978-0-9725657-3-8

Dimensions are given in inches, height preceding width.

Printed in Korea

SERIES CURATOR: Randy Ramer

SERIES EDITOR AND DESIGNER: Carol Haralson

ASSISTANT CURATORS: Carole Klein, Kim Roblin, and Kelly Finegan

PHOTOGRAPHER: Shane Culpepper

ABOVE: PRAY FOR MY PEOPLE, 2006. 8.25 X 37.25, COLLECTION OF THE ARTIST

"Art is a struggle to give meaning to experience. It is a lie which helps us picture the truth."

— CHARLES BANKS WILSON

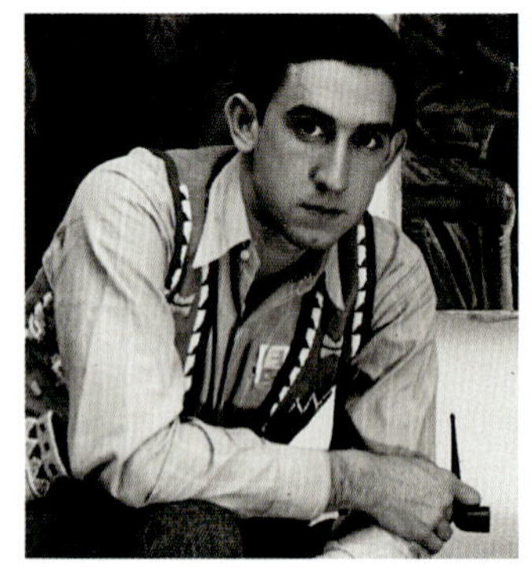

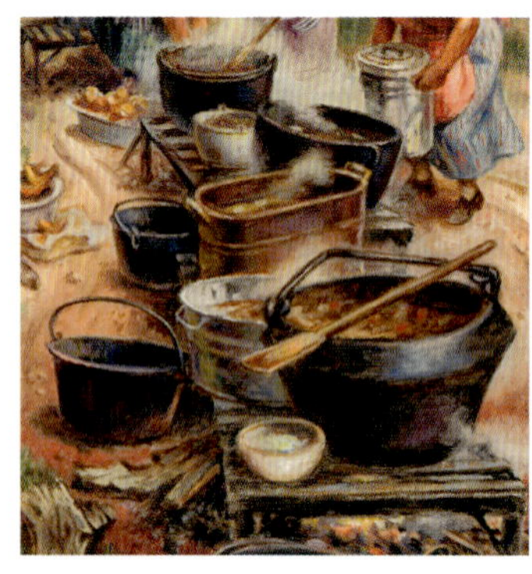

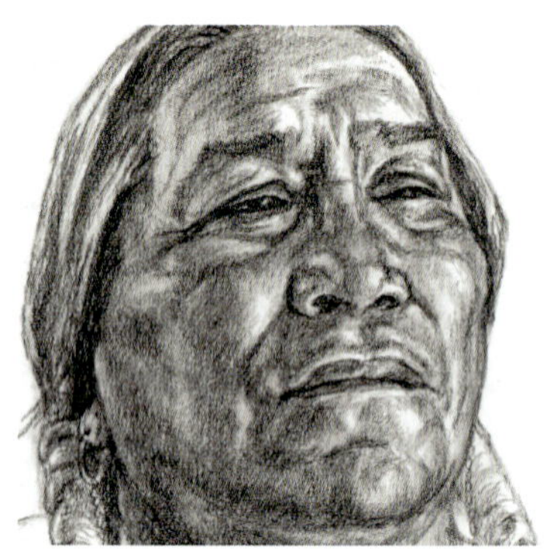

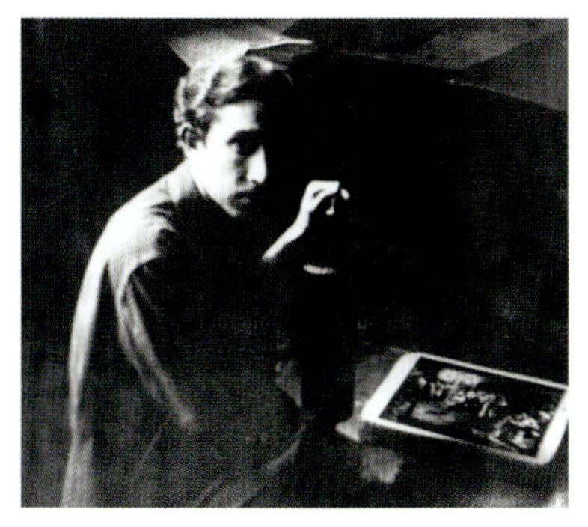

Wilson the Printmaker

119

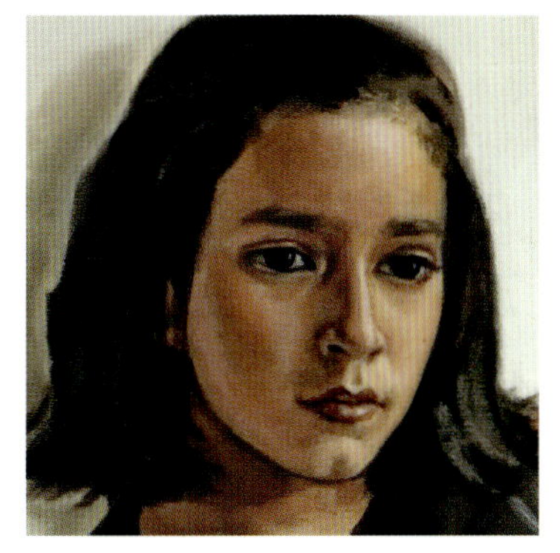

**A Human Face
Is the One Universal
Language**

159

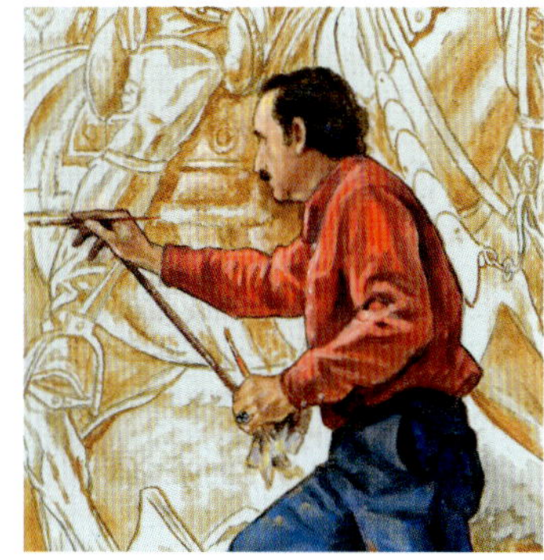

Art Large As Life

179

OKLAHOMA
TO CHICAGO TO
NEW YORK TO
OKLAHOMA

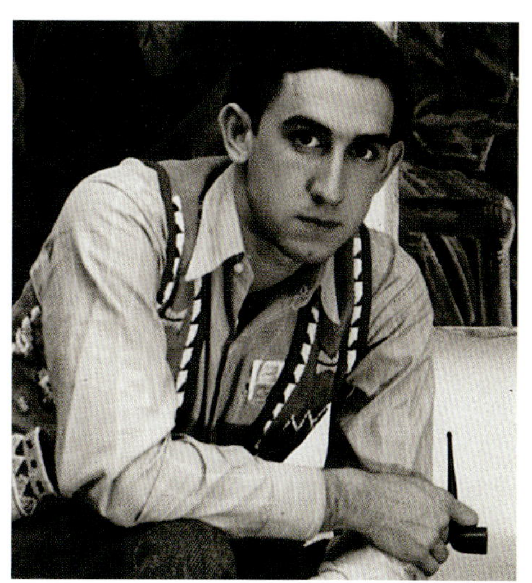

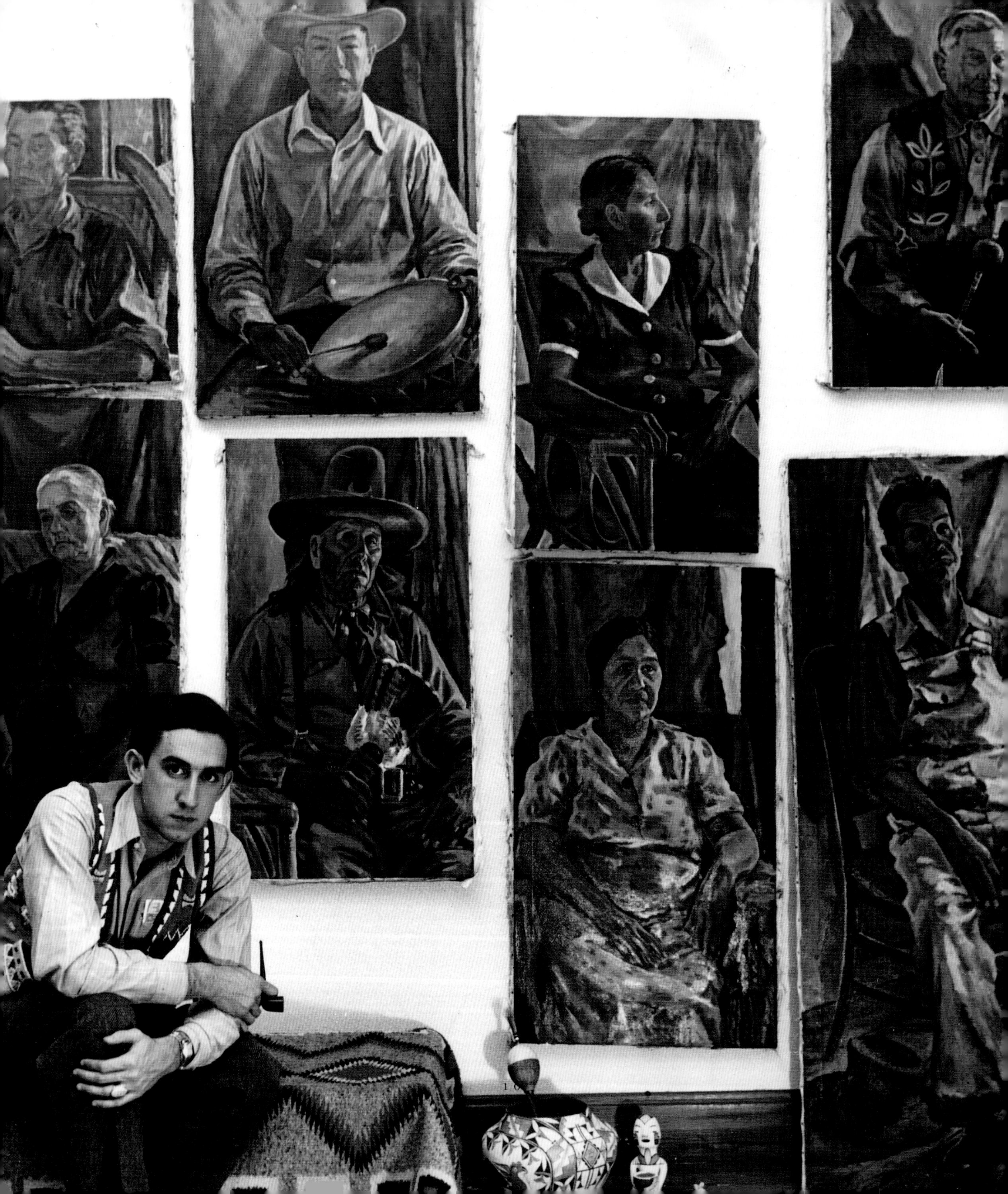

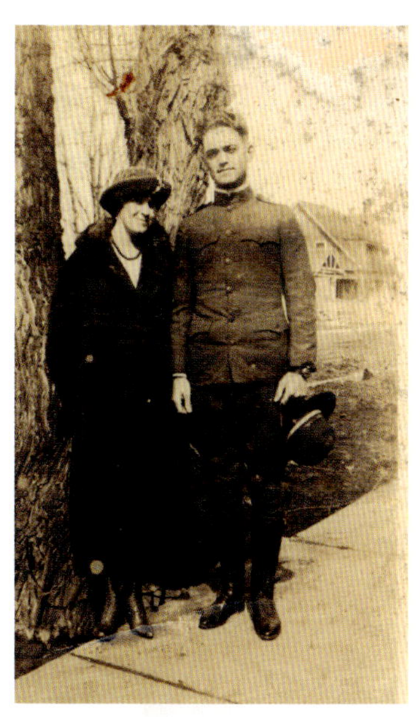

Bertha Banks Wilson and Charles Burtrum Wilson, ca. 1918. FACING: In the summers of 1938 and 1939, Charles Banks Wilson returned to Miami, Oklahoma, from the Chicago Art Institute and painted in a studio above his father's store on Main Street. The portraits seen here are among those completed during that time.

Charles Banks Wilson was born in Springdale, Arkansas, on August 6, 1918. His grandparents were pioneers who had moved to what was then Indian Territory in the early 1900s. Charles's paternal grandfather, John Joseph Wilson, had been a stagecoach driver and trapeze artist before settling down with his family in the town of Miami, in the northeast corner of what is now the state of Oklahoma. John Joseph worked as a house painter while his wife Carrie ran a local restaurant. Their son, Charles Burtrum, studied to be a professional trombone player. He later achieved success with a traveling band called Crawford's Comedians.

Charles Burtrum eventually returned to Miami to marry Bertha Banks, a local schoolteacher, and gave up the life of a traveling musician to work as a house painter. He was called to active duty in the U.S. Army in World War I, serving as a combat stretcher bearer in France. "My father never talked about the war," says Wilson. "I do know it affected him deeply." Indeed the only war story he would ever reveal was of how he received news of his son Charles's birth. Lonely for home and eager for news, men at the front commonly opened, read, and passed around any letters that managed

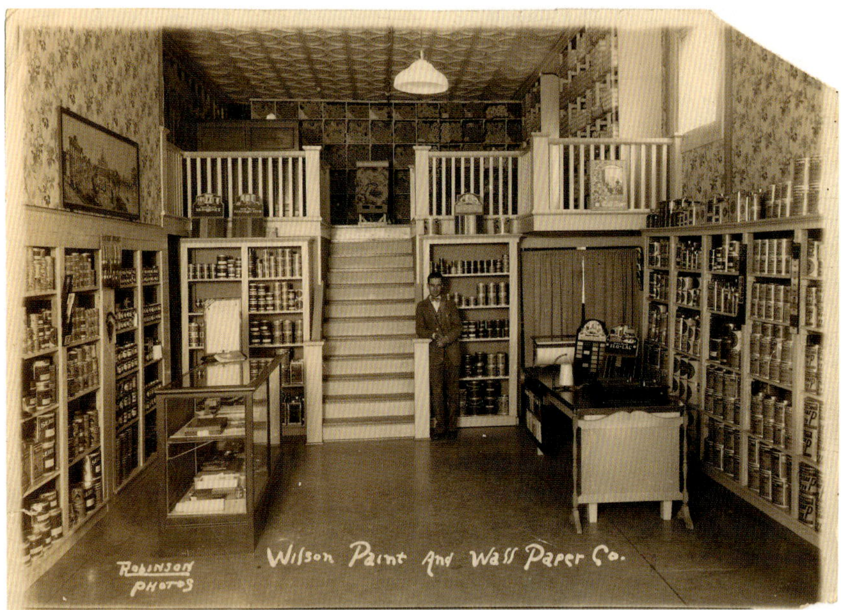

Wilson Paint and Wallpaper Co., on Main Street in Miami, Oklahoma, ca. 1930. BELOW: As a teenager, Wilson was an accomplished trick rope rider—like his idol, Will Rogers—and enjoyed performing in school theatricals.

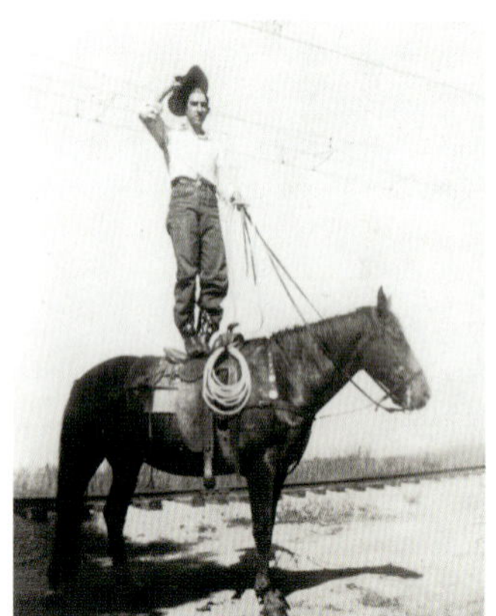

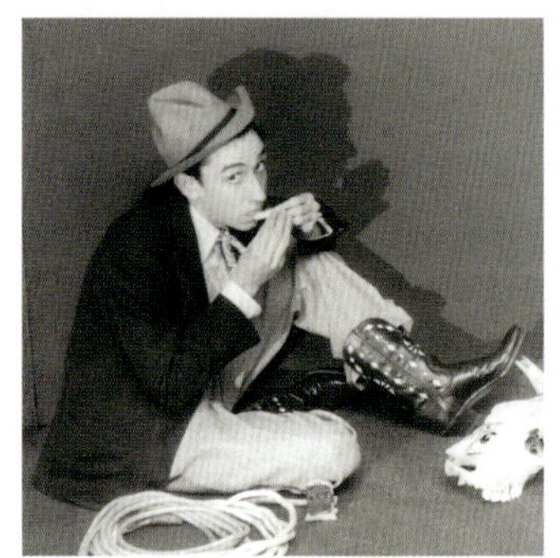

to make it to them. In the trenches, shells exploding around him, Charles's father was the last to read that his son had been born in the home of Bertha's parents in Springdale, Arkansas, where she had been staying the past several months.

Art was always present in Wilson's memories of childhood. Drawing was not something he aspired to do but simply something he did. "I would draw on anything I could get my hands on, the tops of paint boxes, the backs of pictures. I remember standing under the kitchen table—so I had to be very young—drawing on the underside of the table above my head."

Wilson's parents supported young Charles's efforts but it was his father's mother Carrie who would have the greatest influence on his early life. When he was still a boy, his grandmother lost her vision. Carrie and Charles developed a bond as he would sit with her to read the Bible or to listen to her stories. Young Charles became her eyes. As he described for her the people and places around them, Charles developed an attention to detail, the nuances of facial expression and the shapes of seemingly ordinary things in nature, that would later be central to his life's work.

As he grew, life in a town of some 8,000 had an important impact on young Charles's perspective of the world. "People had a great sense of propriety in those days. . . . They paid attention to the little things. . . . I recall my folks' parties with the women wearing evening gowns and the men in tuxedoes. . . . I still feel peculiar going out without wearing a tie." Throughout the 1920s and early 1930s, art remained a

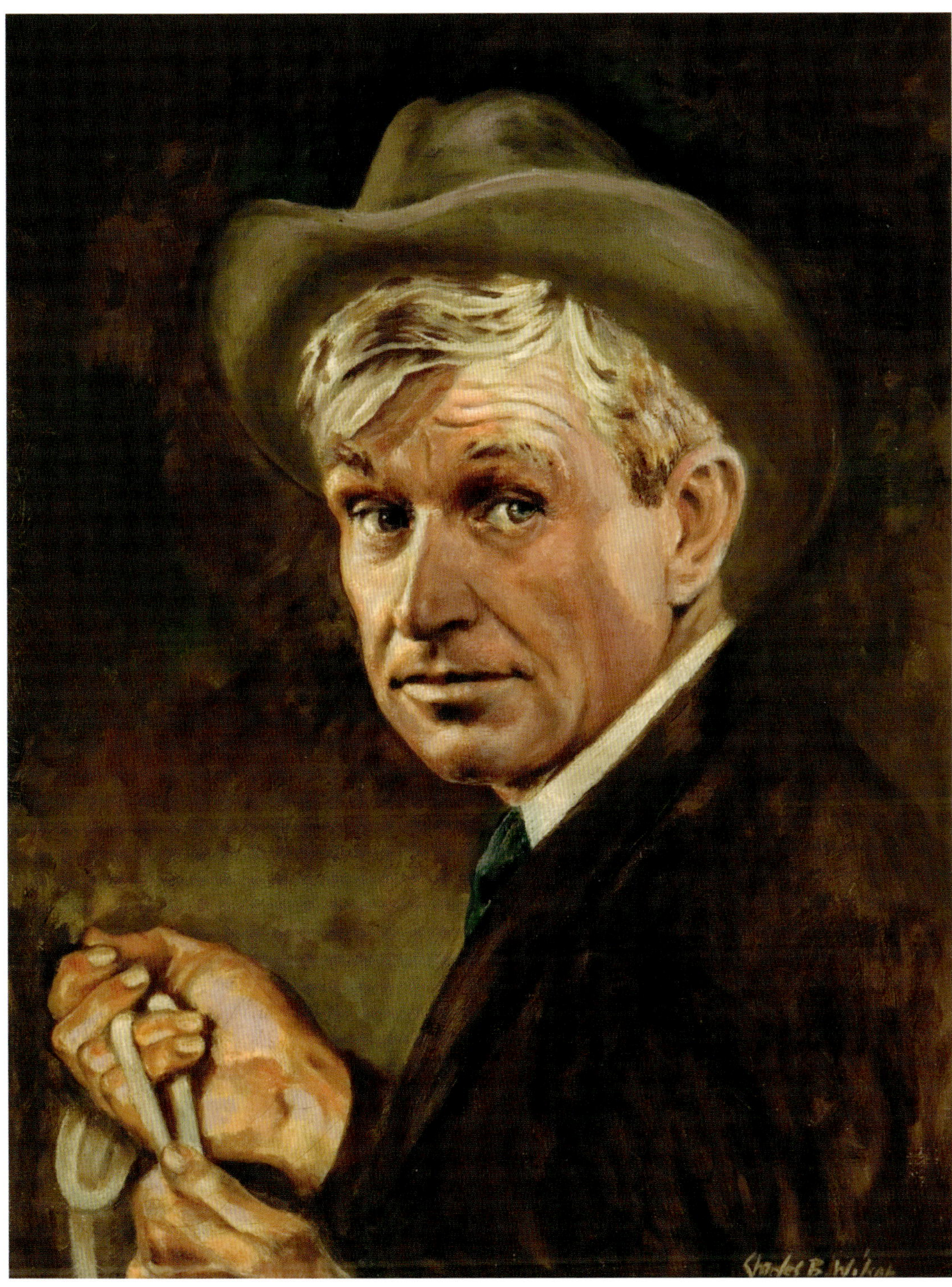

When he was fifteen, Wilson painted this oil of Will Rogers from life (undated, 26 x 18, from the artist's collection). It remains a favorite. CBW: *Some say it's my best. I guess I've gone downhill ever since.*

hobby for Wilson. His abilities did no go unnoticed, however. He drew sketches and cartoons to amuse his classmates and painted posters for the local theater.

Wilson's first painting was of Will Rogers, perhaps the most popular American of the time. "Like most boys my age, I admired Will Rogers immensely. I was simply in love with what he stood for." Like Rogers, Wilson was interested in the performing arts. He acted in local theater and performed in the marching band, even did stunts on horseback. "I think everyone dreams to be something they're not. I wanted to be an actor. Then I wanted to be a musician, like my father. I wanted to be a trick roper. I didn't choose to be in art—it chose me. . . . When I was young, I felt terribly uneducated and unworthy—but the same time capable of success."

Wilson left Miami after graduation in 1936 to attend the Art Institute of Chicago. Based on a sampling of his work, he was quickly enrolled in advanced art classes. "They put me in the upper level, so I missed out on all the basics," he recalls. He washed dishes to pay for his meals. "I had to walk several blocks to the Institute. It was so cold, I had to stop two or three times in stores along the way just to get warm."

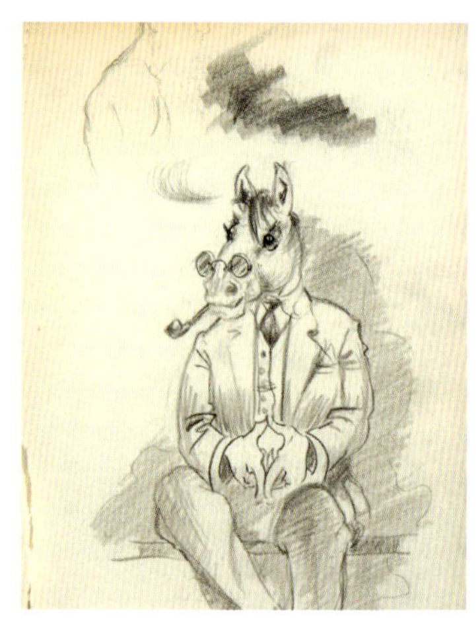

Drawings from the sketchbook Wilson kept at the Chicago Art Institute. CBW: *The line is purely an invention of man. There are no lines in nature, and yet it's the most important element available to the artist.*

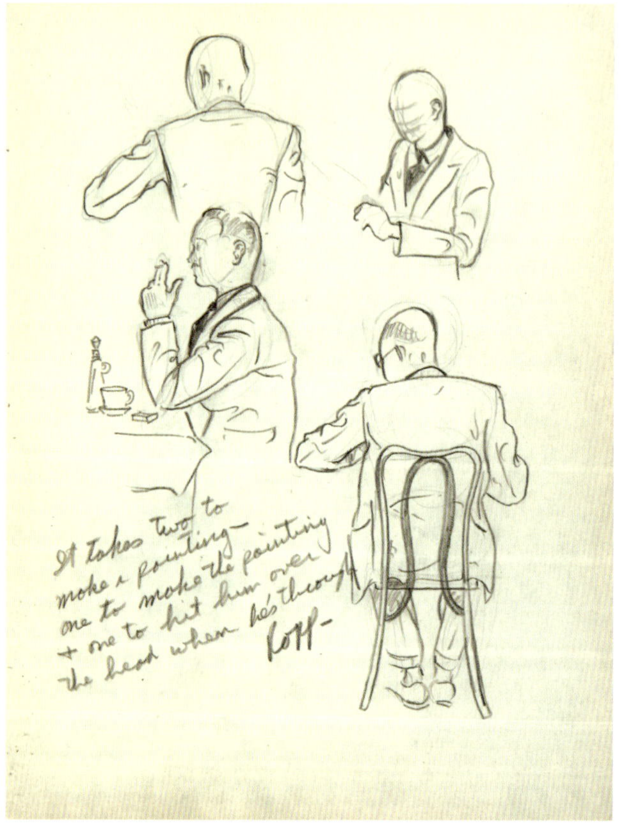

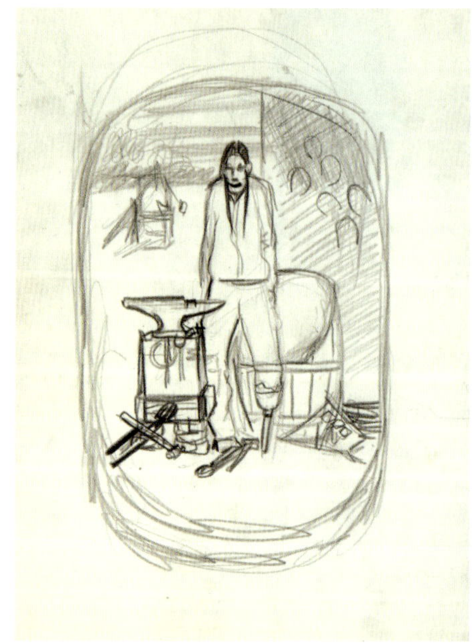

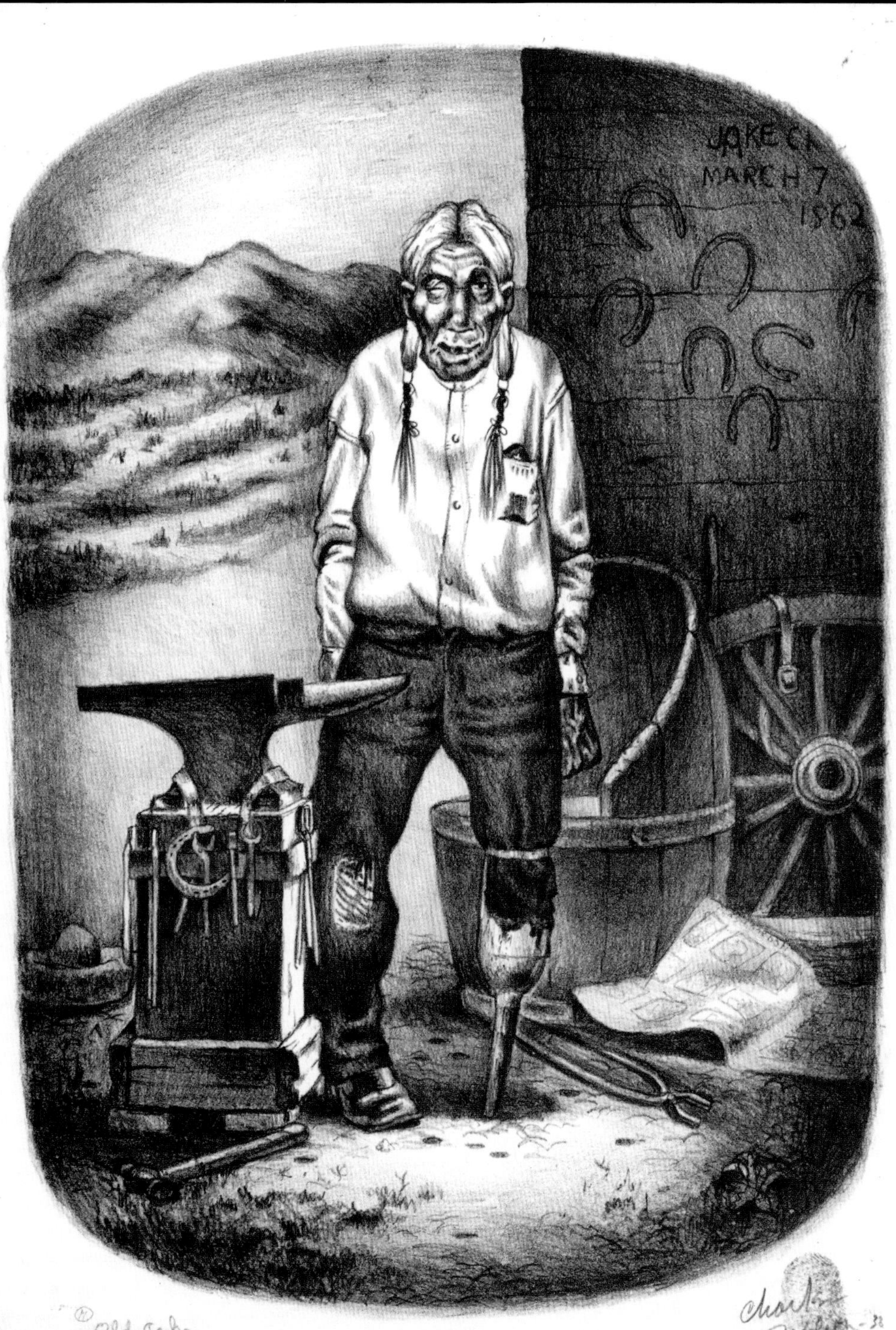

OLD JAKE, 1938

16.5 X 13.

LITHOGRAPH

ON PAPER,

TL2006.13.10

During his early years in Chicago, Wilson's search for subject matter often took him to train stations and other public places—anywhere he could find an interesting pose. He spent countless hours at the Field Museum sketching the people and things around him. "A drawing is essentially a private work related to the artist's own needs," says Wilson. The sketchbooks compiled during his Art Institute days provide a unique record of his needs as an emerging artist. They record his search not simply for subject matter but also his experiments with design. "While a student at the Chicago Art Institute, I took none of the university subjects they offered. To me, time spent in pursuit of any subject other than art seemed precious time wasted."

At eighteen, Wilson was by far the youngest in his class at the Chicago Art Institute. Most of his friends were well into their twenties, and to them, Wilson was something unique. They became fond of hearing his tales of life in the "wilds" of Oklahoma. They were particularly interested in his descriptions of American Indians. "I found myself wanting to show them my world. I wanted them to see it through my eyes."

In 1937 and again in 1938, Wilson returned to Oklahoma for the summer. He set up a studio above his father's paint store in Miami and began to focus on local subjects. Wilson's portrait of James C. Webber, last lineage blood chief of the Delaware, from this period was acquired by Thomas Gilcrease in the mid-1940s. In a letter to Gilcrease in 1950, Wilson wrote: "This is the only picture in existence of Webber, for he told me he had never allowed himself to be photographed. . . . Webber was also a peyote man and I painted him with the medicine feathers. I have always considered it perhaps the better of a dozen or so portraits I did one summer and fall." Wilson's studio was near the bus station in the little town of Miami in northeastern Oklahoma, a place where he had a stream of subjects, whom he would pay twenty-five cents an hour to sit for him. He painted continuously. "Sometimes I believe I select a subject as much for its difficulty as for any other quality it may possess. This is particularly obvious when I view my early work."

Well into his studies at the Art Institute, Wilson still had no clear sense of direction regarding a career as an artist. Grandmother Carrie had long suggested that he pursue work as a cartoonist. In 1940, he was also encouraged to pursue cartooning by Carey Orr, political cartoonist for the *Chicago Tribune,* who was impressed with samples of Wilson's work. Later that year, Wilson left the Art Institute for New York City and an apprenticeship with the *Chicago Tribune-New York News* syndicate. At twenty-one, he was eager to get to work. The work, however, was not quite what he expected. "I was fairly disappointed," says Wilson. "My job was to ink in the drawings that other people had done." After a week, he lost all interest. "It just wasn't art." Wilson returned to Chicago, the notion of becoming a professional cartoonist now well behind him. "I was relieved. I simply had to get it out of my system."

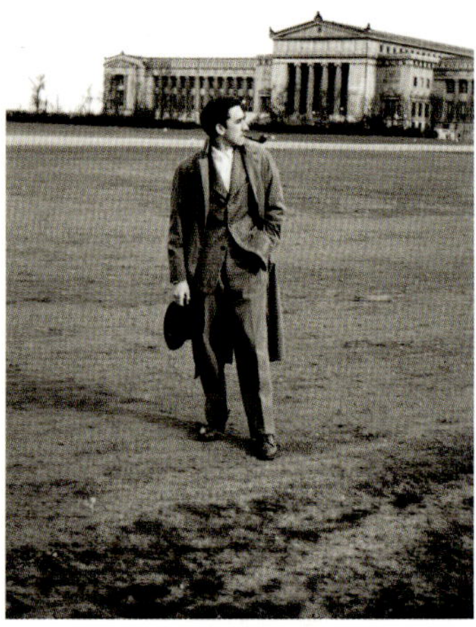

In front of the Field Museum in Chicago, ca. 1937. Wilson spent countless hours at the museum sketching what he called "random victims." CBW: *In front of a painting, the spectator tends to identify himself with the subject — in front of a drawing he identifies himself with the artist and has the experience of seeing as through the artist's eyes.*

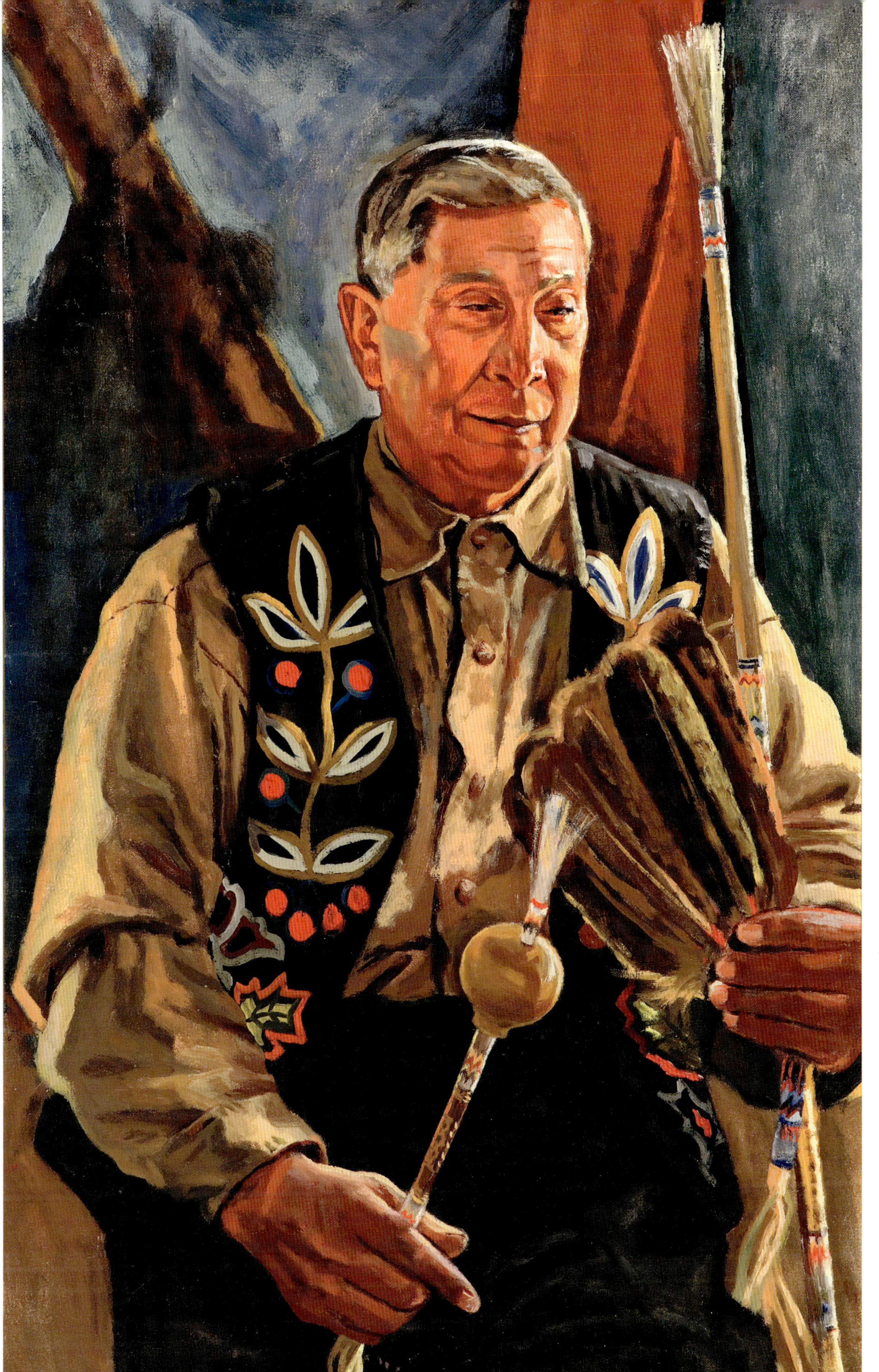

JAMES C. WEBBER,
DELAWARE CHIEF,
1939.
36.625 X 22.75,
OIL/CANVAS,
0127.1465

Wilson's achievements as an artist were continuing to build. He had received the purchase award in 1939 from the Chicago Society of Lithographers and Etchers and had exhibited in the U.S. Office of Education in Washington, D.C. In 1940, three of his lithographs were featured in *Coronet* magazine to illustrate an article on American Indians. This was Wilson's first presentation of Indian subjects to a national audience.

Back in Chicago, artist Aaron Bohrod encouraged Wilson to send some of his prints to the Associated American Artists in New York. Wilson did, and the work caught the eye of Thomas Hart Benton, who suggested the AAA commission a work from him. The group invited him to New York to create a print. Wilson accepted the commission, eager to move forward with his career. But first he returned briefly to Miami with something else on his mind—a young Quapaw woman named Edna McKibben he had met at a local powwow three years before. "I thought she was just the most beautiful girl I had ever seen," says Wilson. In 1941, only hours before leaving for his commission in New York, the two were married in a small ceremony in the Miami First Presbyterian Church. In New York, the young couple took up residence in the attic of a large boarding house. The newlyweds' new home was small, but suited them nicely. It had a single bedroom and a kitchenette. More importantly, it had enough room for Charles to set up his studio and begin work.

Wilson's career would soon go in new directions. The lithograph, *Comanche Portrait,* that he produced for the AAA was printed by a well-known lithographer, George Miller, and Wilson began visiting Miller's studio on a regular basis. There, he met Alan Crane, fellow lithographer and illustrator of children's books. Crane would introduce Charles and Edna to New York life in a way that few could. He took the young couple from Oklahoma clubbing in Manhattan and directed them to good restaurants known to the locals. They went to parties with John Steinbeck, Robert Henri, and John Sloan. "Once you live in New York, you never get that out of your blood," Wilson remembers. Barely into his mid-twenties, the artist found himself good friends with Lynn Riggs, Marquis James, and Woody Guthrie—all fellow Oklahomans then living in the city. Wilson's opportunities to work as an artist continued to expand. He was asked to provide illustrations for an upcoming book called *The Hill* by poet David Greenhood. Greenhood's wife was Helen Gentry, art editor for Holiday House, the children's book publisher. The Greenhoods were impressed with Wilson's work, and the young artist was eventually offered more work as an illustrator than he could have imagined. During the next few years, Wilson worked as an illustrator but also pursued painting and lithography.

With the outbreak of the Second World War, his lithograph called *Freedom's Warrior* was shown at the Metropolitan Museum of Art's invitational *Artists for Victory* exhibition. His prints were featured in *Collier's* magazine, and he took an assignment writing articles and producing posters for the Office of War Information.

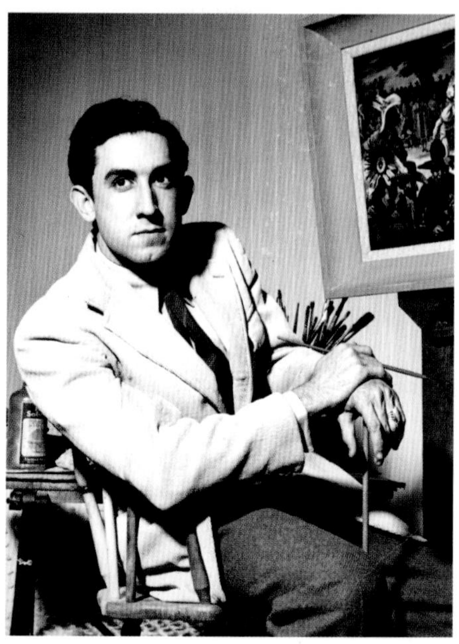

Wilson in the 1930s. CBW: *My art students often asked — What is the difference between a commercial artist and a fine artist? My answer was, the fine artist is still getting money from home.*

COMANCHE PORTRAIT, 1941. 12.625 X 16.75, LITHOGRAPH/ PAPER, 1427.265

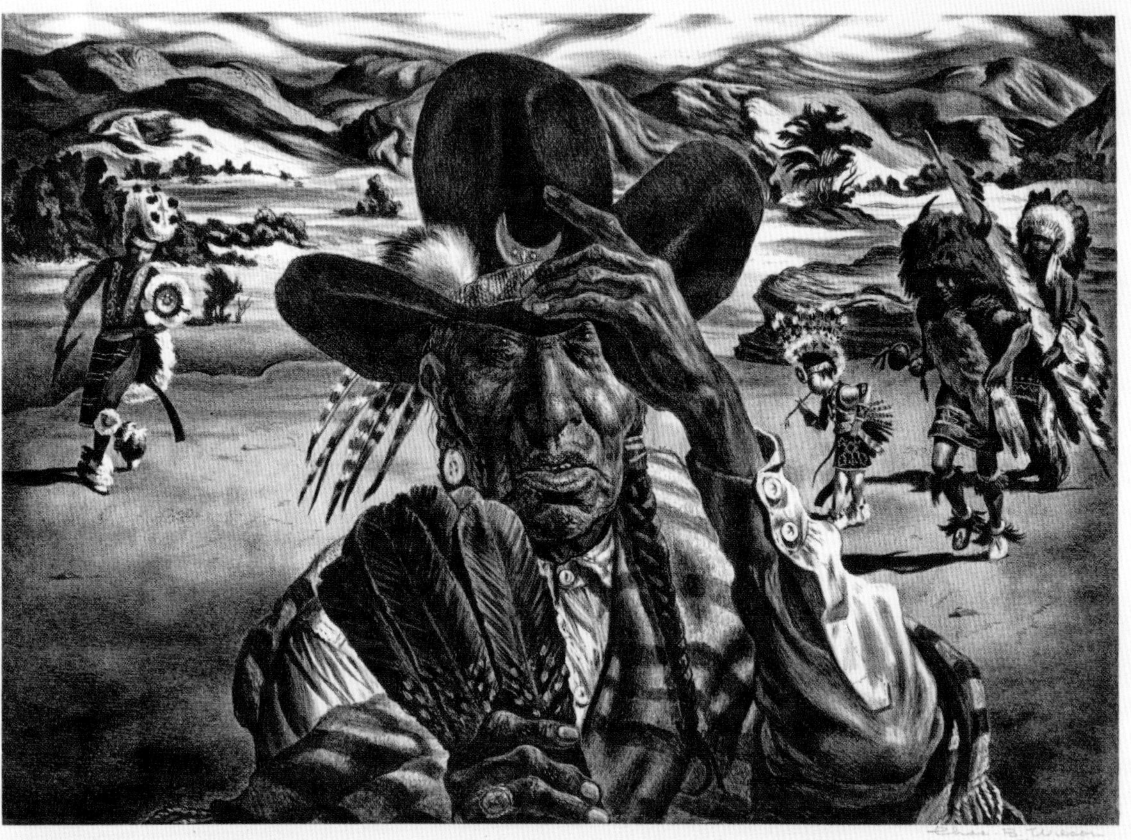

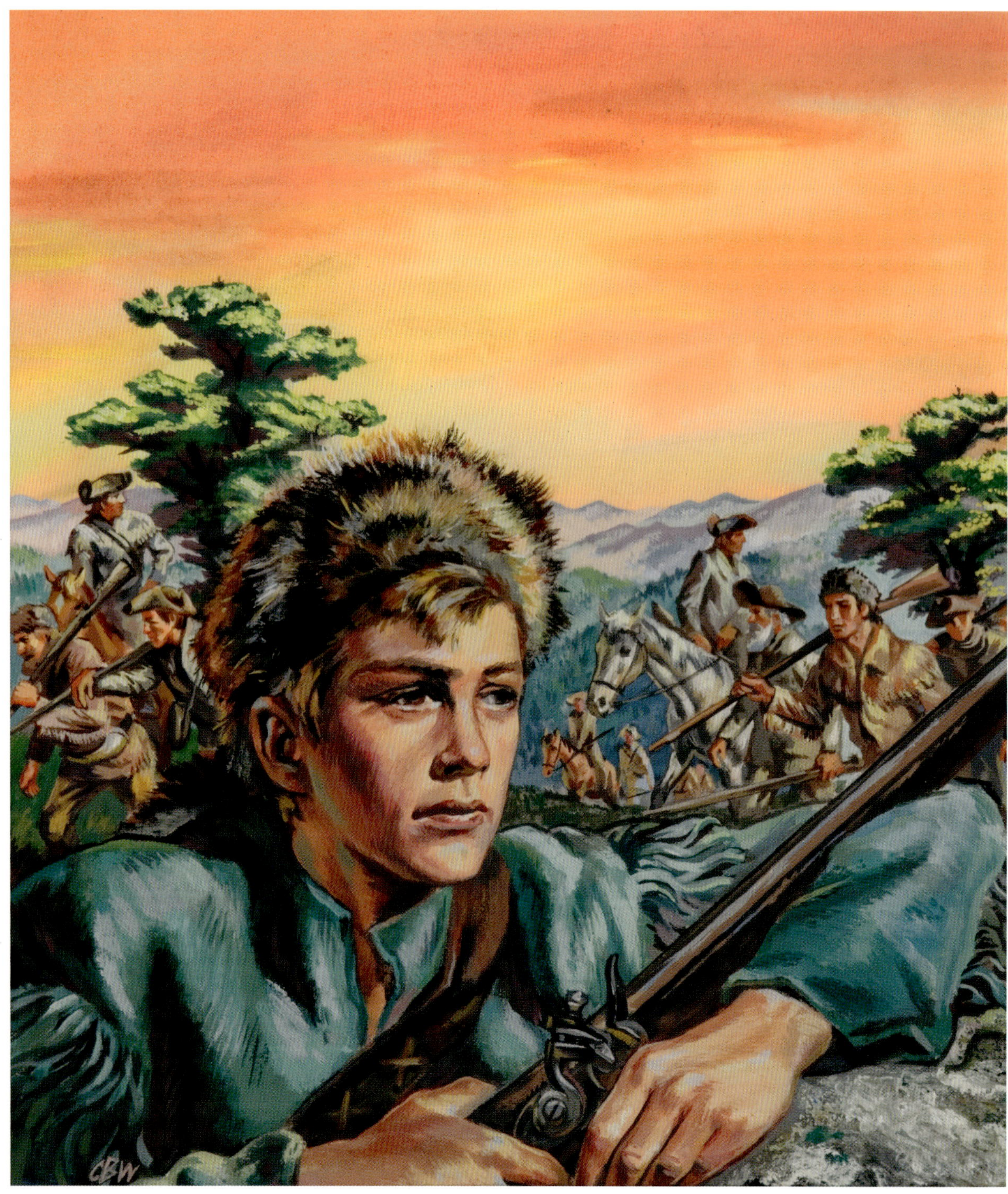

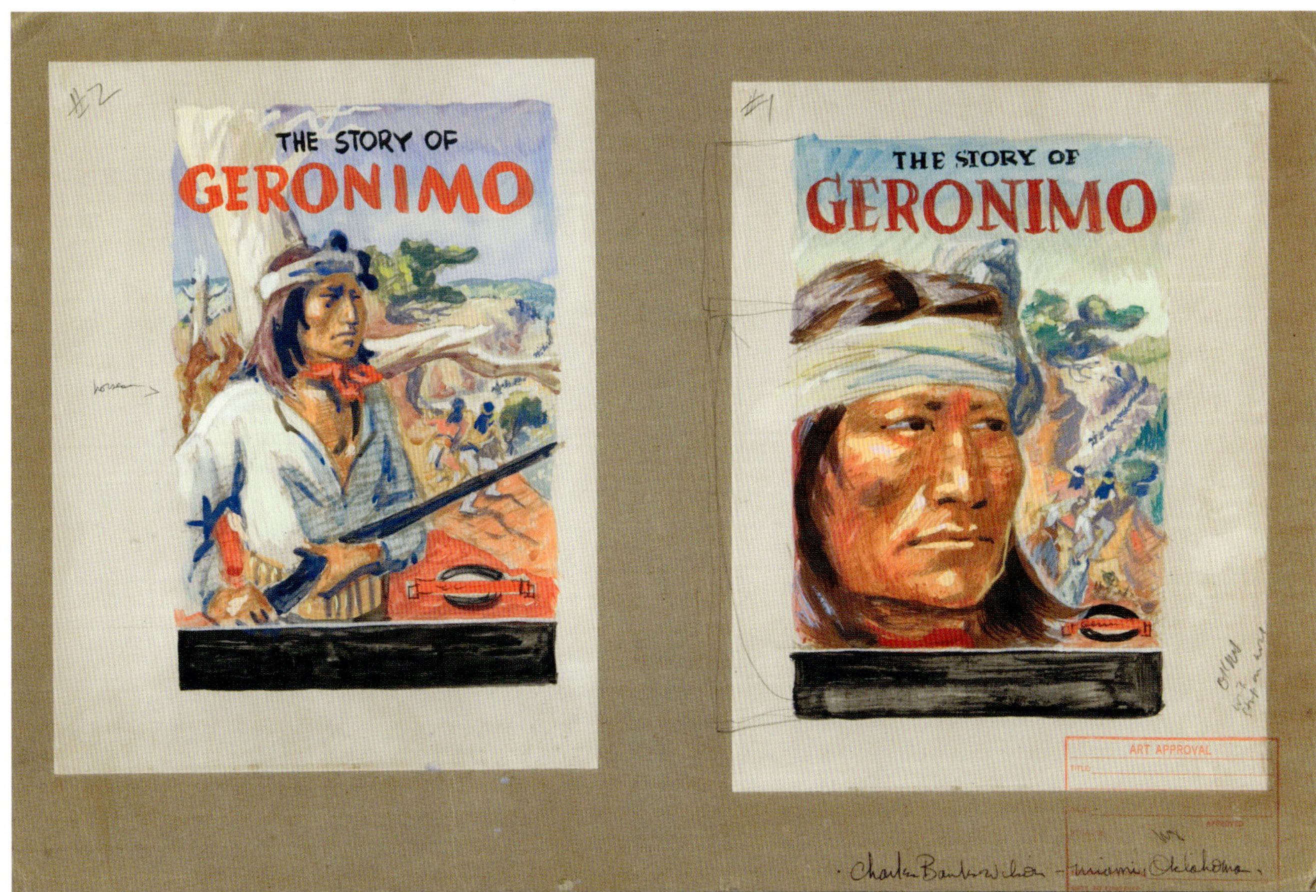

ARTWORK FOR *THE STORY OF GERONIMO*, 1928. 11 x 8.625, TEMPERA/BOARD, 0227.1928 (LEFT); 0227.1929 (RIGHT)

REBEL SIEGE, WATERCOLOR/PAPER, 0227.1756

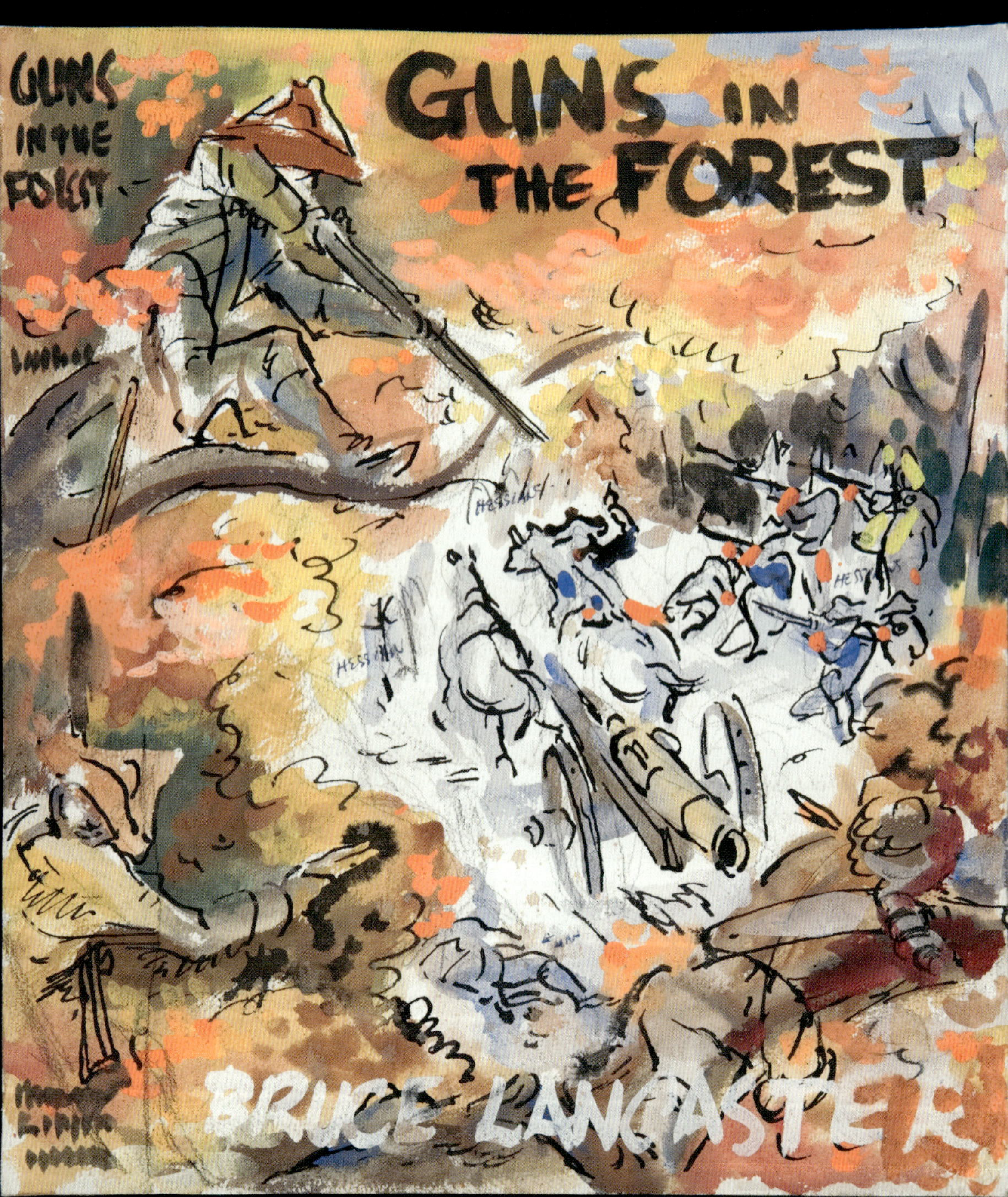
GUNS
IN THE
FOREST
GUNS IN THE FOREST
HESSIANS
HESSIANS
HESSIANS
BRUCE LANCASTER

As the war continued to escalate, Wilson was certain that he would soon be called to serve. "I didn't want to be drafted in New York," he says. He wanted to go in with young men from backgrounds similar to his own. In 1943, the Wilsons returned to Oklahoma where Charles went in for his physical examination at the regional induction center in Tulsa. He was told, however, that he would not be immediately called to service due to a foot injury he had sustained on the track field in high school. Wilson found himself back where he started, the studio above his father's downtown Miami paint store. "I was feeling quite down, I recall," says Wilson. "But happiness and unhappiness are both productive." For the next several years, Wilson continued to be productive as an illustrator, providing drawings for over a dozen books including J. Frank Dobie's *The Mustangs* and the Robert Louis Stevenson classic *Treasure Island.*

The 1940s were a productive time with regard to painting as well, culminating with his masterpiece *Shawnee Ribbon Bets* completed in 1948. Book illustrations paid the bills, however, and Wilson would eventually become one of the most widely sought after and highest paid illustrators in the United States. —RANDY RAMER

By the late 1940s, Wilson had become one of the most sought-after book illustrators in the United States. CBW: *Children's books reflect not so much a child's feelings about other children, animals, and nature as the attitudes of adults about infancy.*

A WORKING SKETCH FOR *GUNS IN THE FOREST*, 1931. 11 X 8.625, WATERCOLOR/ PAPER, 0227.1931

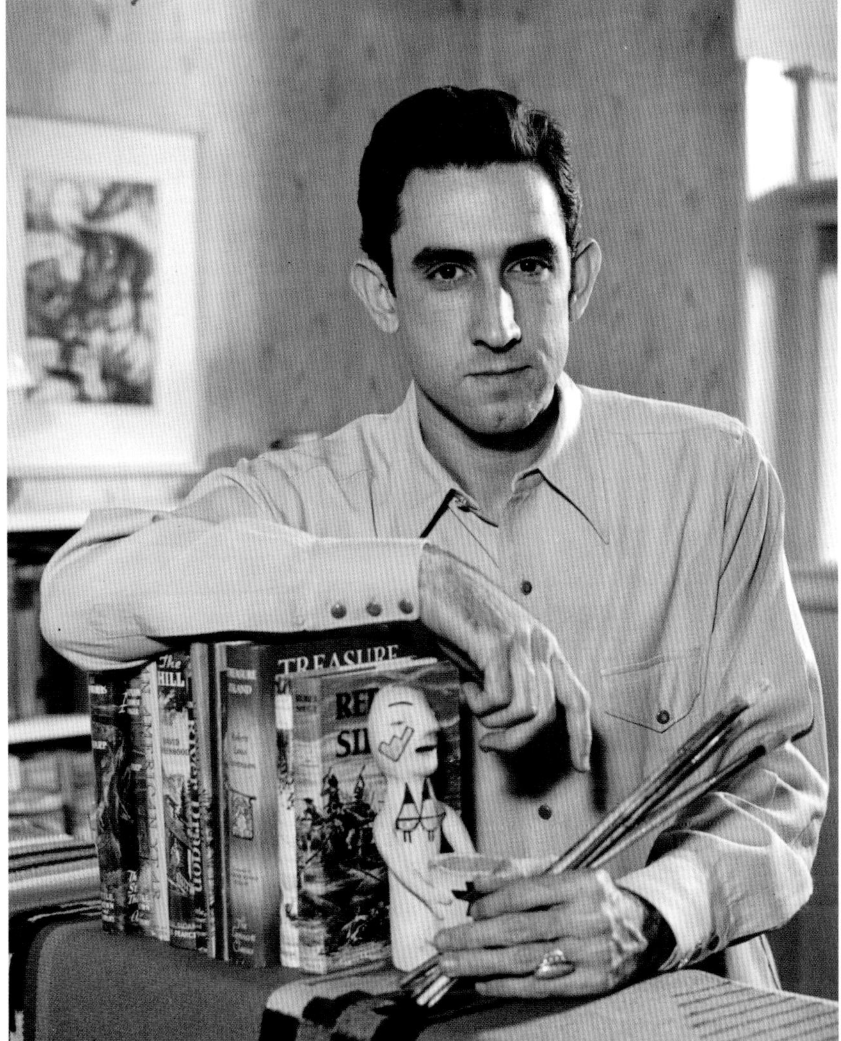

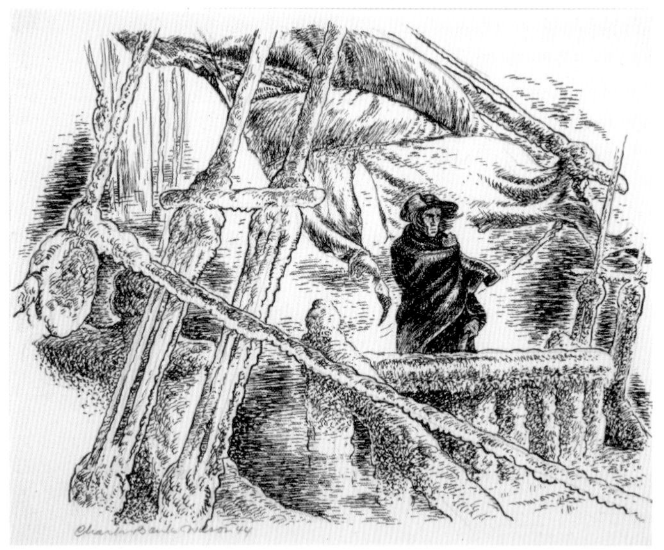

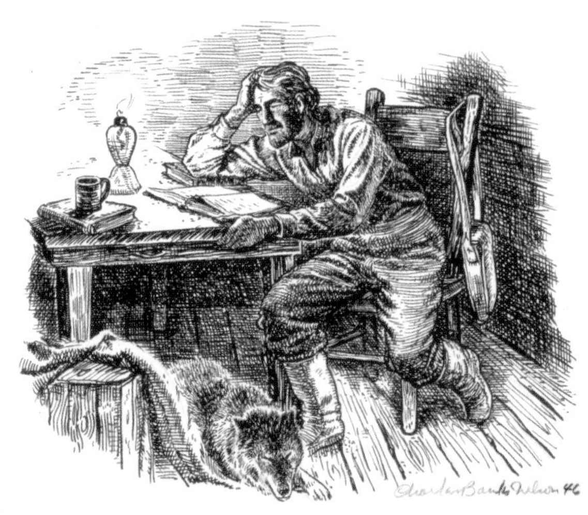

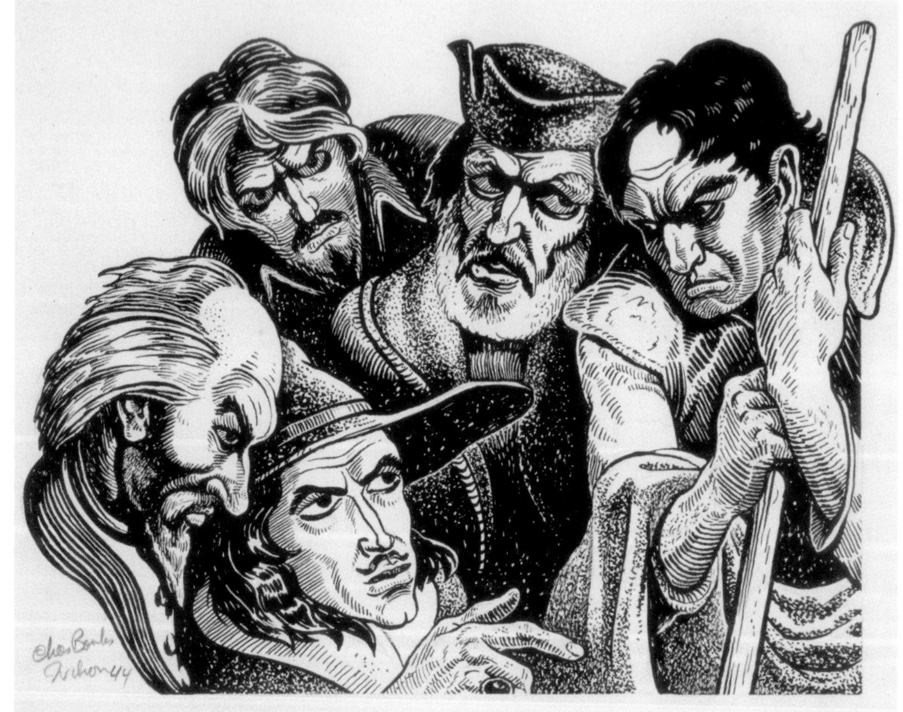

CLOCKWISE FROM UPPER LEFT: A JOURNEY'S END FROM *COMPANY OF ADVENTURERS*, 1944. 12.375 X 14.125, PEN/INK ON PAPER, 1327.2172; THE COMPANY SURRENDERS FROM *COMPANY OF ADVENTURERS*, 1946. 11.75 X 13.75, PEN/INK ON PAPER, 1327.3174; THE MURDER PLOT FROM *CHAMPLAIN: NORTHWEST VOYAGE*, 1944, 12.5 X 14.25, PEN/INK ON PAPER, 1327.2191

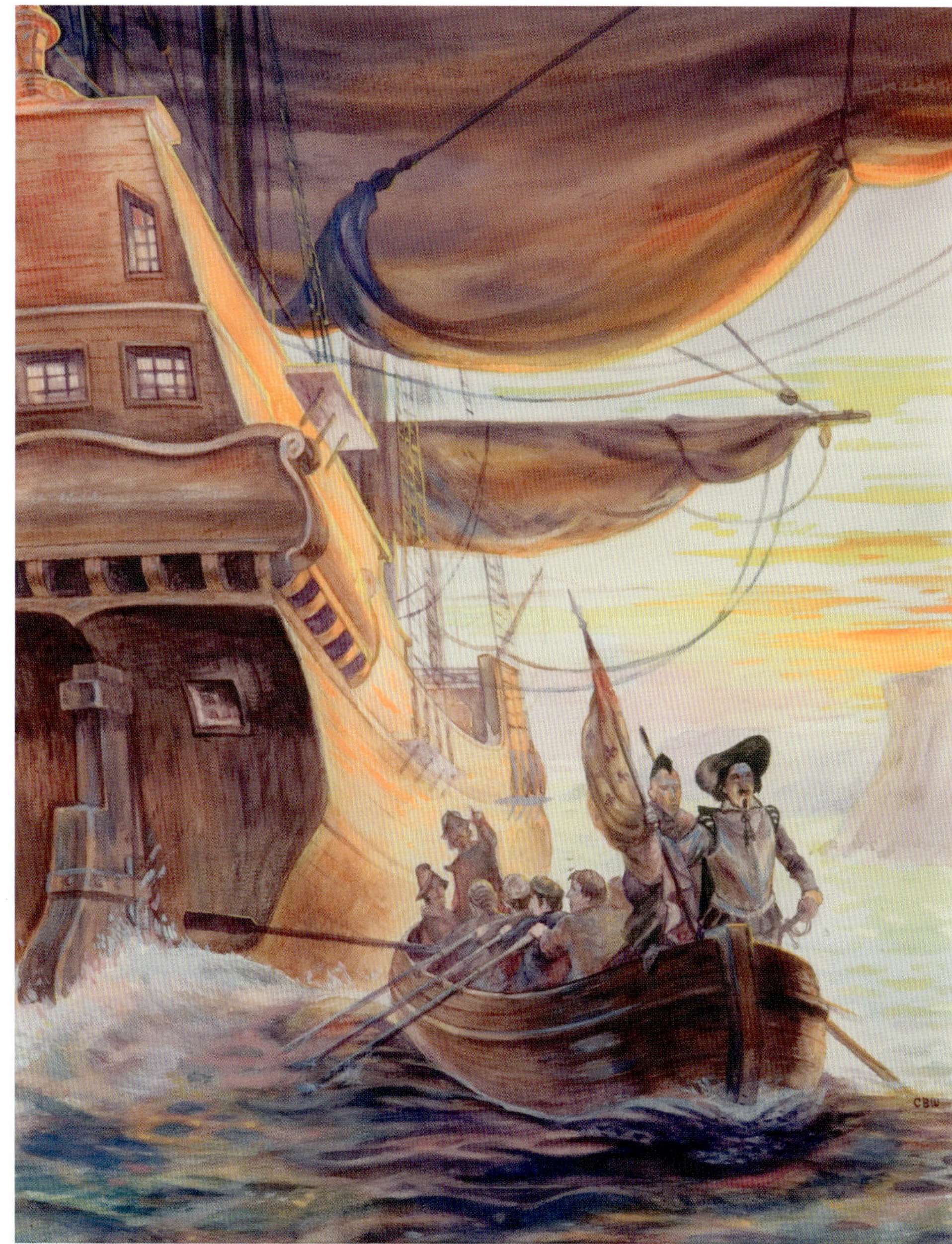

BOOK COVER
FOR *CHAMPLAIN:
NORTHWEST
VOYAGE*, 1944.
CASEIN/BOARD,
0227.1757

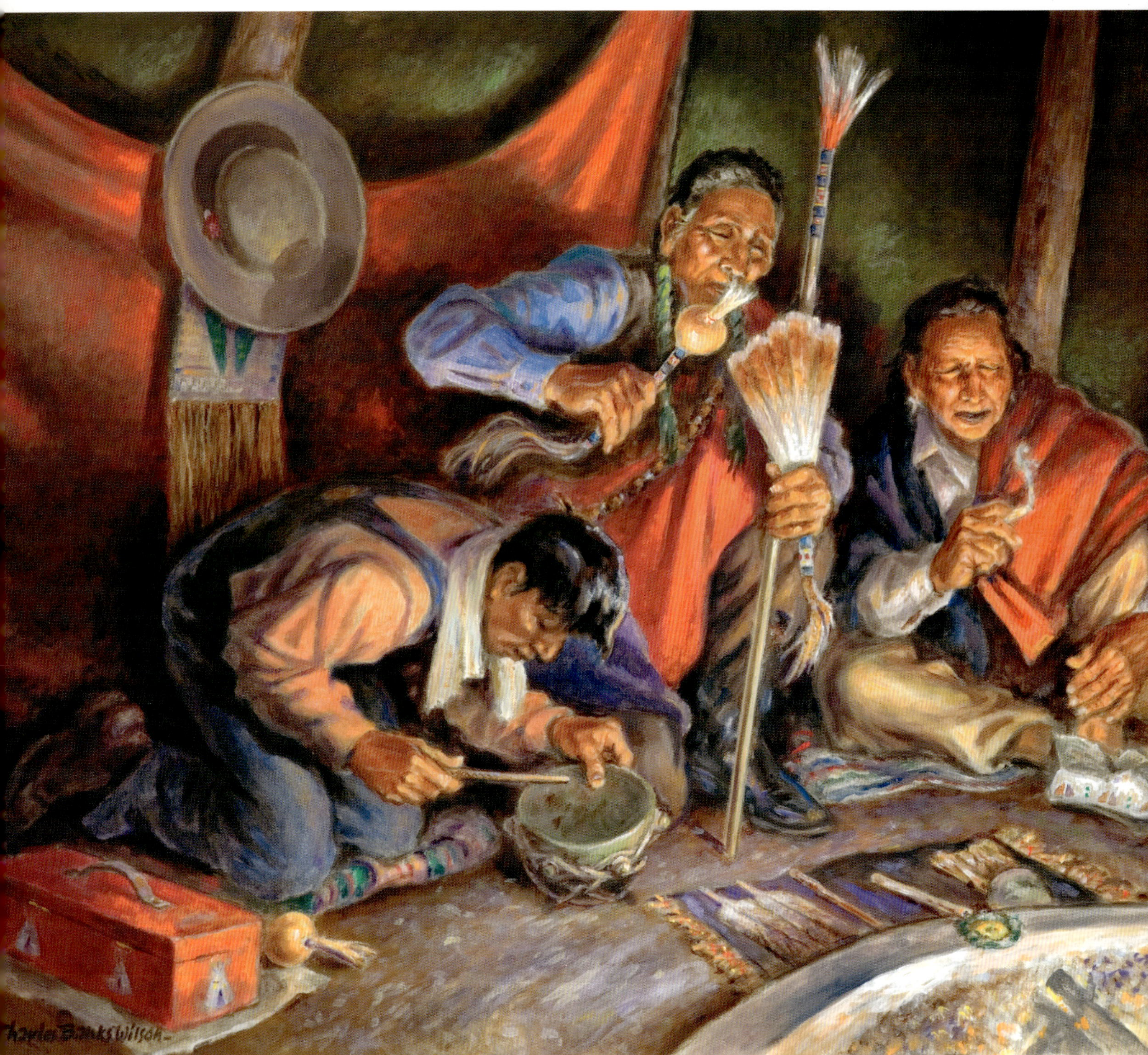

GUS MCDONALD,
1940. 24 X 22,
OIL/CANVAS,
COLLECTION OF THE
ARTIST

INDIAN PEYOTE
CEREMONY, 1996.
16.5 X 19,
OIL/CANVAS,
0127.2492

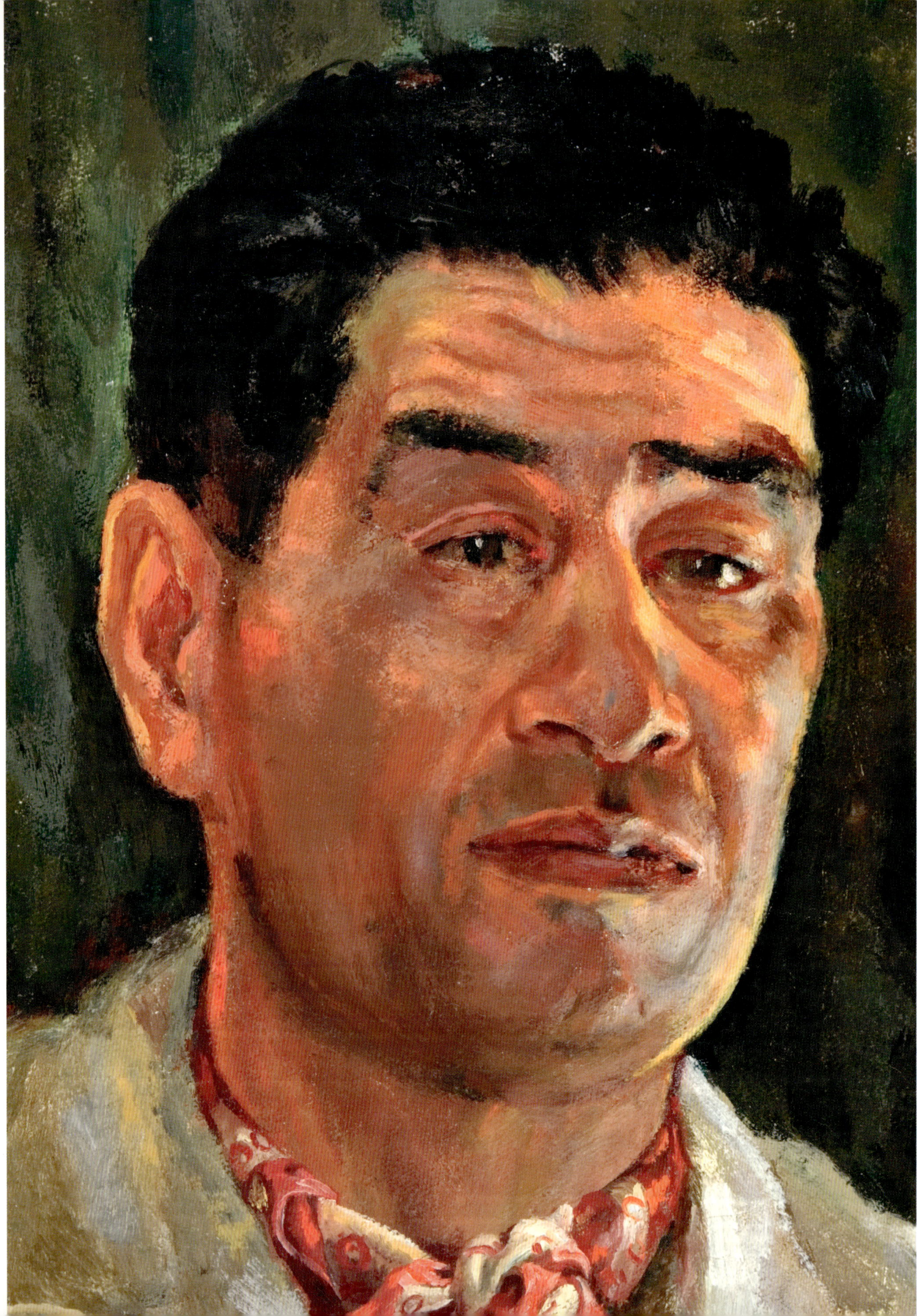

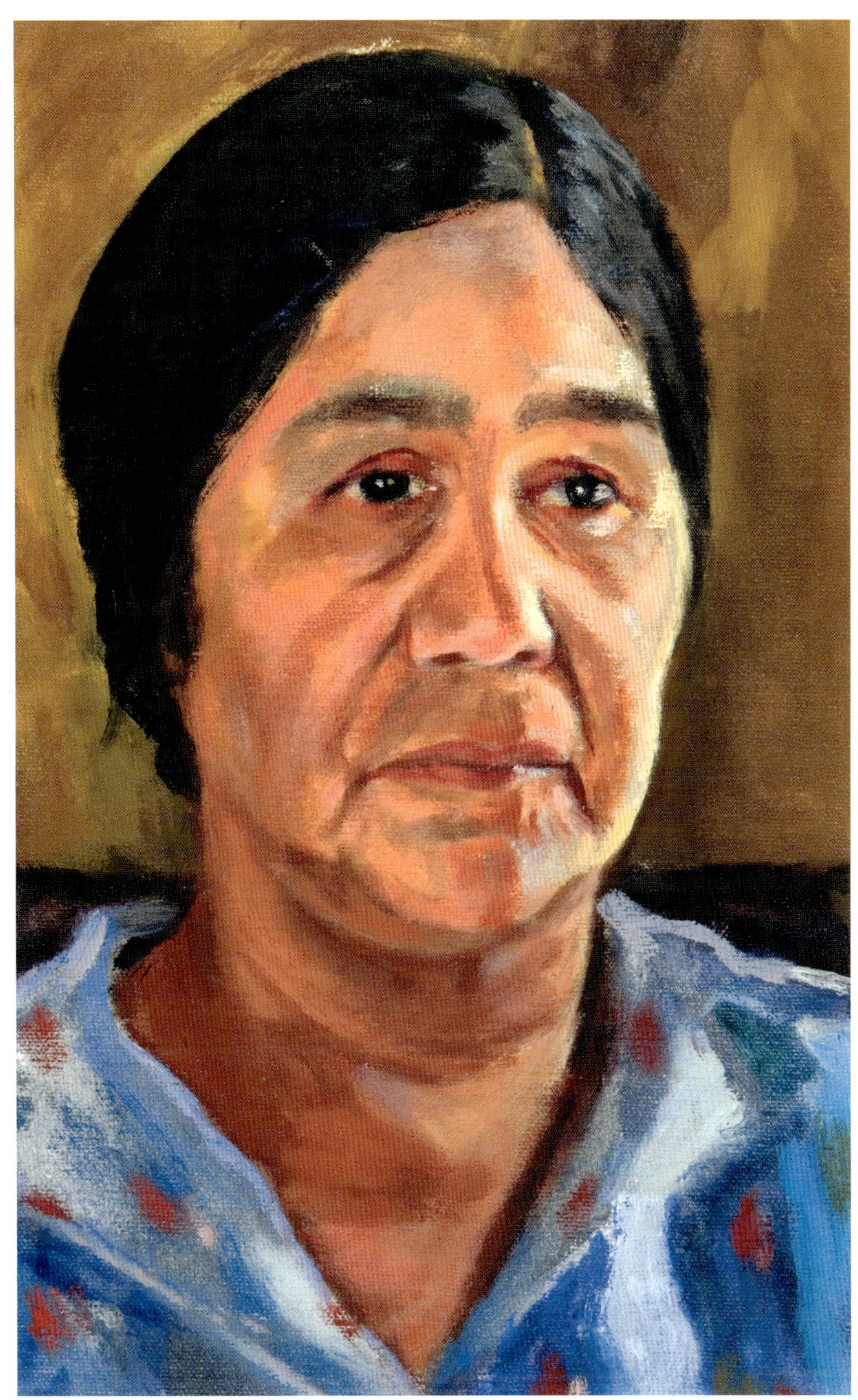

SARAH, MOHAWK/
SHAWNEE, 1939.
13 X 9,
OIL/CANVAS,
COLLECTION OF THE
ARTIST

FREEMAN BOLT
CHEROKEE, 1939.
13 X 9,
OIL/CANVAS,
COLLECTION OF
THE ARTIST

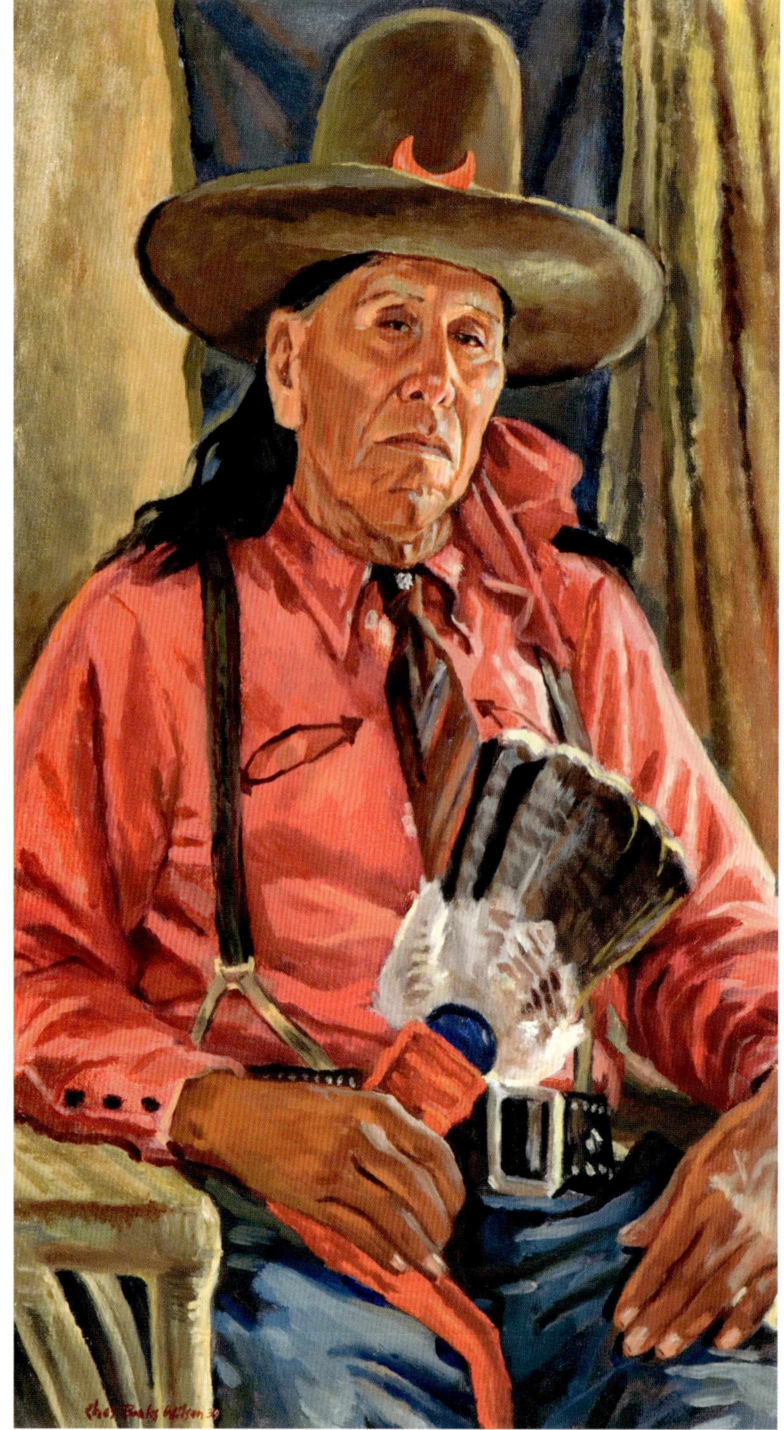

LOUIS FEATHERMAN,
CA. 1939. 36.25 X 20.25,
OIL/CANVAS,
COLLECTION OF THE
ARTIST

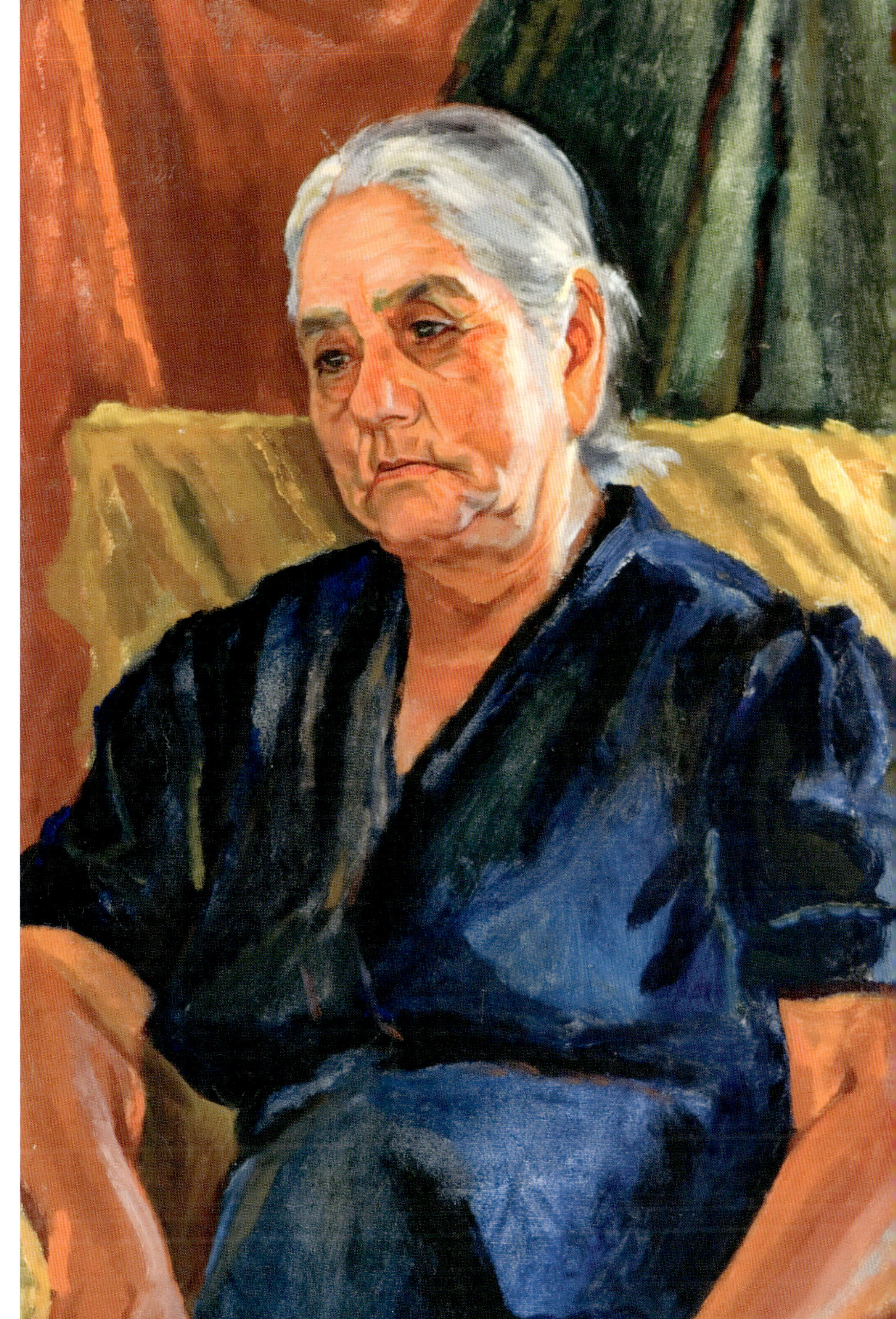

ALICE BLACKHOOF,
CA. 1939. 39.75 X 17.5,
OIL/CANVAS,
COLLECTION OF
THE ARTIST

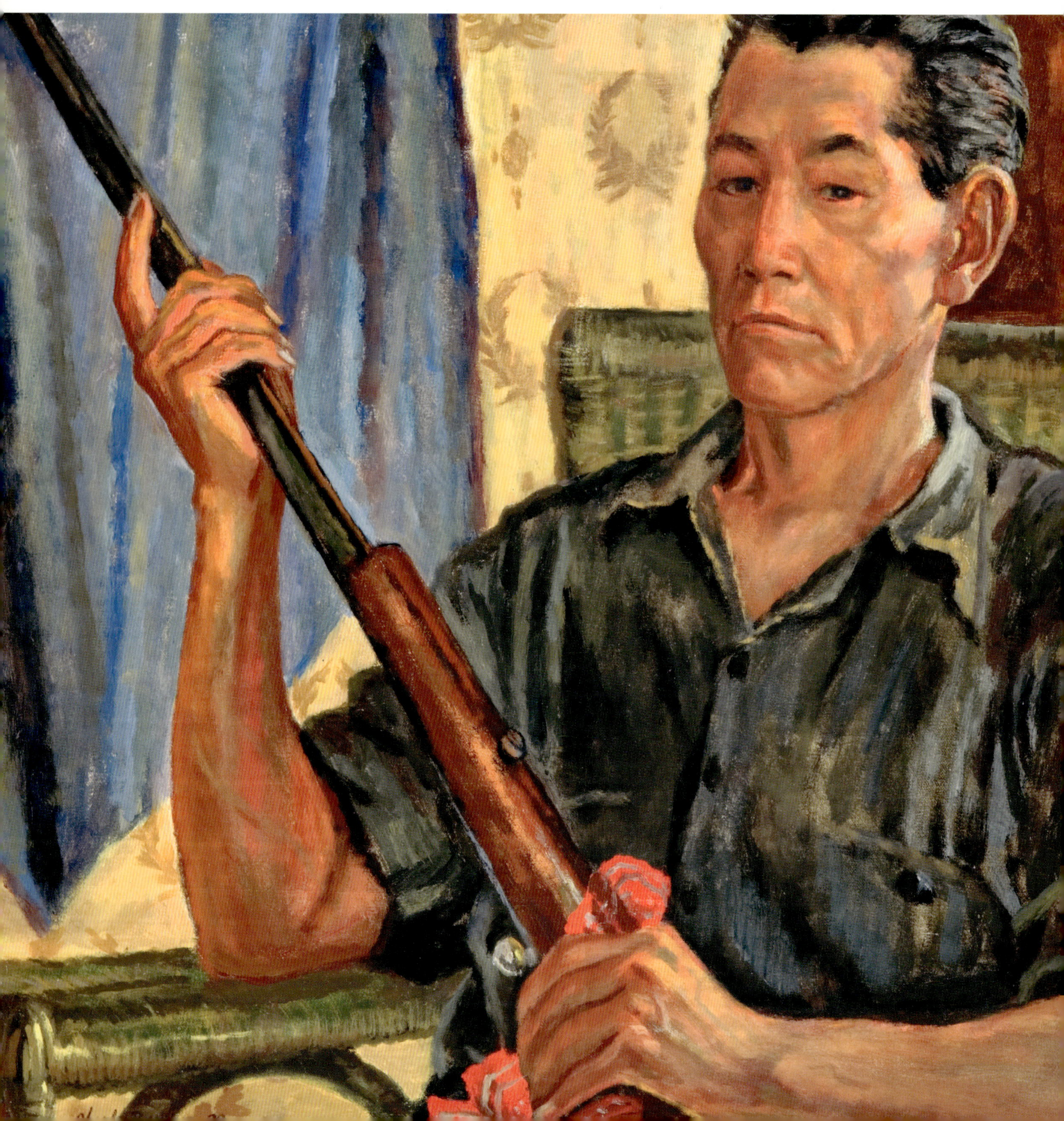

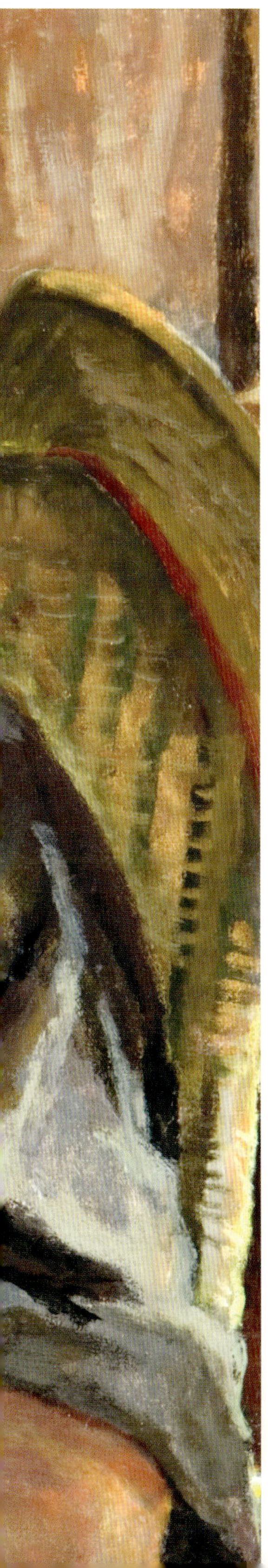

WALTER BEARSKIN,
CA. 1939. 24 X 30,
OIL/CANVAS,
COLLECTION OF
THE ARTIST

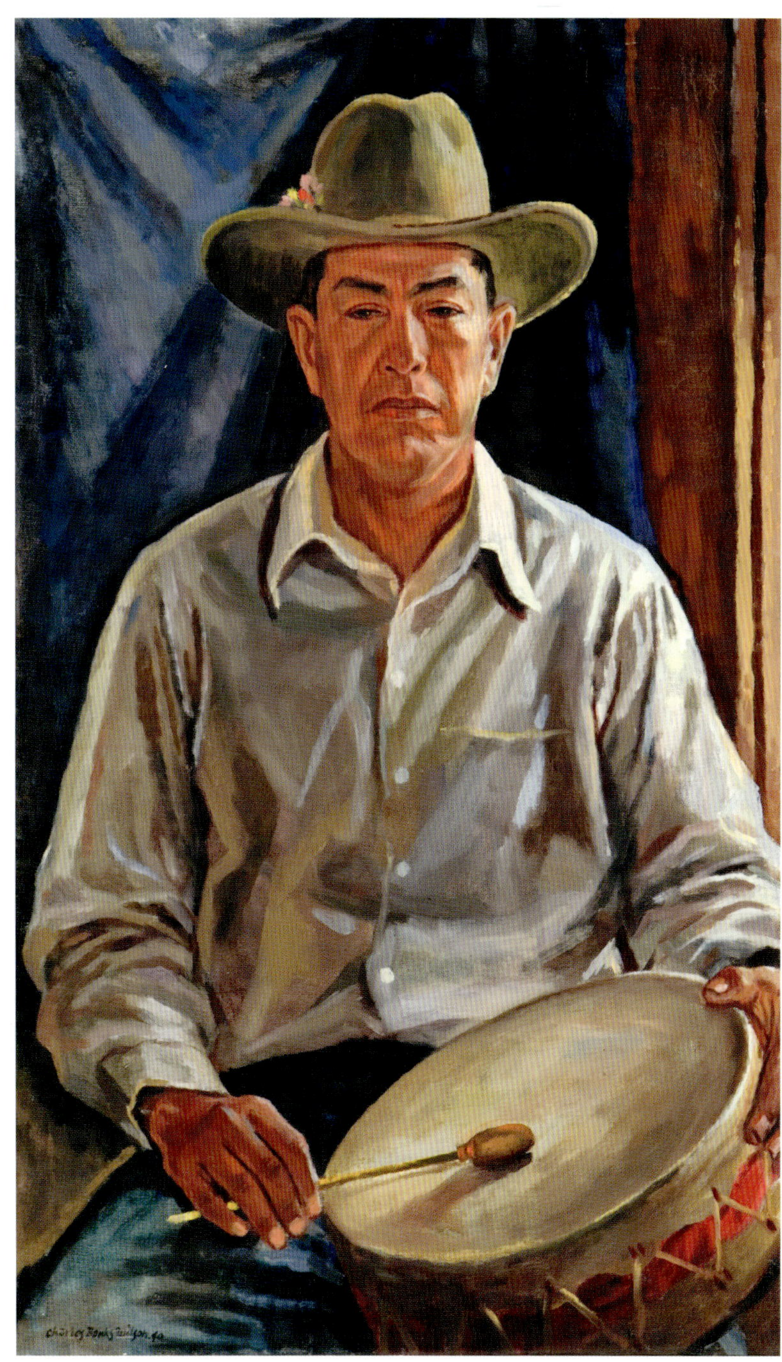

BILL, SHAWNEE,
CA. 1939.
24 X 30,
OIL/CANVAS,
COLLECTION OF
THE ARTIST

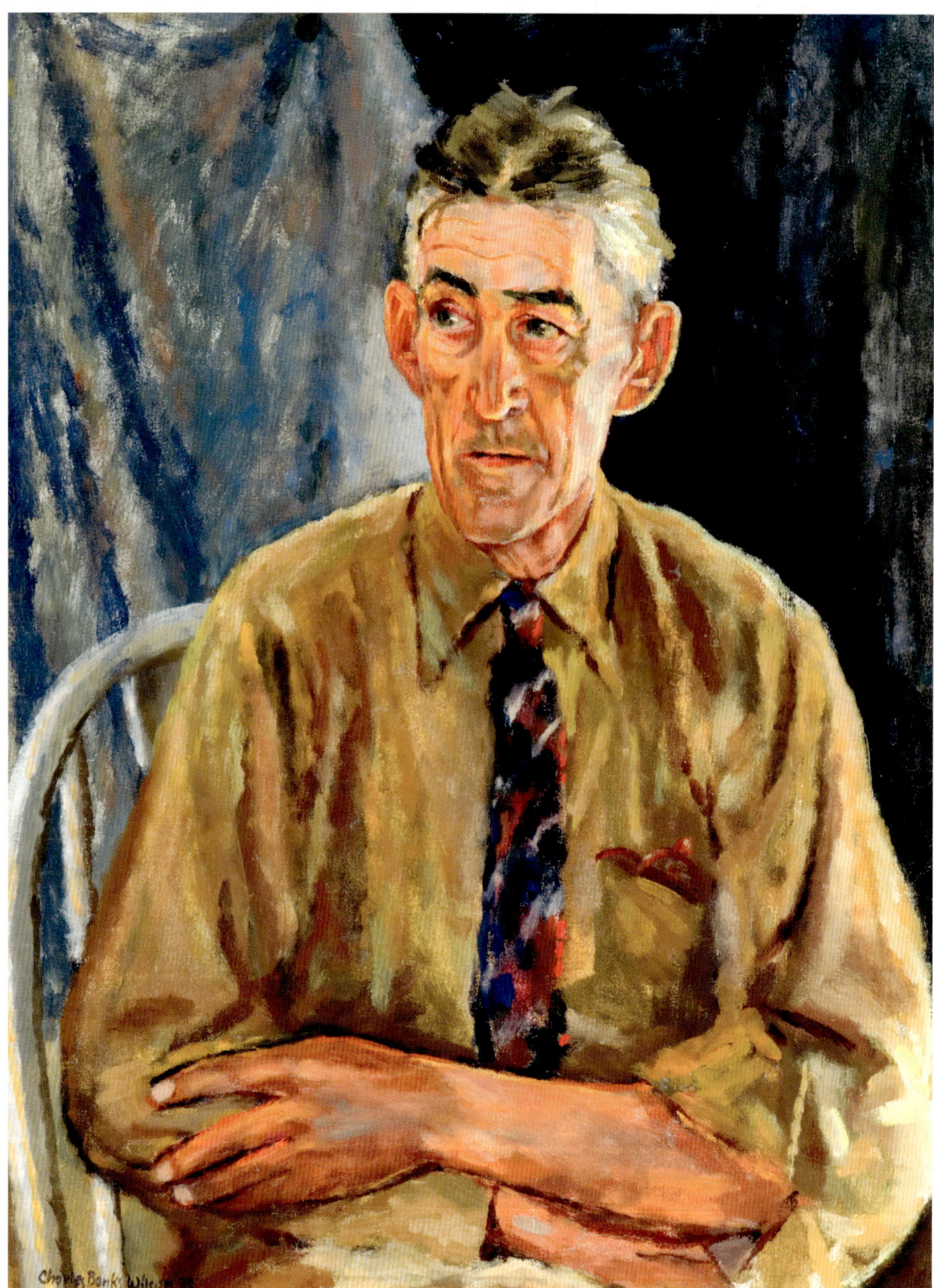

MINER WITH ONE
HAND, CA. 1939.
31.5 X 24,
OIL/CANVAS,
COLLECTION OF
THE ARTIST

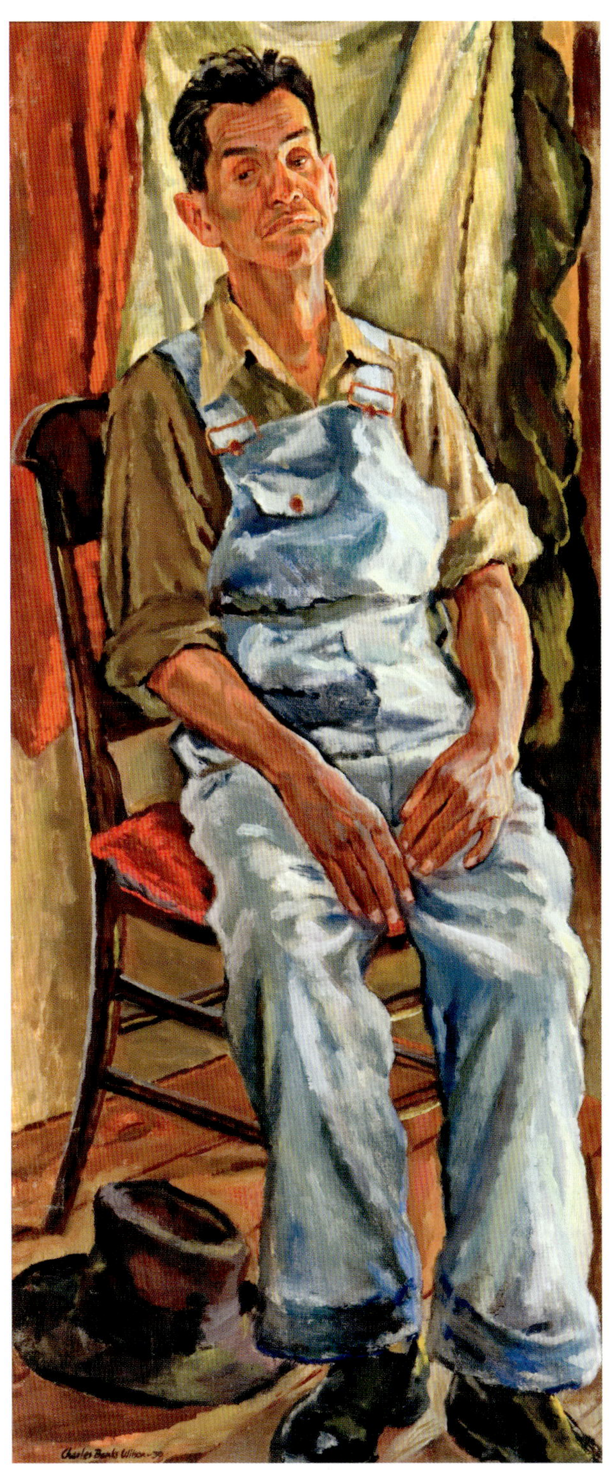

PETE BUCK, CA. 1939.
59.5 X 25.5,
OIL/CANVAS,
COLLECTION OF THE
ARTIST

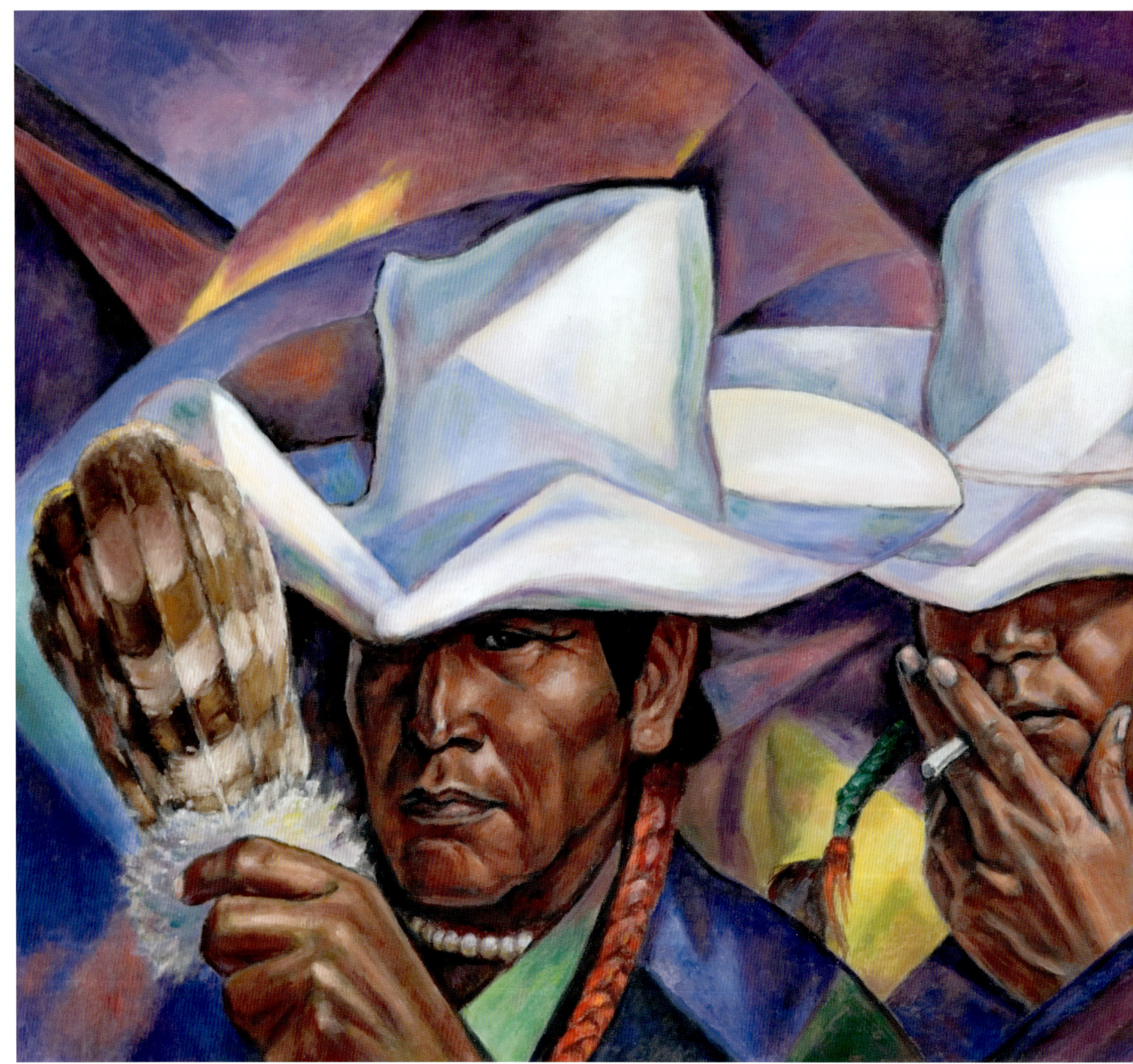

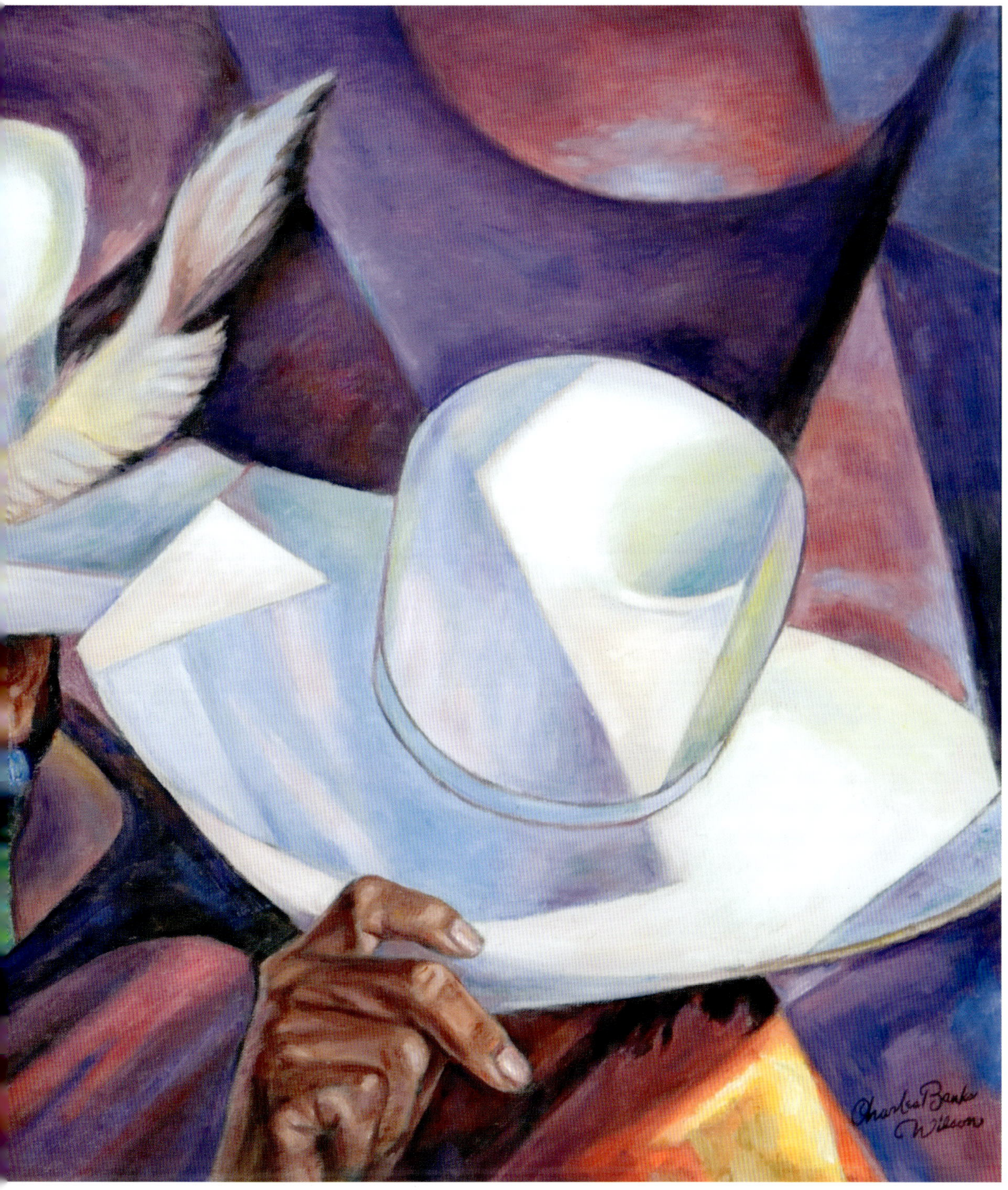

WHITE HATS,
21.5 X 43.5,
OIL/CANVAS,
COLLECTION OF
THE ARTIST

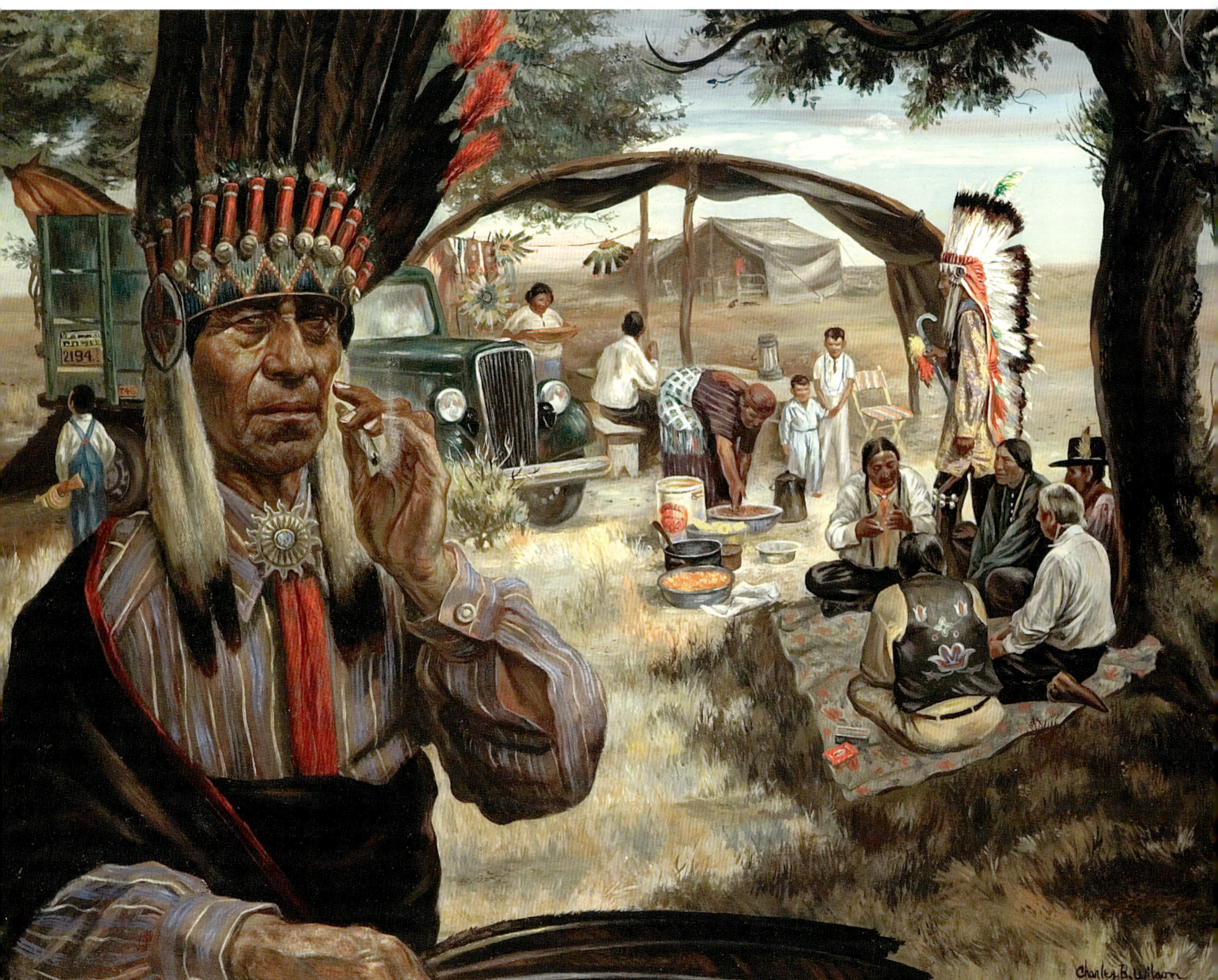

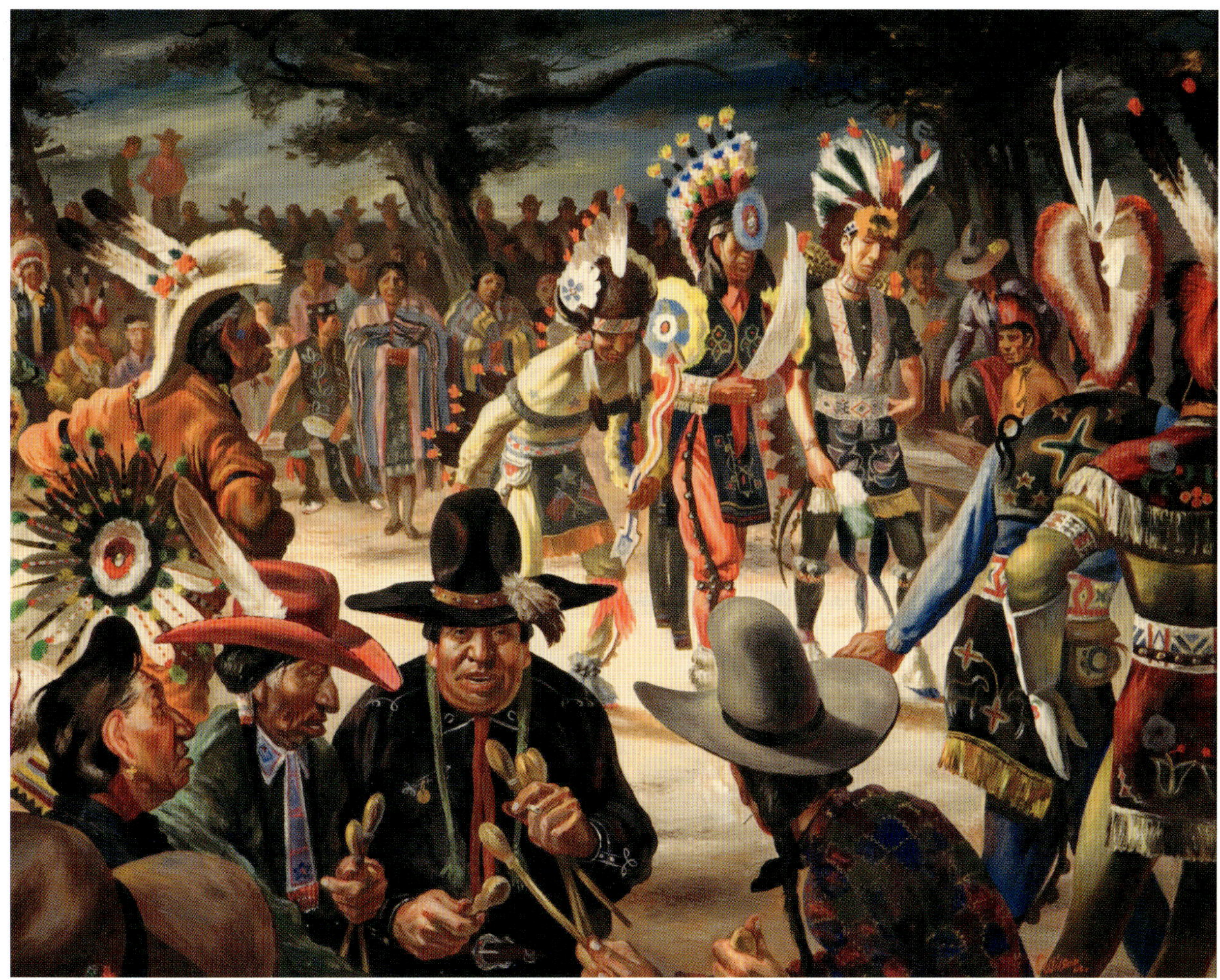

QUAPAW
POWWOW, 1942.
20.5 X 24.5,
OIL/CANVAS,
0127.2512

COMANCHE
CAMP, 1942.
18 X 23.5,
OIL/CANVAS,
COLLECTION
OF THE ARTIST

FAMILIAR PATHS : PAINTING EVERYDAY LIFE

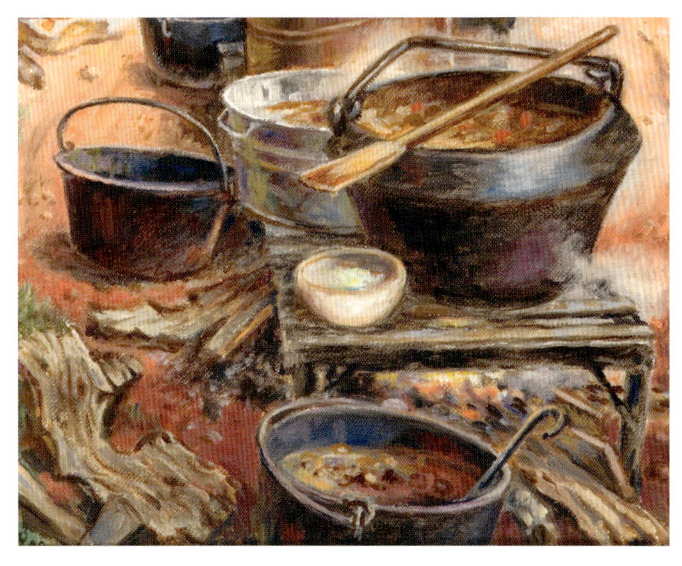

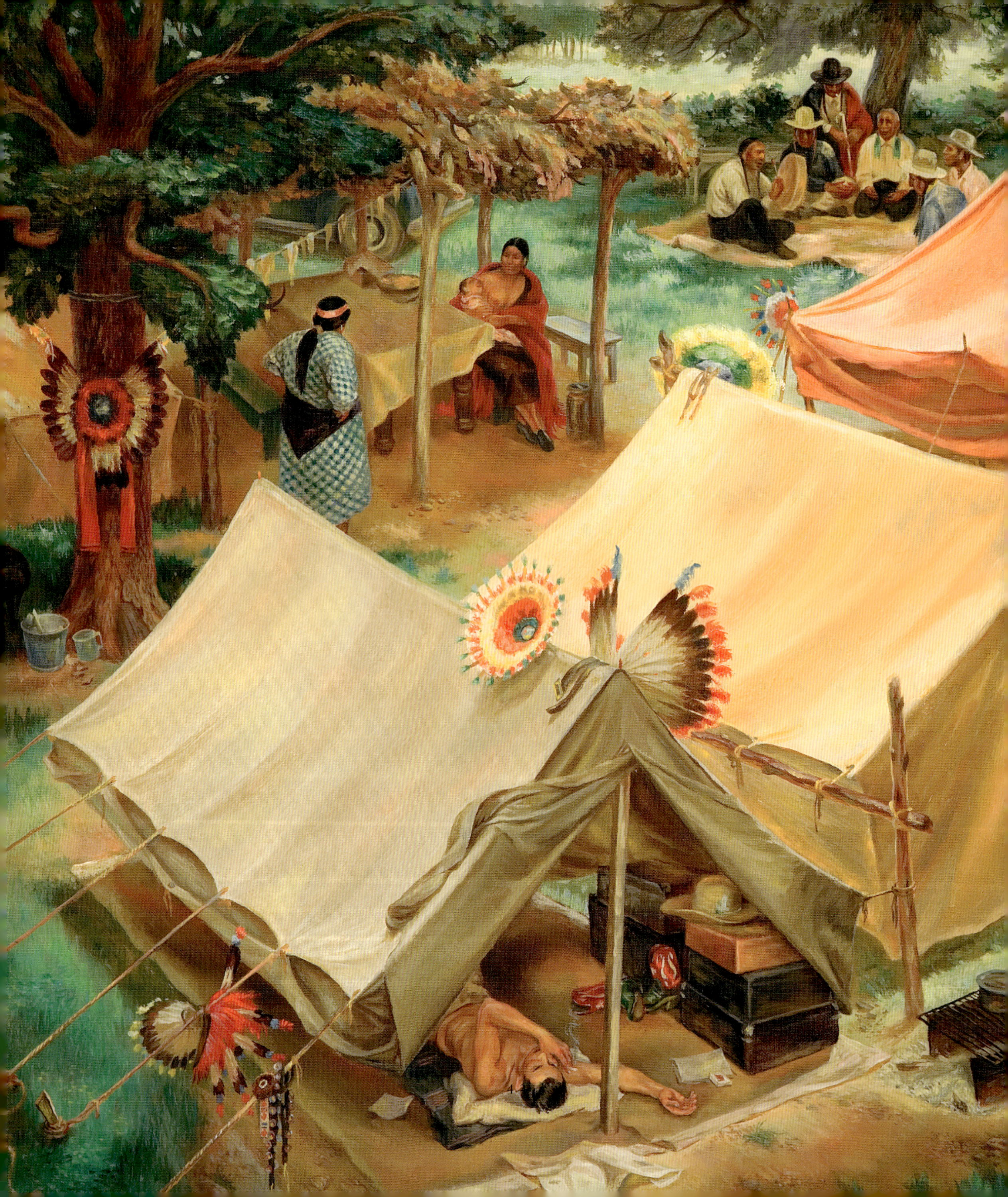

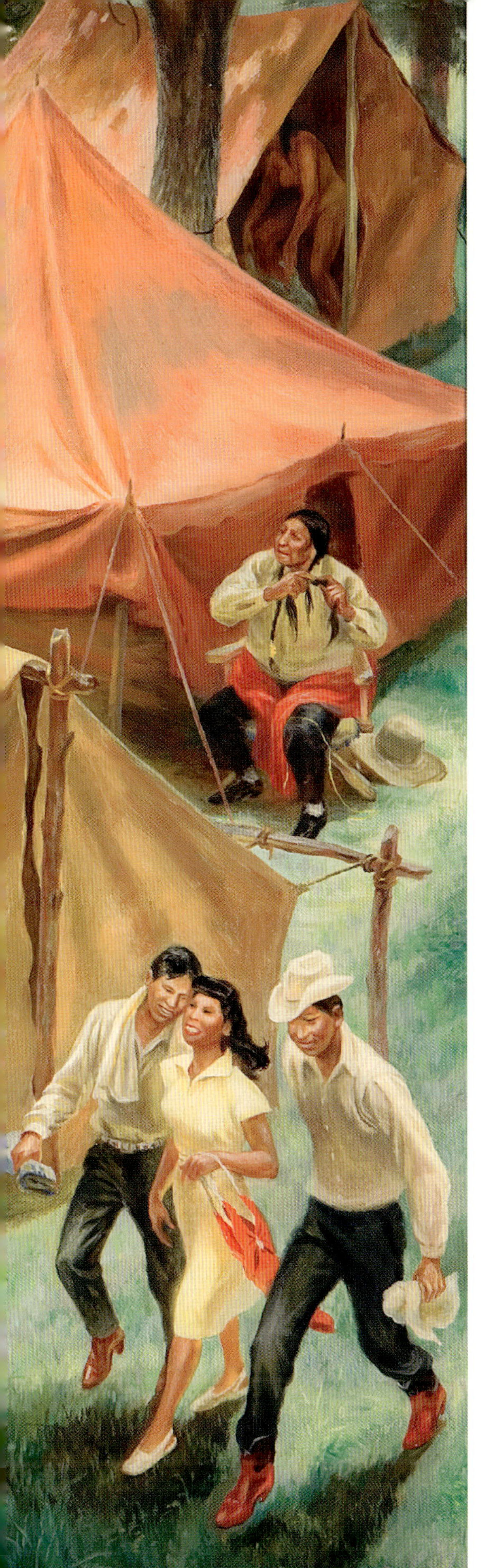

"I believe — as I look back — every drawing I made and every painting — is a sentimental observation of people and places."

harles Banks Wilson creates important works— portraits that honor great Oklahomans, murals that pay tribute to the history of Indian Territory and his home state, and a long-running series of portraits of Native Americans that rivals the work of George Catlin and Joseph Henry Sharp in significance and execution. On the basis not only of subject matter but also of technical expertise and aesthetic genius, these works guarantee Wilson's rank among American painters. It is his work of a more humble nature that assures him a place in the hearts of Americans and in the company of the great regionalists such as Thomas Hart Benton, Grant Wood, and John Steuart Curry.

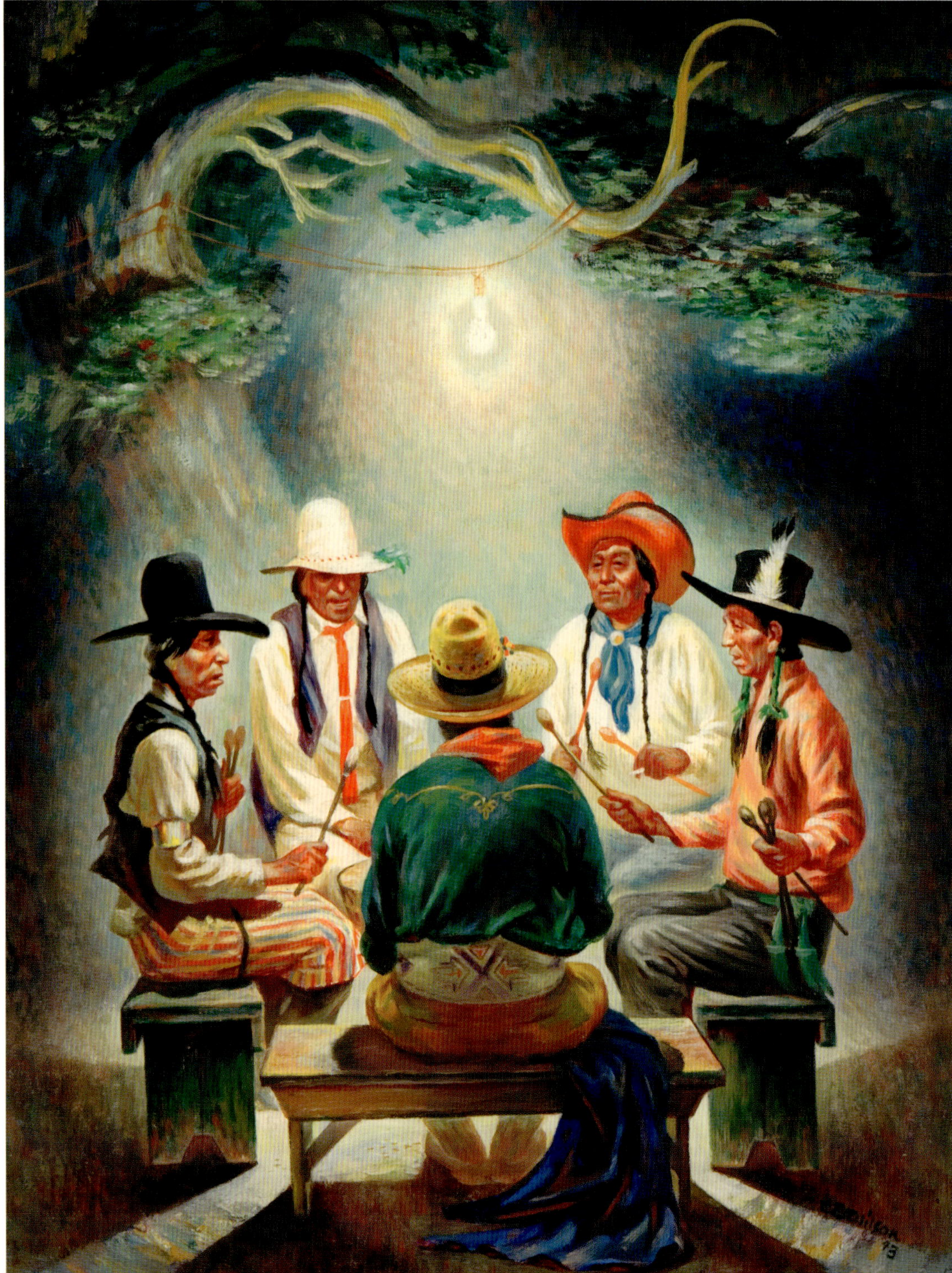

PRECEDING PAGES:
POWWOW AFTERNOON,
1947. 21.75 X 24.5,
OIL/CANVAS,
0127.1464

OKLAHOMA MELODY,
1943. 14 X 11,
OIL/CANVAS, 0127.466

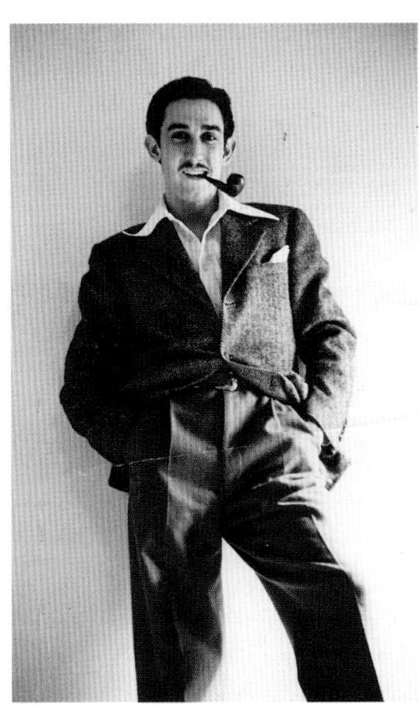

Wilson, ca. 1937.

Wilson's images of rural twentieth-century America, specifically Oklahoma and Arkansas, pay homage to the hard work, the determination, and the times of celebration and joy of the people who inhabit this world. In his paintings of the lives of those who follow the "familiar paths" Wilson is not a photographer, but an observer concerned with relaying his impressions of nature and the land in form and line. His art reflects his youth—one might consider it modern America's youth—growing up in rural Oklahoma, doing chores, fishing and swimming in creeks and ponds, going to local powwows. Gilcrease Museum is fortunate to have one of the most significant and diverse collections of Wilson's work.

After training at the Art Institute of Chicago in the 1930s and a stint in New York in the 1940s, Wilson returned to his home in Miami, Oklahoma. Even while he had been away from the heartland, his summers had been spent attending, observing, and making sketches at local powwows, focusing on the bystanders rather than the dancers in their regalia. *Oklahoma Melody* (1943), for example, features not the dancers, but the virtual heartbeat of the powwow, the drummers. Technically, the star of the composition is its lighting. Wilson chose an interesting—and challenging—lighting source. He remarked, "At the time I did this, it wasn't uncommon for lighting at powwows to consist of only one light bulb or 3 or 4 at most, suspended from a pole or tree, providing the barest illumination." This "barest illumination" meant that only the colors and forms that received the most direct light from the single bulb were accentuated. Intense shadows form behind the seated men, and the surrounding environment dissolves into darkness just inches away from the illuminated figures.

In 1947 he finished an oil painting that could only have come from his long experience as an observer, one that reveals the intimate side of traditional powwows and demonstrates Wilson's mastery of design in a densely-packed and vitally-interesting composition: *Powwow Afternoon.* Wilson described the painting for Thomas Gilcrease:

> The time after the noon meal is a lazy period at the powwow, but it also is a wonderful time for visits with friends and the swapping of old songs as well as old stories. Kids go swimming, old men hunt the shady side of a tree, the young war dancer, tired from a night long round-dance or stomp session, lolls in his tent, and the dogs just nose about.

Paintings such as *Powwow Afternoon* might seem documentary in nature, and certainly Wilson relays a great deal of information in a small rectangular space. However, in this kind of work, Wilson's interest and intent is the feeling of a time and place. He says, "This is not a picture of any exact spot. . . . It is memories of many powwows which are embedded in my experience."

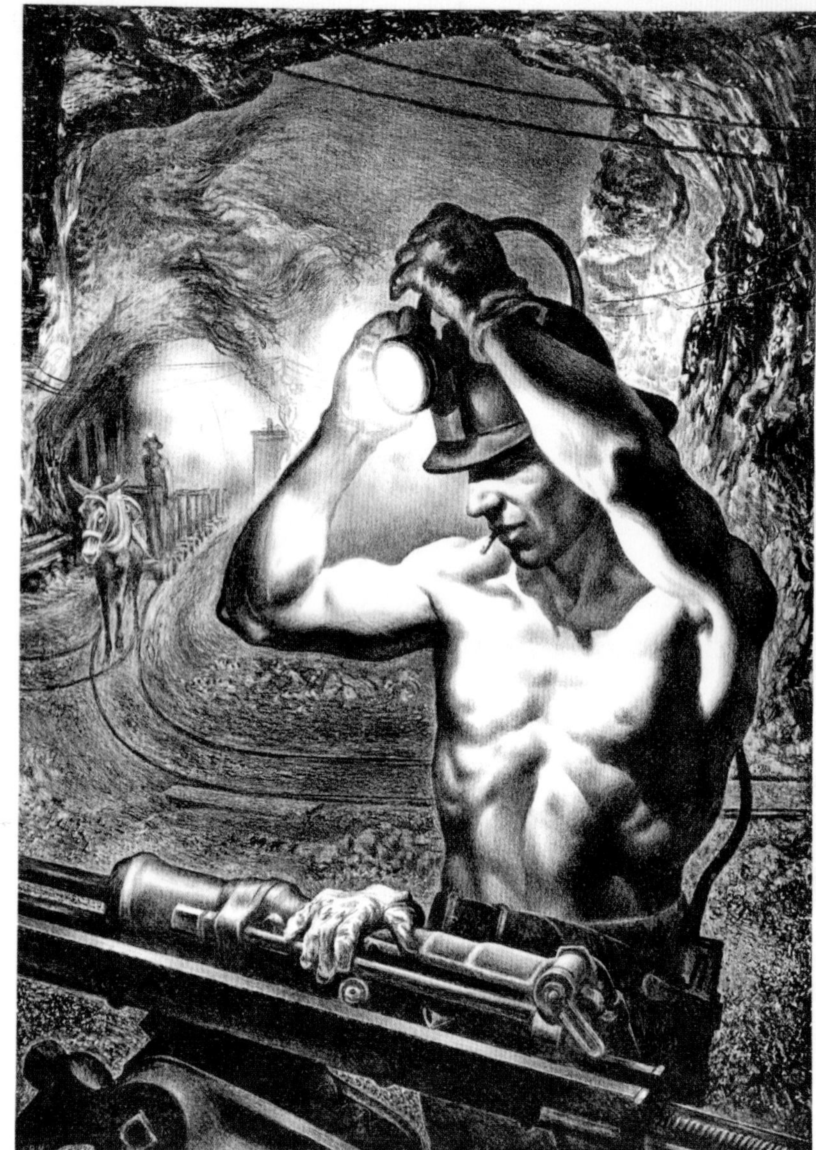

HARD ROCK, 1943.
17.125 X 13.4,
LITHOGRAPH/
PAPER, 1427.773

From his earliest days as an artist, Wilson sought authenticity in his work. In the late 1930s he spent much of his time during the summers executing sketches in the lead and zinc mines of northeastern Oklahoma. Photo by Orrick Sparlin.

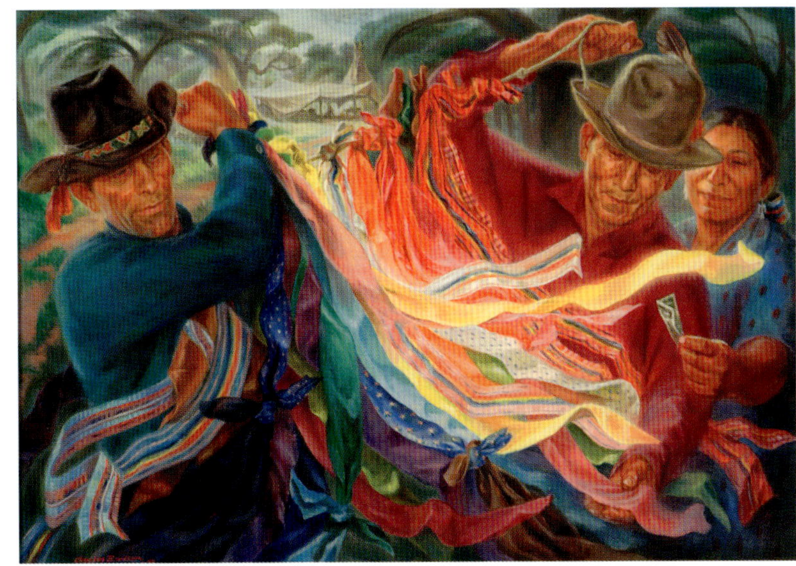

Perhaps Wilson's consummate design-over-subject painting is *Shawnee Ribbon Bets,* painted in 1948. The rich, succulent colors of the ribbons and their dynamic flow contrast with the esoteric human activity. The actual subject of the painting is so obscure that Thomas Gilcrease asked Wilson to explain it:

> A part of the costume of the women has long been the wide colorful hair ribbon tied to the single braid which is worn trailing down the back. For one reason or another, this developed into the main article for betting and many Indians of this region now carry with them an extra ribbon for just this purpose.
>
> Prior to the contest, usually at a special ceremony or powwow such as the Seneca Green Corn or the Shawnee Bread Dance, two men go about the camping grounds gathering the articles to be bet. As a bet is offered it is tied to the cord they carry. If that bet is in turn 'called' the second bettor ties his ribbon to the ribbon he is hoping to win. Sometimes scarves and even clothing is bet and so tied on. When money is offered it is tied into the corner of a 'called' scarf or ribbon. The painting portrays this gathering of the Ribbon Bets. On the right can be seen a woman handing the men a dollar bill to be bet against a certain ribbon.

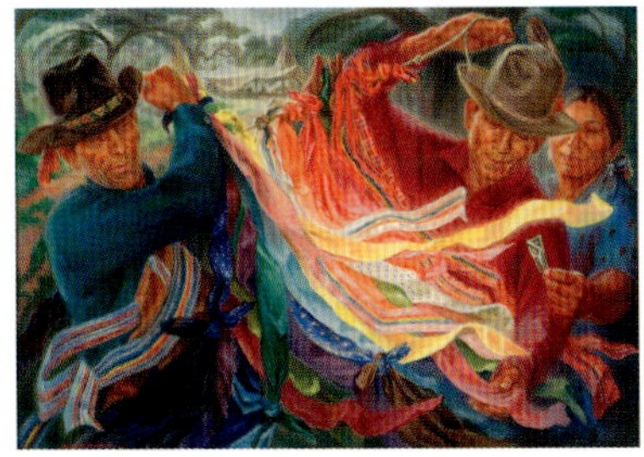

ABOVE AND FOLLOWING PAGES:
SHAWNEE RIBBON BETS, 1948. 27.25 X 35,
OIL/CANVAS, 0127.1468

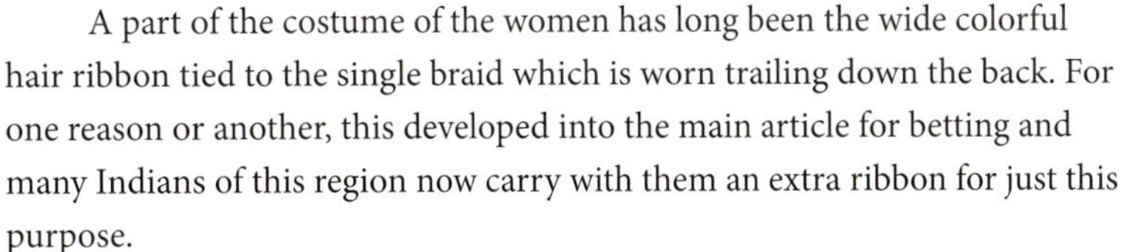

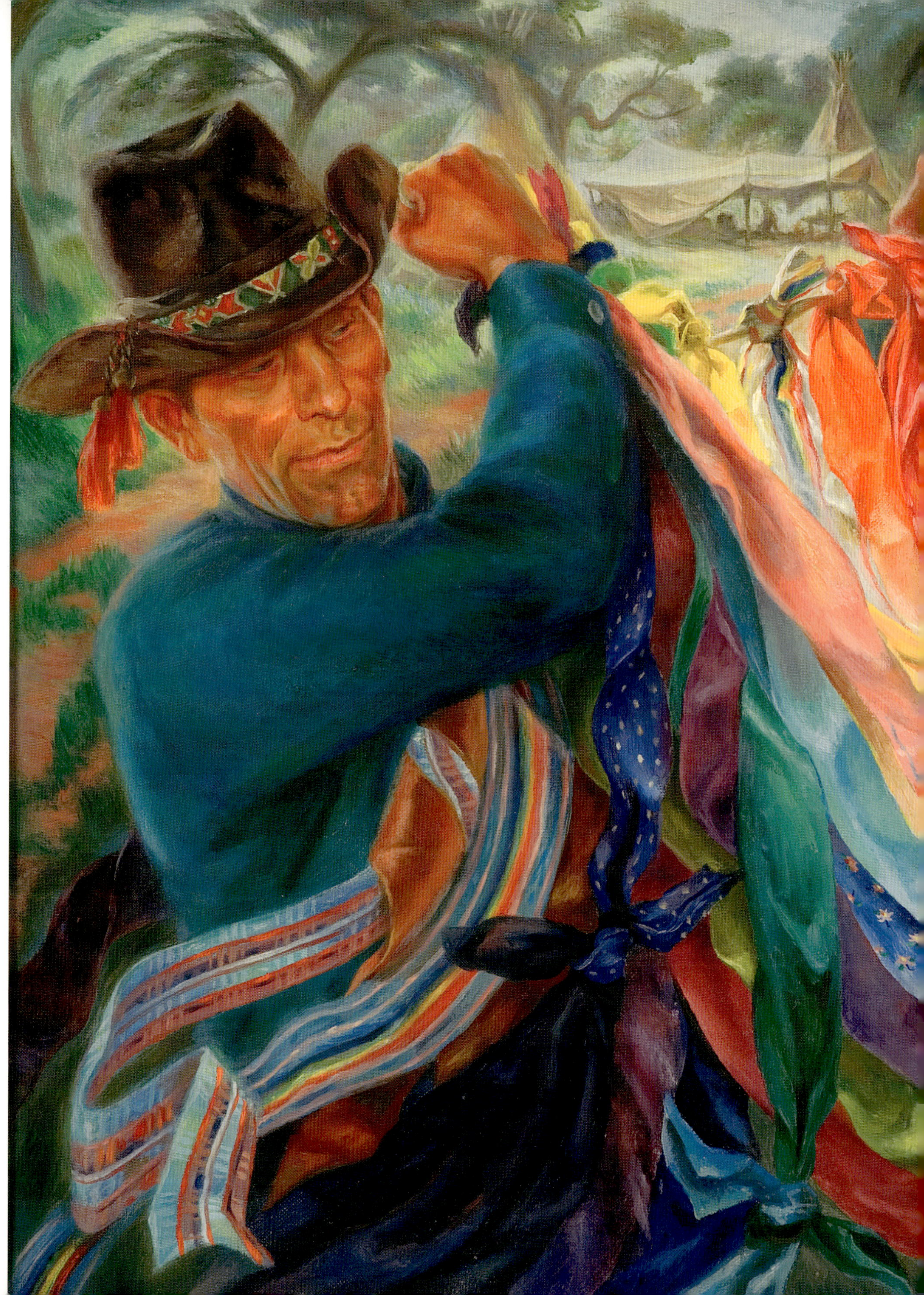

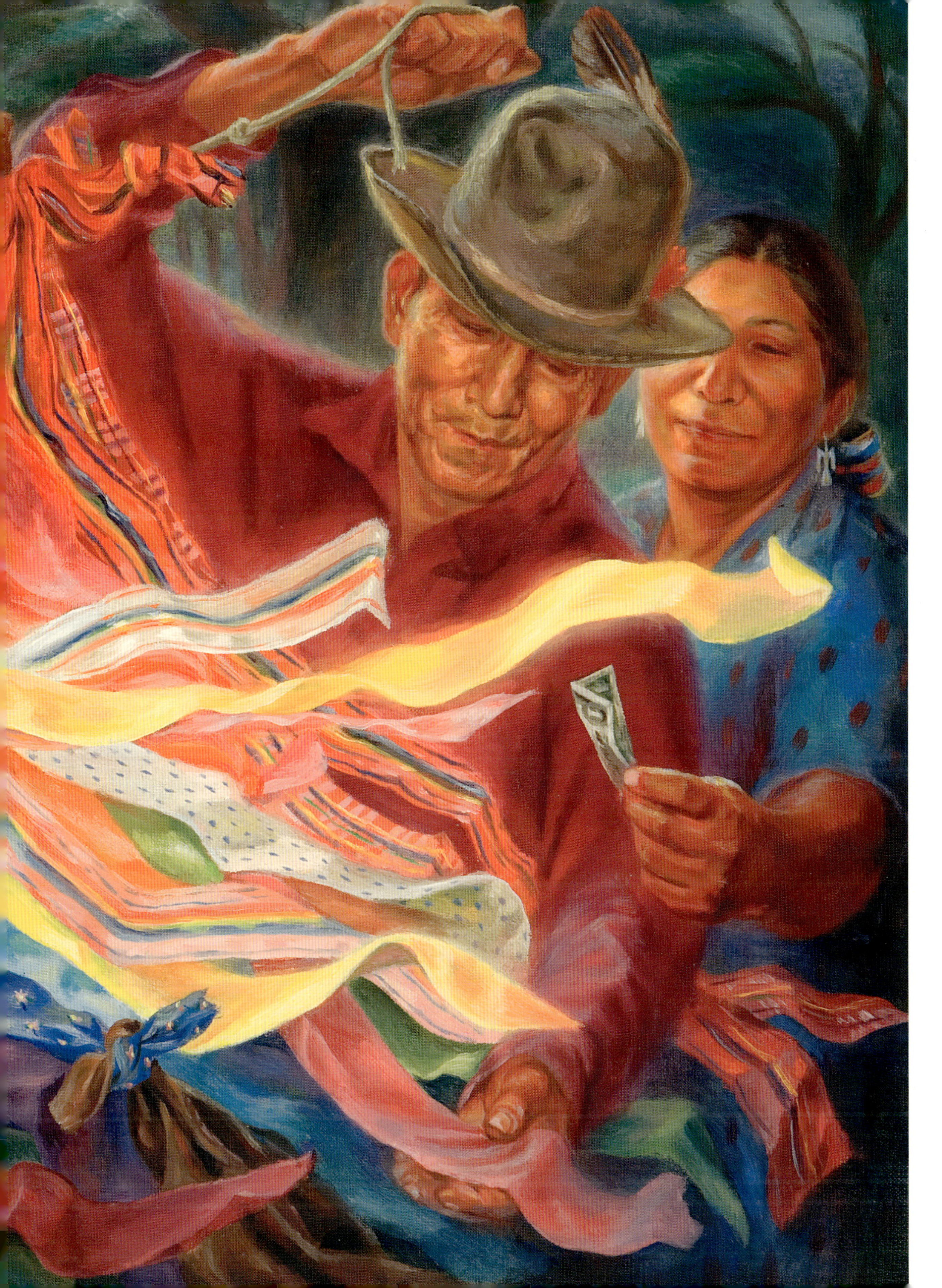

Wilson went on to explain that because the ribbon bets is an incident rather than part of the ceremony, this painting is probably the only visual record that exists.

In perhaps the most obvious tribute to the observer, Wilson painted *Ceremonial—Some Come Just to Watch* in (2001). In the 2004 interview, he spoke about what he likes best, the people:

> One of the things I enjoyed was this little girl. While the ceremonial dancers and the drummers and the people are singing back in the shadows, the little girl is dancing… The little blond headed boy is flirting with the little blond headed girl. And back over here is Joe Benny and I always put a dog in… In the corner on the right hand side is the fellow who posed for the center figure in one of the capitol murals —Joe Benny Mason, a Quapaw.

Artistically, Wilson can make the most commonplace thing a source of wonder for the viewer who takes the time to really examine a painting like *Ceremonial;* the representation of the rusting metal roof, with its play of light and color, is nothing short of amazing.

As with *Shawnee Ribbon Bets* in the 1940s, Wilson continued in the 1990s to look at vital aspects of native ceremonial life that rarely if ever are noticed outside the culture. As with any family and community gathering, food is central. "Women do more than anyone in keeping the Indian heritage alive," Wilson observed. And he paid homage to them in *Powwow Cooks* (1996), an unusual vertically composed painting that implies the complexity of the creation of a meal and represents Indian women as the backbone of the culture.

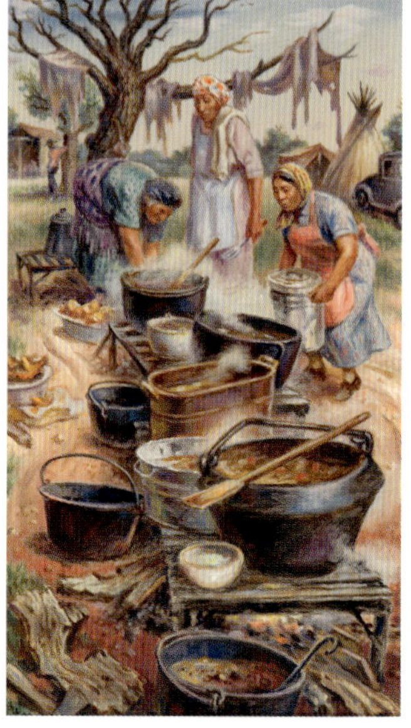

ABOVE AND FACING:

POWWOW COOKS, 1996. 10.375 X 16.75, OIL/CANVAS, 0127.2491

CEREMONIAL—SOME COME JUST TO WATCH, 2001. 9.813 X 27.5, OIL/CANVAS, 0137.2523

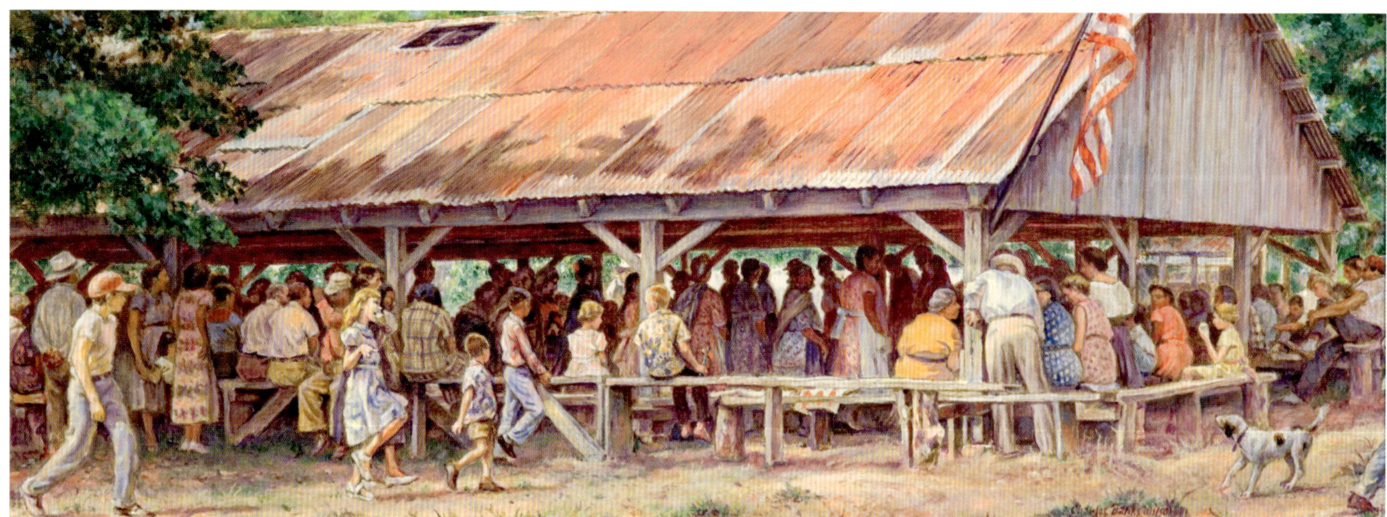

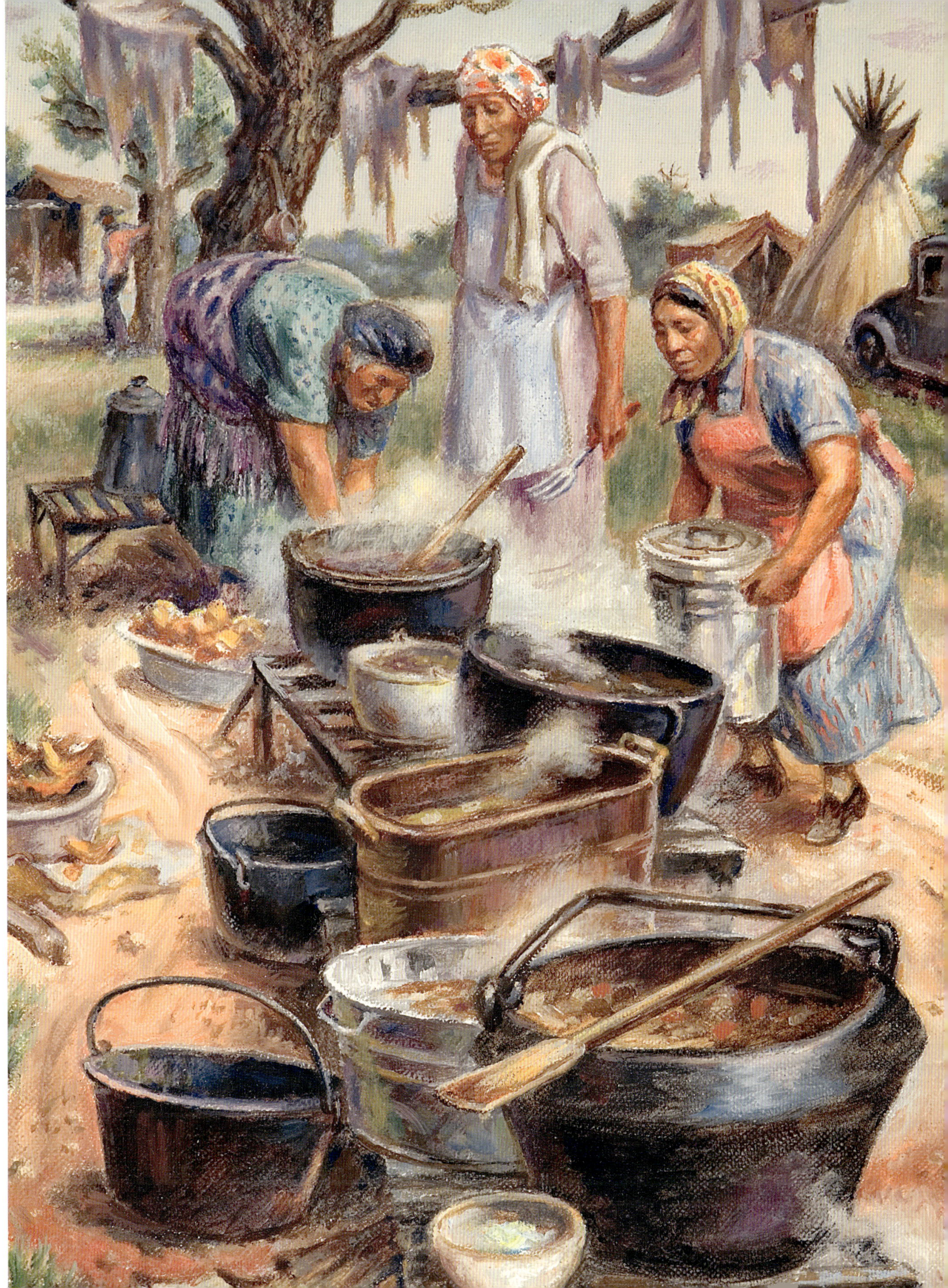

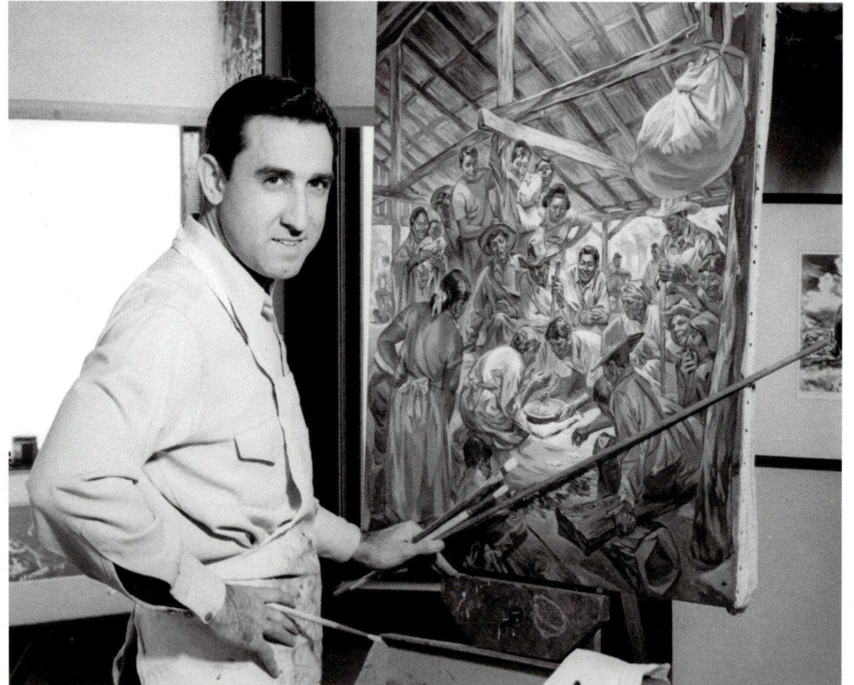

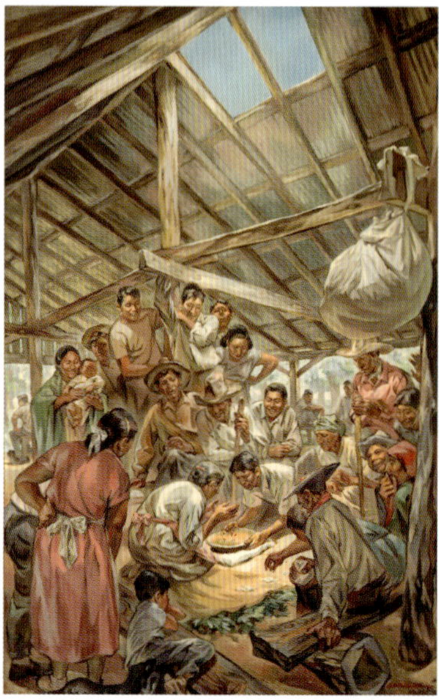

Gilcrease Museum has continued to acquire significant works, including a pair of paintings Wilson created in 1954, *Seneca Thanksgiving Ceremony* and *Dividing the Offering.* As is Wilson's custom, in these scenes from the Seneca Green Corn ceremony, he focused less on formal activities than on details of the communal energy sustaining the gathering. *Seneca Thanksgiving Ceremony* depicts the peach seed game, played in the longhouse. "God is watching the game through the skylight," Wilson says. "And when God gets tired of the game he lets one side or the other win. The bag up to the right holds their clothes, their bets. The clothes that they bet are the clothes that will be waiting for them when they get to heaven. So they were encouraged to bet their best clothes." An integral part of Green Corn is sharing bounty; again Wilson:

> They bring a little bit of everything they raised during the summer to share with the rest of the tribe. This is called Dividing the Offering. They're all sitting there with their baskets and tubs to carry back their share of the offering. Everything that they shared is something with seeds, watermelon, cantaloupe, tomatoes, and cucumbers. I put a dog over there sniffing the watermelon because no Indian ceremony would be complete without a dog.

ABOVE AND FACING:

SENECA THANKSGIVING CEREMONY,

1954. 53.5 X 38.5,

OIL/CANVAS, 0127.2476

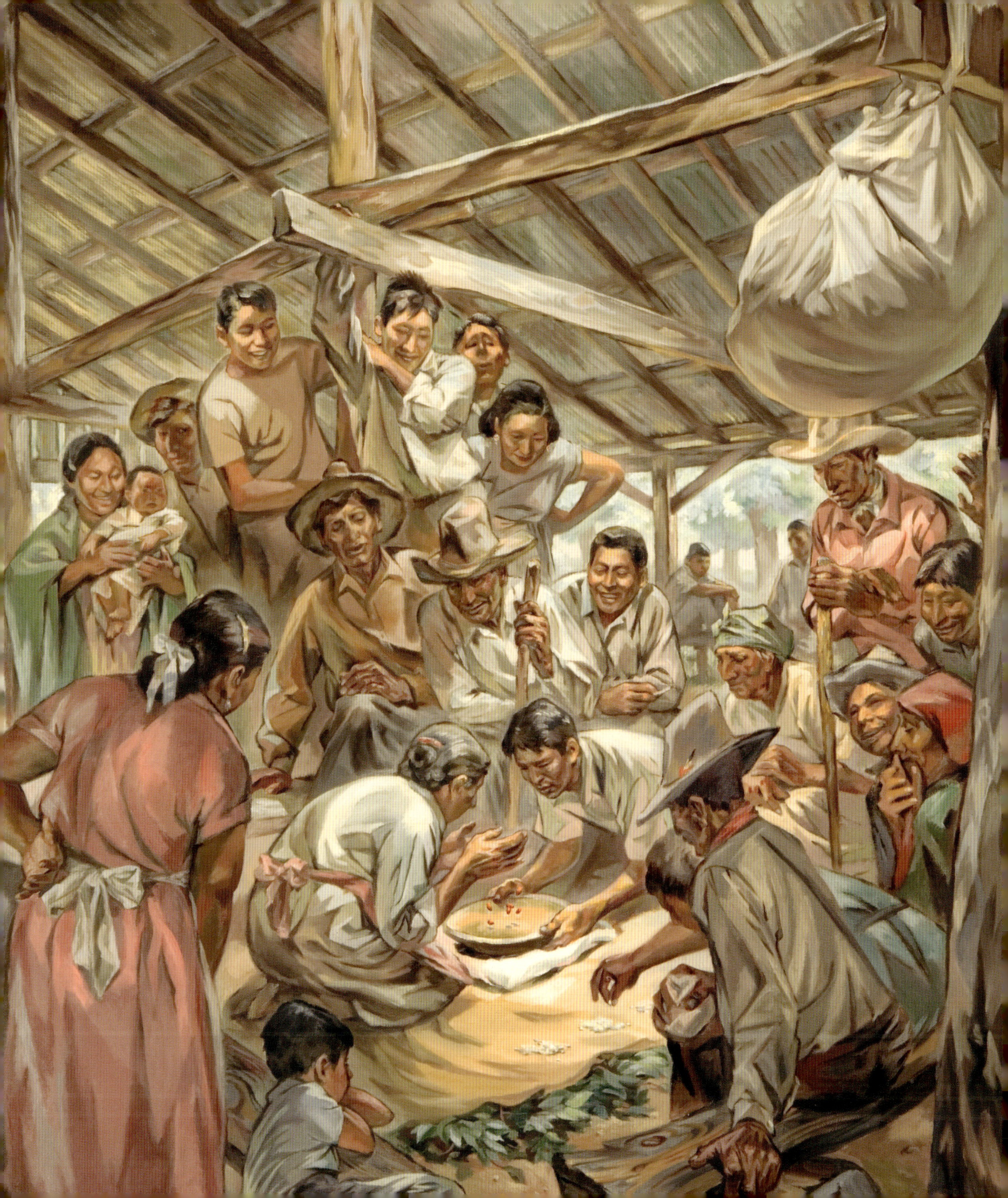

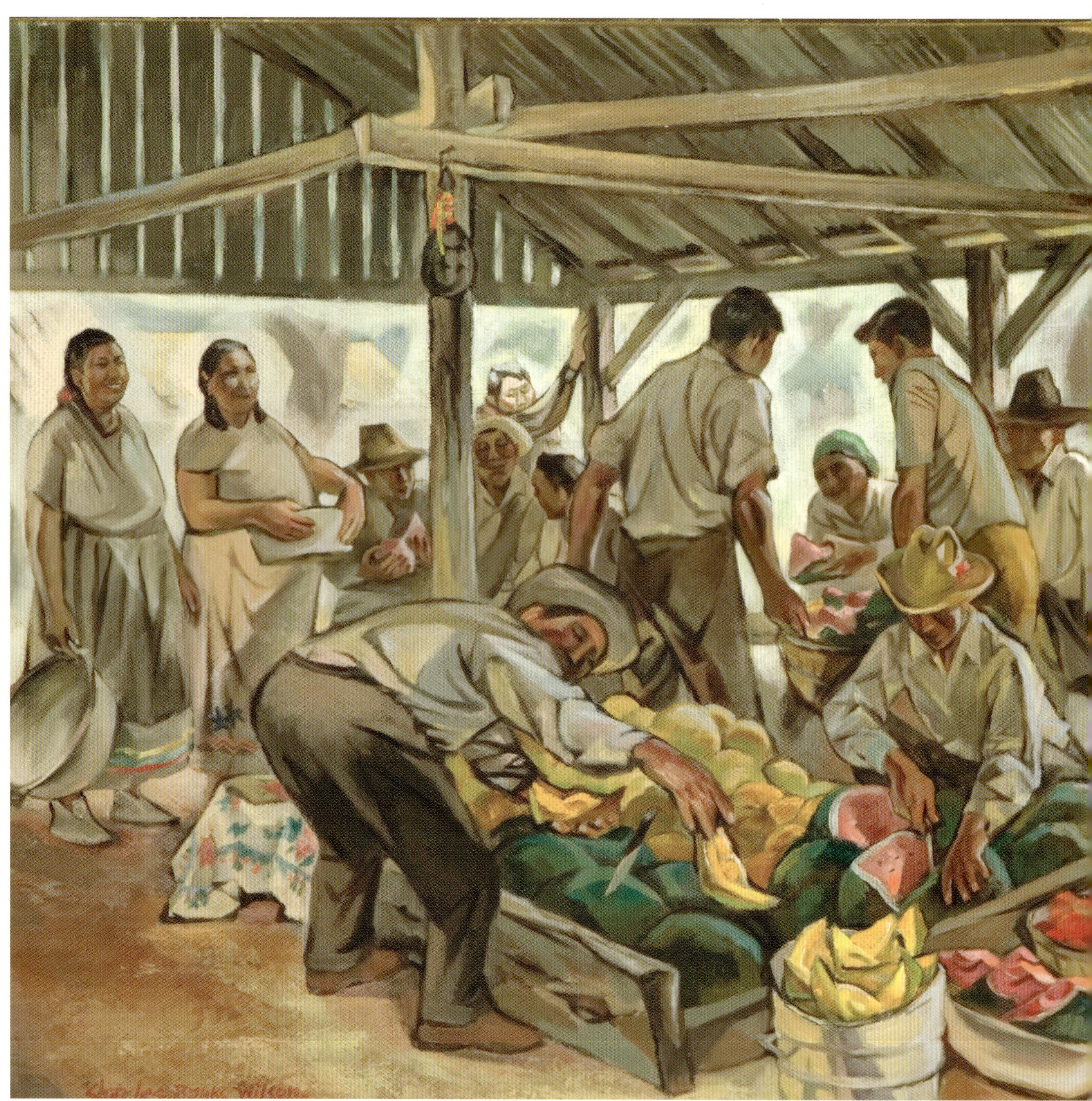

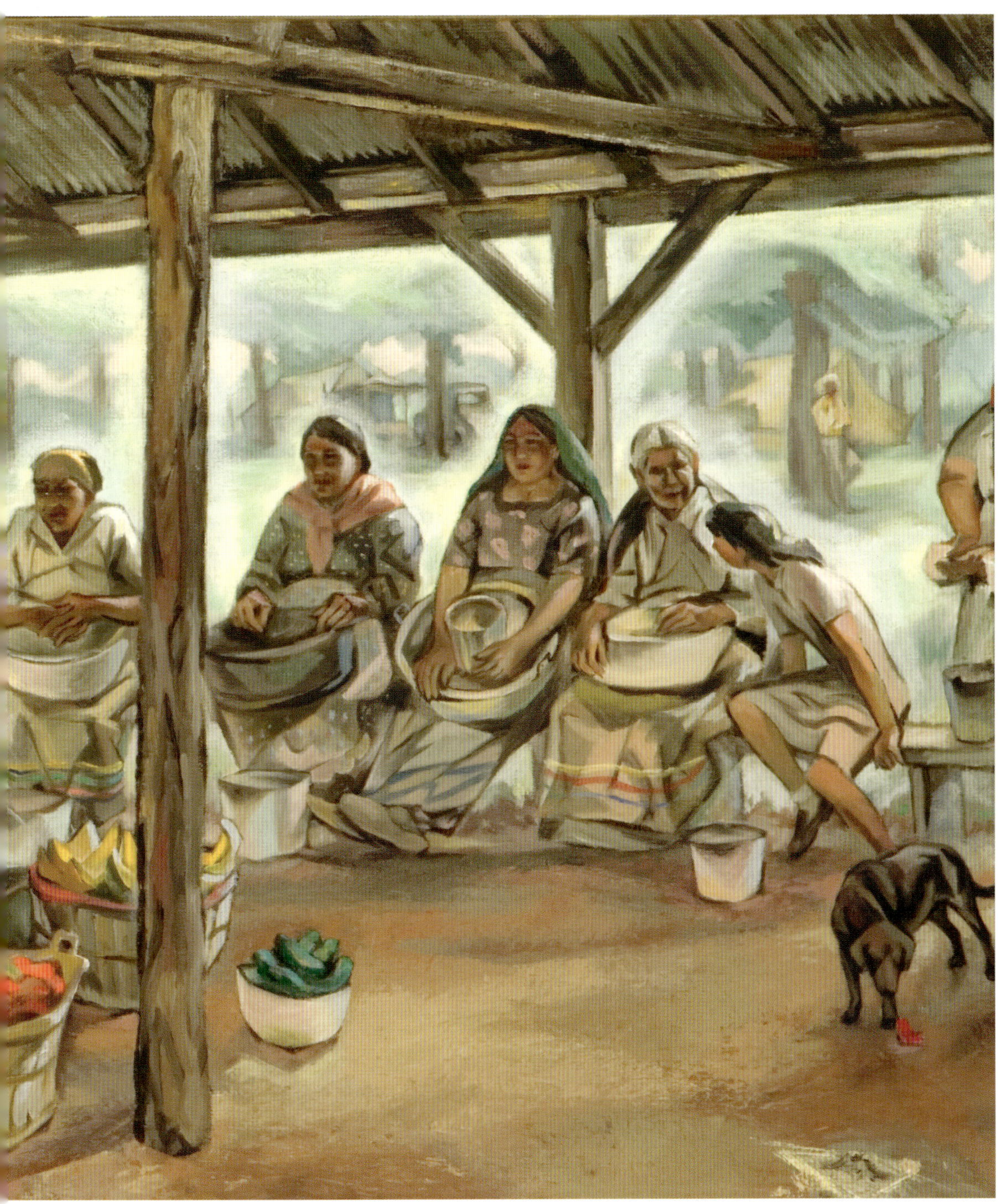

DIVIDING THE
OFFERING, 1954.
30.5 X 50,
OIL/CANVAS,
0127.2477

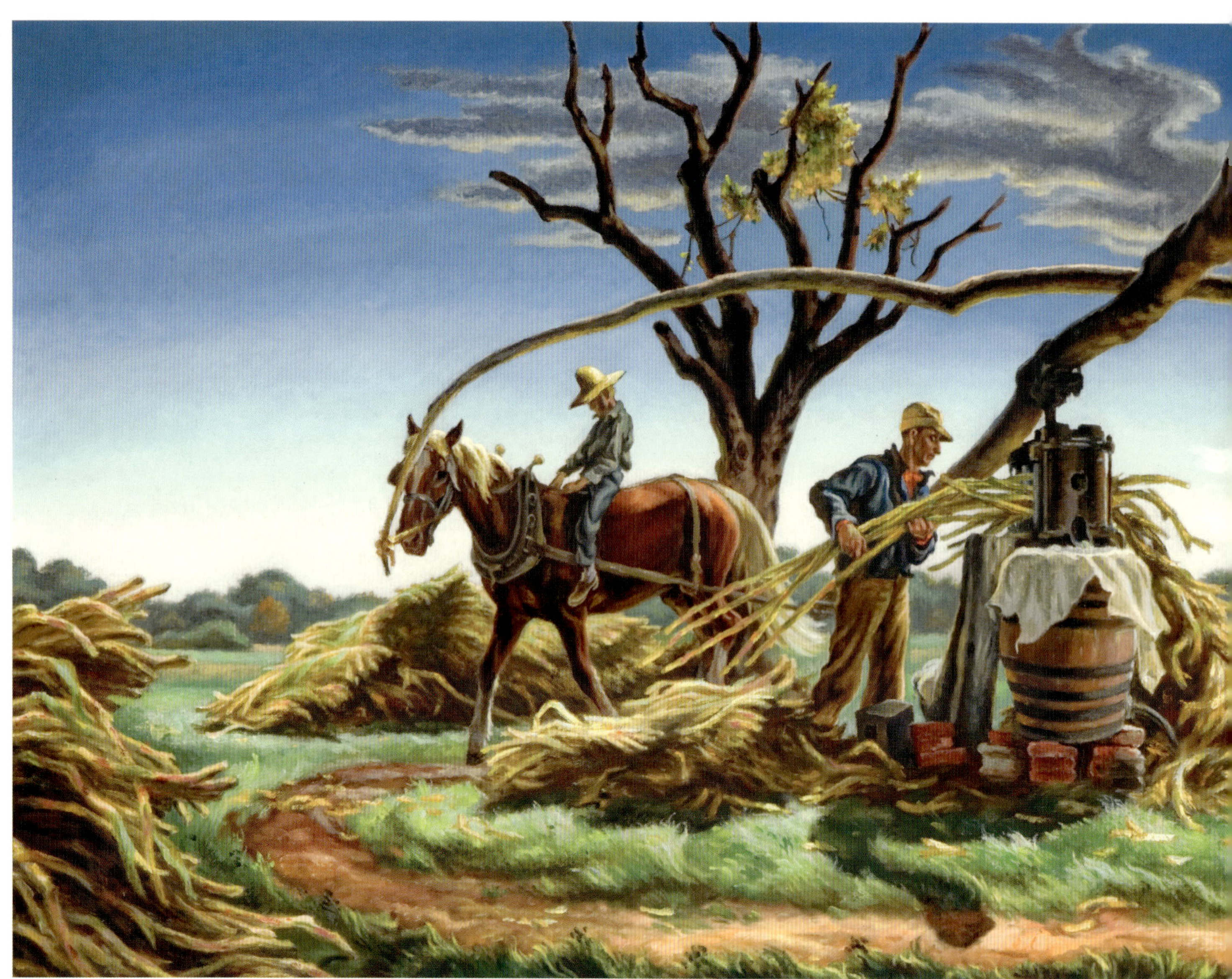

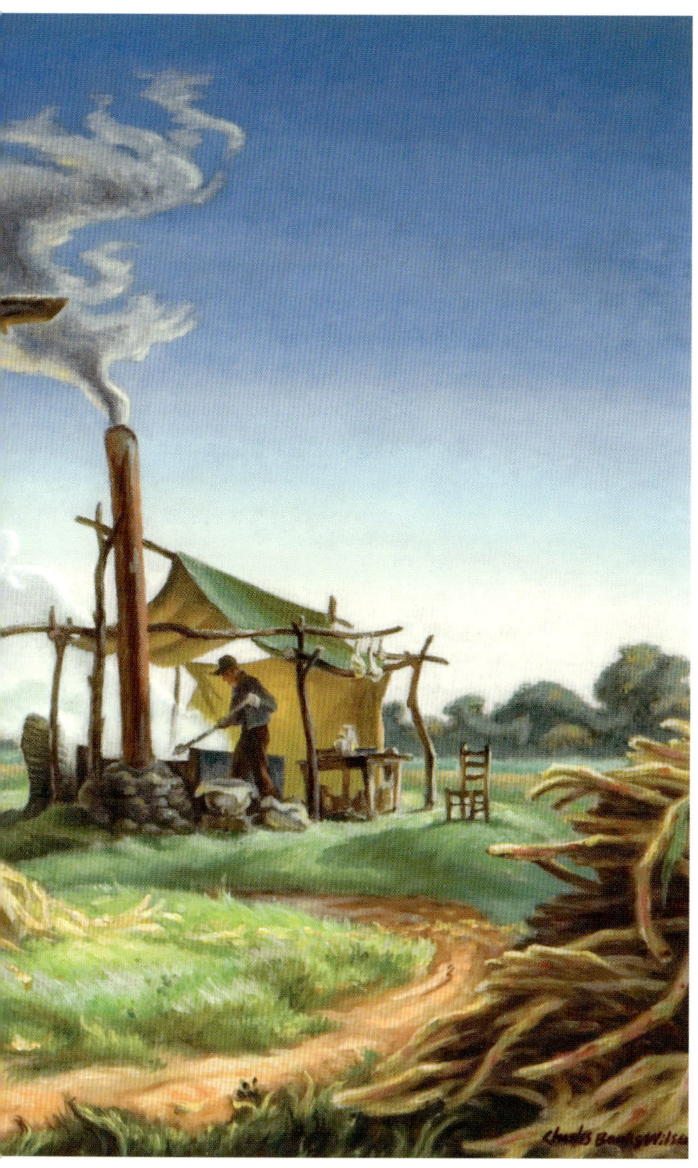

SORGHUM MILL

AT 10 AM, 1960.

29.55 X 49.75,

OIL/CANVAS, 0127.2455

In the 1950s, Wilson turned to a project that shifted his attention away from ceremonial to everyday life, that of farmers and rural families. For a commission from *The Ford Times,* Wilson painted more than ninety watercolors of Oklahoma's lakes, streams, and farms. Concentrating on design over story, he gathered ideas for a lifetime of paintings, especially of things seldom seen today that trigger memories fond and not so fond. Without resorting to sweetly nostalgic (and unrealistic) images of America's past, Wilson reminds us that people worked hard and that their hard work resulted in both successes and failures.

Sorghum Mill at 10 AM (1960) documents the process of extracting juice from sorghum cane so that it can be cooked down to syrup. Sorghum was an important crop during America's lean times of the early and mid-twentieth century. It was drought-tolerant, a good rotational crop, and could be harvested for animal forage as well as processed into syrup for human consumption. "I am amazed at how many people tell me of their experiences in making sorghum molasses. One fellow set me straight when he told me, 'It ain't picturesque, it's damn hard work,' " Wilson recalled.

The painting is a classic example of regionalist sensibility. Wilson diverts attention from the demanding yet tedious character of the job to the beautiful, sinuous forms— including such unlovely realities as the carbon-laden smoke emitted from the cookshack.

In rural America, then as now, children were an important source of family labor. But the reward for hard work was rural life itself, with animals, trees to climb, woods to explore, fishing and swimming holes. In his travels, Wilson often observed children at work and at play. *Morning Chores* (1969) is an example of the sometimes serendipitous nature of plein-air work. While sketching a cabin, trees, road, and distant landscape, the artist says, "I took little notice of the boy who came outside a number of times to get wood from a freshly cut pile. When I did recognize what he was doing, I knew he had given my picture a subject." Without the boy, the picture would have been technically excellent, but lack human interest, which is central for rural genre.

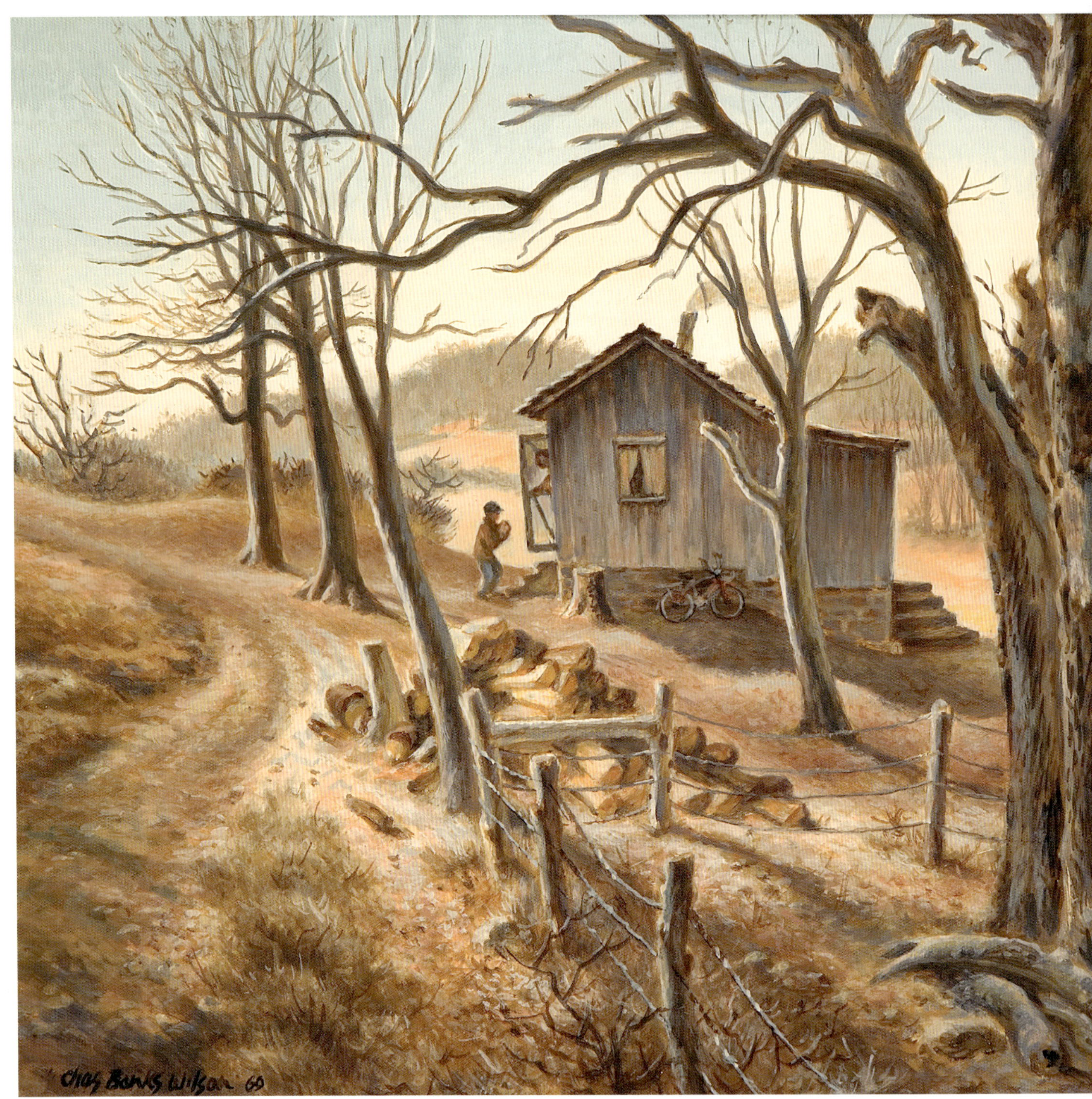

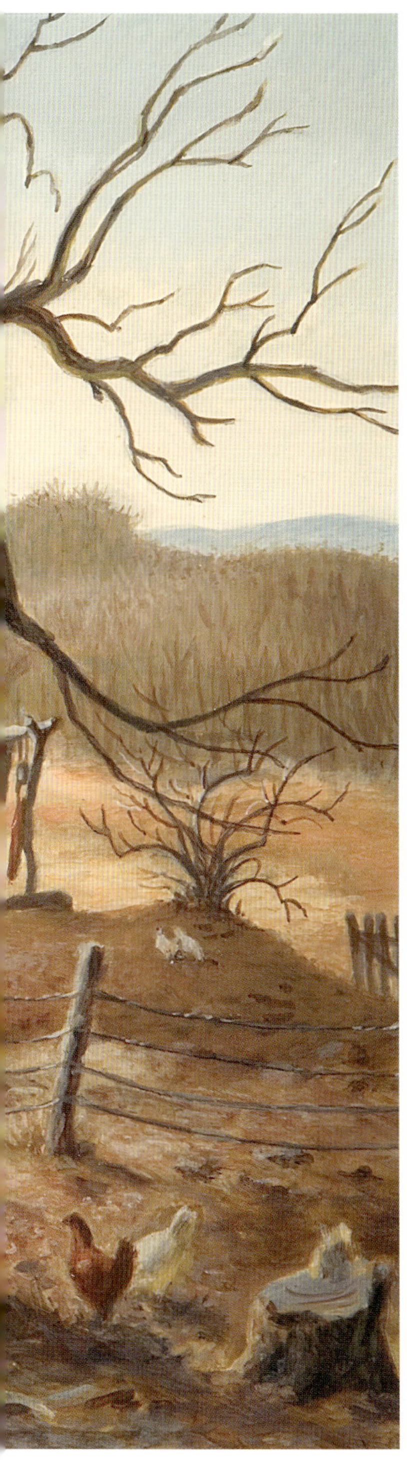

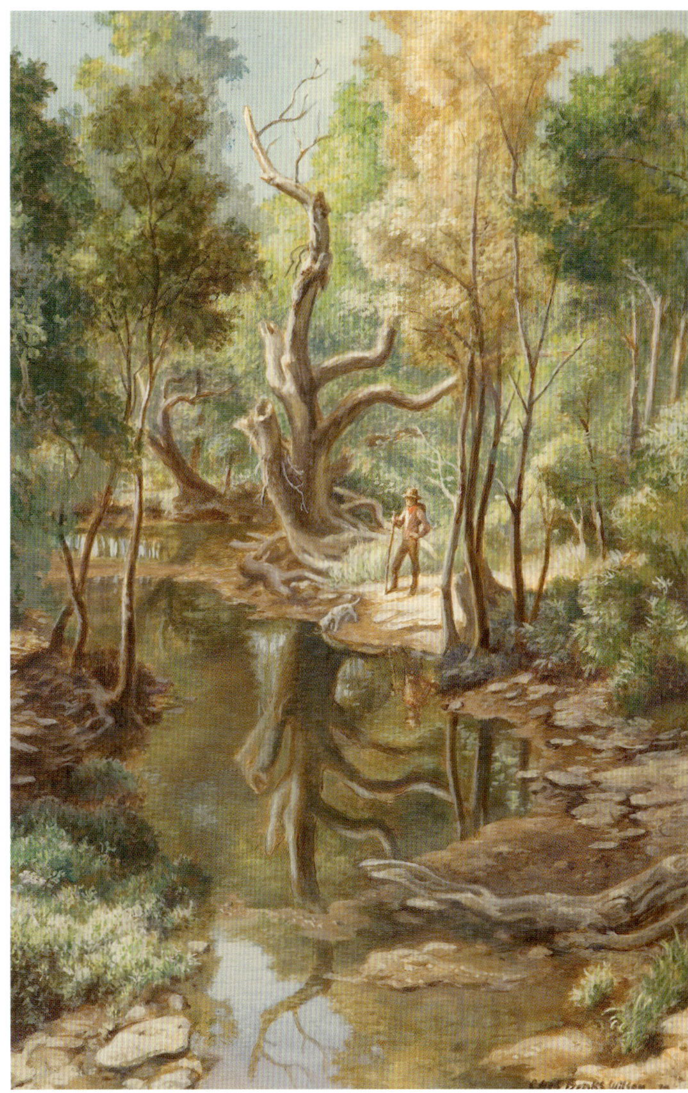

REFLECTIONS,
1979. 27.5 X 21,
EGG TEMPERA,
0137.2458

MORNING CHORES, 1969,
21.5 X 26, EGG TEMPERA,
0137.2470

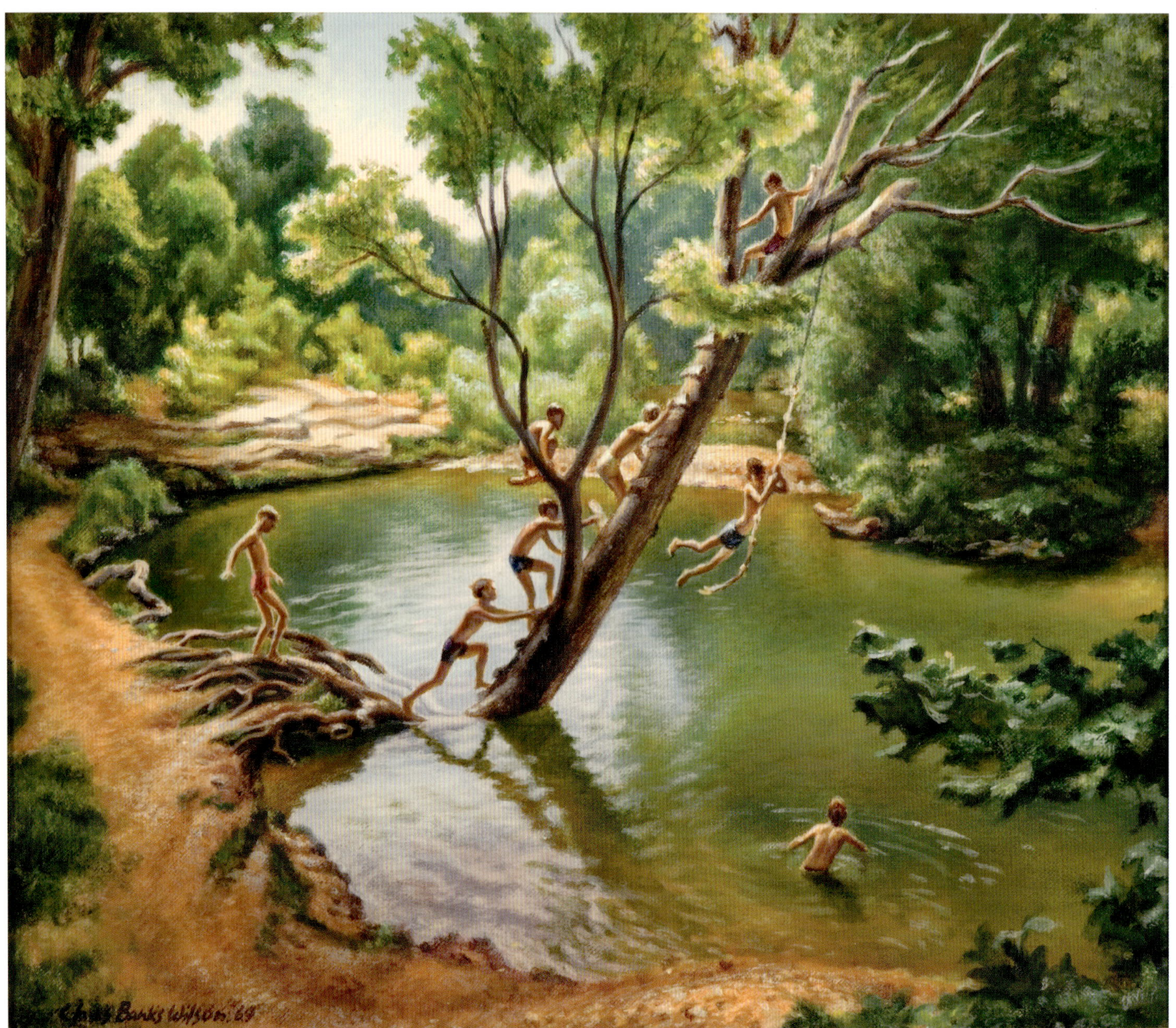

Of course the compensation for a job well done is play. Summers in Oklahoma before air conditioning were made bearable by a good swimming hole—especially if the water was spring-fed and cold. A good tree at the right angle meant a rope swing. In *Any Summer Afternoon* (1969) we can enjoy the delight of the children, feel their shock at dropping through the stifling air into the sparkling, icy water, and hear their shouts of joy. Wilson was not immune to the call: "Most good swimming holes feature a tree such as this, and when I run across one, a decision has to be made—to sketch or go swimming!"

A fascinating aspect of Wilson's approach to his work is his ability to interest us in the most mundane aspect of life. *Family Album* (1949) resulted from his ongoing quest for "Indian stuff," and a visit to a family who told him there might be some in their trash heap a ways down from the house.

> I looked at all the stuff there and I think what really turned me on were the shapes and colors. The rust of the barrels and things made the green of the spring look twice as green. . . . I made a lot of sketches there and bought some of the things like the baby walker which has no value and I noticed a little blue potty in the barrel and figured there was a boy in the family and no boy would throw away wheels. I had a friend who had a tintype album and I put that in the corner and that's why I call it the family album. The history of the family is in the things they throw away. An old chair over here with no stuffing in it carved on the back, and I could imagine when they first got that chair how proud they were. . . . The thing I'm most proud of as an artist is there was an old bottle of hair oil and you can tell there had been oil in that bottle. It takes a damn good painter to do that—paint the inside of a bottle.

And "a damn good painter" he is. For all the historical and cultural importance intrinsic in his work, Wilson is first and foremost an artist. Draftsmanship, composition, use of materials, an understanding of color theory and light—all these things can be learned as the "craft" of art. What cannot be learned or acquired is the "art" of art—the ability to see with more than the physical eyes. Few possess this gift. As an artist, Wilson exists on that rarified plane among those few. Yet, as a man, to those of us fortunate enough to spend time with him and call him friend, he is as genuine as his portraits, as high-spirited as his scenes of childhood fun, and as unpretentious as the people he has chosen to observe and document.

—ANNE MORAND

ANY SUMMER
AFTERNOON,
1969. 24 X 26.125,
ACRYLIC/CANVAS,
0137.2465

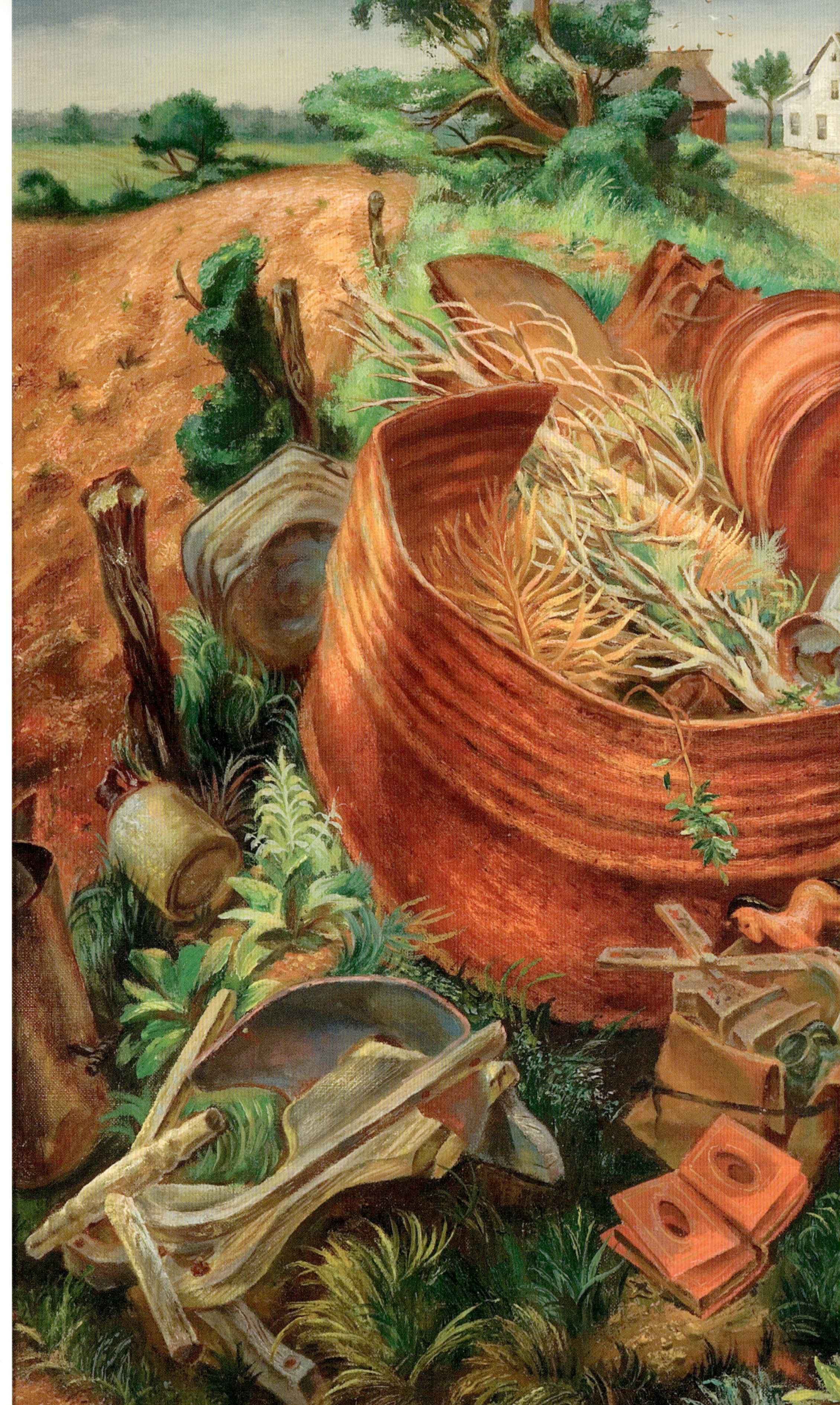

FAMILY ALBUM, 1949.
35.5 X 23.5, OIL/
CANVAS, 0127.2509

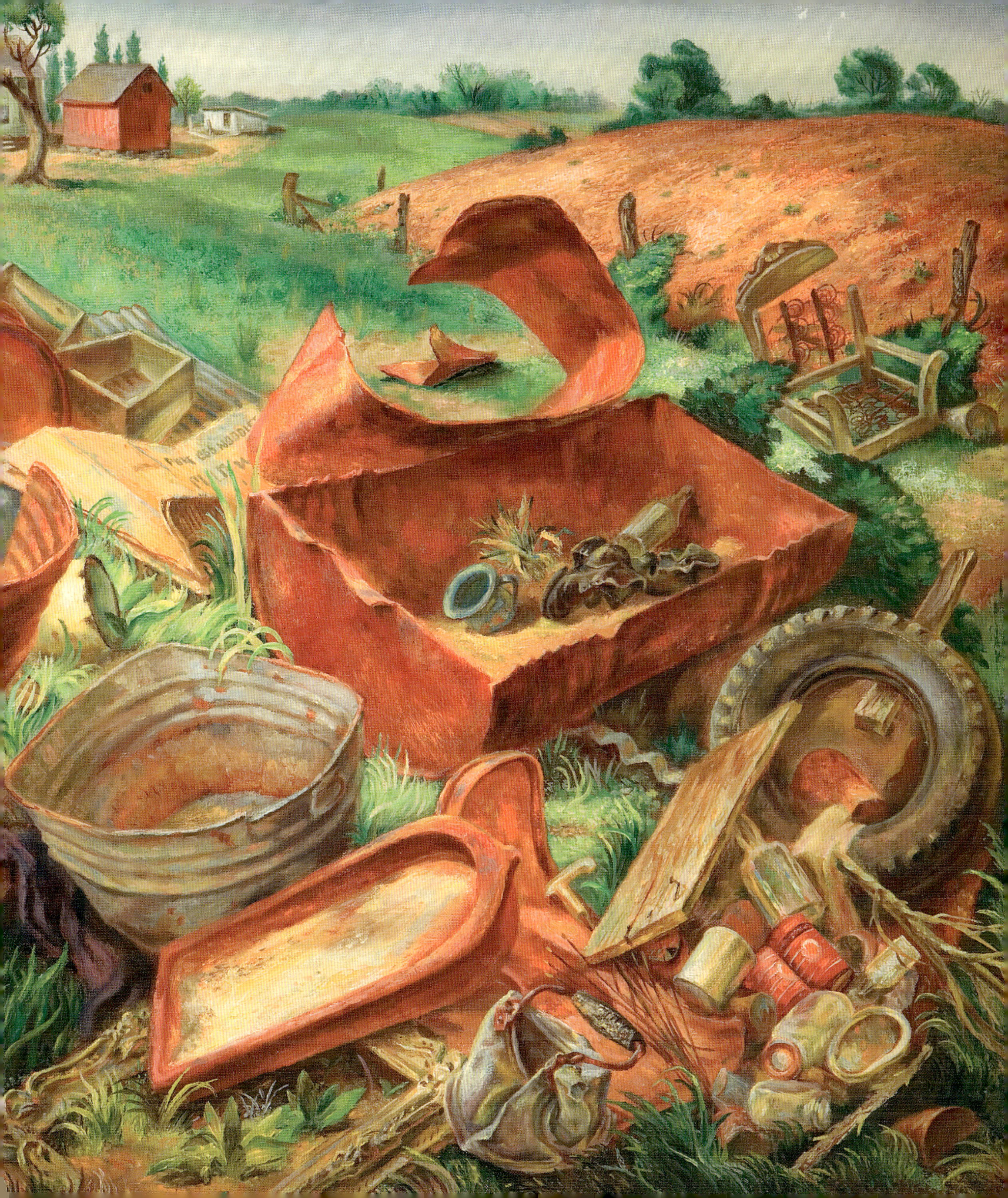

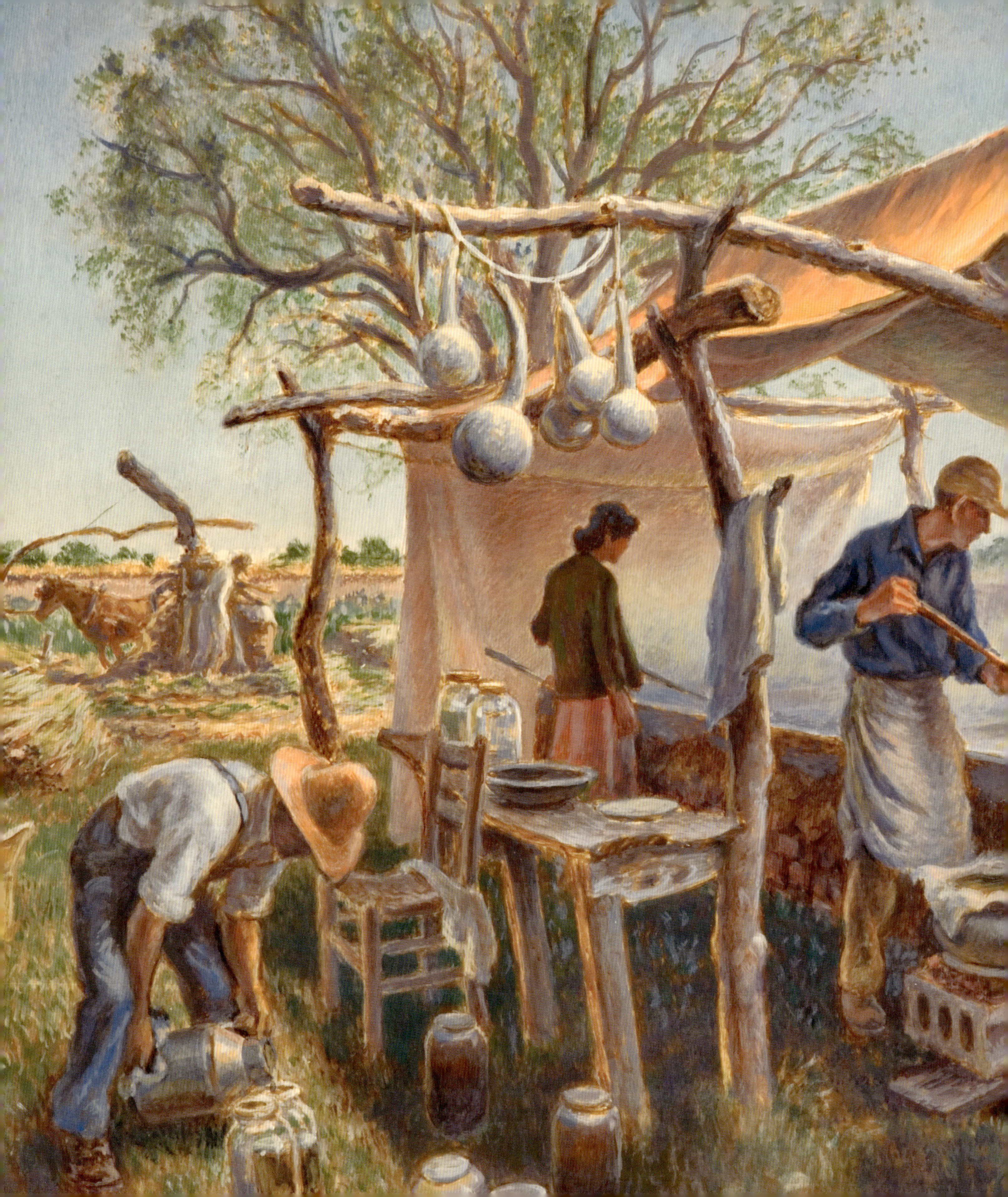

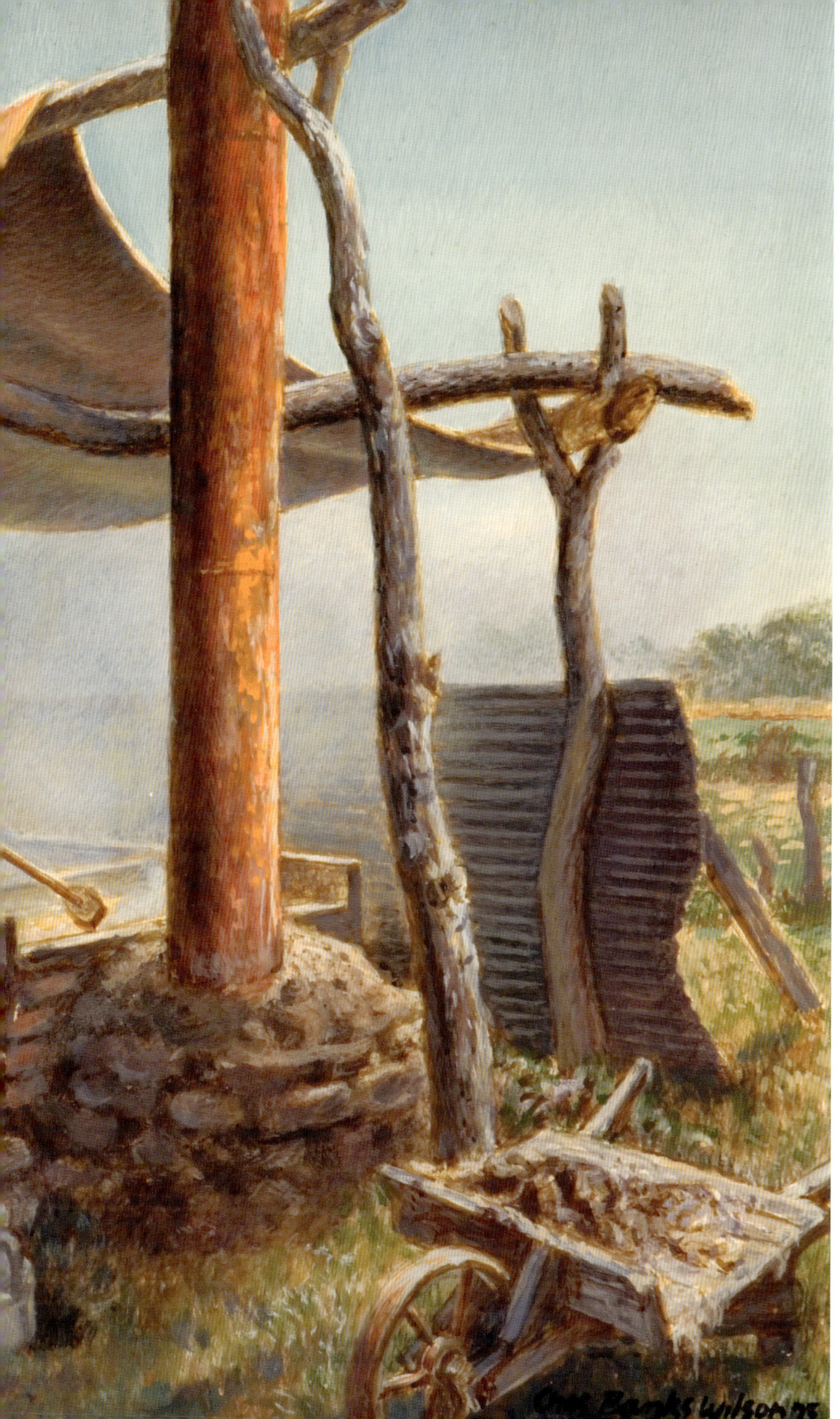

COOKING SORGHUM,
1975. 19.625 X 25,
EGG TEMPERA,
0137.2459

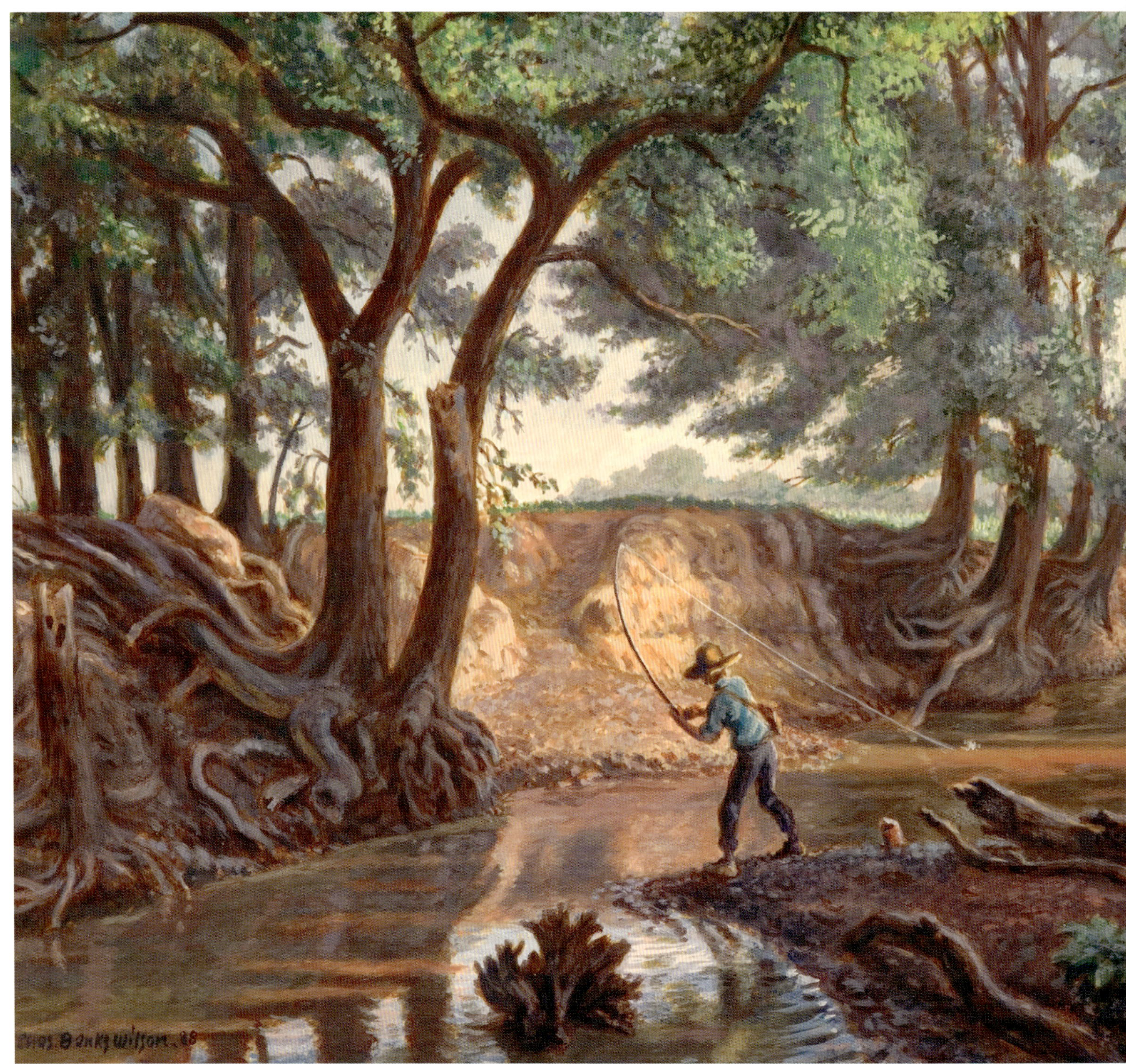

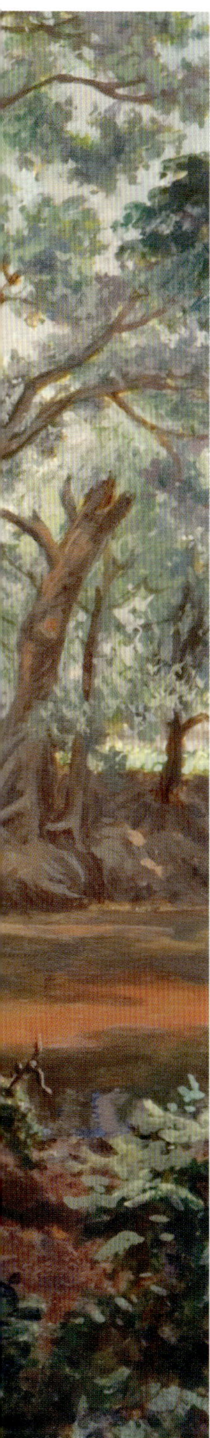

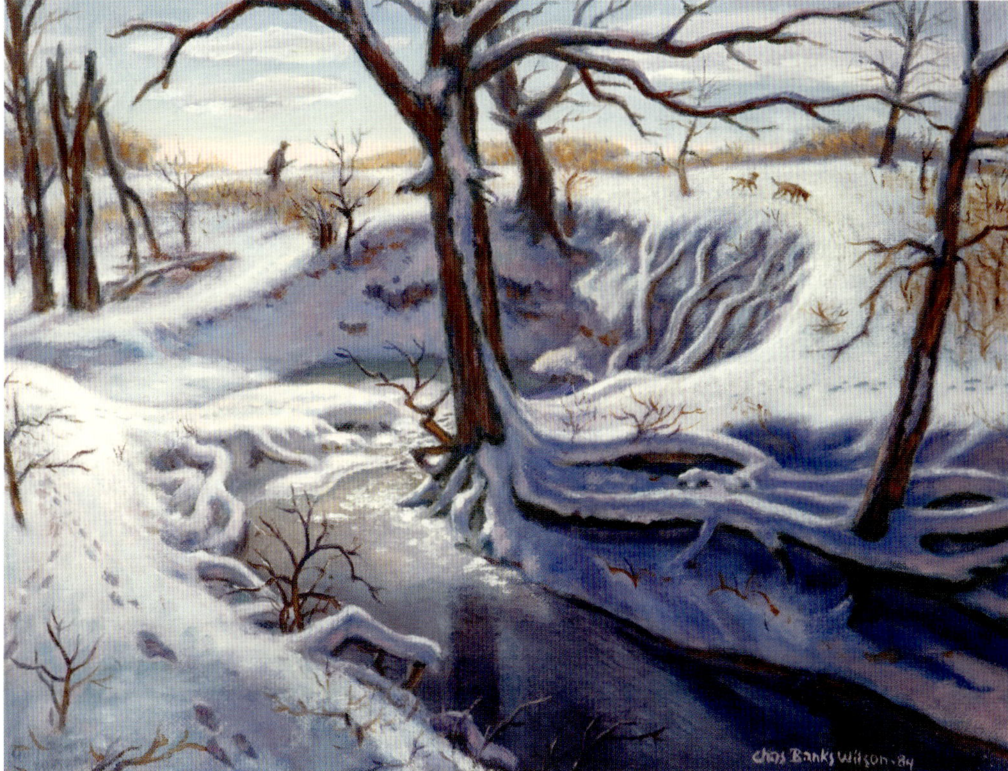

RABBIT TRACKS,
1984. 16.625 X
19.875, OIL/
CANVAS,
0137.2566

CBW: *The basic elements of all aesthetic quality are primitive!*
That is why aesthetic quality and the notion of progress are alien to each other.

SHADOWS ON THE CREEK,
1988. 18.75 X 22.375,
EGG TEMPERA,
0127.1468

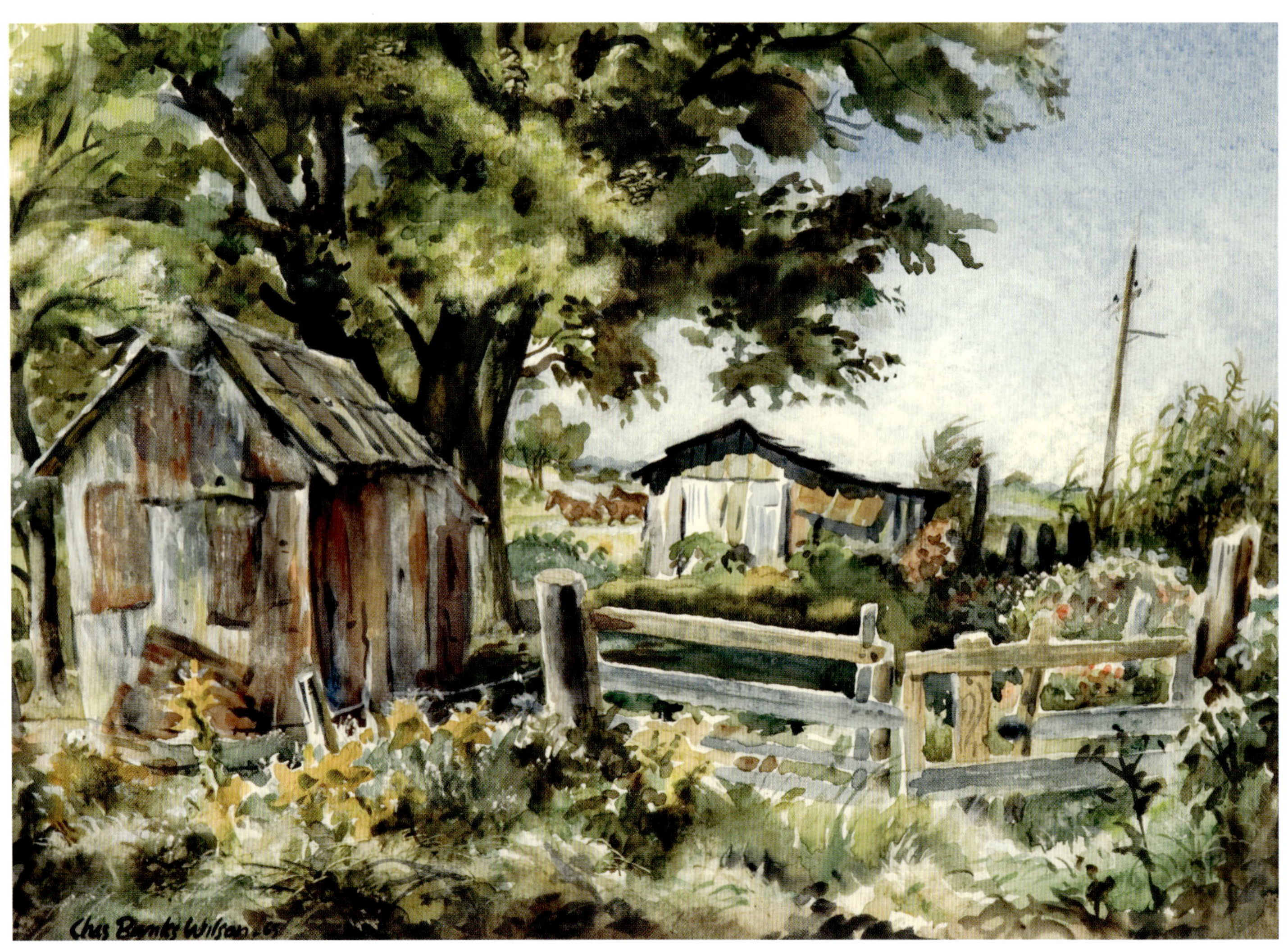

THE OLD FARM,
1965. 22 X 28,
WATERCOLOR/
PAPER 0227.1751

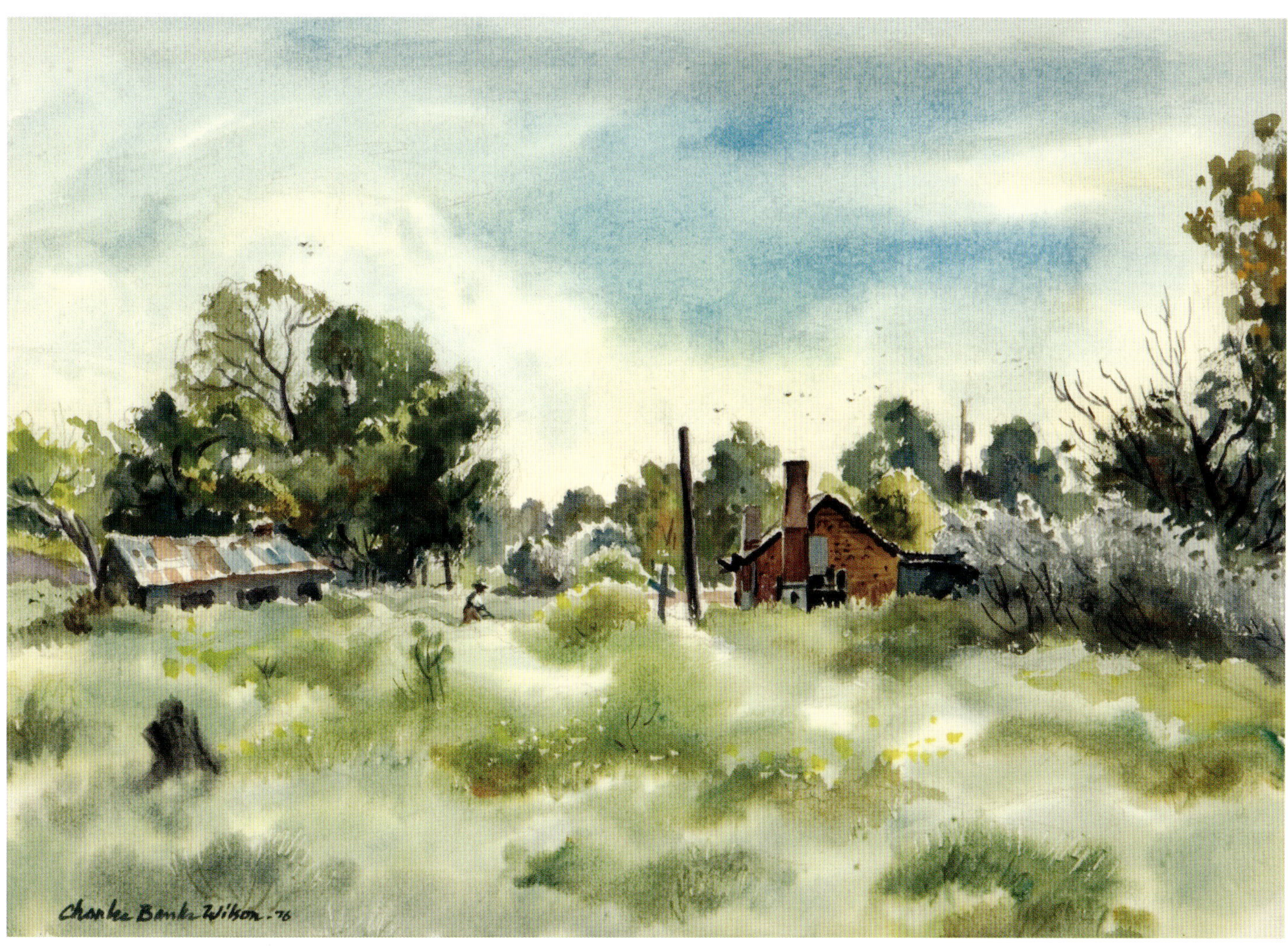

FARMER CUTTING

GRASS, 1976. 21 X 27,

WATERCOLOR/PAPER,

0227.1753

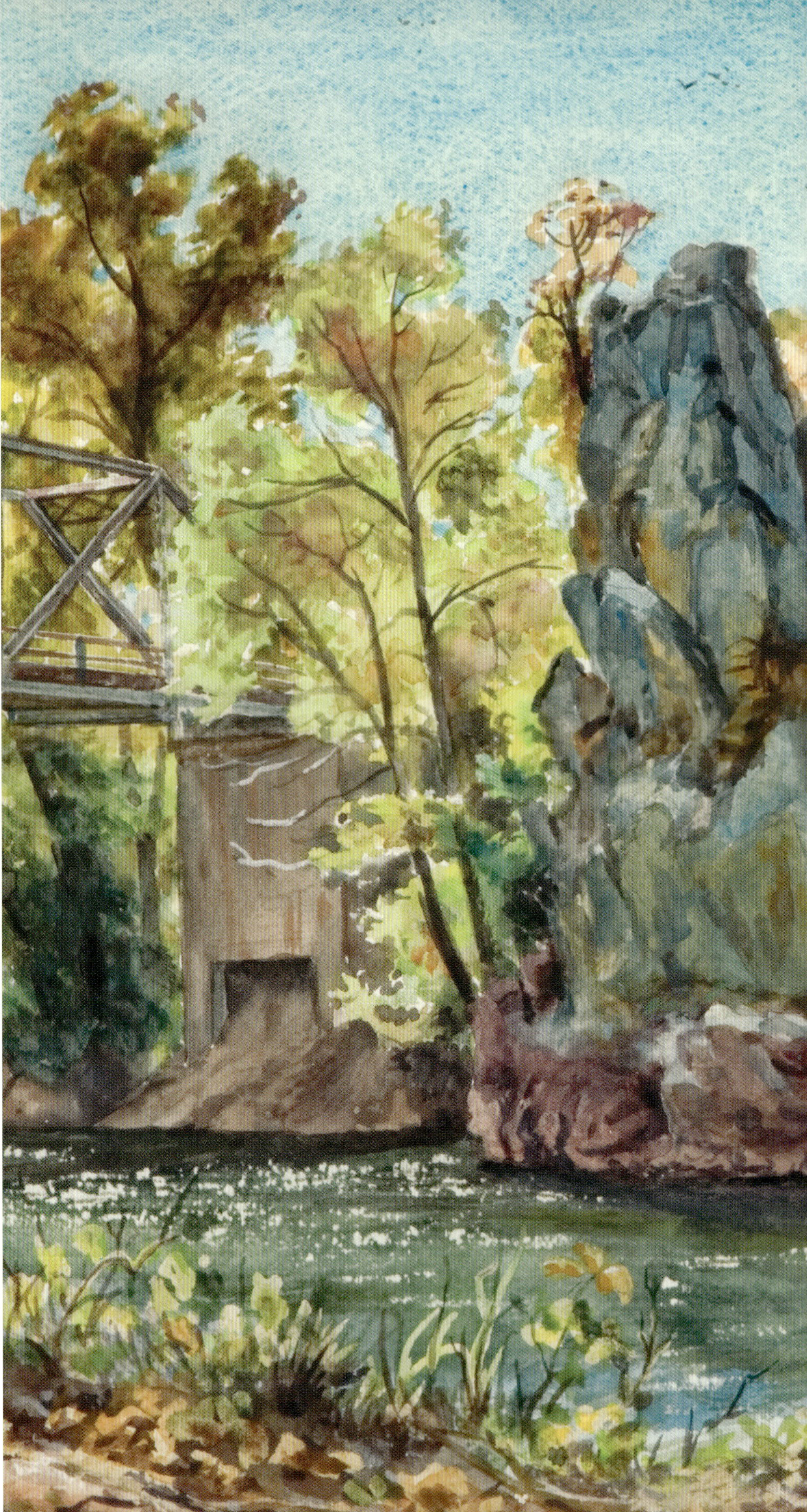

LOVER'S LEAP AT 5 PM,
1976. 23.5 X 28.75,
WATERCOLOR/PAPER,
0227.1750

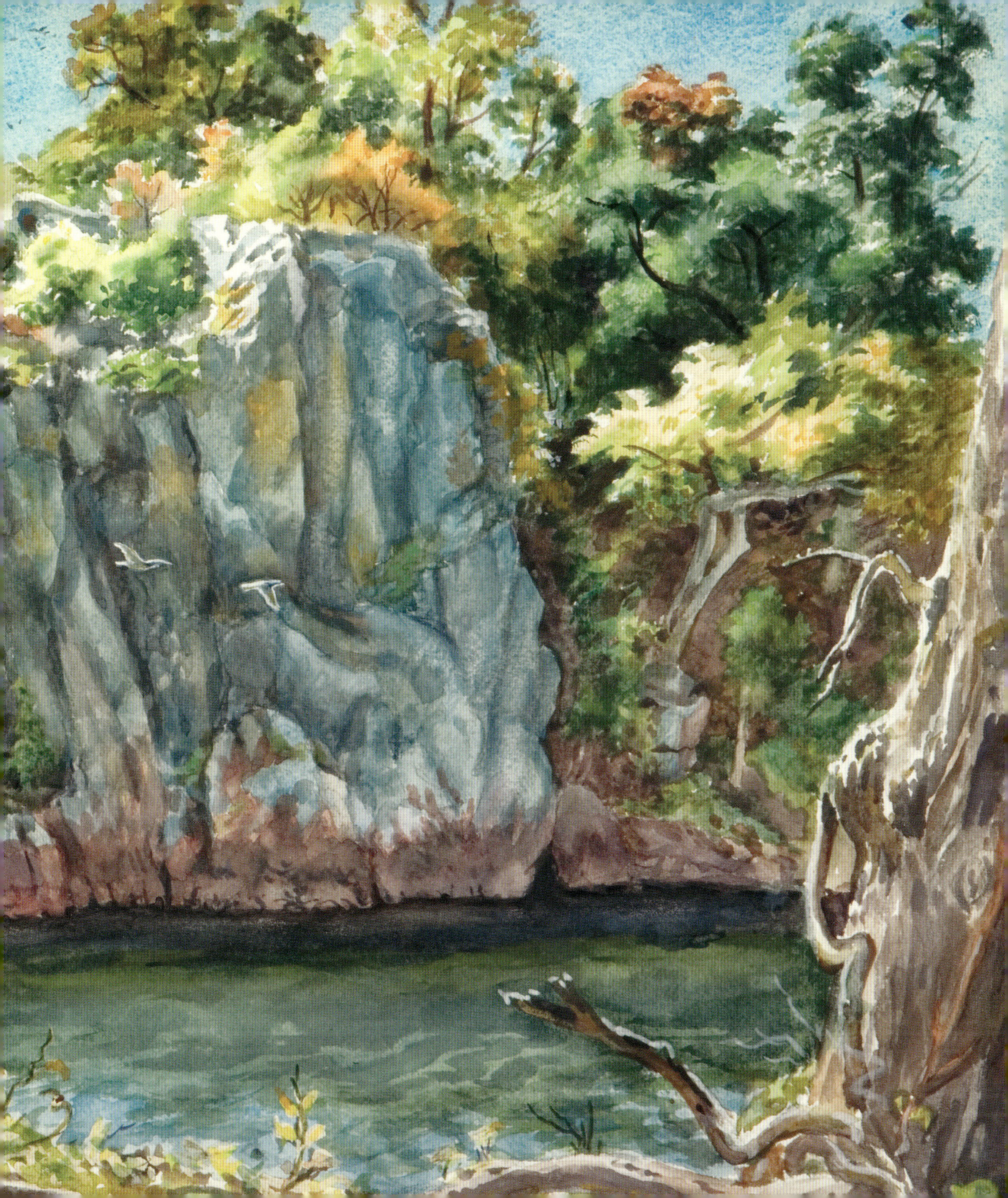

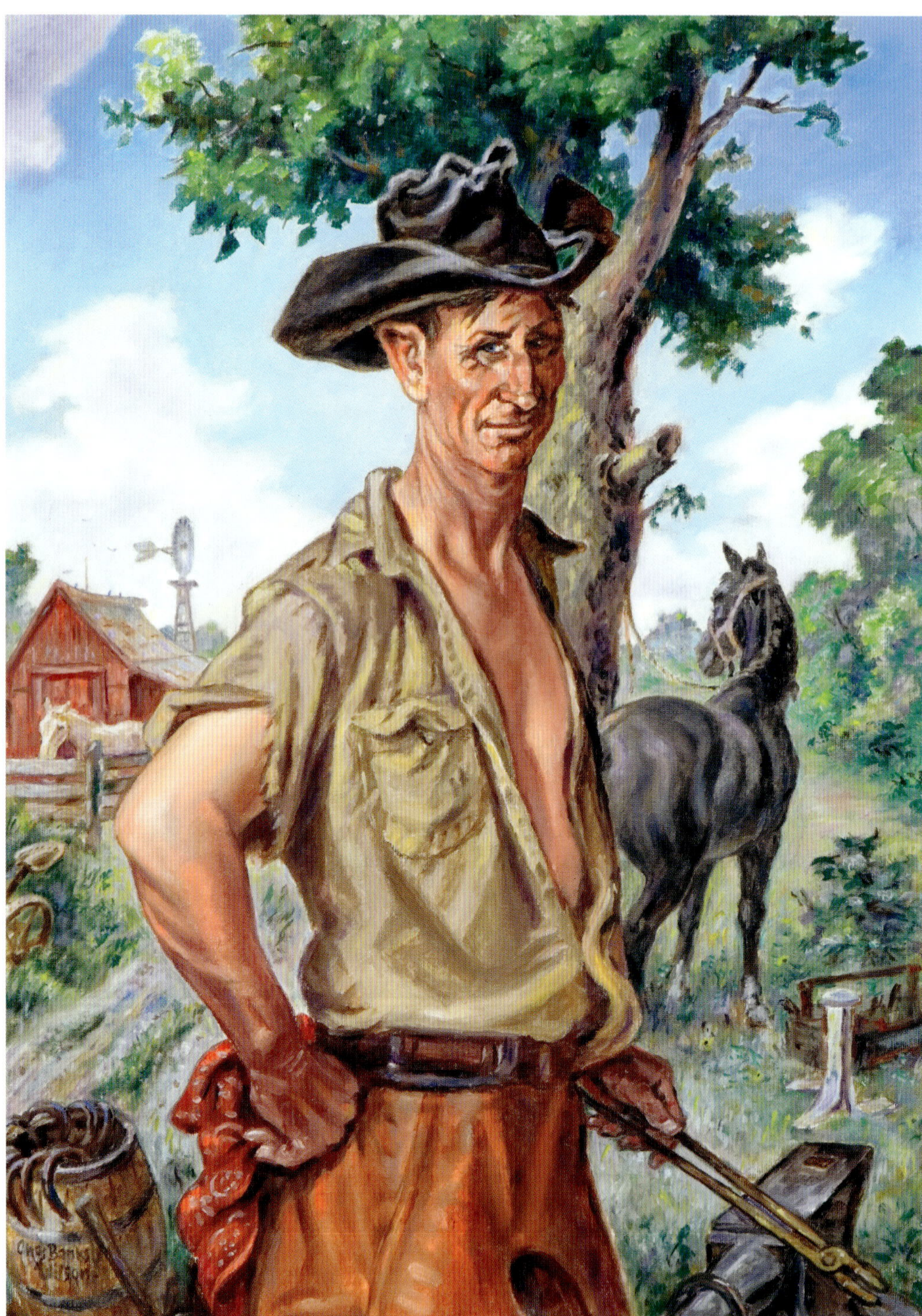

JIM ARCHER, 2004.
21.5 X 15.75,
EGG TEMPERA,
COLLECTION OF
THE ARTIST

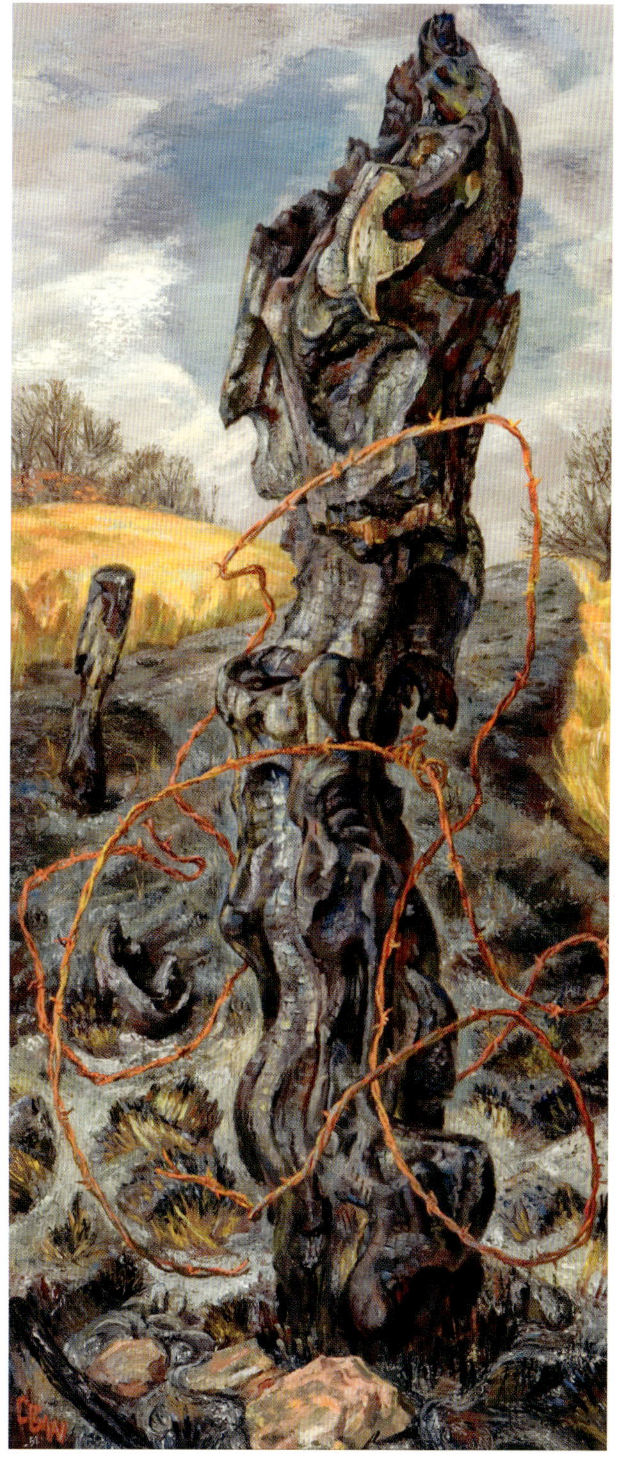

TOTEM, 1950.
39.25 X 17.75,
OIL/CANVAS.
COLLECTION OF
THE ARTIST

THE OLD
TRUCK IN
SHANTY TOWN,
1968. 19.5 X
22, PEN/INK
ON PAPER,
0227.1759

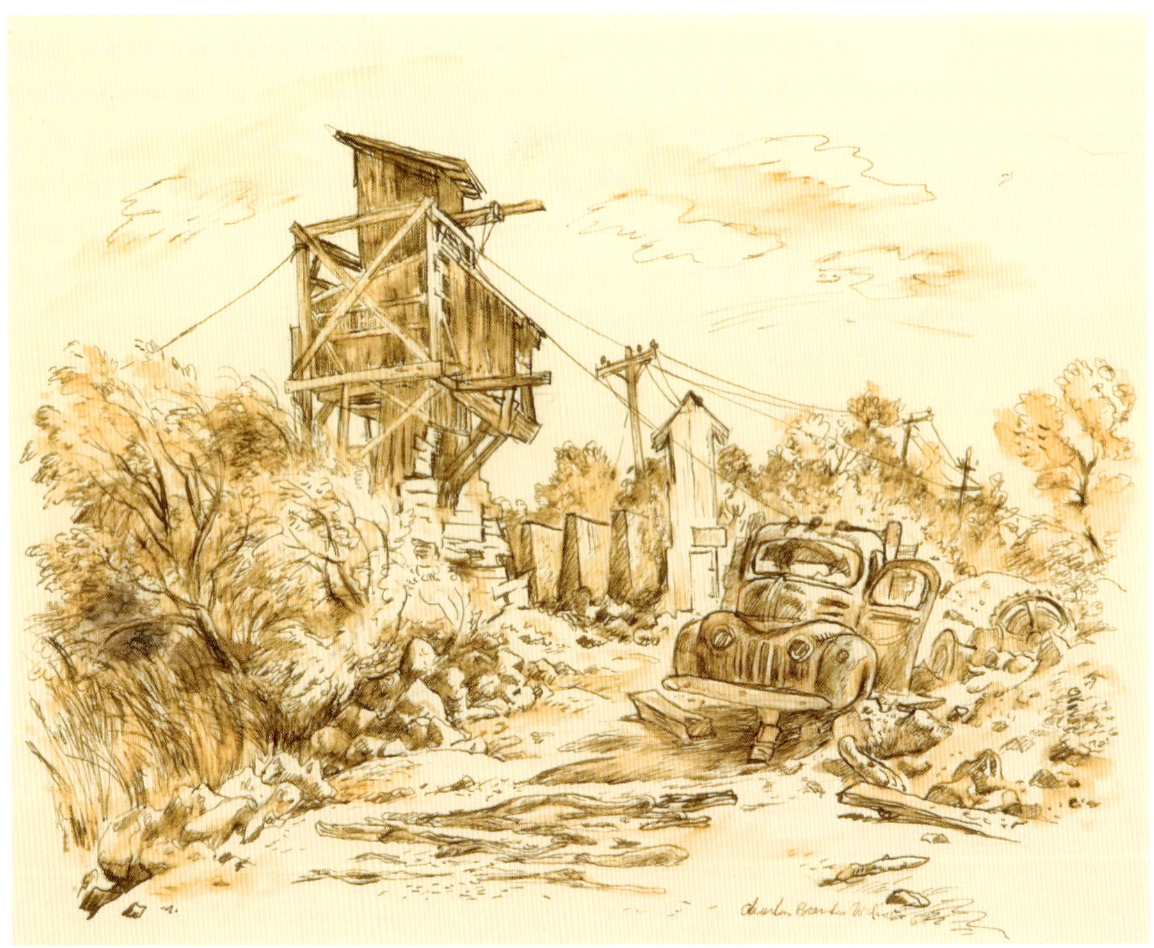

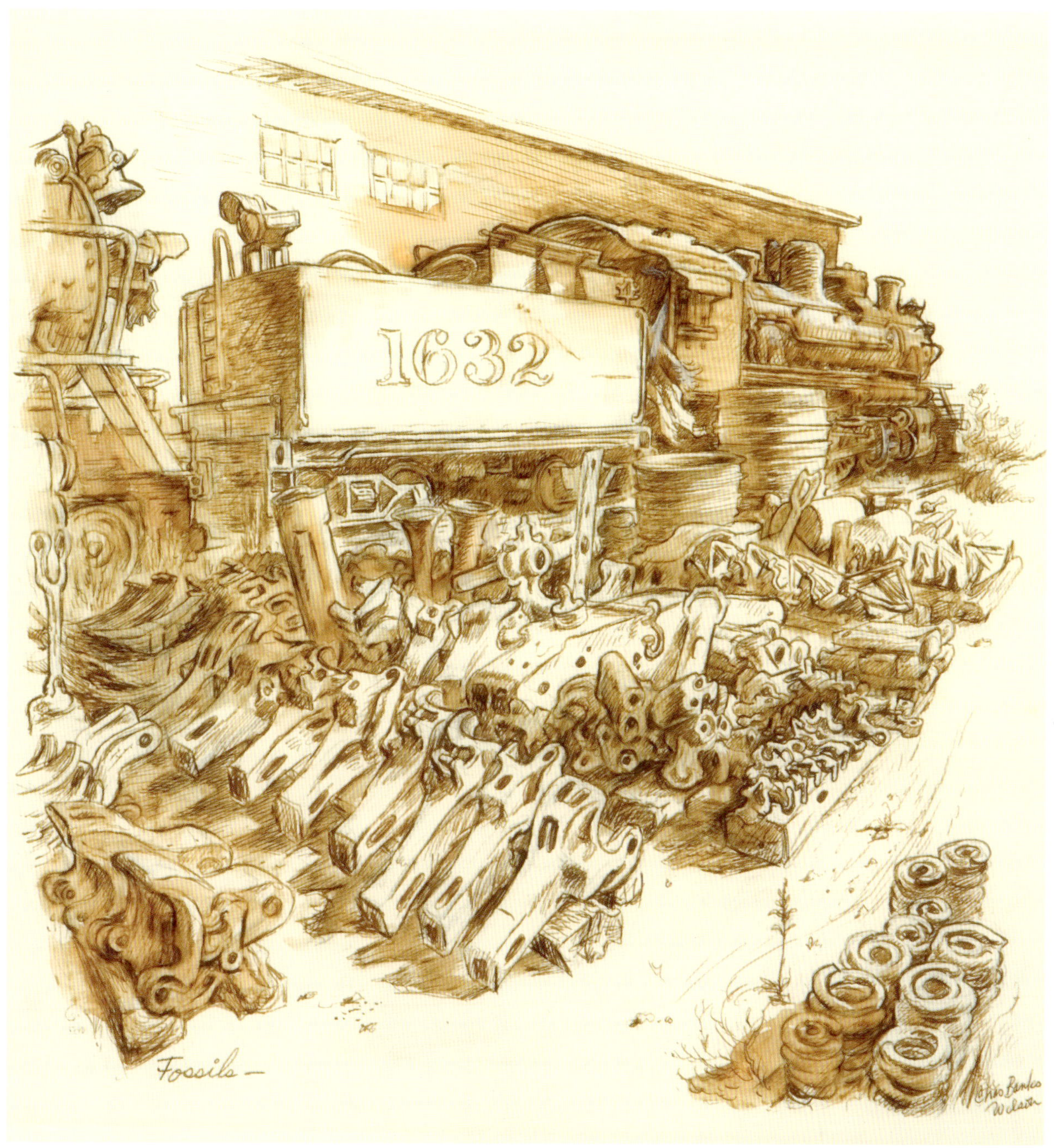

FOSSILS, 1968.
23.375 X 22.5,
PEN/INK ON PAPER,
0227.1758

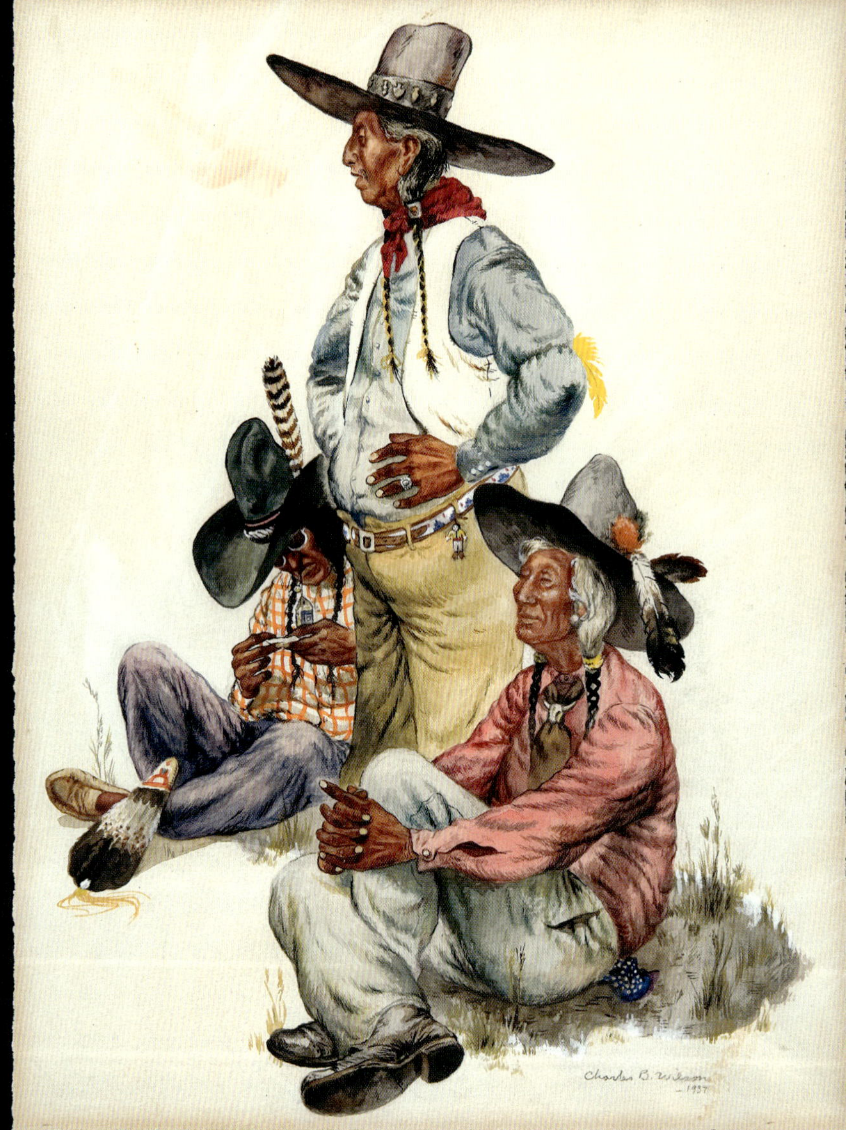

THREE INDIAN MEN IN CONTEMPORARY CLOTHING, 1937. 14.625 X 11, WATERCOLOR/ PAPER, 02.1995

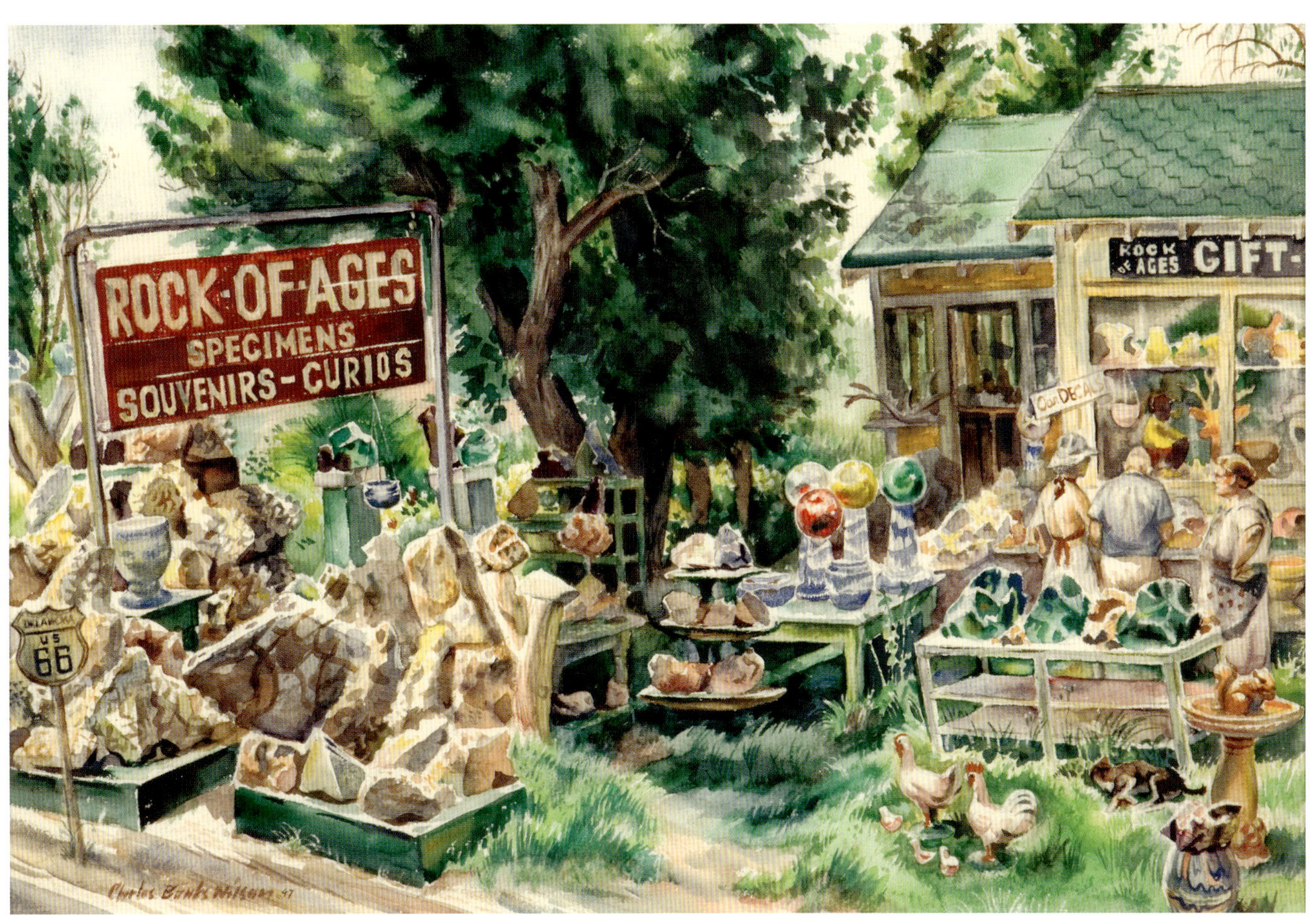

ROCK OF AGES,
1947. 22.5 X 29.75,
WATERCOLOR/
PAPER, 0227.1749

OVERLEAF, DETAIL:
CELEBRATION, 1990.
22 X 50, OIL/CANVAS,
COLLECTION OF THE ARTIST

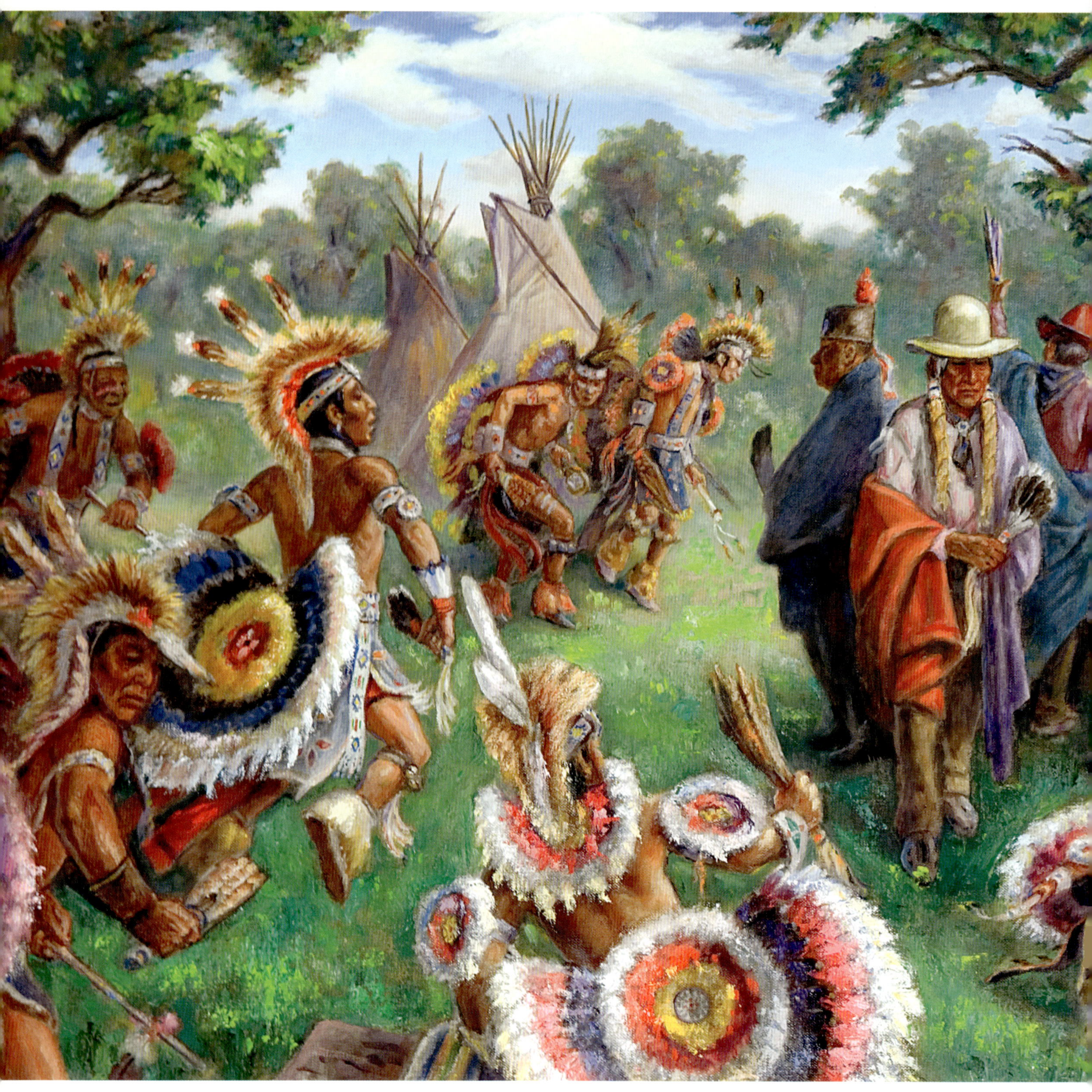

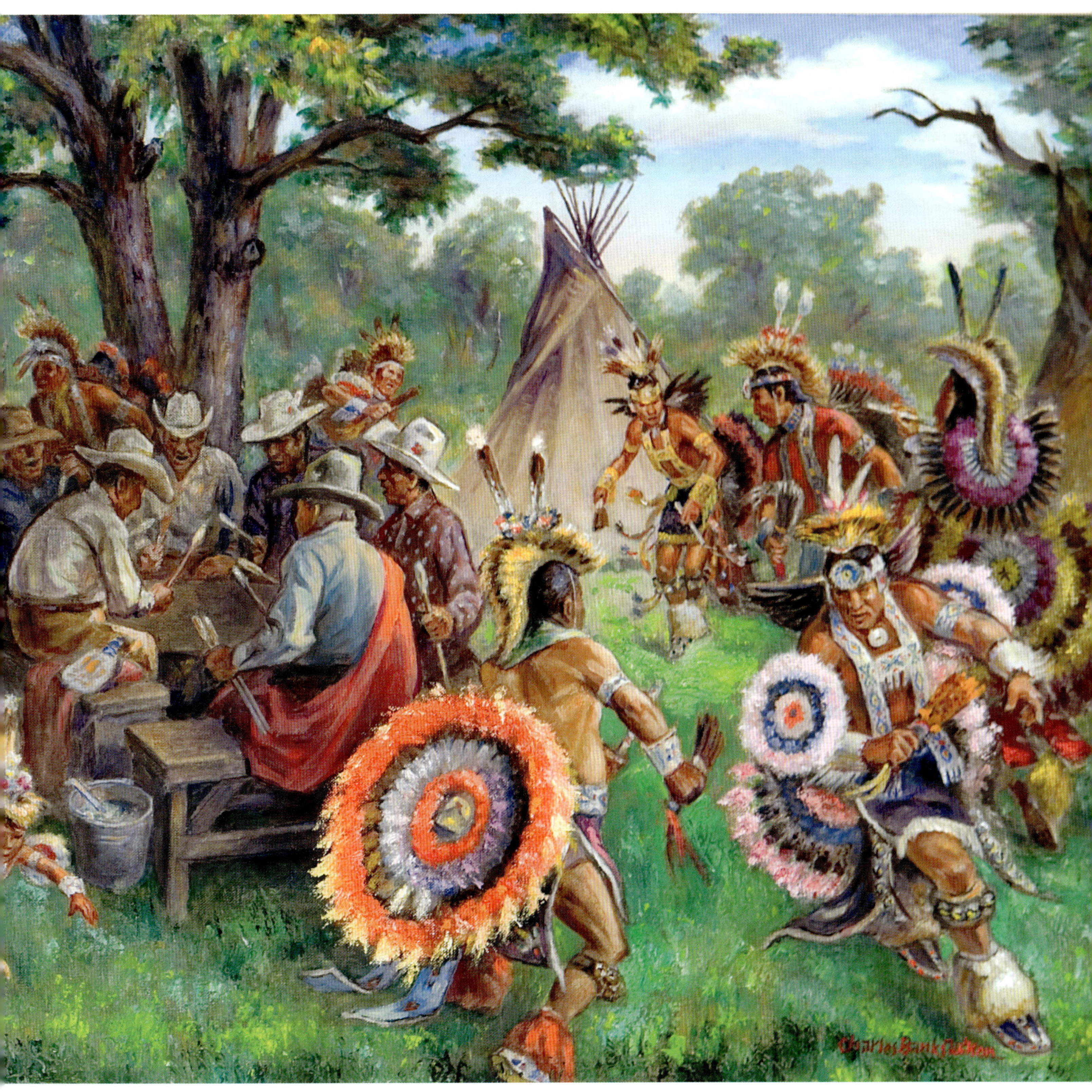

SO IT WILL
BE KNOWN
THAT I HAVE
LIVED :
SEARCHING
FOR THE
PUREBLOODS

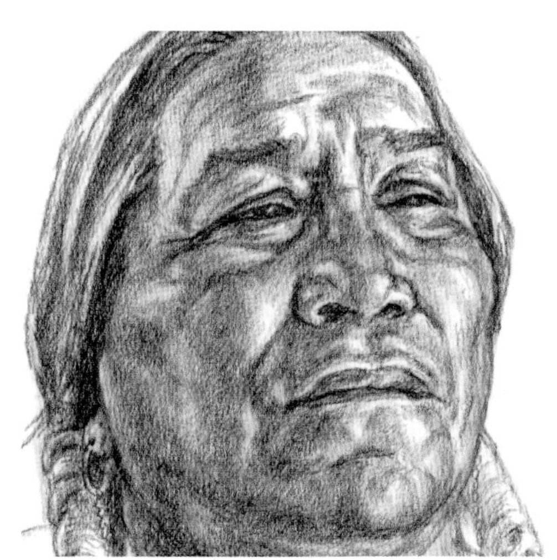

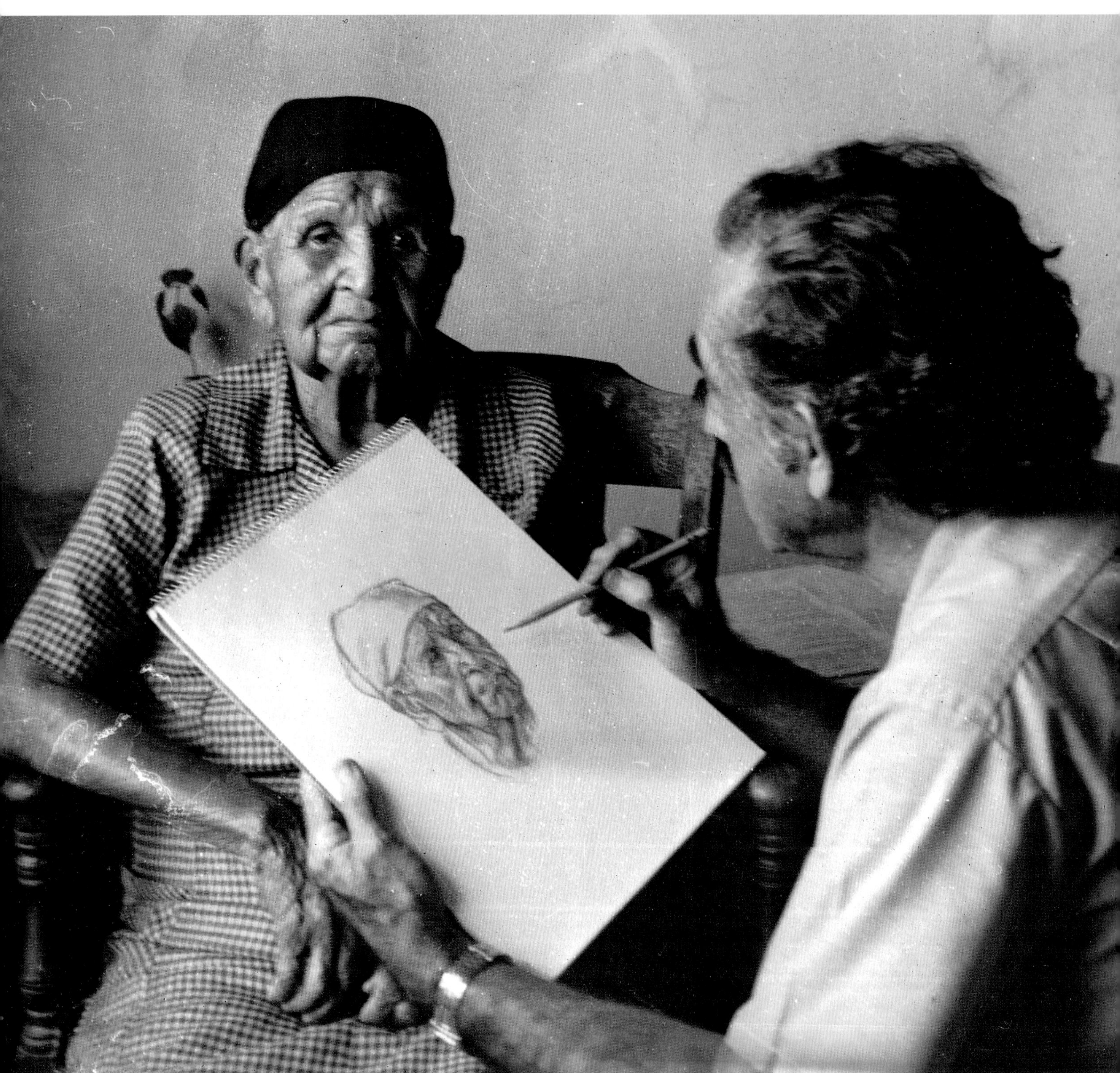

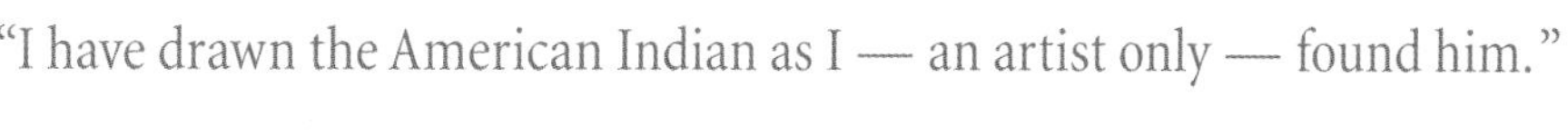

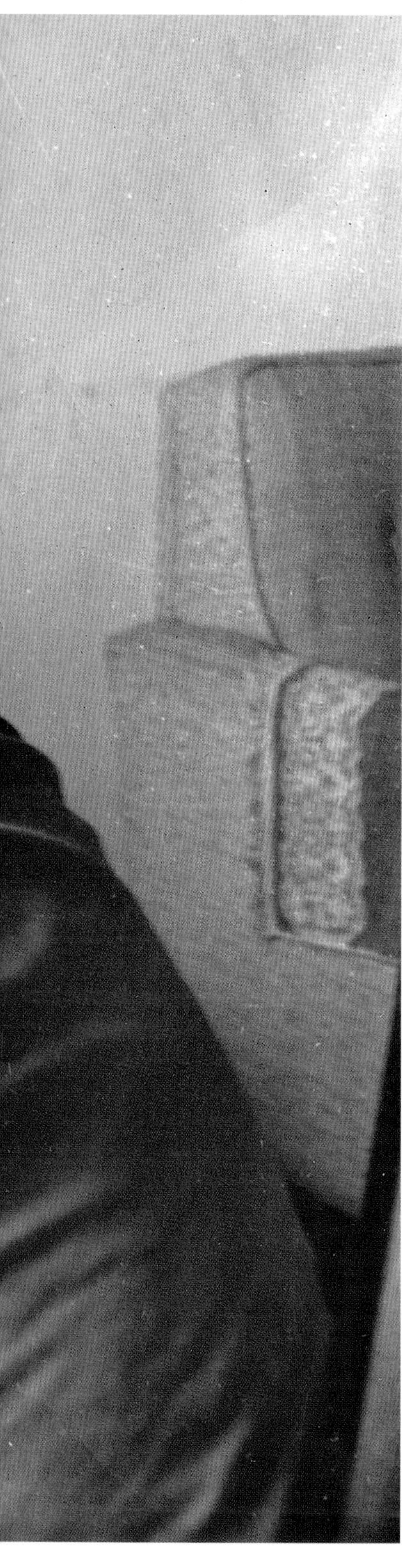

n searching for and creating portraits of pureblood American Indians, Charles Banks Wilson found himself well within the artistic philosophy he still owns today—that subject matter is paramount, and that it should reflect the artist's own time and place. The portrait has a special place in the history of art. From early beginnings to contemporary times the likenesses of people have played an important role in recording not only the persona and temperament of individuals but the complexion of an age, of a society in any given time. Multiple portraits of individuals within an ethnic group form a kind of gauge by which one can measure not just specific physiognomy, attitude, and gesture, but generalities such as time, place, and the state of these individuals in their environment. History, in other words, can be seen in faces.

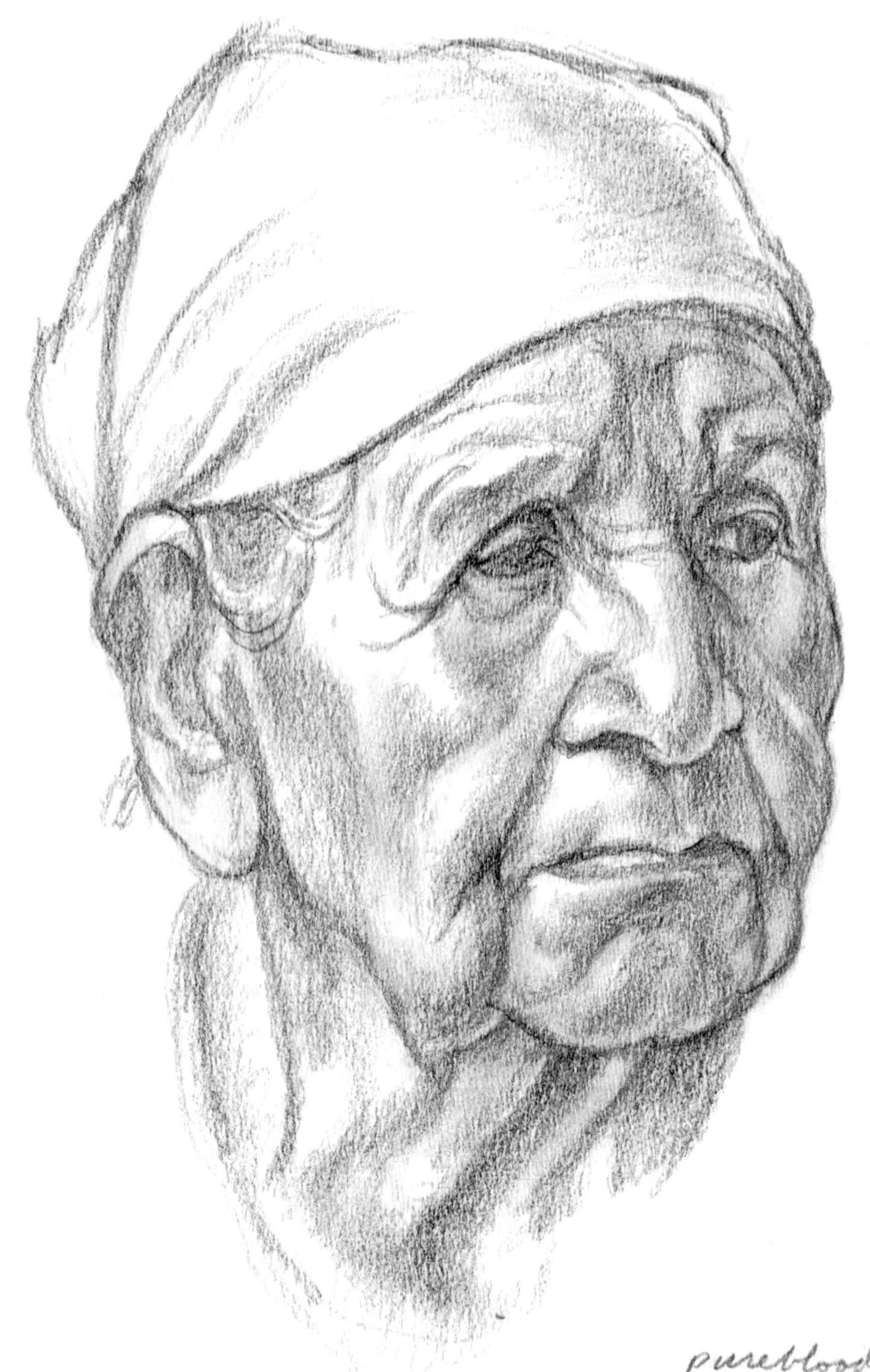

pureblood Euchee
age 90 —
CBW - 80

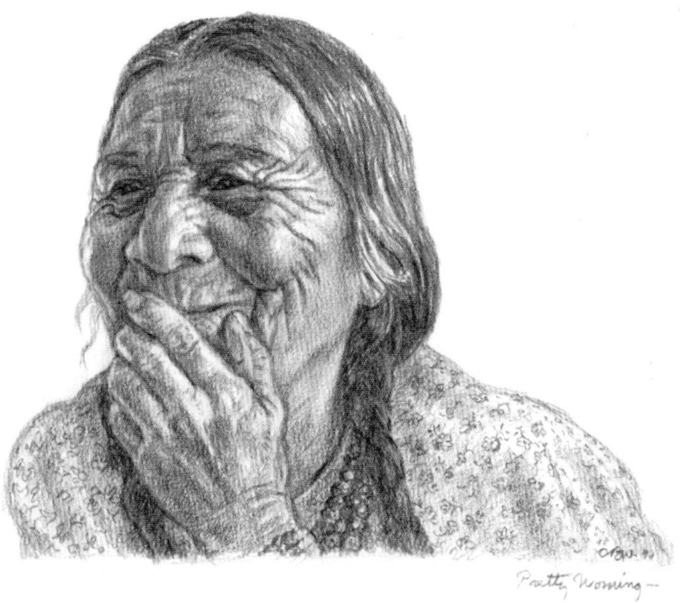

It is rare for an artist to devote his entire life to portraying a specific group of people whose individual personalities speak so eloquently. In 1938 at the age of nineteen, Wilson rendered his first portrait of a pureblood Indian, Henry Turkeyfoot, a Shawnee. Thus began an evolution of successive portraits made possible from his continuing quest for the few remaining pureblood Indians. Wilson calls this process "Search for the Purebloods." Purebloods are individuals of only one tribal lineage. Wilson explains the presence also of mixed bloods in the series of portraits: "Some tribes have had no purebloods in my lifetime. In a number of cases, it was necessary to settle for a person who had more of that tribe's blood in his or her veins than anyone else."

Present-day Oklahoma has a rich American Indian heritage. As a result of federal policy, tribes were moved to the territory from their ancestral lands in all parts of America beginning in the early 1800s. They often made long and difficult journeys, losing many members along the way. Currently 8 percent of Oklahoma's population is descended from the sixty-seven tribes who inhabited Indian Territory. Wilson understood the historical significance of his place and time, and, realizing that no one was portraying the unique American Indian purebloods still remaining, he made a serious commitment to record them. He recounts:

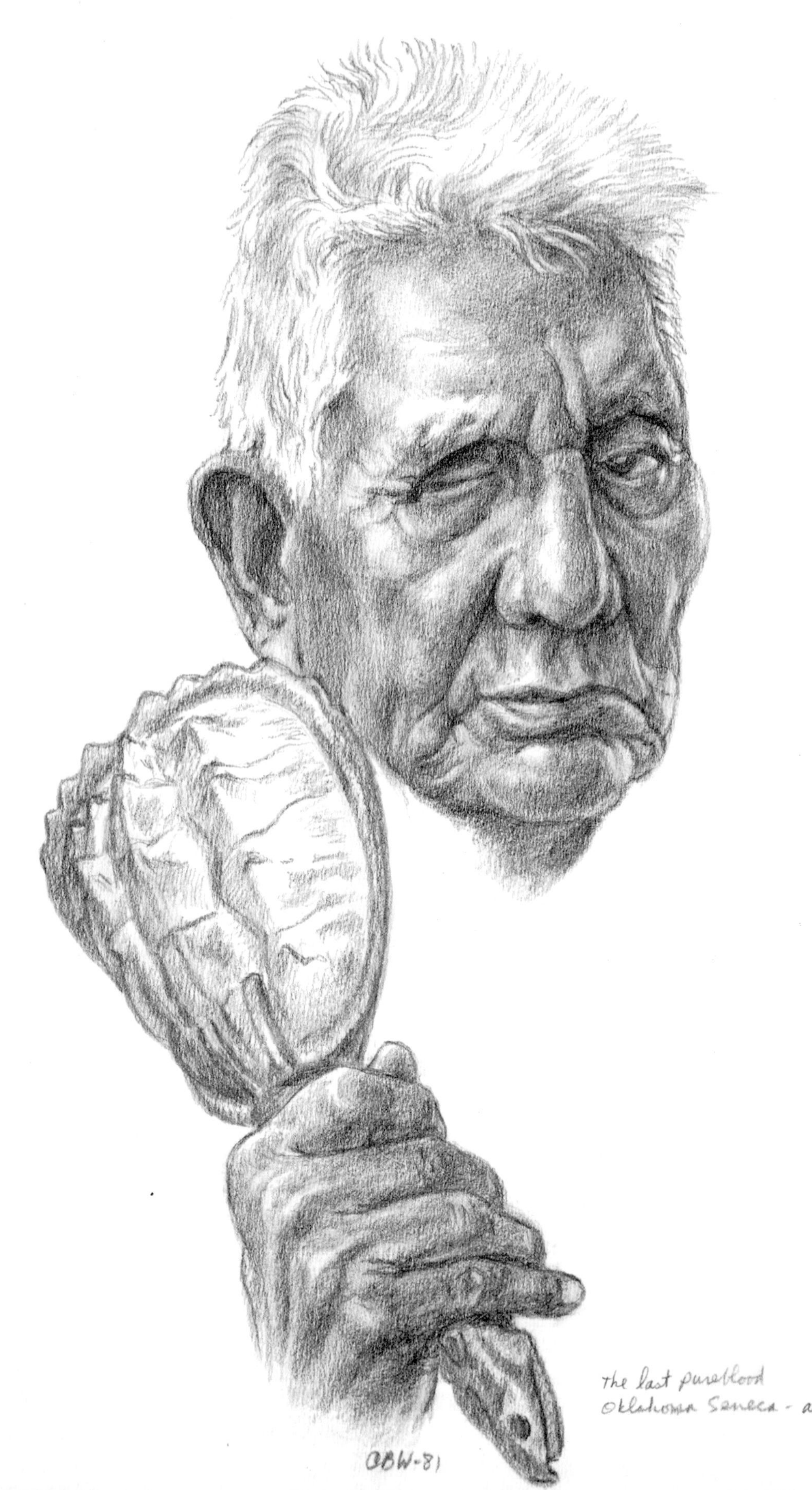

the last pureblood
Oklahoma Seneca - age 79
OBW-81

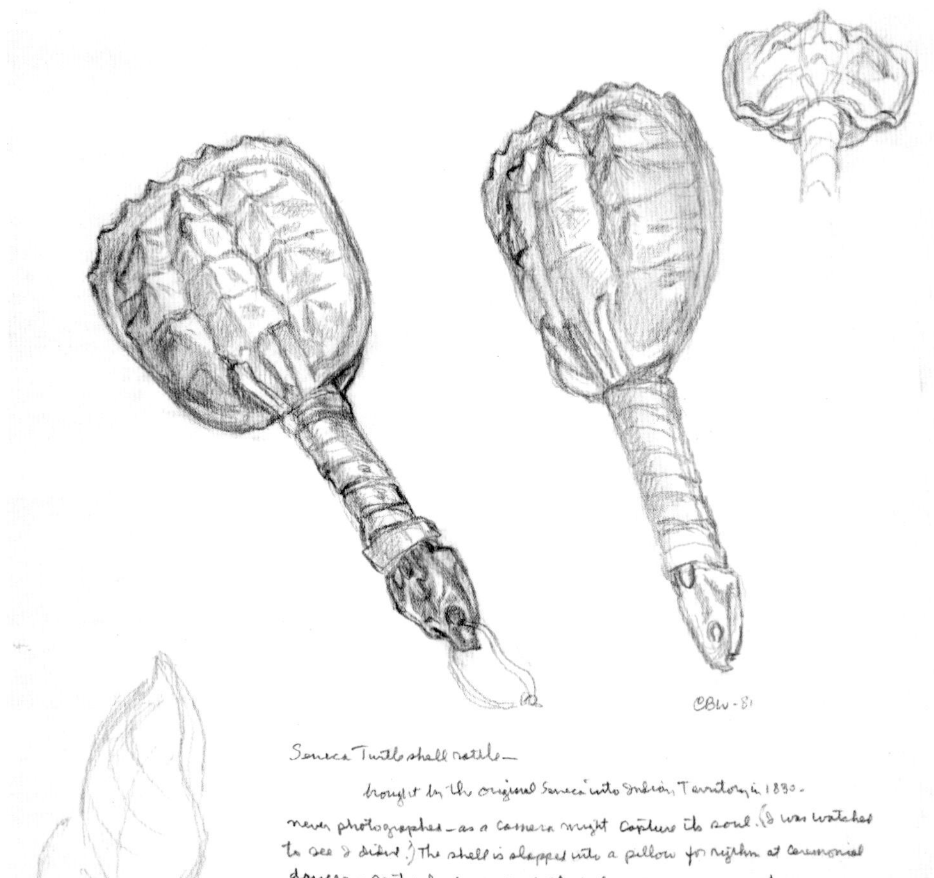

THE LAST PUREBLOOD
OKLAHOMA SENECA,
1981. 12.75 X 9.875,
GRAPHITE/PAPER,
1327.2098

SENECA TURTLE
SHELL RATTLE, 1981.
14 X 11,
GRAPHITE/PAPER,
1327.2046

A mishap literally jarred me into making a decision about the pureblood project. I fell off a ladder and nearly killed myself. The fall made me realize that I was mortal and, if I had something important to do, I had damned well better get it done. From that moment there was no doubt about my future; nothing I could do would be more important, and nothing was I better prepared for, as an artist, than my search for the remaining purebloods. It is a project I am obligated to complete.

A portrait can be defined as a "likeness" of a particular individual—that which reveals who he is and distinguishes him from another. "Likeness" cannot be captured by rendering only shapes, form, and color, but must contain the spirit—something that speaks of personality and pulsates beneath surface appearance. The artist's response to the sitter requires him to make choices about what is important in order to distill essence. Wilson allows one to see the soul of his sitters. This unique body of work by a single artist provides an opportunity to explore and compare the facial features and countenance of individuals of many tribes. Wilson created his drawings from life, rather than from photographs. When asked about the convenience of photography, he shares this viewpoint:

> As excellent a piece of machinery as is the camera, it has its limitations when compared to the artist's mind. Film in the photographer's camera is not influenced by a previous photo, while the artist's mind is consciously and sub-consciously aware of all past experiences and can select differences or similarities because of them.

The search led Wilson to the far reaches of the state and sometimes outside it; he went wherever he needed to go to find the purebloods. Sometimes they came to his studio, but "more often I went to them—drawing wherever they could be found: at their home, in a hospital, a bar, back porch, a tent, on a river, in jail, in church, at a ceremony." He went to many ceremonies and powwows. Speaking about his approach to drawing at these events, he explains:

> At first I drew Indians in their fancy trappings as they appeared in the dance space —chiefs wearing buffalo-horn headdresses, dancers outfitted in beautiful feathers—but gradually I became aware of the people outside the arena. They were Indians too—Indians watching Indians be Indians. These spectators were trying to live in a white world. A chief might have long, braided hair, but he might be wearing a derby. He might have a blanket draped around him, but his shirt might be pleated in front, with ruffled cuffs.

CBW: *The artist should recognize that a subject (landscape) has beauty for him because it expresses a thought which to him is good! (In a portrait he must inscribe the character — and not just the features.) . . . . A portrait is more than the reproduction of a face.*

WINNEBAGO PUREBLOOD
– 85, 1984.
11.125 X 10.5,
GRAPHITE/PAPER,
1327.3847

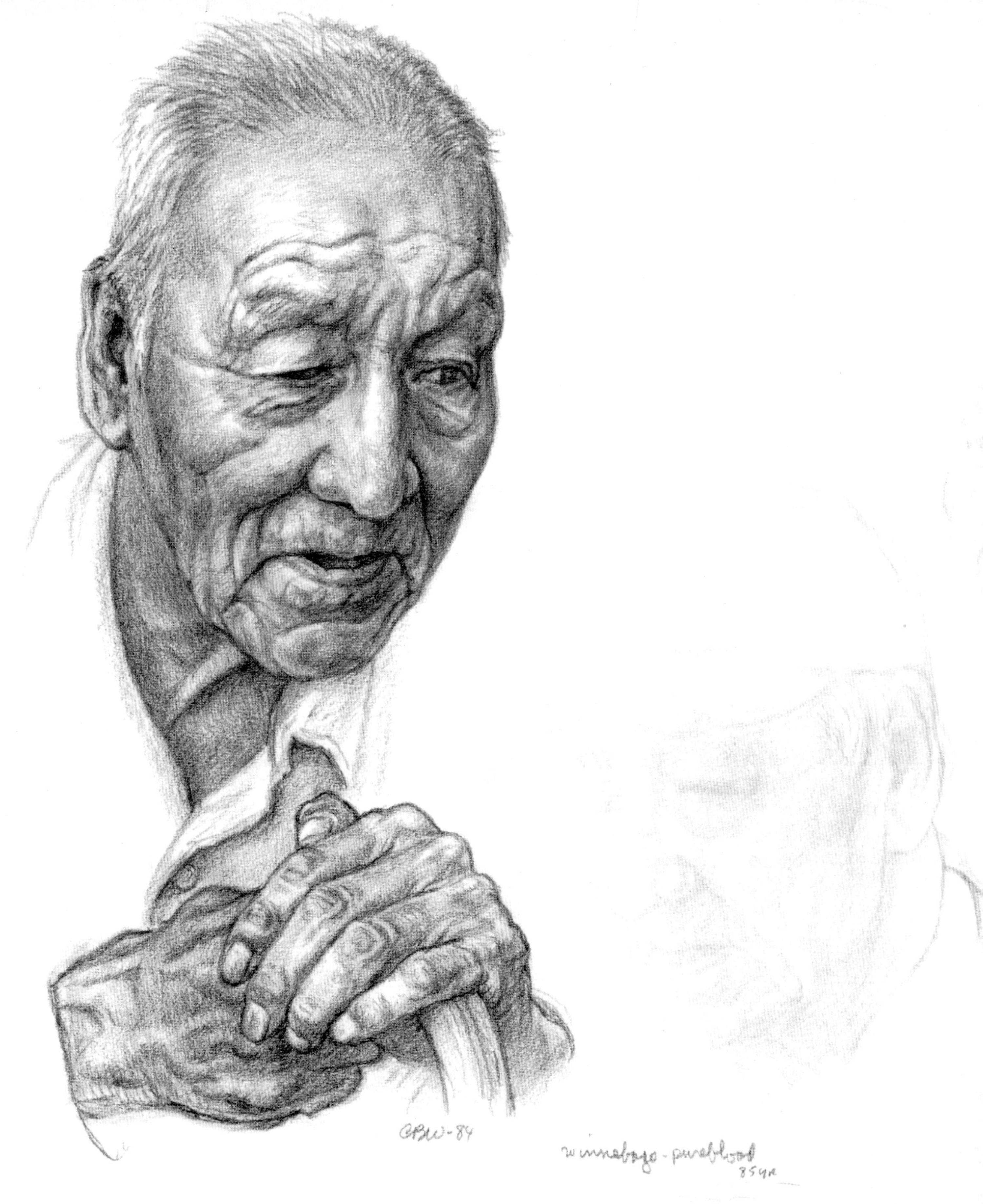

CPW-84
winnebago - pureblood
85 yr

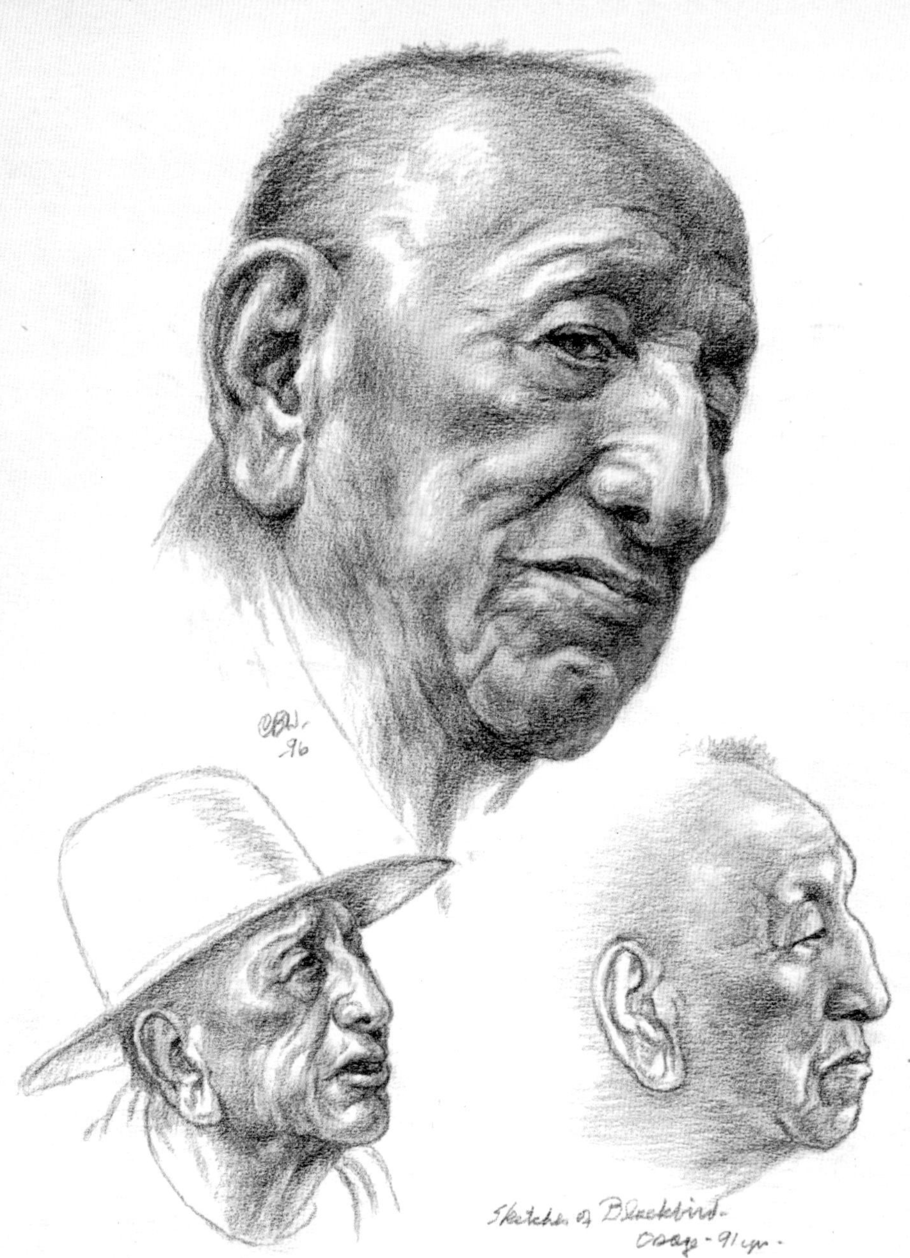

Sketches of Blackbird.
Osage - 91 yr.

Wilson was moved by this visible convergence of cultures in the lives of his subjects both on the human level and in terms of his artistic philosophy. His engagement and personal interaction with his subjects no doubt contributes to the astounding glimpse one has into these faces and lives. He recounts his first meeting with Henry Turkeyfoot:

> As we eyed each other in a small clearing in the blackjack trees growing along the river, I felt every inch the intruder who has some explaining to do. 'I'm an artist', I began. 'I was here once before, and I hope to paint your picture.' In a high-pitched voice, Henry Turkeyfoot confessed he had seen me before, but not knowing my business, had hidden in the brush, as was his habit when strangers came around unannounced.

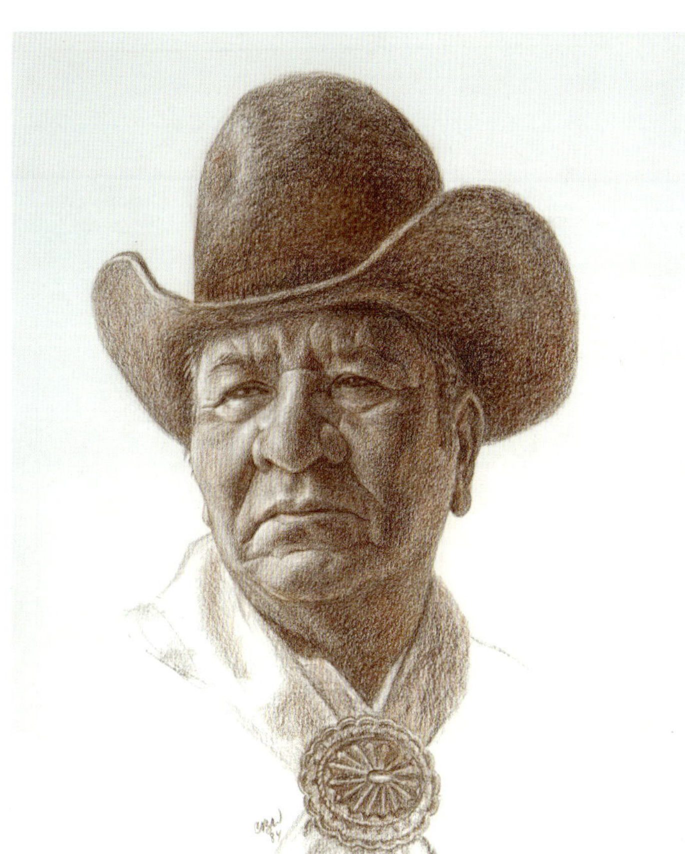

YANKTON SIOUX, 67 YEARS, 1984. 14 X 12, COLOR PENCIL/PAPER, 1427.2105

SKETCHES OF BLACKBIRD, OSAGE, 1996. 12 X 9, GRAPHITE/PAPER, 1427.3847

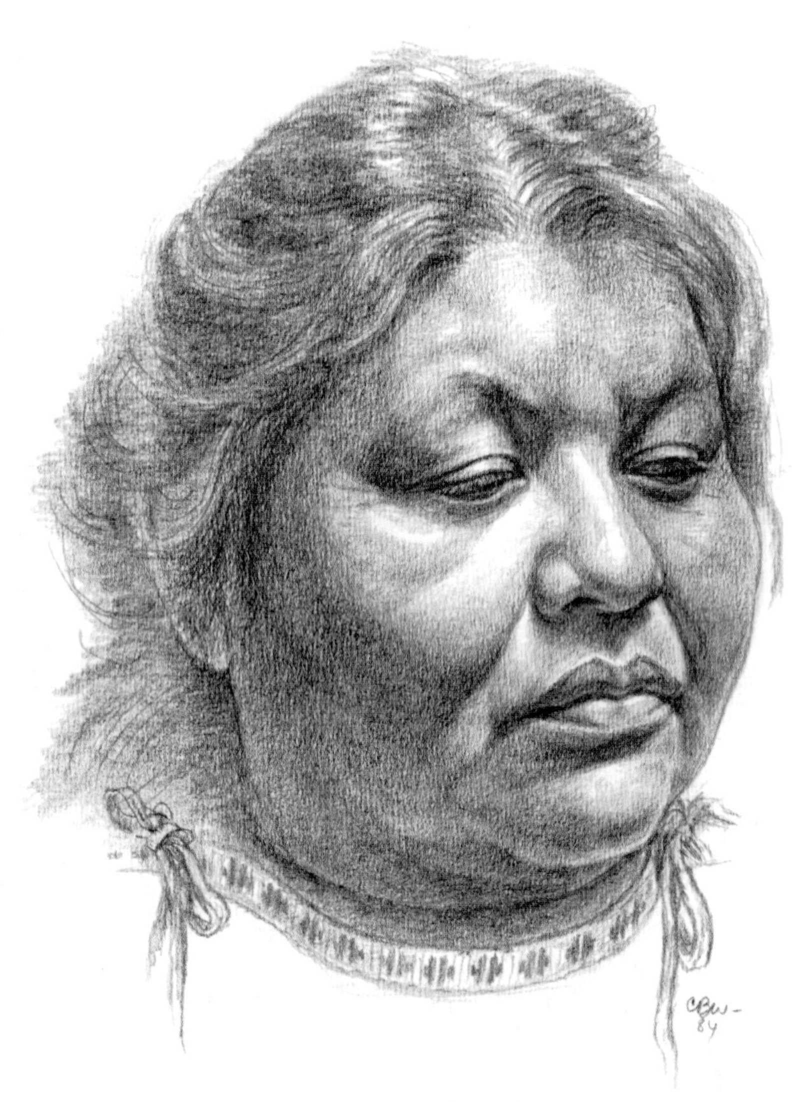

yakima pureblood woman - 44 yrs

Henry Turkeyfoot eventually became good friends with Wilson, as did many others. A Modoc man would often leave handmade gifts at Wilson's door and disappear. His sitters gave him their trust and small gifts of themselves, sharing their thoughts and bits of their lives with the artist who would memorialize them. One of the last Pureblood Kaws, an old man who had no one with whom to speak his language told Wilson: "God gave the Kaw this language, so when I talk to people I speak English, but when I talk to God I speak His language." On the portrait of a Delaware, Wilson wrote that the man, in his earnestness to pose, had fainted. "I figured for a time I had killed the last Delaware," noted Wilson. And then there was Woogie Watchetaker, who was called "Rainmaker" and, according to Wilson, for good reason. "It often rains when he is at a powwow, and when it does people are apt to say, 'Woogie, go home!'" There was a story for every portrait, and like life itself, they contained a mix of happiness, sadness, and humor.

These portraits could not have been created without the effort and patience of the sitters themselves. They were exacting taskmasters, as it mattered to them that their likenesses were good ones, and Wilson's hand and heart responded. Nathan Goldstein, in *The Art of Responsive Drawing,* says: "Responsive drawing is choosing and relating wisely from among the parts and impressions that constitute our subject: it is the ability to join percept to concept, to fuse thinking and feeling, to merge inquiry and intuition…"

Wilson possesses an artistic ability to synthesize the details of the human face with the elusive qualities of spirit. He has given life to the important characteristics of his Native American subjects. With an extraordinary perception for human significance, he has preserved the heritage of many tribes in Oklahoma, giving them a proper place in the larger context of Oklahoma, as well as American history. Louis Featherman, a Sioux from South Dakota who knew he was dying and had come to Oklahoma to visit his relatives, asked Wilson to paint him "so it will be known that I have lived." So it is with all the individuals who come to life in this series and will continue to live because of the vision of Charles Banks Wilson. —CAROLE KLEIN

YAKIMA PUREBLOOD
WOMAN, 44 YEARS, 1984.
18.75 X 14.75,
LITHOGRAPH/PAPER,
1427.2138

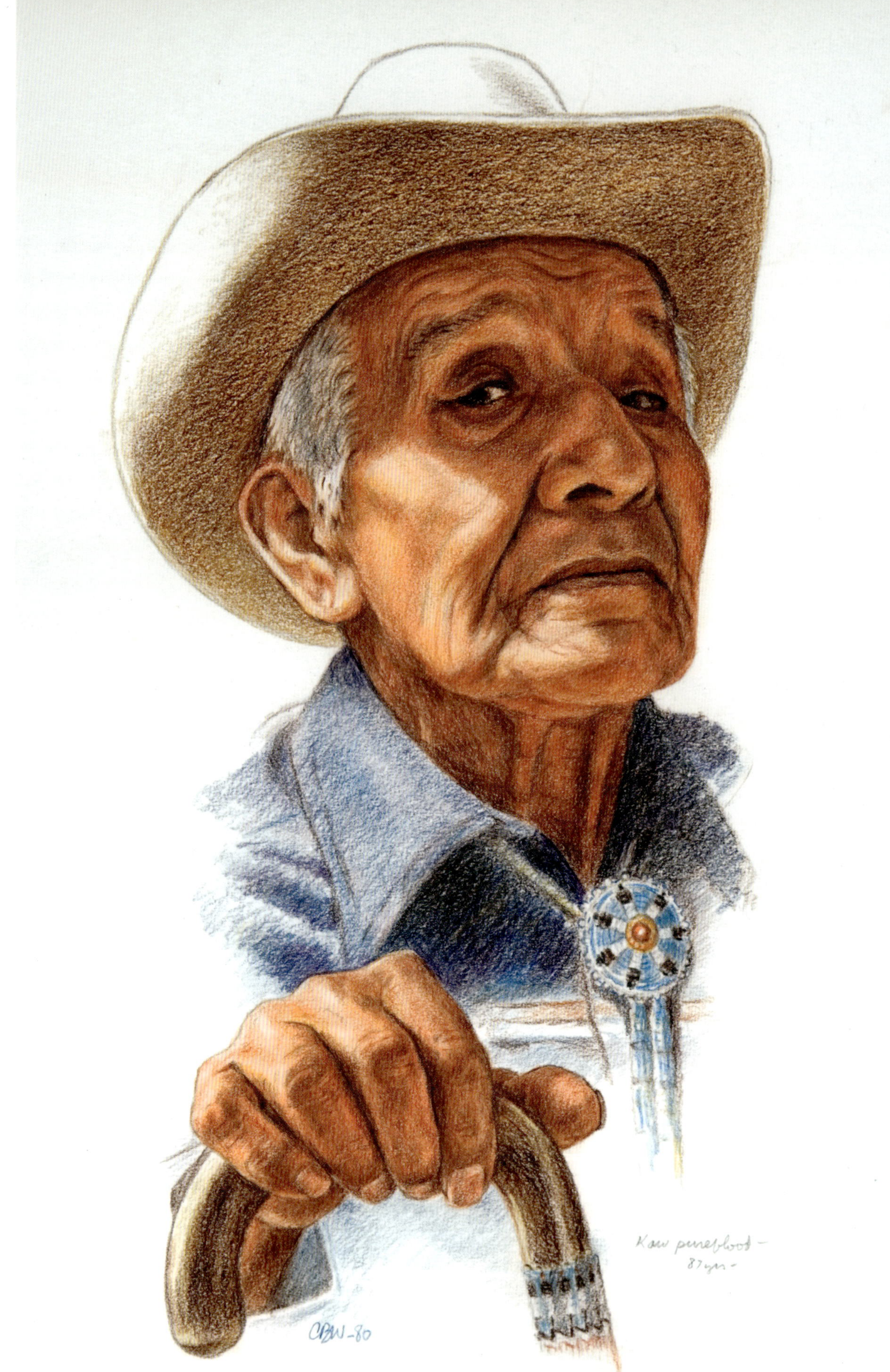

KAW PUREBLOOD,
87 YEARS, 1980.
14 X 10.25,
COLOR
PENCIL/BOARD,
1427.2078

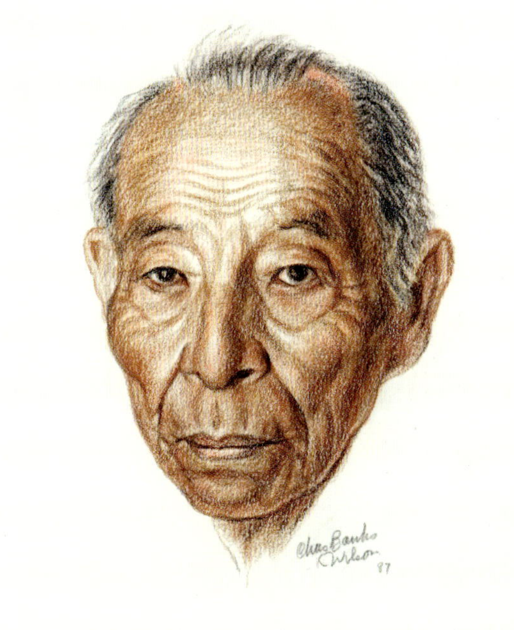

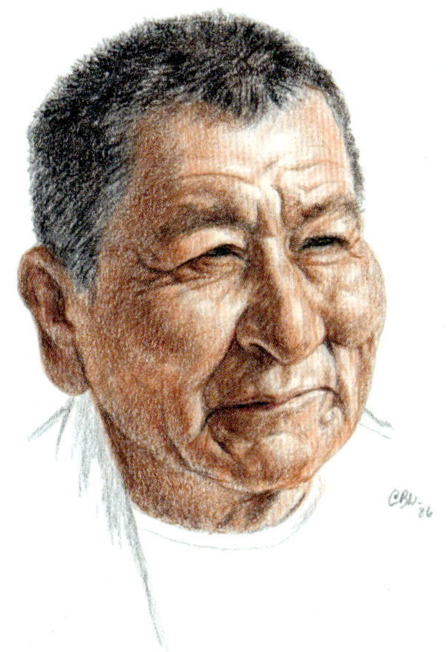

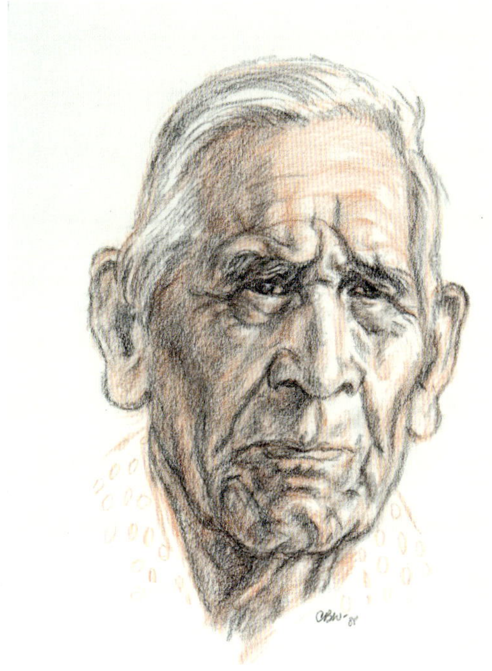

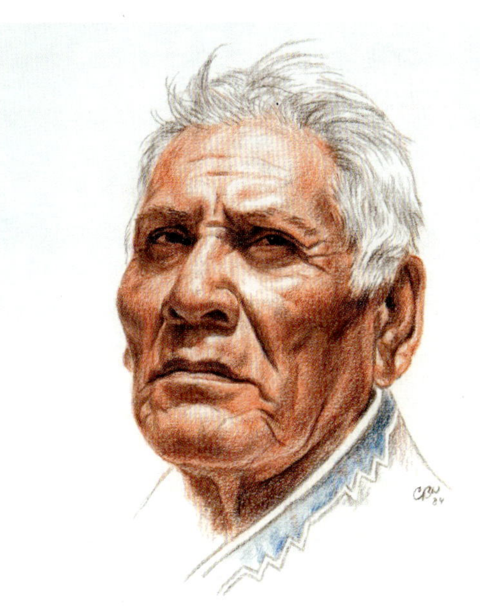

CLOCKWISE FROM UPPER LEFT: PEORIA CHIEF (WEO BLOOD) – 78 YEARS OLD, 1987. 17 X 10.625, CONTÉ CRAYON/ PAPER, 1327.2026

BRULE (SIOUX) – 63 WITH A SUMMER HAIRCUT, ROSEBUD, S.D., 1986. 17 X 10.625, COLOR PENCIL/PAPER, 1327.2223

WICHITA PUREBLOOD – 65 YEARS, 1984. 14.625 X 10.75, COLOR PENCIL/PAPER, 1327.2124

CREEK PUREBLOOD, 1988. 14 X 10.625, CONTÉ CRAYON/ PAPER, 1327.2025

CBW: *The artist must never disregard what is true.*

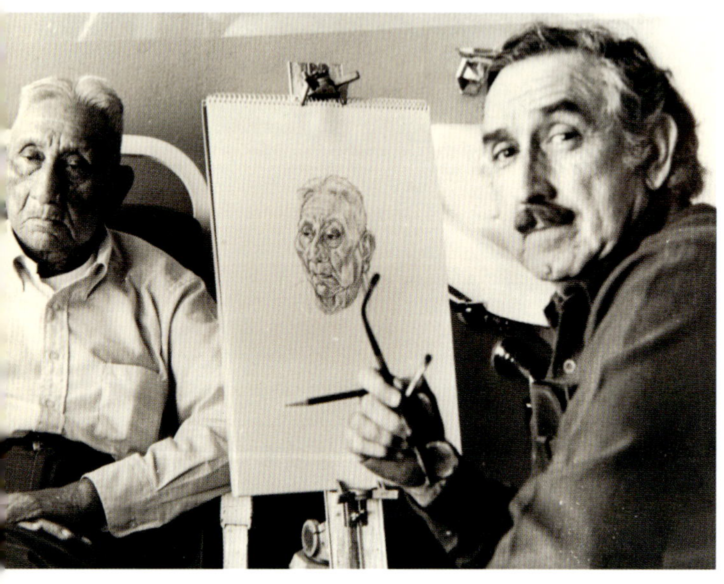

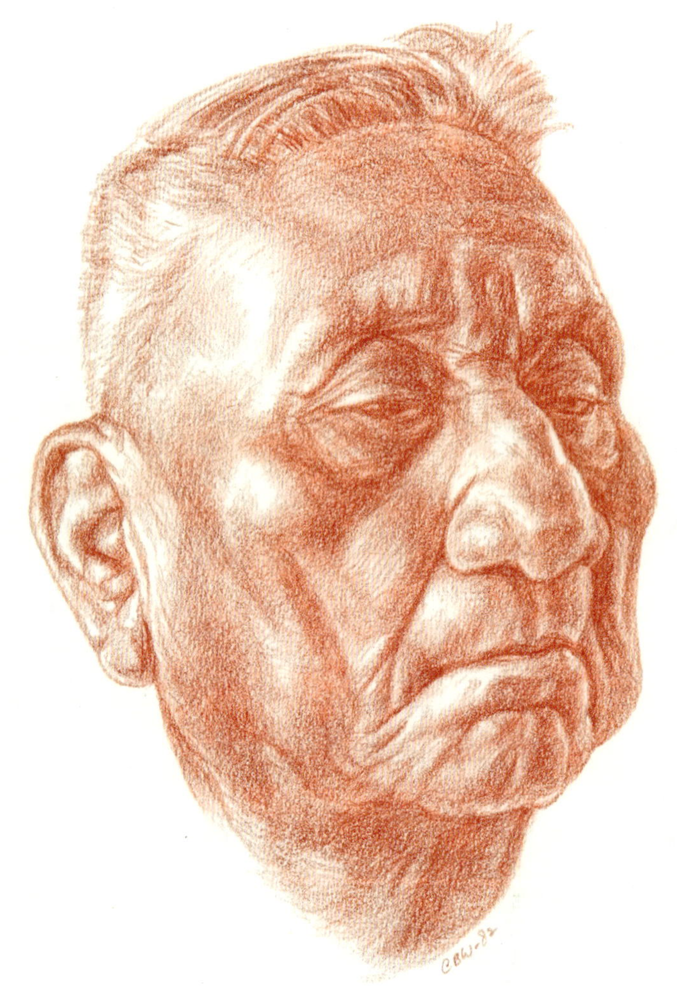

SEMINOLE PUREBLOOD
MEDICINE MAN–
AGE 87-98-103?, 1982.
13.125 X 10.125,
COLOR PENCIL/PAPER,
1327.2120

SKETCH OF CHARLES
WHITEHORN – OSAGE
ORATOR, 1960.
16.75 X 13.625,
GRAPHITE/PAPER,
1327.2100

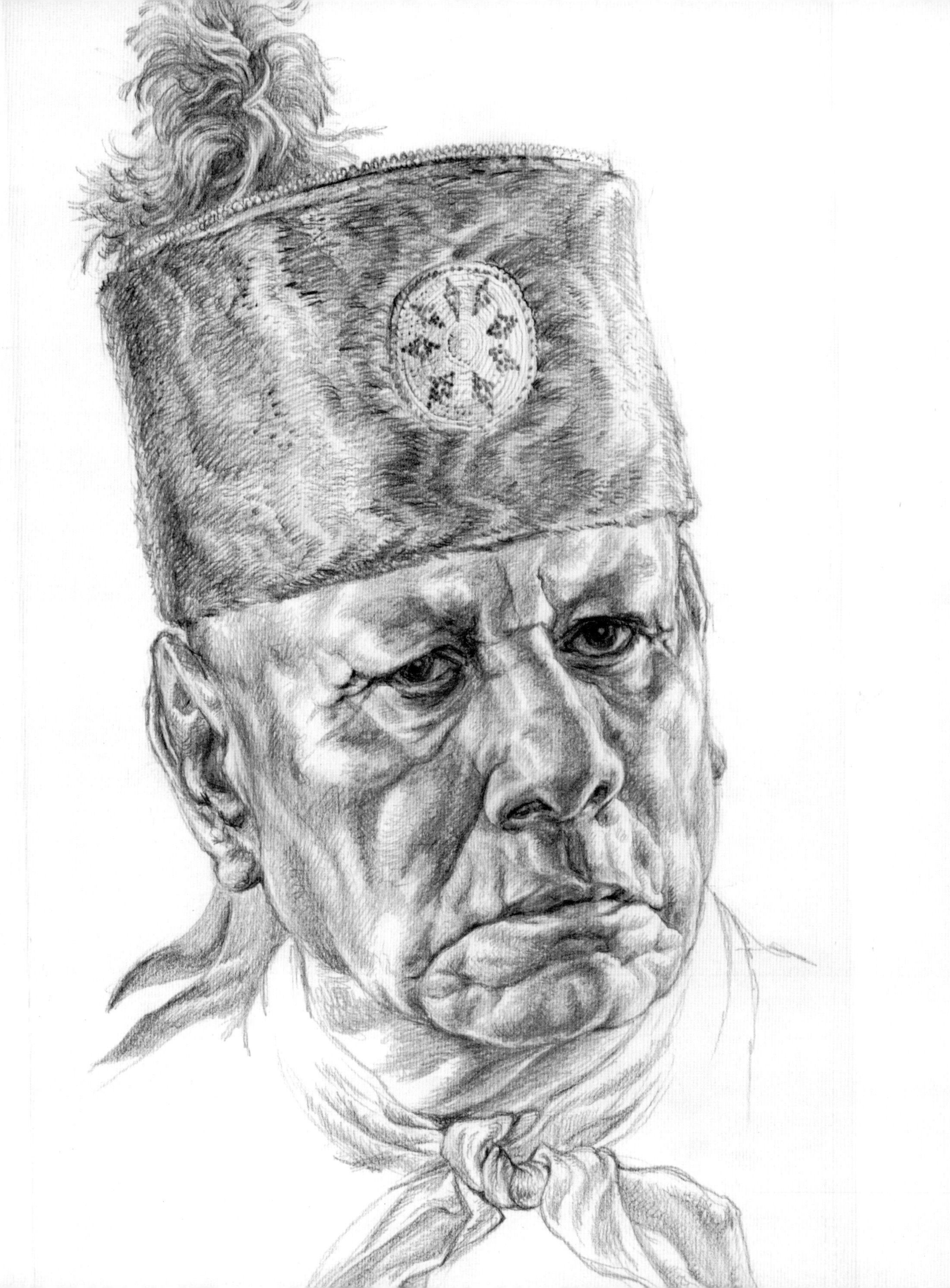

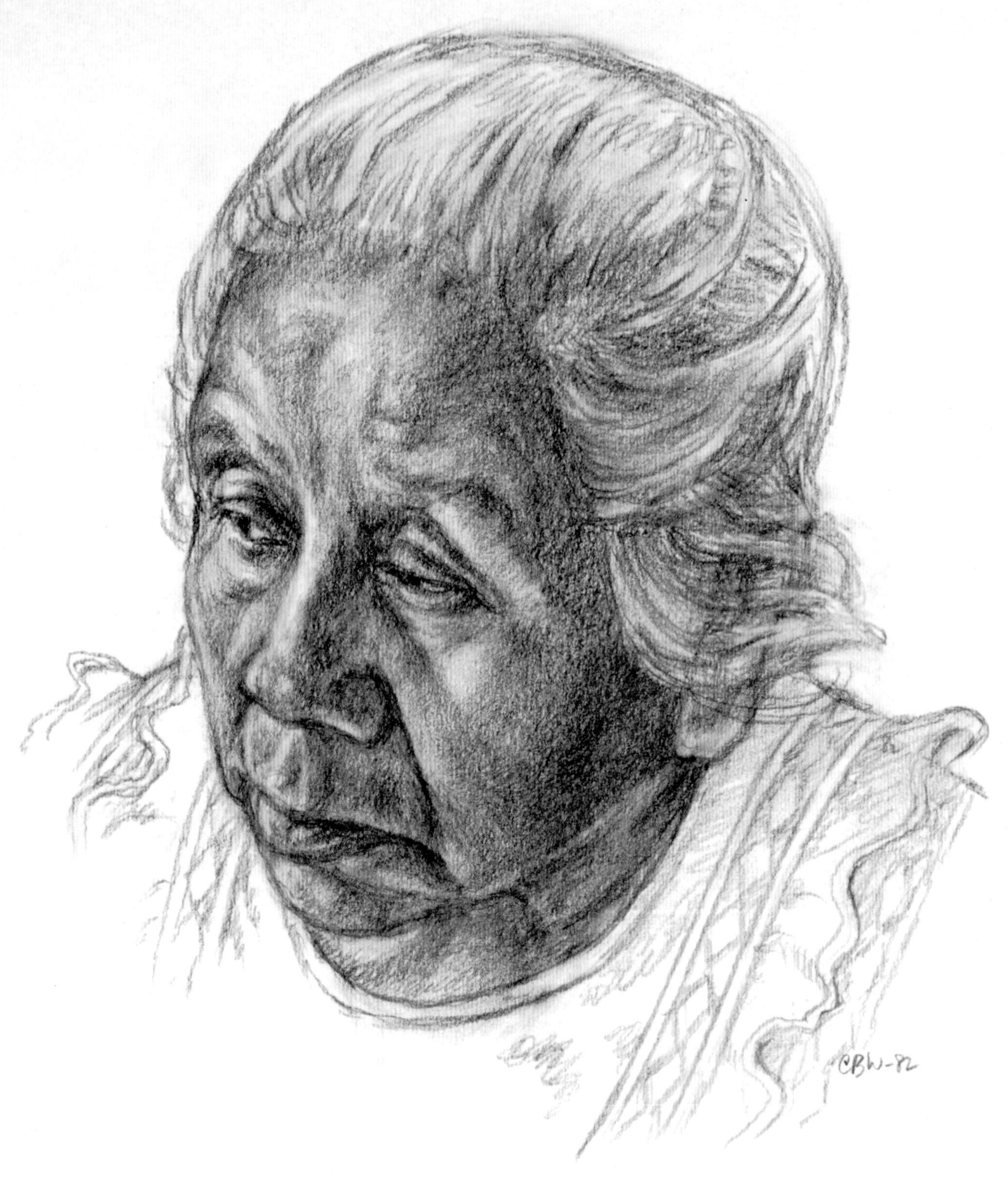

Choctaw woman - 80 yrs.

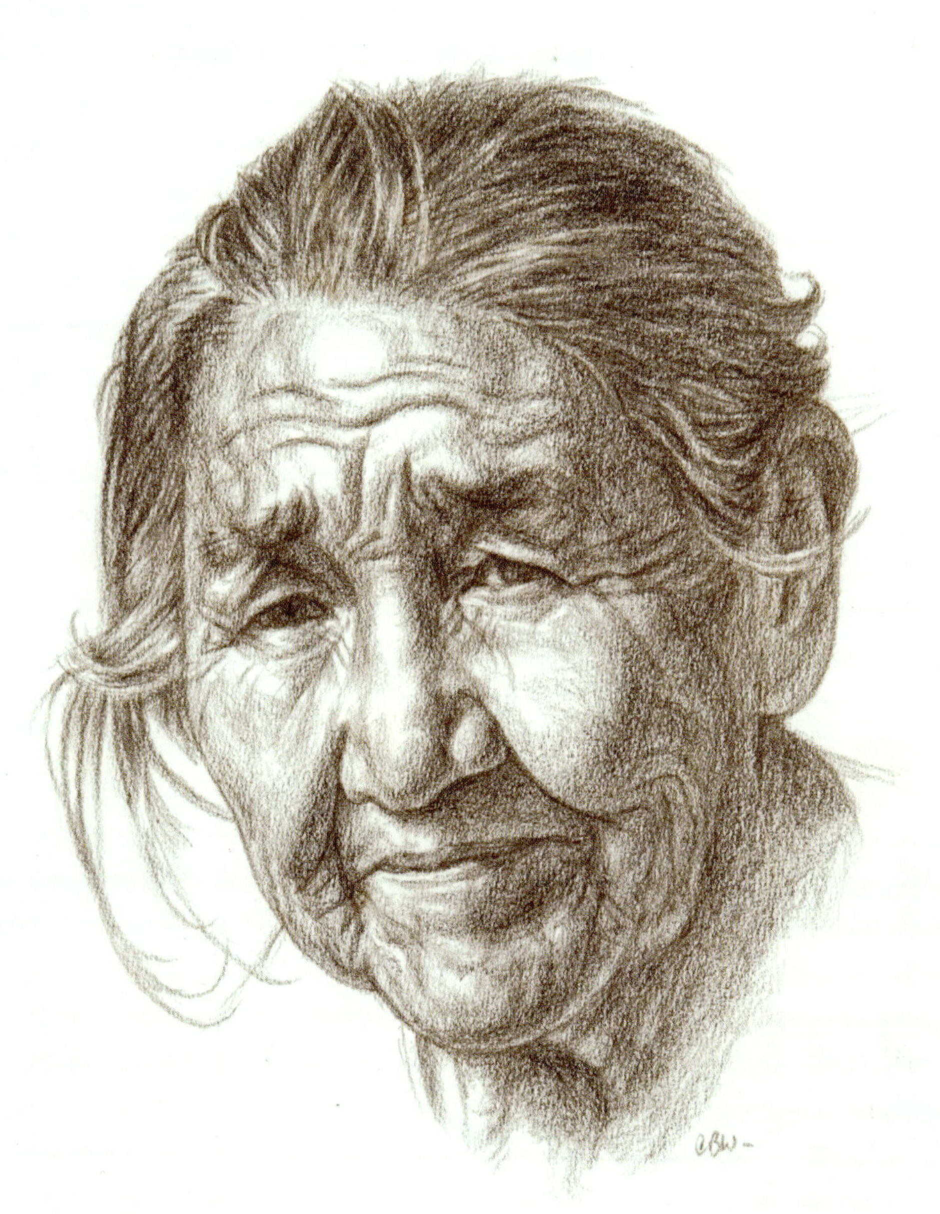

CHOCTAW WOMAN –
80 YEARS, 1982.
12.75 X 11.875,
CHARCOAL/PAPER,
1327.2018

OTTAWA WOMAN –
72 YEARS.
13.875 X 10.25,
GRAPHITE/PAPER,
1327.2079

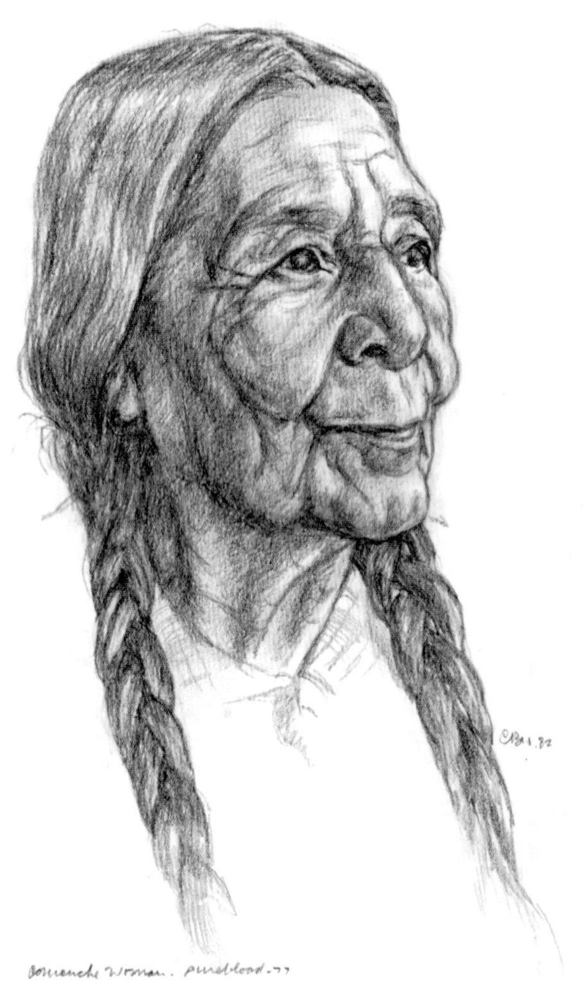

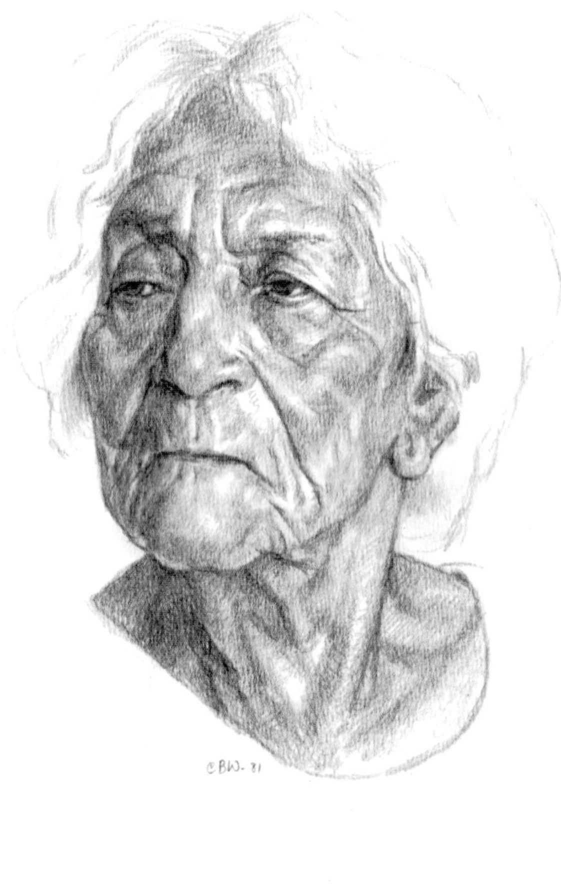

COMANCHE WOMAN – PUREBLOOD – 1982. 77. 12 X 10.5, GRAPHITE/PAPER, 1327.2099

MIAMI WOMAN, 1981. 12 X 9.75, GRAPHITE/PAPER, 1327.2130

CREEK WOMAN – PUREBLOOD – 77, 1984. 13.125 X 11, GRAPHITE/PAPER, 1327.2134

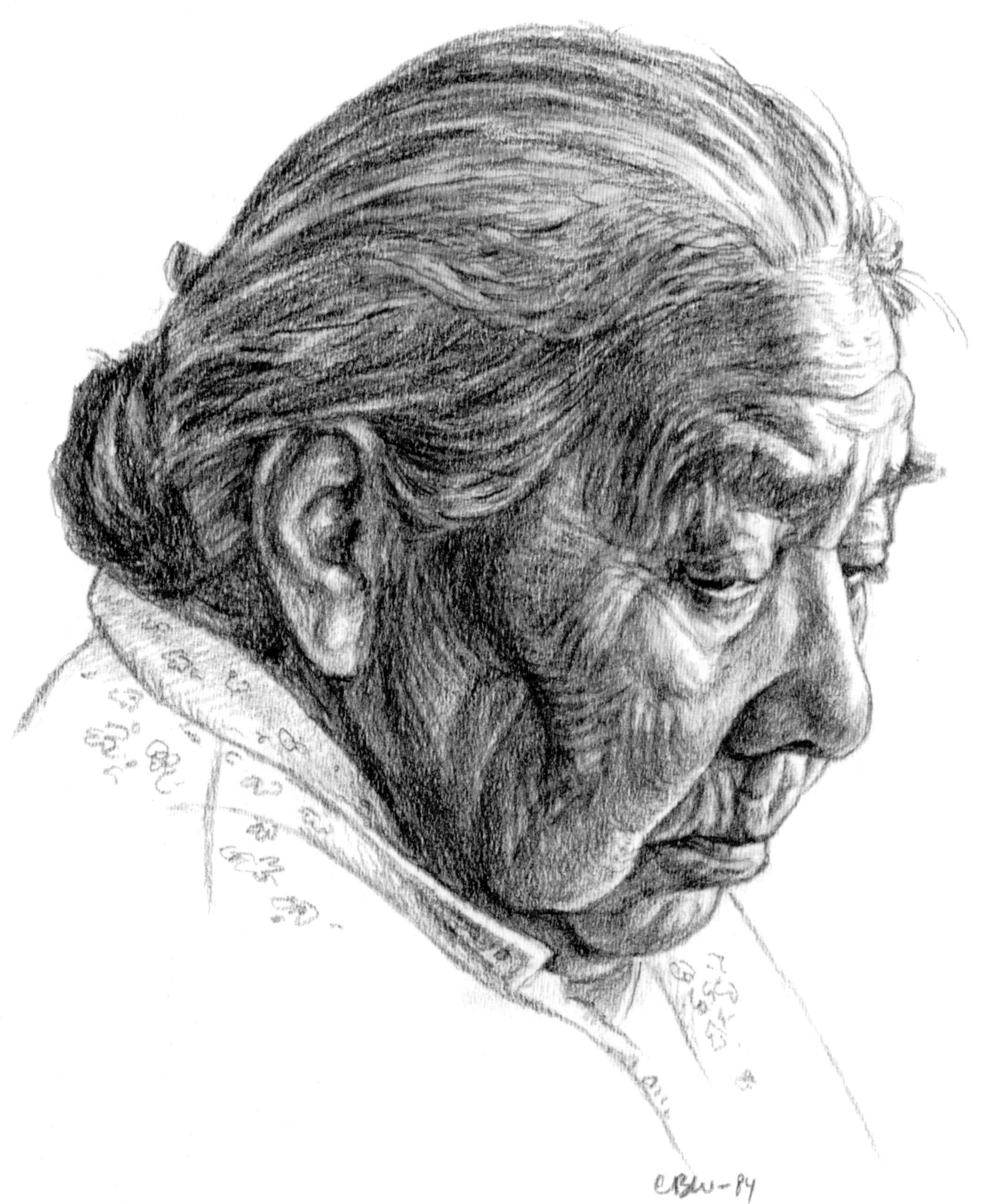

CBW-84

FEELIN' GOOD!
MODOC.
13.25 X 11,
GRAPHITE/
PAPER,
1327.2126

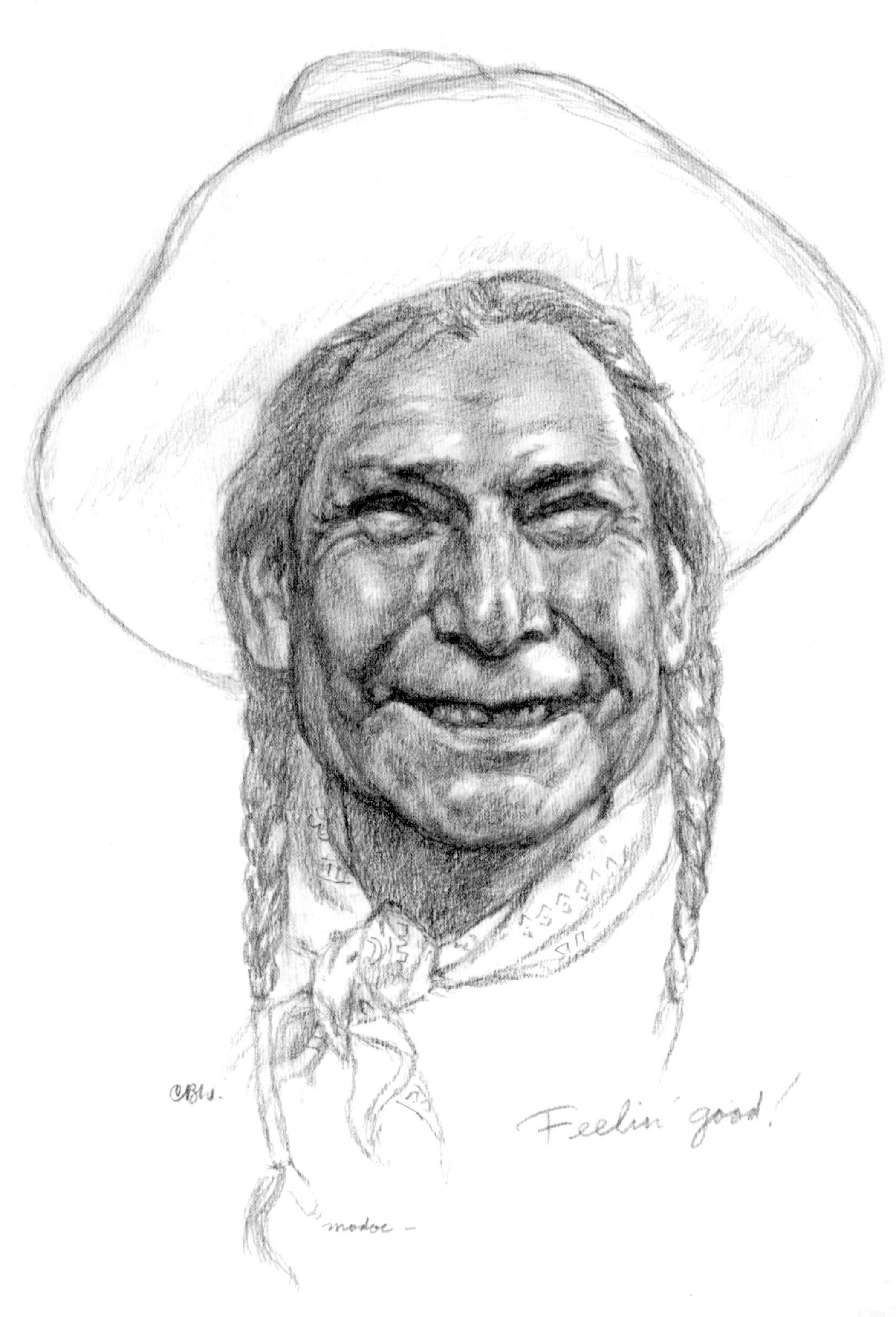

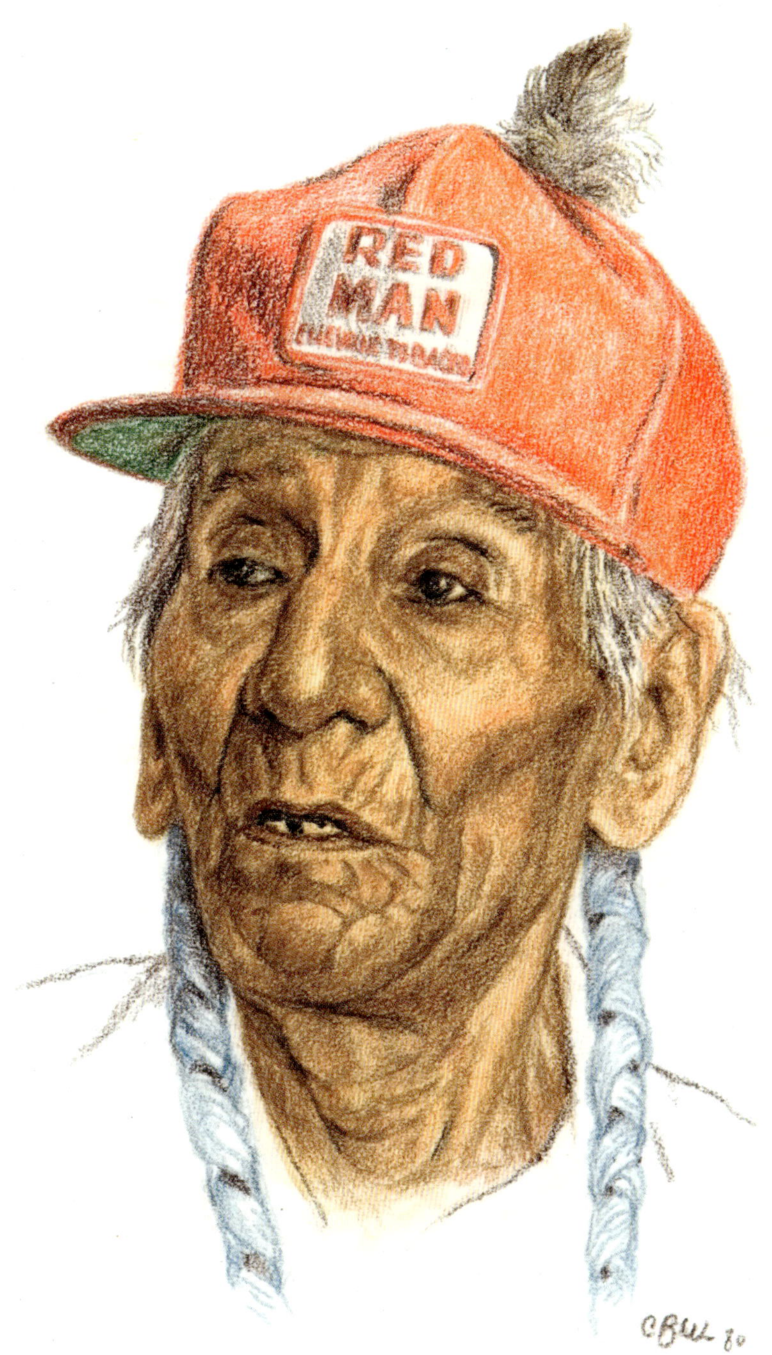

MENOMINEE
– 80 YEARS,
1980.
12.125 X 8.75,
COLOR
PENCIL/PAPER,
1327.2131

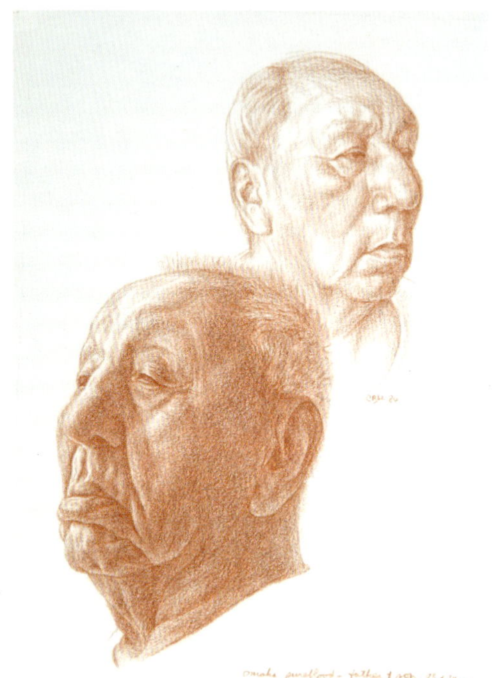

OMAHA PUREBLOOD
– FATHER AND SON
– 93 AND 74 YEARS,
1984. 13.25 X 10.25,
COLOR PENCIL/PAPER,
1327.2106

QUAPAW PUREBLOOD
MAN – 72 YEARS,
1985. 10.25 X 13.25,
GRAPHITE/PAPER,
1327.2104

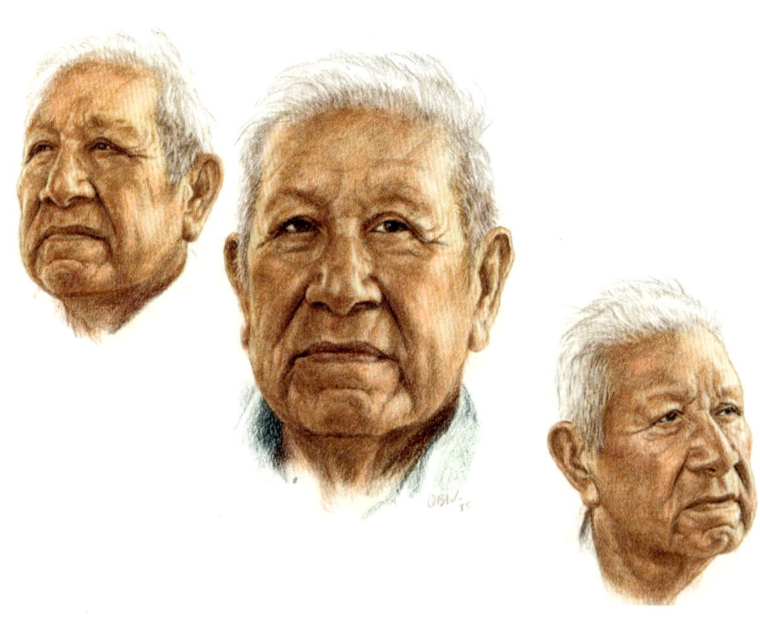

KIOWA PUREBLOOD,
1982. 15.25 X 11.25,
COLOR PENCIL/PAPER,
1327.2101

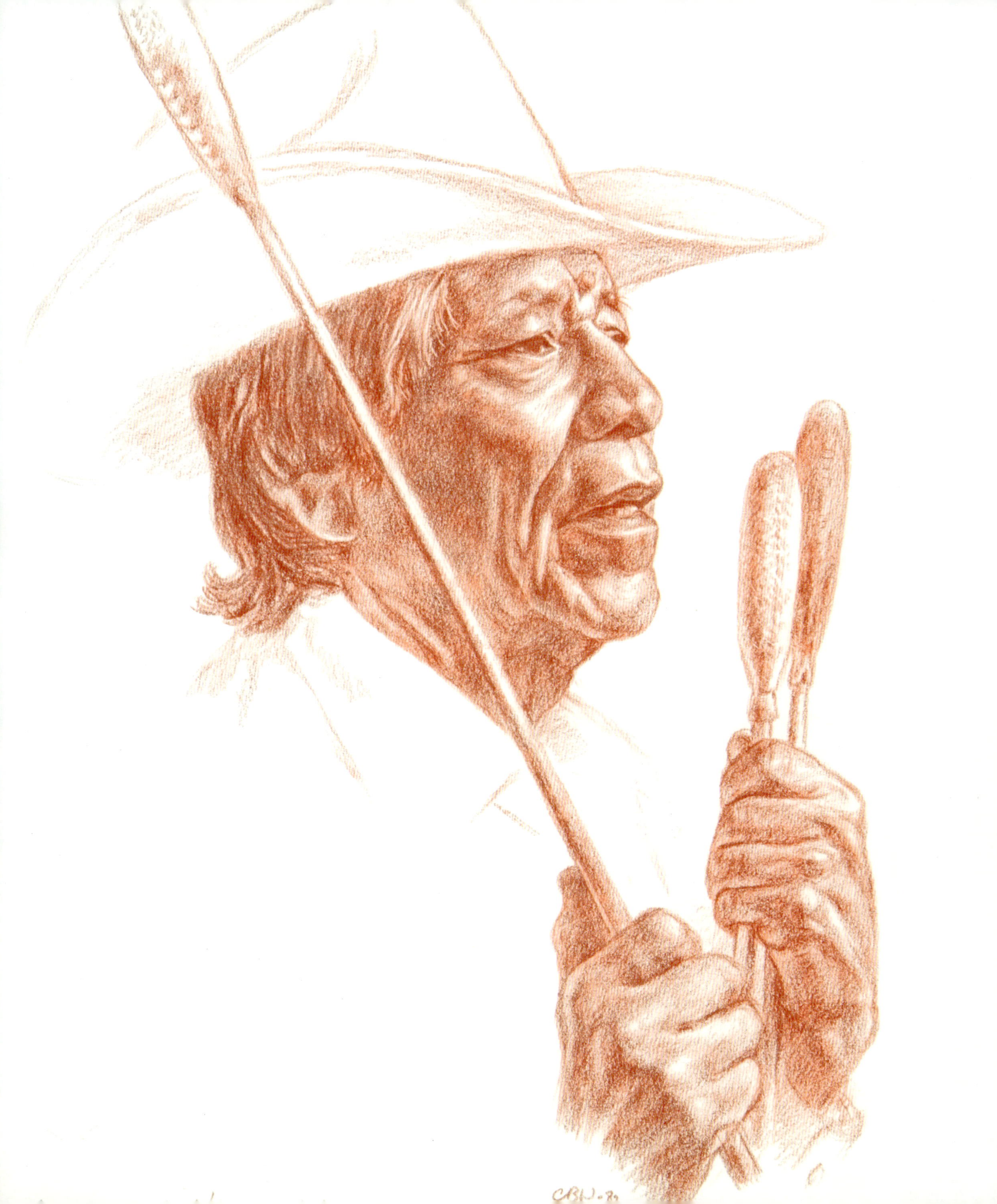

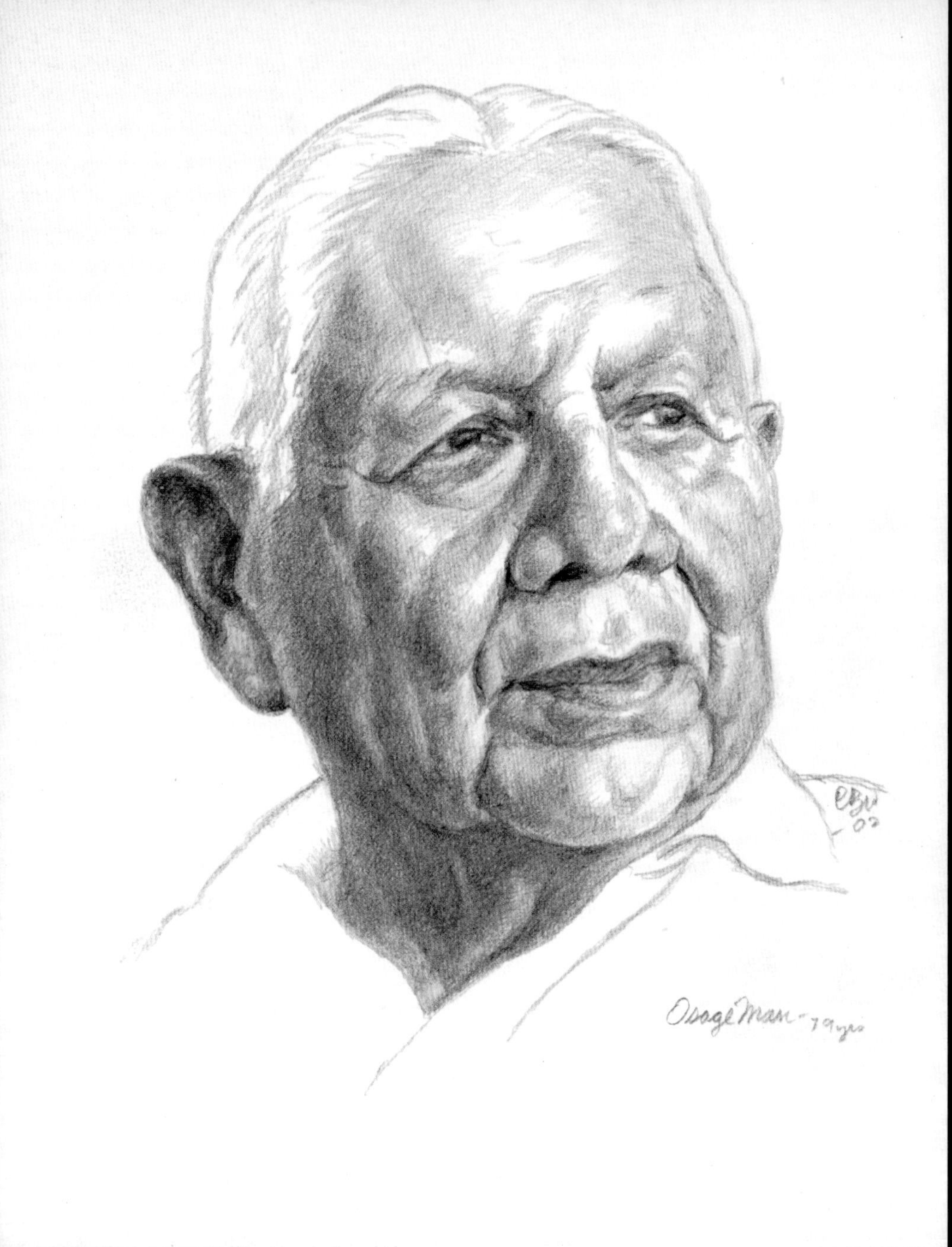

OSAGE MAN – 79 YEARS

– MAURICE HAMILTON, 2002.

14 X 11,

GRAPHITE/PAPER, 1327.3880

COMANCHE PUREBLOOD – 65

YEARS, 1981. 14 X 10.25,

GRAPHITE/PAPER, 1327.2208

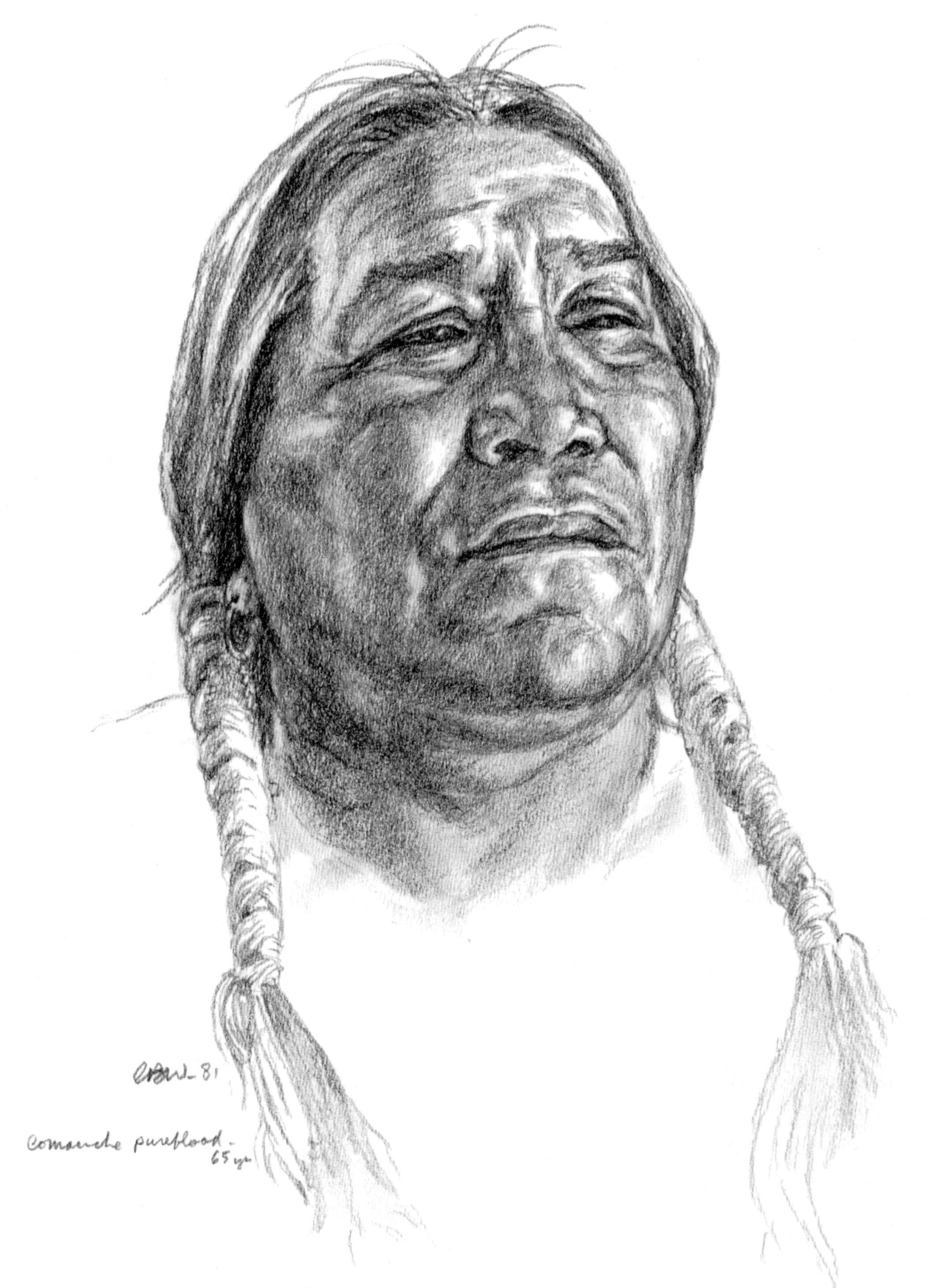
CBW-81
Comanche pureblood.
65 yr

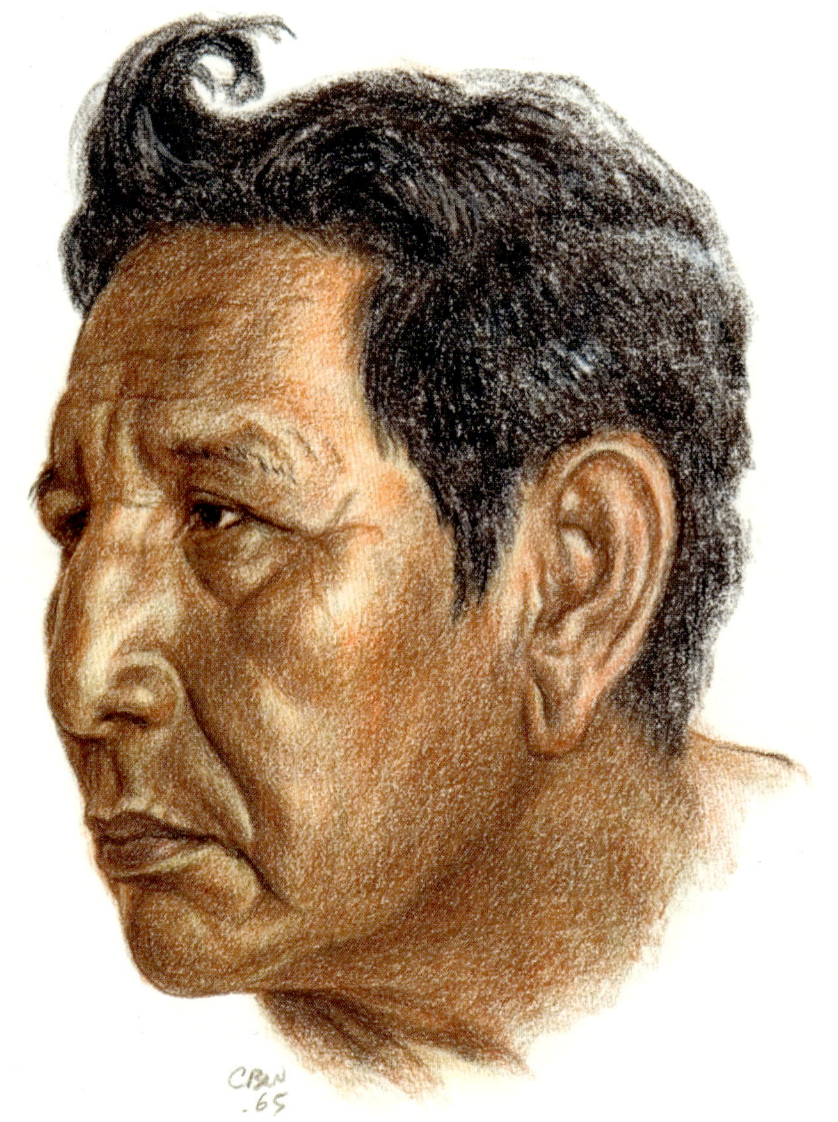

CHEYENNE,
1965.
13.25 X
7.125,
COLOR
PENCIL/
PAPER,
1327.2205

JOHN HOOF
– ARAPAHO, 1960.
14.125 X 11.25,
UMBER WASH, INK/
PAPER, 1327.2102

FRANCIS EAGLE
– PONCA, 1961.
UMBER WASH,
16.75 X 11.5,
INK/PAPER, 1327.2103

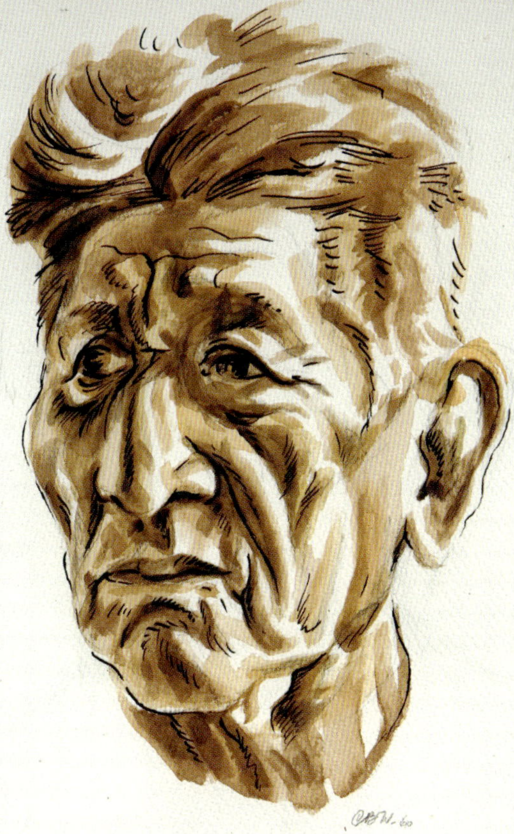

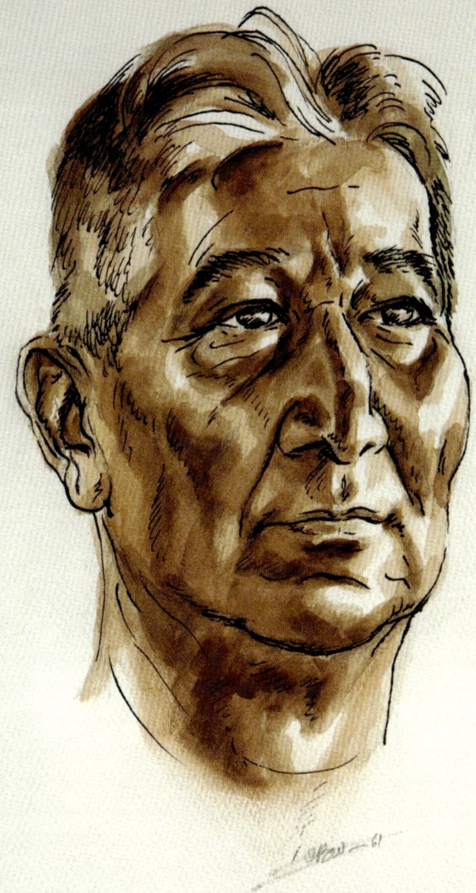

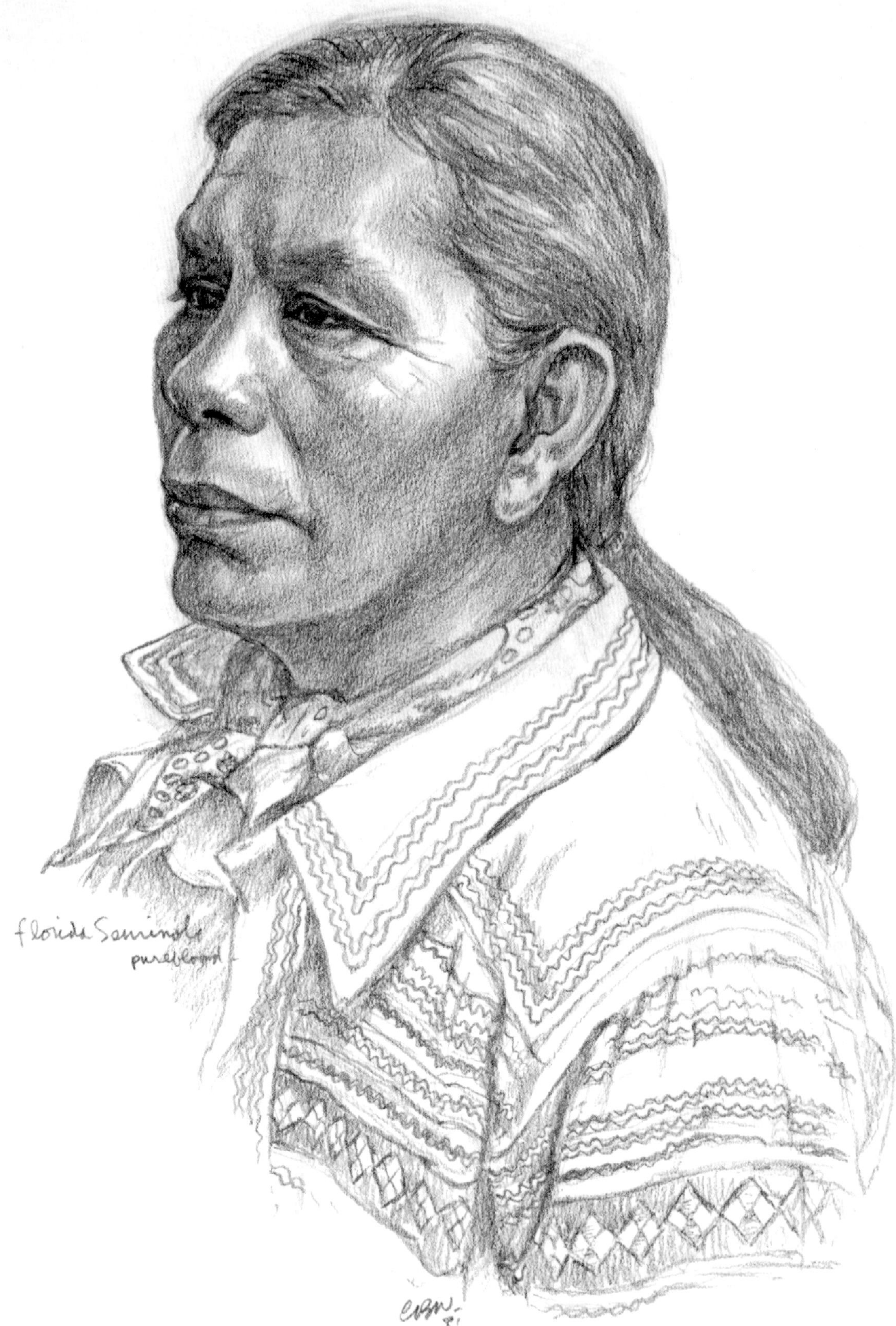

FLORIDA SEMINOLE

PUREBLOOD, 1981.

14.375 X 10.375,

GRAPHITE/PAPER,

1327.2092

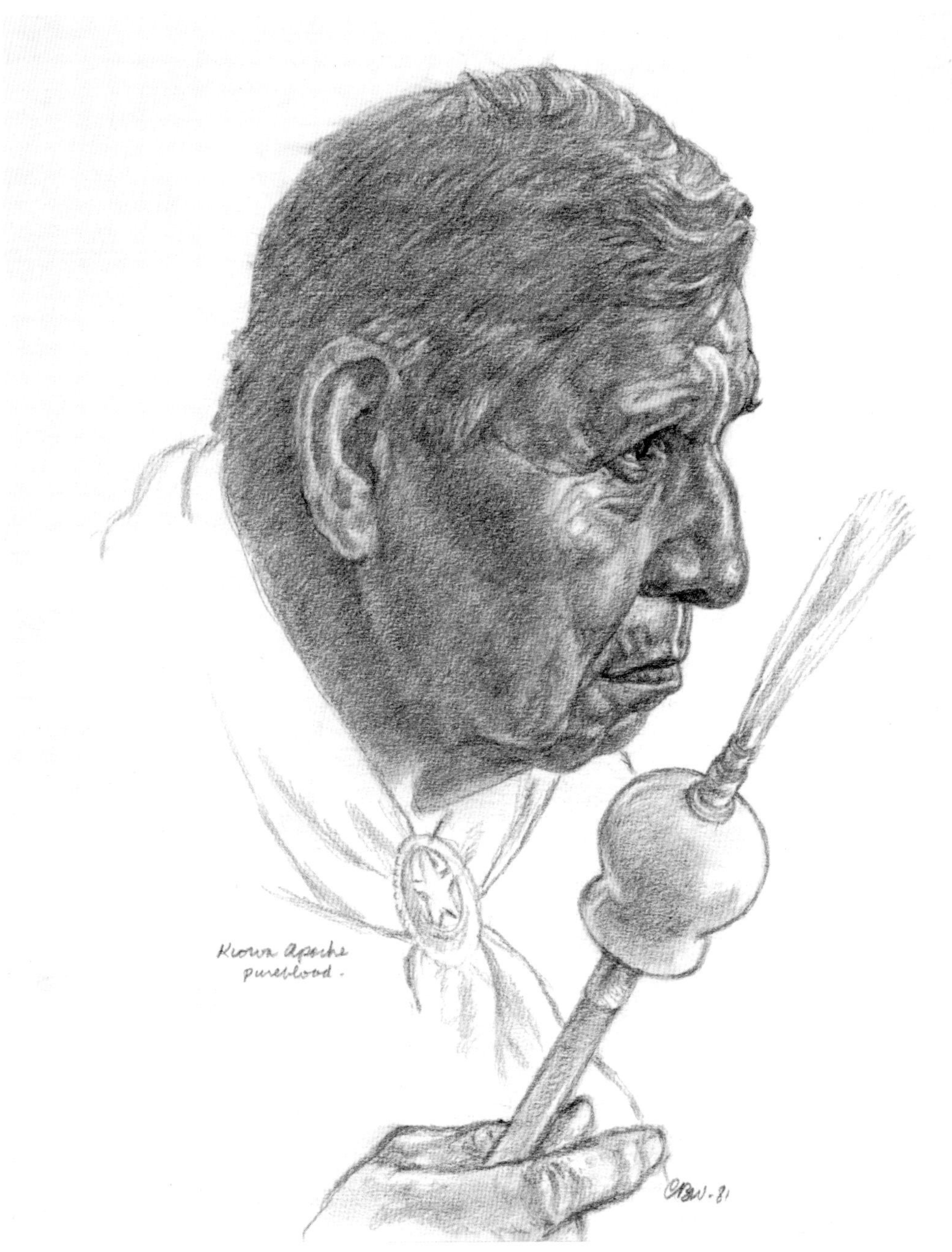

KIOWA APACHE
PUREBLOOD, 1981.
18.75 X 14.75,
GRAPHITE/PAPER,
1327.2135

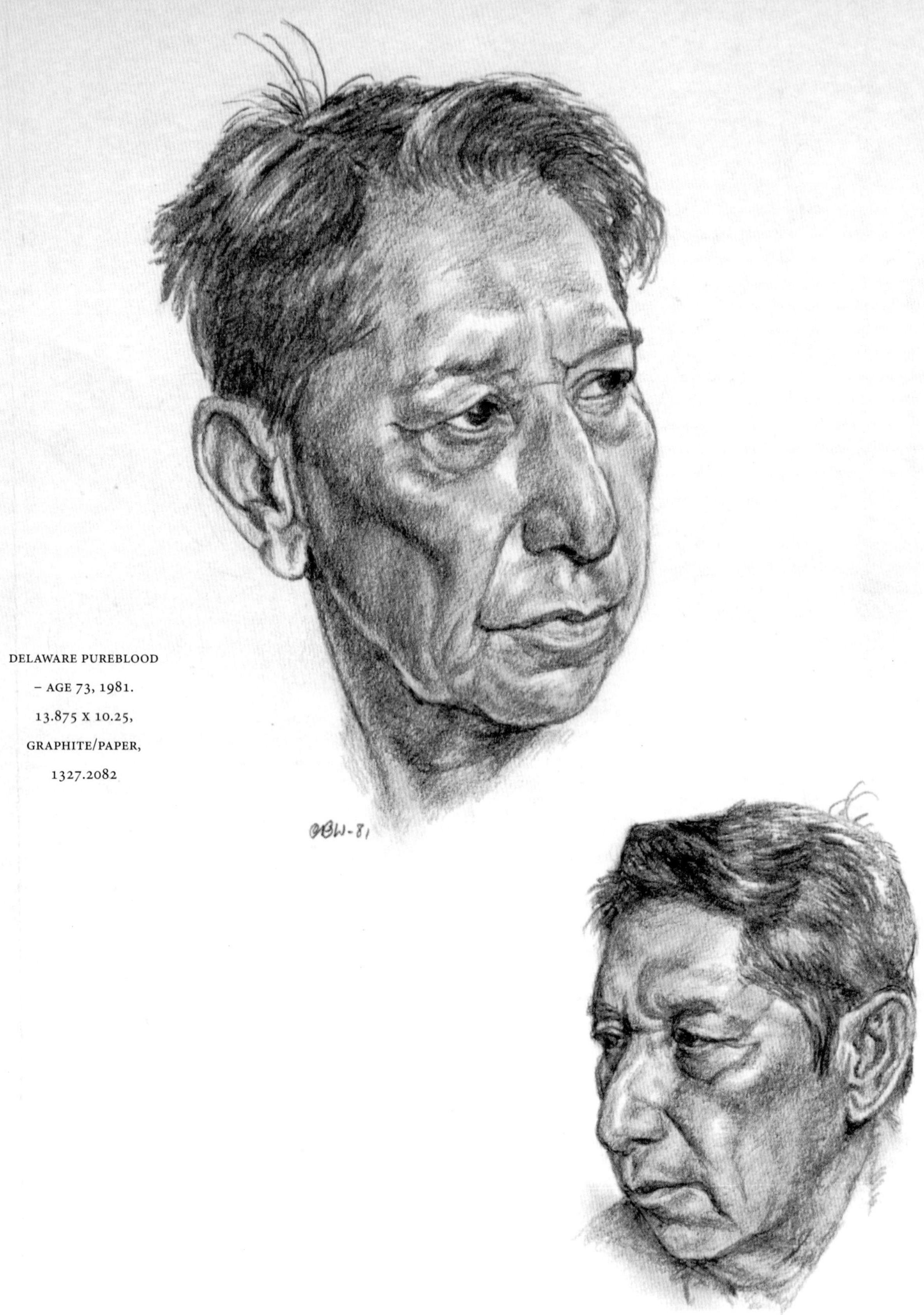

DELAWARE PUREBLOOD
– AGE 73, 1981.
13.875 X 10.25,
GRAPHITE/PAPER,
1327.2082

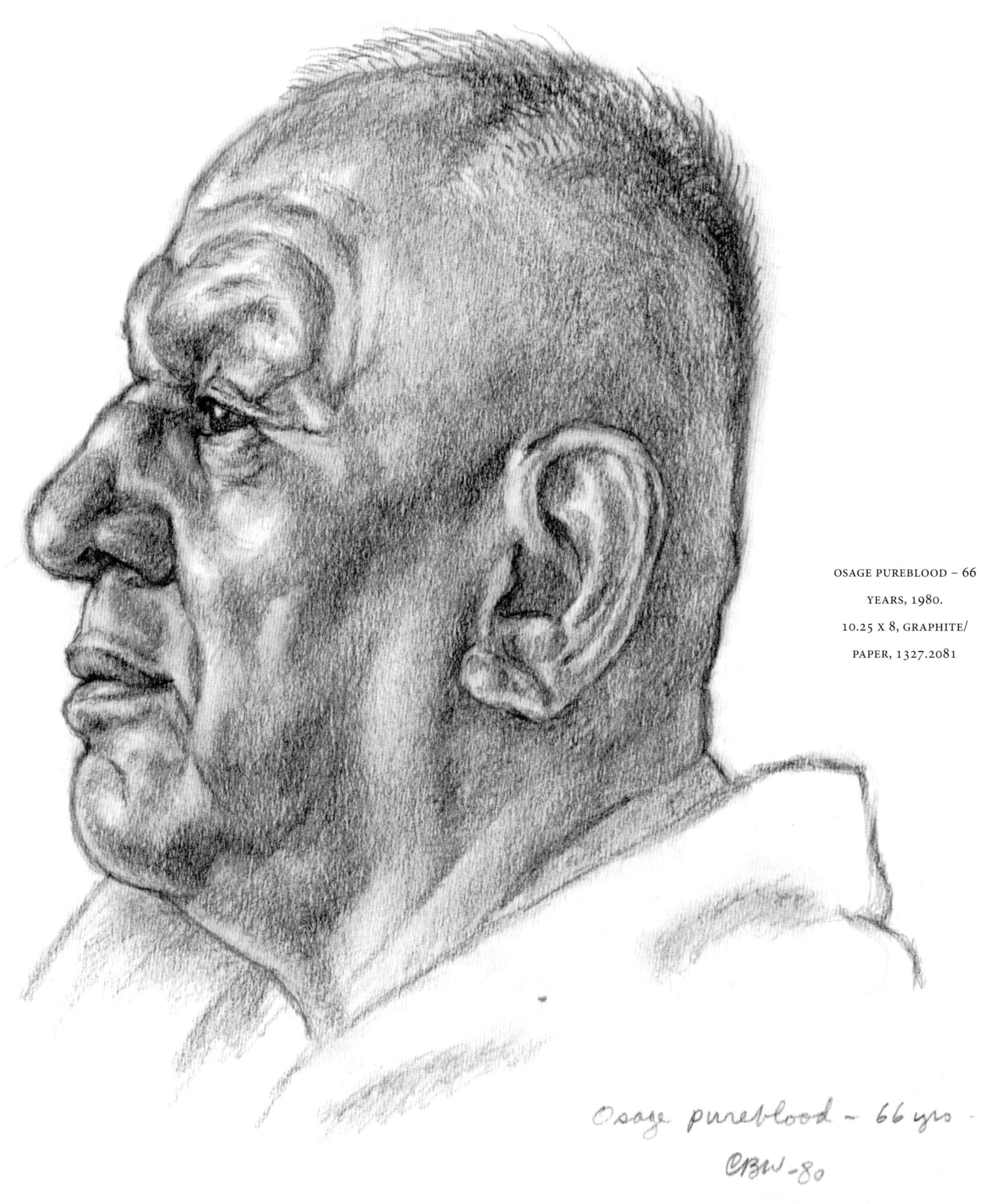

OSAGE PUREBLOOD – 66
YEARS, 1980.
10.25 X 8, GRAPHITE/
PAPER, 1327.2081

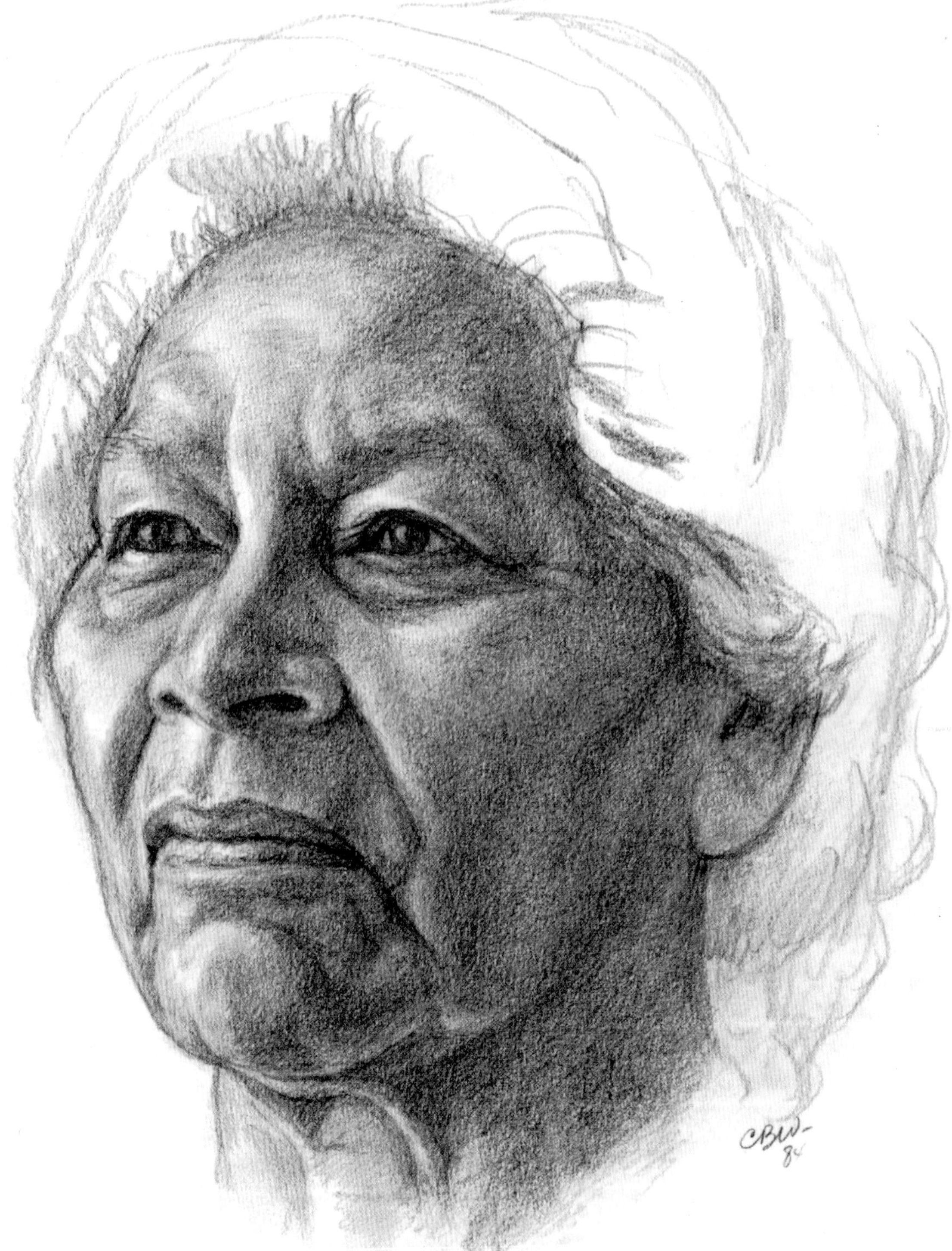

CHEROKEE WOMAN

– PUREBLOOD –

63 YEARS, 1984.

14.25 X 10.125,

GRAPHITE/PAPER,

1327.2109

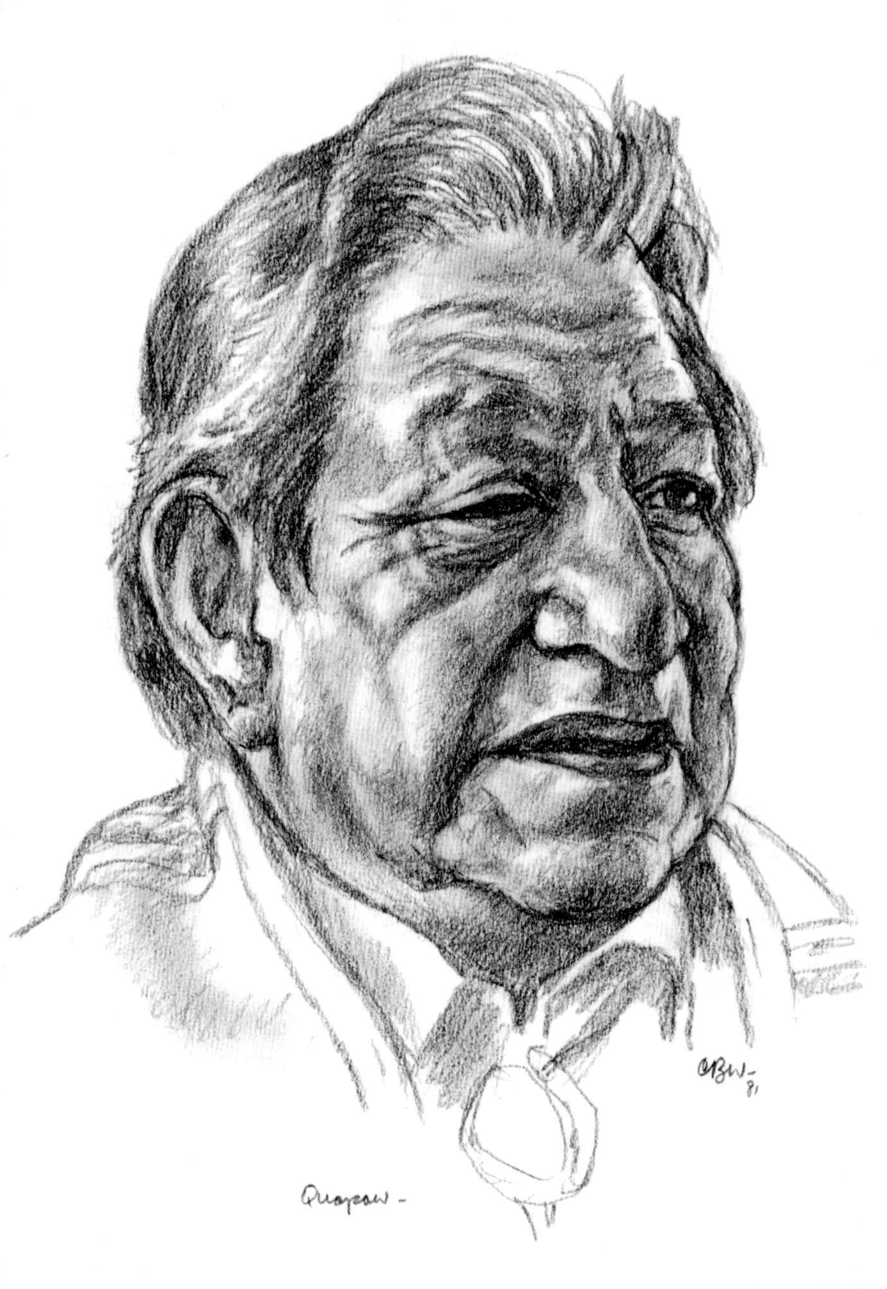

QUAPAW, 1981.

14.125 X 10.375,

GRAPHITE/PAPER.

1327.2209

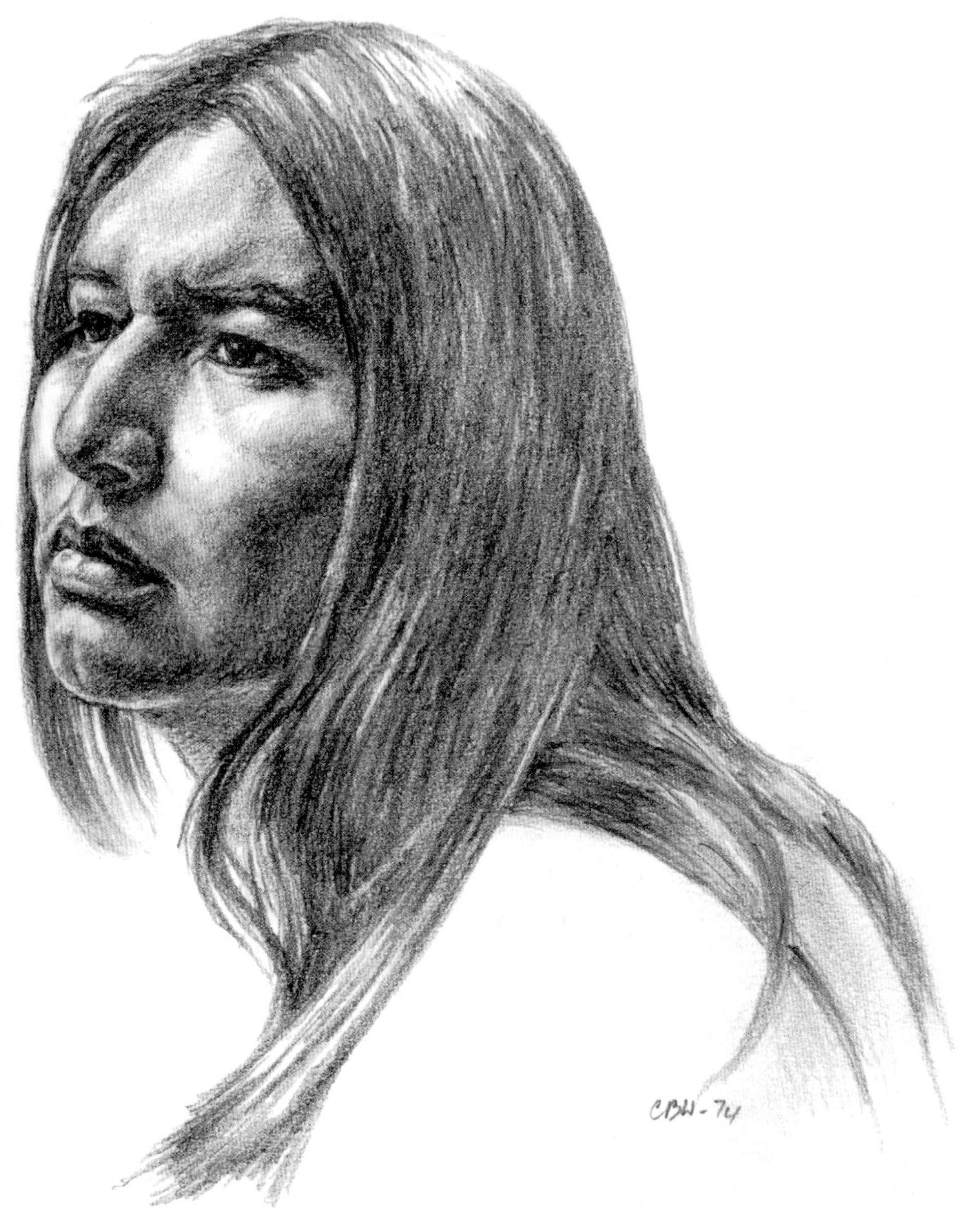

CBW-74
Taos - man - ag 23

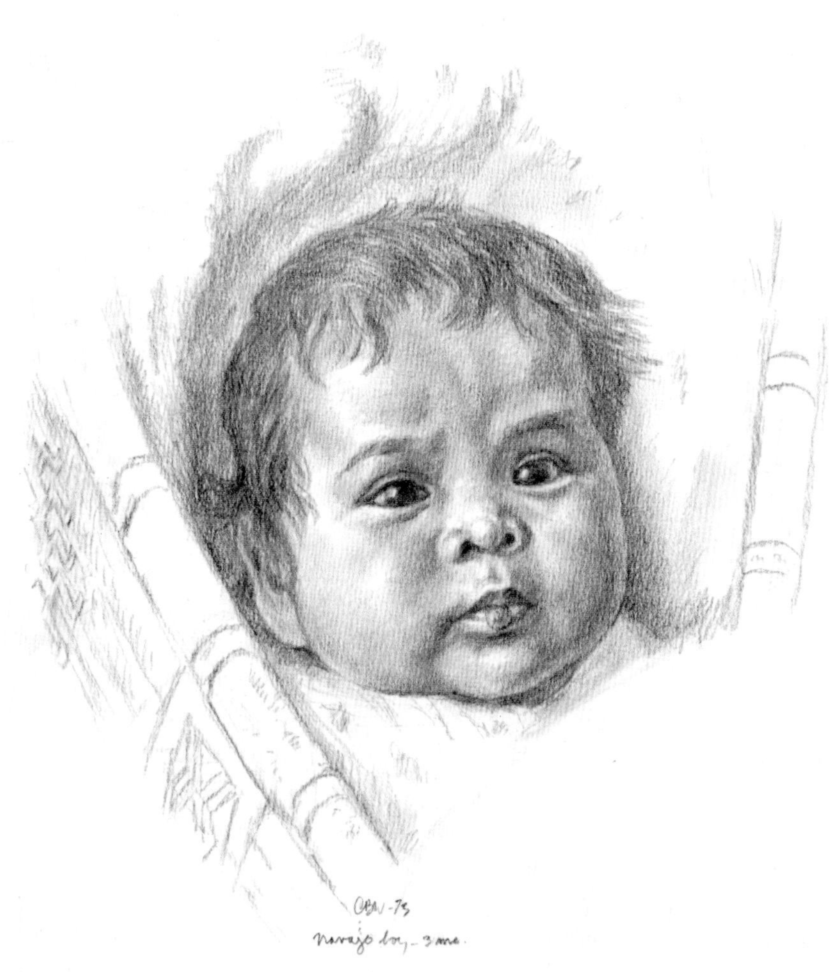

TAOS MAN – AGE 23, 1981.
GRAPHITE/PAPER,
1327.2094

NAVAJO BOY –
3 MONTHS, 1973.
GRAPHITE/PAPER,
1327.2210

WILSON THE PRINTMAKER

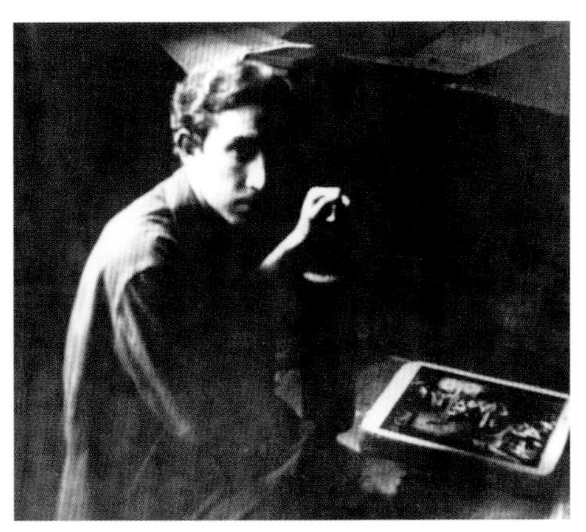

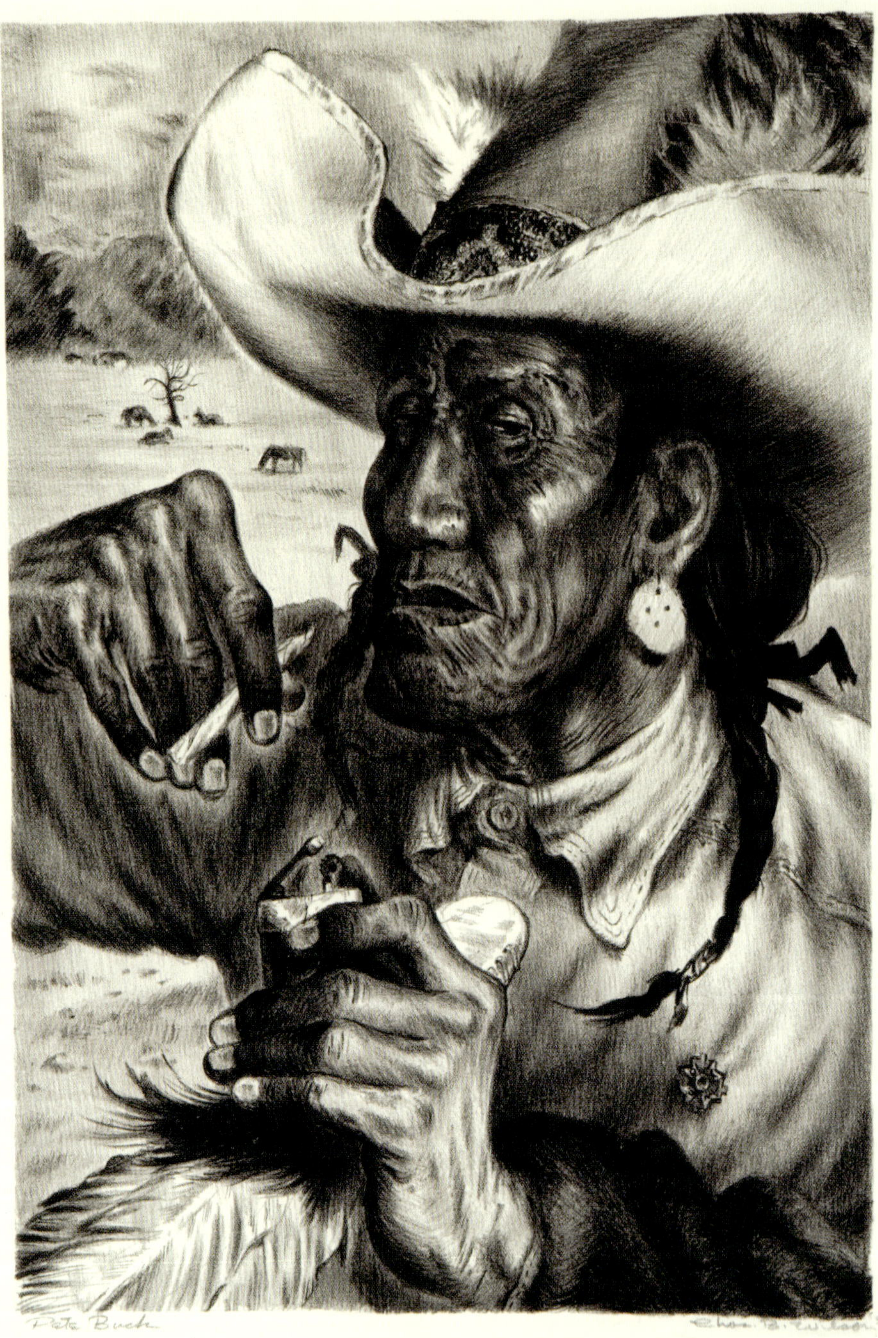
Pete Buck

Lithography has been part of Charles Banks Wilson's life since his initial exposure to the medium at the Chicago Art Institute when he was not yet twenty: "As I learned it, lithography is a very physical medium, especially the process of drawing directly on the stone.... The stone's natural grain, its feel as my pencil or crayon passes over it, is almost sensual. It inspires me as I draw. Of course, being able to print multiple images of a drawing does offer a commercial incentive to do lithographs, but that is not the reason I love the medium above all others."

The heart of the medium is a heavy rectangular slab of gray Bavarian limestone. Before the artist draws on it, it is made completely smooth and level by grinding it in a rotating motion against a similar stone, with a layer of fine grit, wet sea salt or grainy quartz, sandwiched between the two. The smoothed stone is drawn upon with a lithographer's black grease pencil or crayon. Then a coating of gum arabic solution is smoothed over its surface and it is allowed to dry for a day. When the gum arabic is washed away, the drawing disappears to the eye, but, like a memory, is retained in the

PETE BUCK, 1939.
15.75 X 11.25,
LITHOGRAPH/PAPER,
1427.717

stone. Next comes inking. Oil-based ink is rolled onto the moistened slab with a hide-wrapped hand roller. The oily ink clings to the drawing but is rejected by the watered stone, and again the drawing is visible. Then the stone is placed on the bed of the lithography press. Damp paper is draped over it, pressure is applied, and the movable press bed is cranked forward under a scraper to transfer the image to paper.

Many, many things can go wrong at any stage of the process—from concept to cranking to the lifting of the newly-born print from the press: too much pressure flattens and spreads the ink, the stone may be imperfectly surfaced, the paper may be too damp or too dry. Even the temperature in the room may be wrong. Only an unbroken strand of luck and skill produces a perfect print.

"Creative lithography is an unrelenting medium," says Wilson. "Every phase requires concentrated effort. Because I am acutely aware of the work that is necessary to successfully complete an original lithographic edition, I usually consider only my very best work suitable for the stone." As a result, Wilson sometimes translated an iconic image from a different medium to the stone, for example his *Madonna of the Plains,* drawn from a mural commissioned for the Oklahoma State Capitol, and *Shawnee Ribbon Bets,* originally an oil on canvas. As a result, we are beneficiary of a doubled pleasure, along with insights into the character of alternative media, how Wilson approached them, and his rope-trick versatility.

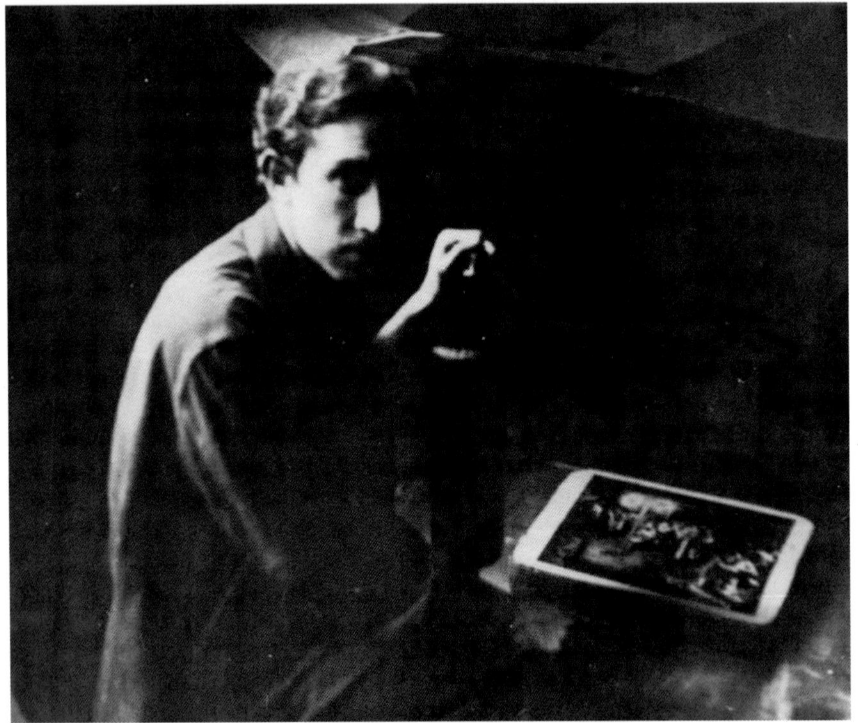

Wilson at the Chicago Institute of Art in 1940 looking up from his work on an early lithograph. CBW: *There are all kinds of lives to be lived — there should be all kinds of art to express them.*

HANDGAME FEAST
– QUAPAW, 1941.
11.375 X 17.25,
LITHOGRAPH/PAPER,
14.881

TRIBAL BAND,
LITHOGRAPH/PAPER,
1939. 12.5 X 18.25,
LITHOGRAPH/PAPER,
1427.764

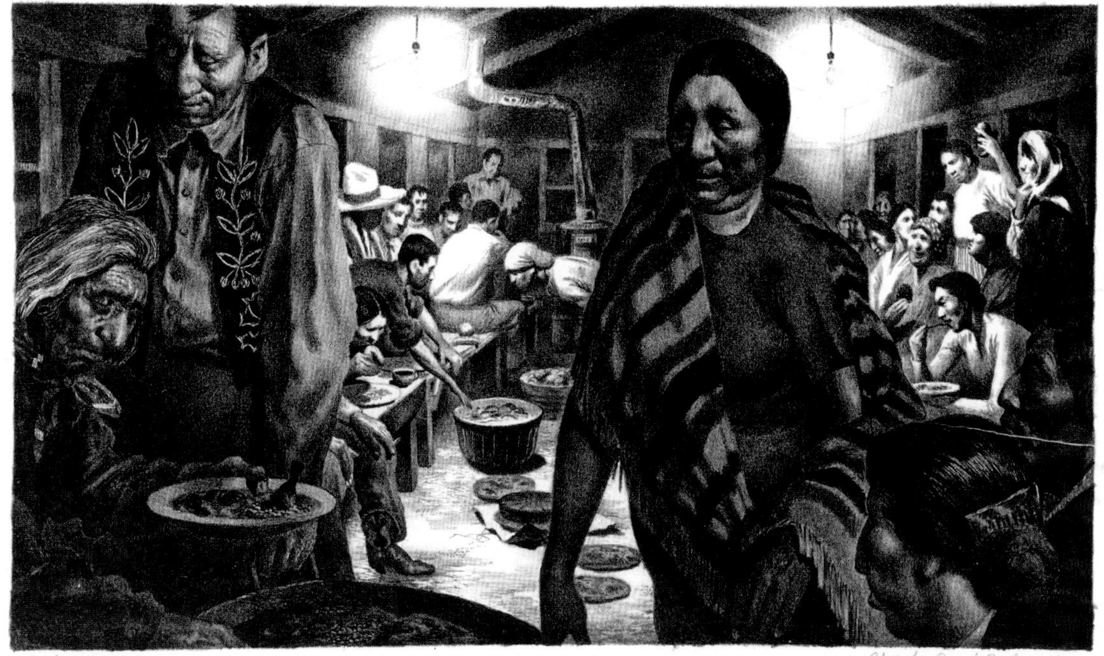

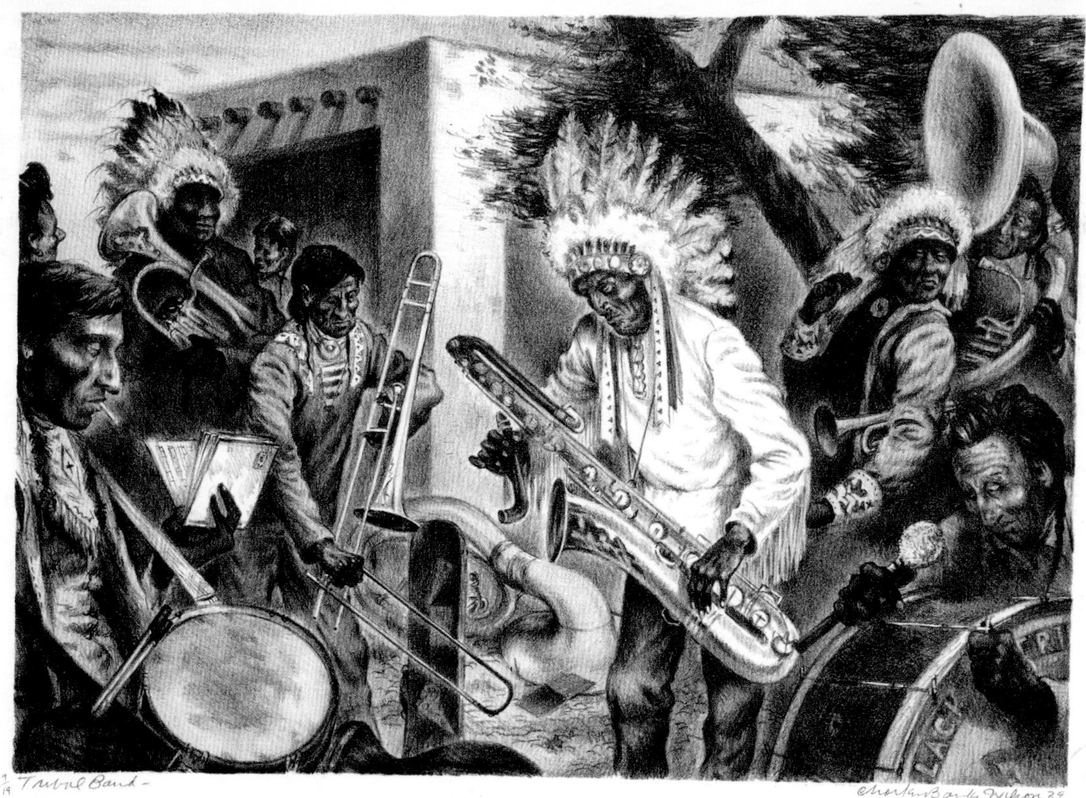

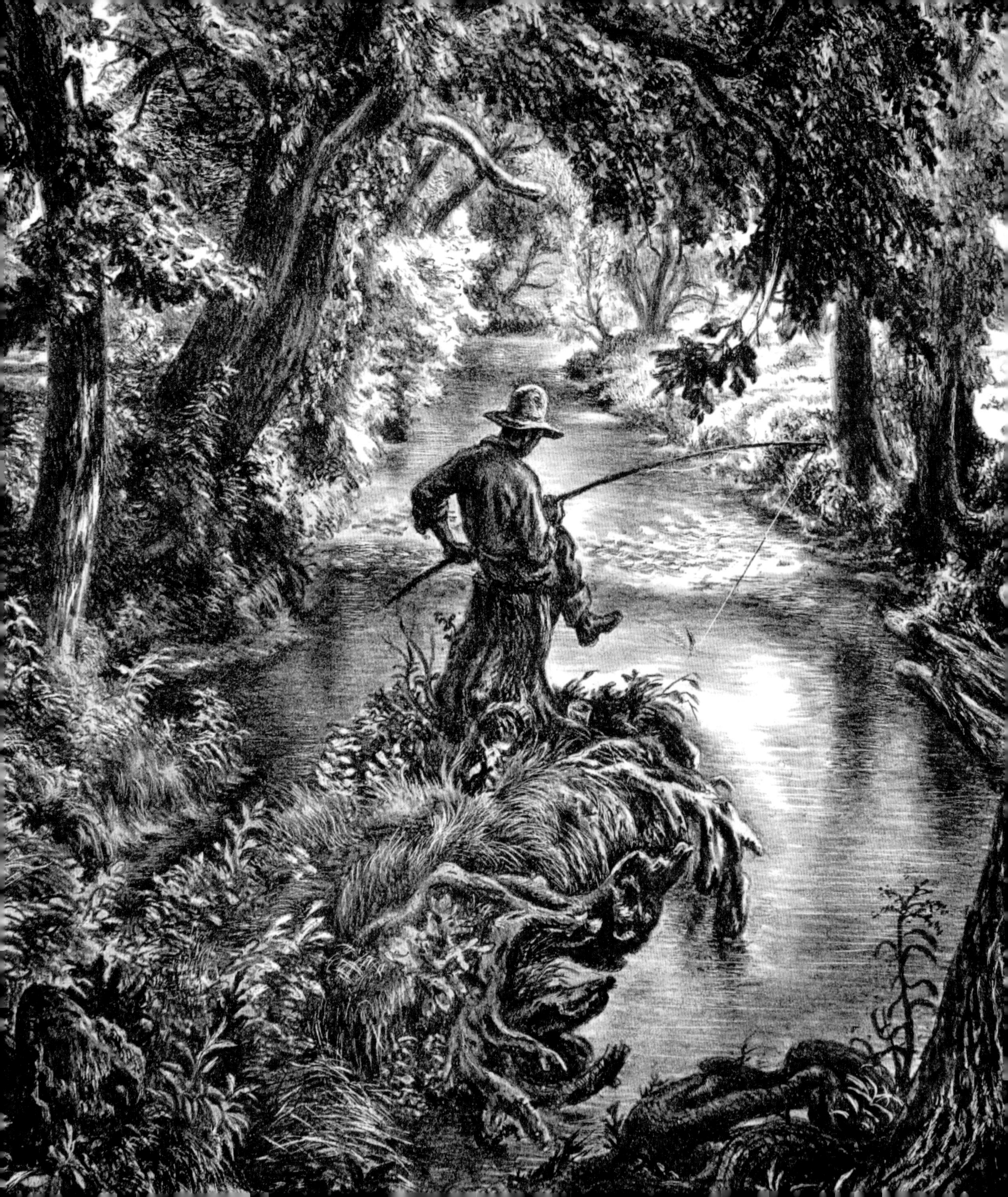

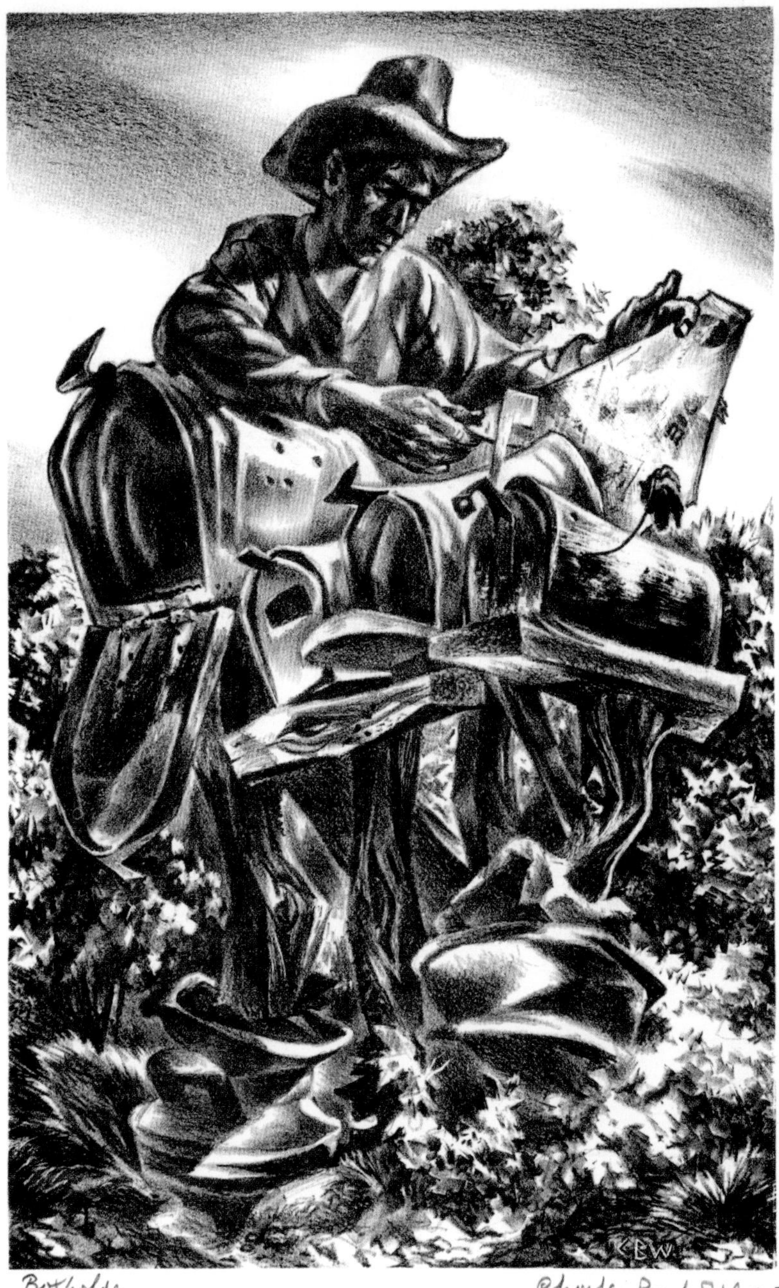

BOXHOLDER, 1954.

19 X 11,

LITHOGRAPH/PAPER,

1427.776

MORNING ON THE

CREEK, 1967.

19.875 X 13,

LITHOGRAPH/PAPER,

1427.787

Wilson learned lithography from Francis Chapin during his study at the Art Institute of Chicago, and, in Wilson's words, "It may have been the best thing that ever happened to me." Two flows of energy converged: the youthful Wilson, strong and evolving in his art, met a medium he would love for life. The American public, lean and inward-looking in the Depression years following the market crash of 1929, sought a new understanding of its collective experience. Regional schools of art arose that documented the lives of the common people, along with renewed respect for the power and intimacy of hand labor. It was the perfect moment in American history for the medium of printmaking to emerge—fine-art multiples are by their nature egalitarian, and a celebration of craft. Though each pulled print is a unique entity, the stone can speak in one voice to many eyes.

Wilson was invited to produce a lithograph for the Associated American Artists in 1941 through the intercession of Thomas Hart Benton, whose prints were sold by the group in its New York gallery, department stores, and by mail order. Established in 1934, Associated American Artists sought to democratize art by making it available to Americans with varying resources in a broad range of social settings. The group commissioned original prints, most with regional subjects, by artists such as Benton, Reginald Marsh, and George Bellows, and sold them for as little as five dollars each. Many were printed by the master lithographer George Miller in New York. Miller printed Wilson's lithograph for the Associated American Artists commission. For the next ten years, Wilson continued to make lithographs with Oklahoma themes, but they were printed in New York by Miller as Wilson had no press of his own.

Then, in Miami, Oklahoma, in 1951, two things happened. Adolph Naglins, a Latvian immigrant working on a nearby farm, came to Wilson and offered his services. Naglins, who had once worked in a print shop in Europe, had learned of the man in the loft-like upper room above a Main Street paint store who made lithographs. Shortly after, Wilson heard about a lithography press for sale in Springfield, Missouri, which would turn out to be identical to Miller's own in New York. Technical challenges lay ahead in perfecting prints in the Miami studio, but Wilson's course was set. In 1964, Tony Mayer began to assist Wilson in the physically taxing aspects of the work; it was a productive relationship that continued many years.

The response of an artist to a particular medium is as mysterious as any other form of falling in love, and the best of the resulting relationships lasts a lifetime. For Charles, everything about lithography—the silky limestone surface, the pungent gum arabic, the creak of the press lever, the cool breath of the dampened paper in the warm Oklahoma air—combined with everything the print represented, technical challenge, drive for perfection, and democracy of distribution, into one harmonious whole. His stones may have been quarried in Bavaria, but they were as native to him as the lifetime of images he would draw upon them. —CAROL HARALSON

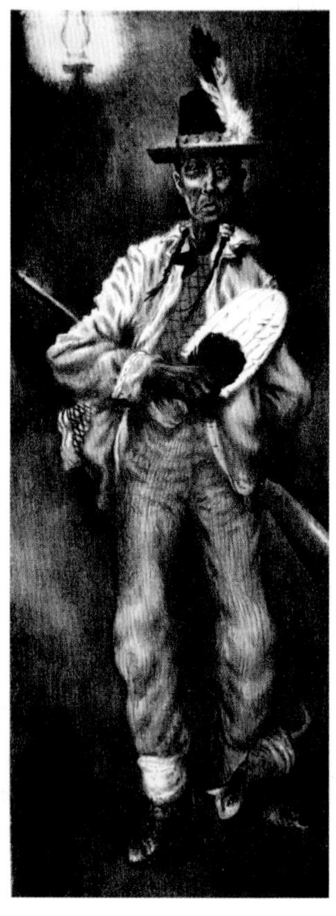

WHITE TREE, 1939. 17.25 X 7.75, LITHOGRAPH/PAPER, 1427.719

HENRY TURKEYFOOT, 1940. 11.5 X 15.75, LITHOGRAPH/PAPER, 1427.713

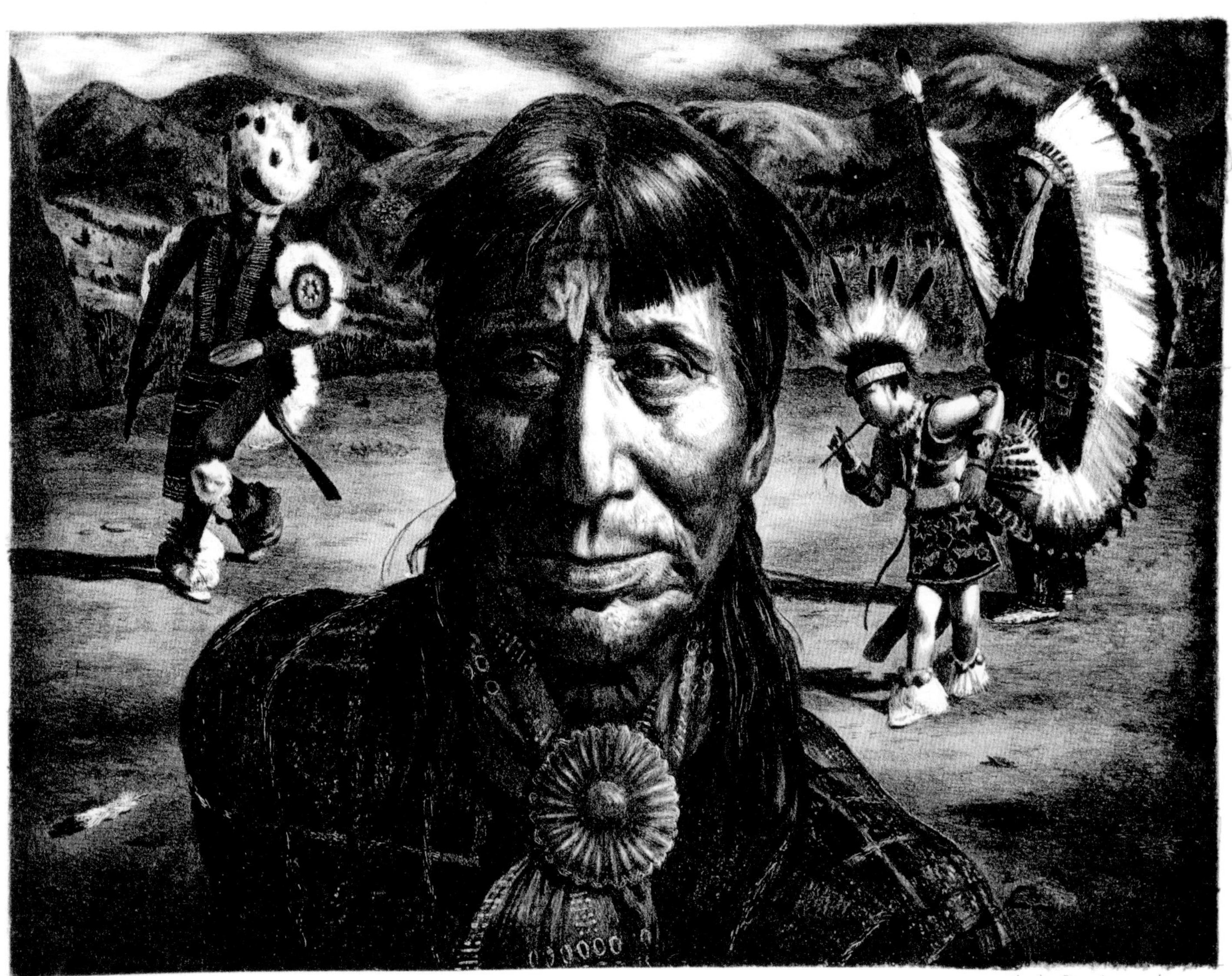
Henry Turkeyfoot
Charles Banks Wilson

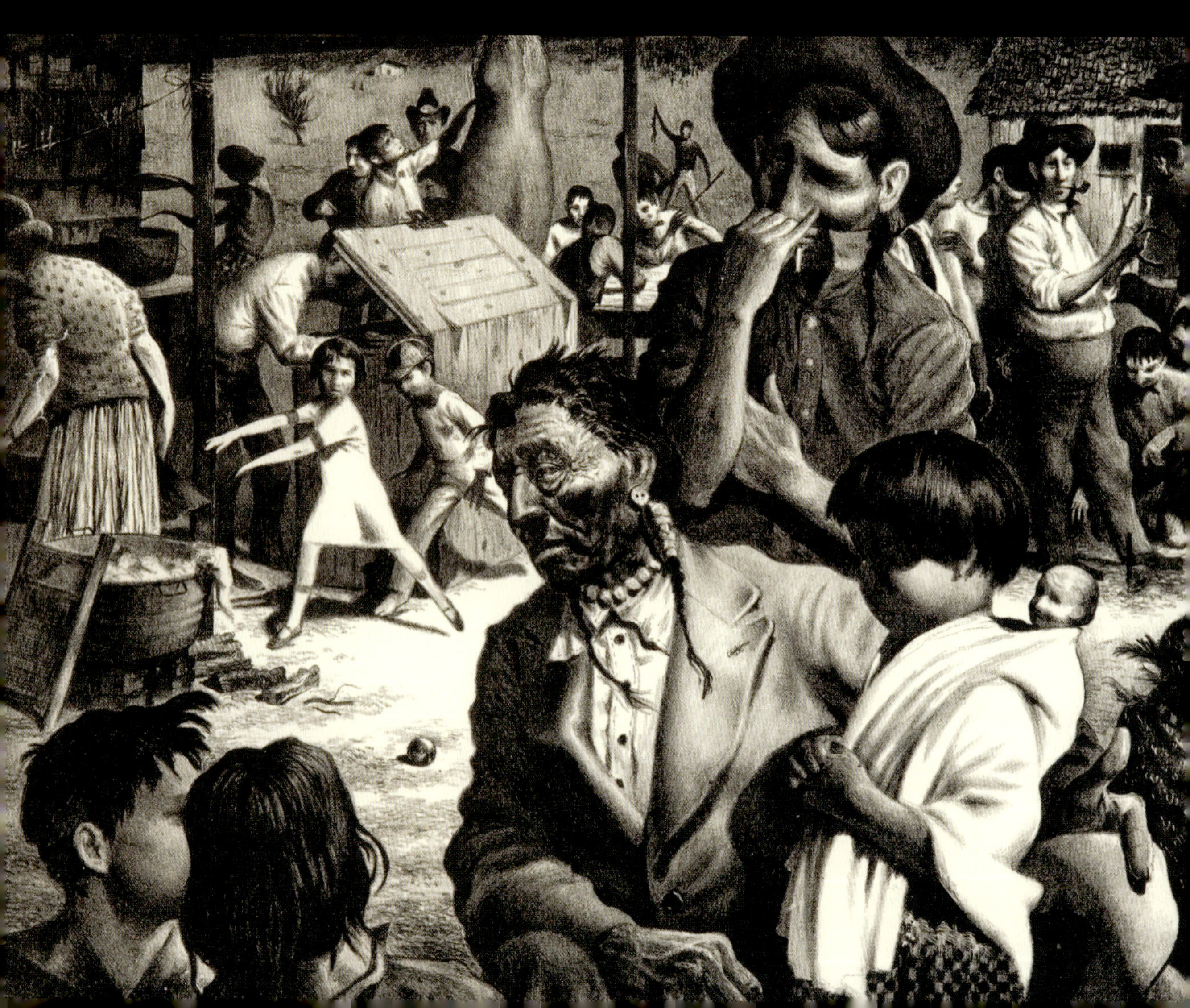

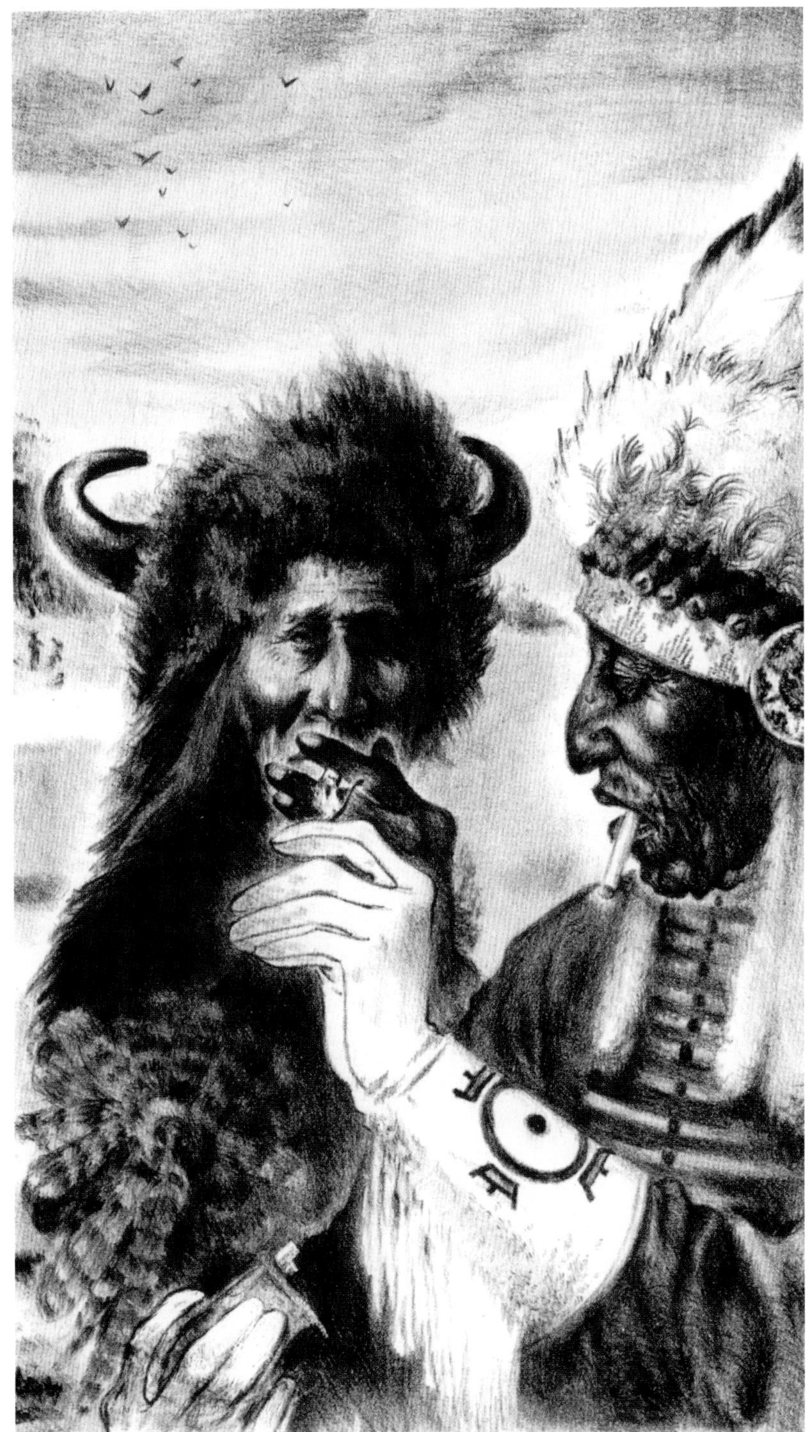

INDIAN SMOKE, 1940.
14 X 7.5,
LITHOGRAPH/PAPER,
TL2006.13.6

THE STORY TELLER, 1939.
11.25 X 15.75,
LITHOGRAPH/PAPER,
14.880

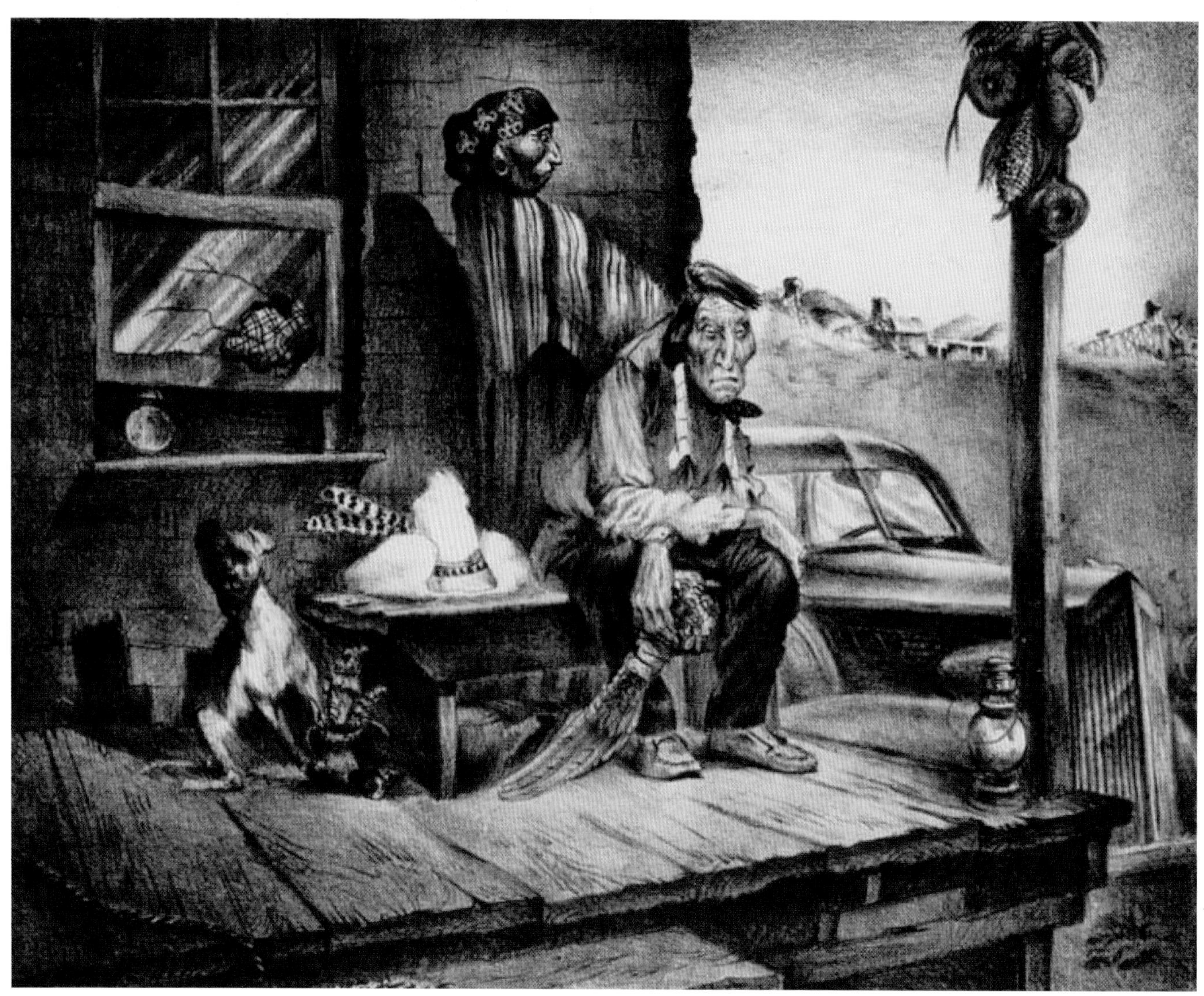

THE NEW RICH, 1939.
12.25 X 16.625,
LITHOGRAPH/PAPER,
1427.765

MAN WITH A PLOW,
1939. 17 X 12.75,
LITHOGRAPH/
PAPER, 1427.763

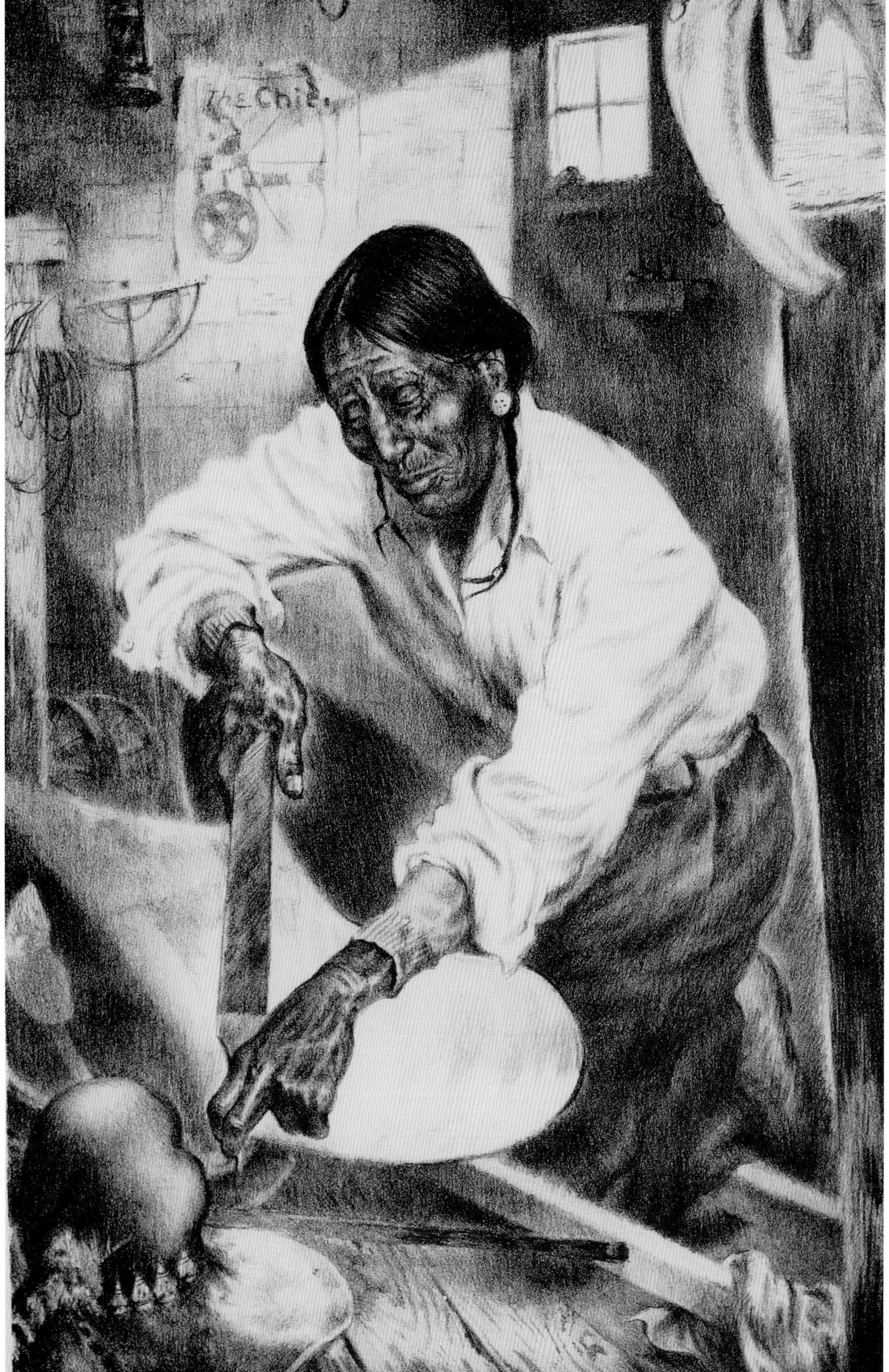

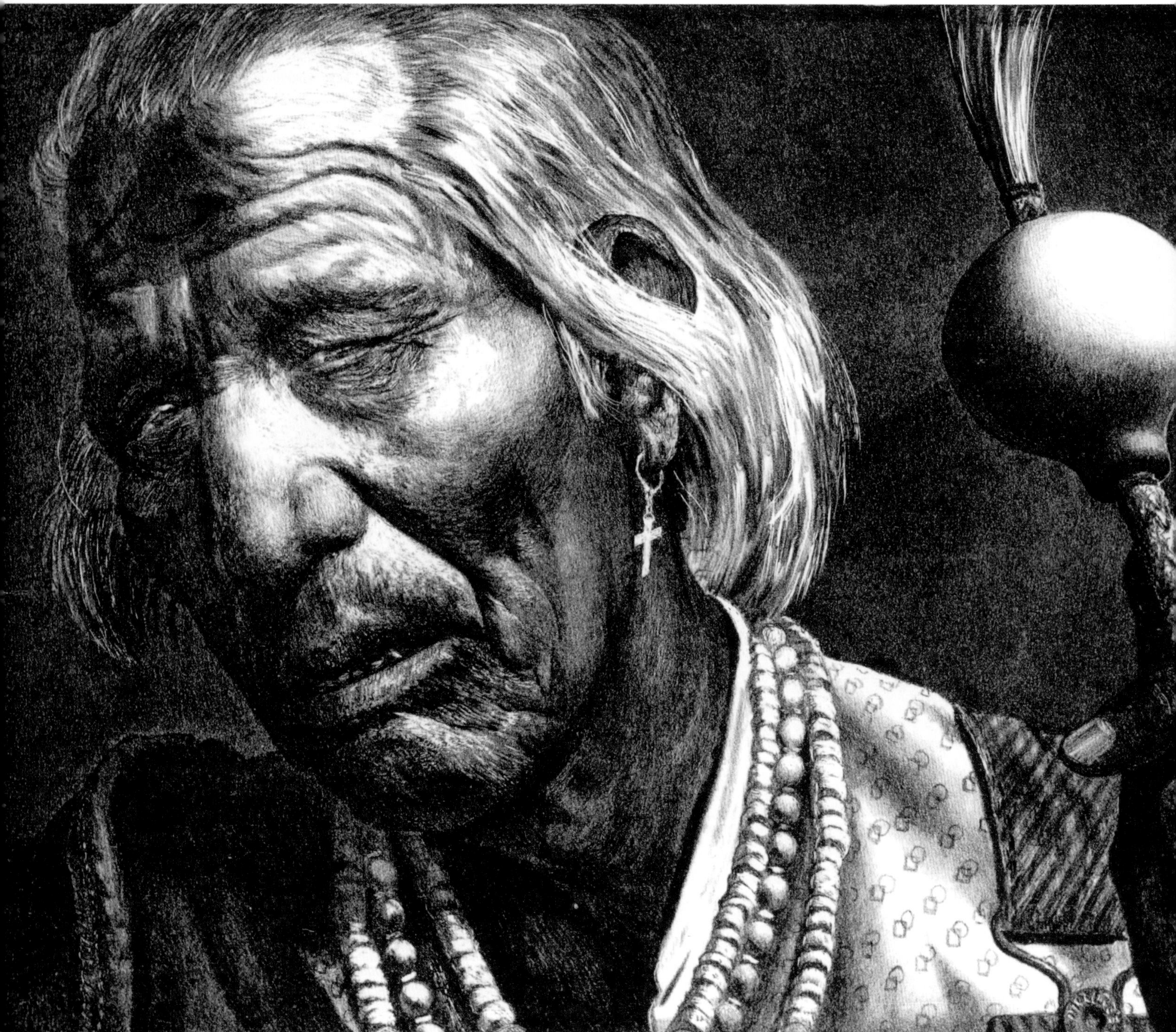

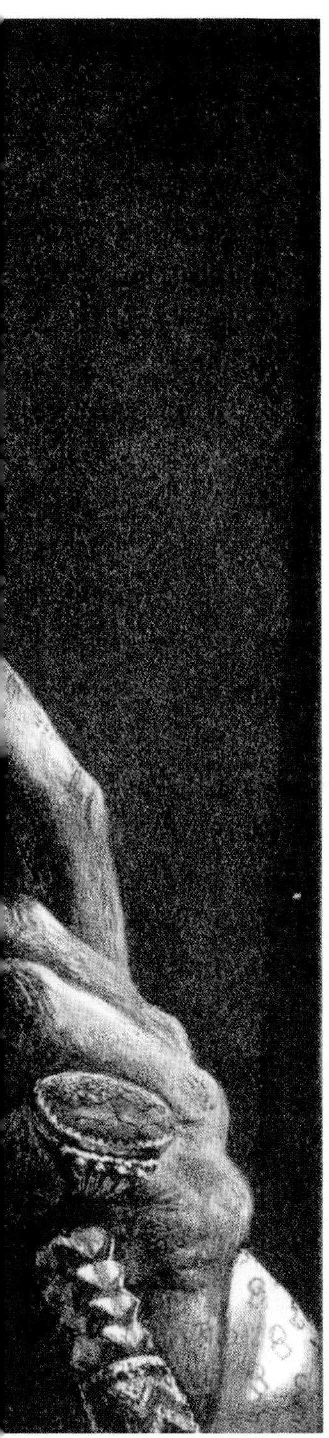

OLD MEDICINE SINGER, 1941.

11.25 X 16,

LITHOGRAPH/PAPER, 1427.718

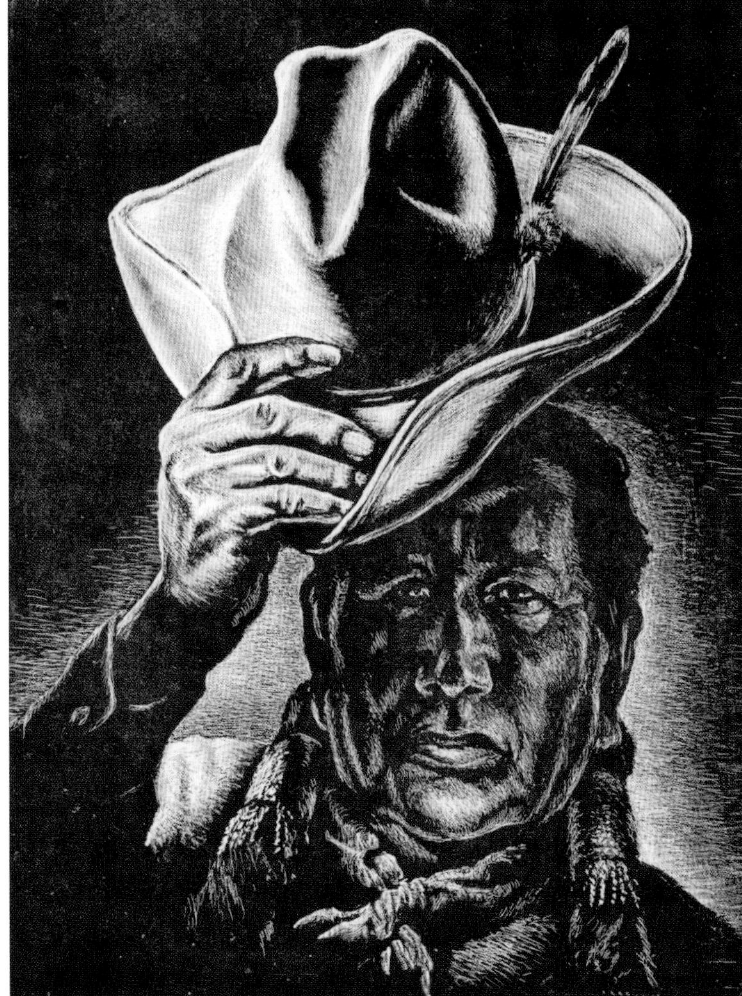

BLACKOWL,

1967. 11 X 10,

LITHOGRAPH/

PAPER,

1427.725

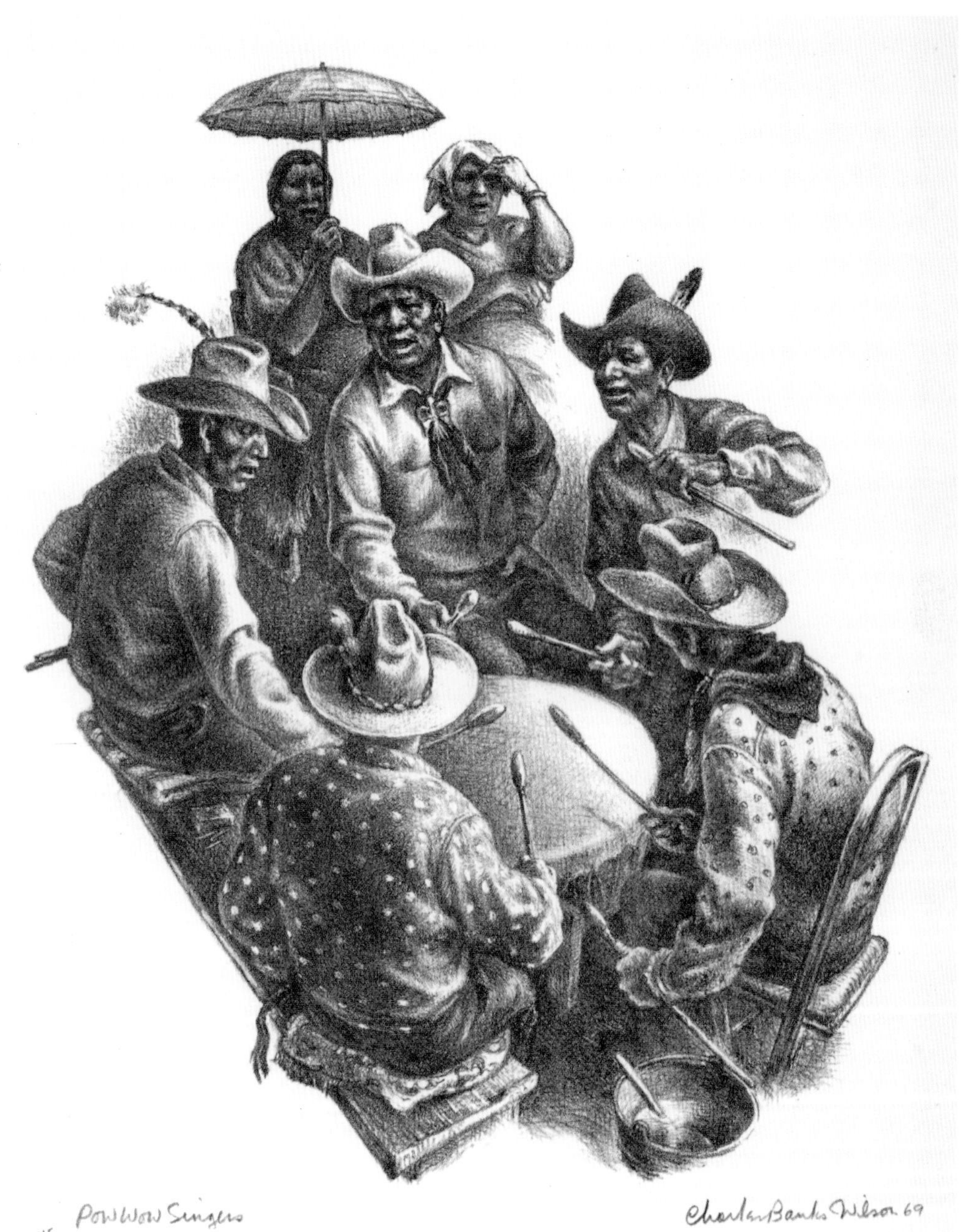

POW WOW SINGERS,
1969. 20 X 13,
LITHOGRAPH/PAPER,
1427.731

OKLAHOMA MELODY,
1985. 15.125 X 11.125,
LITHOGRAPH/PAPER,
1427.743

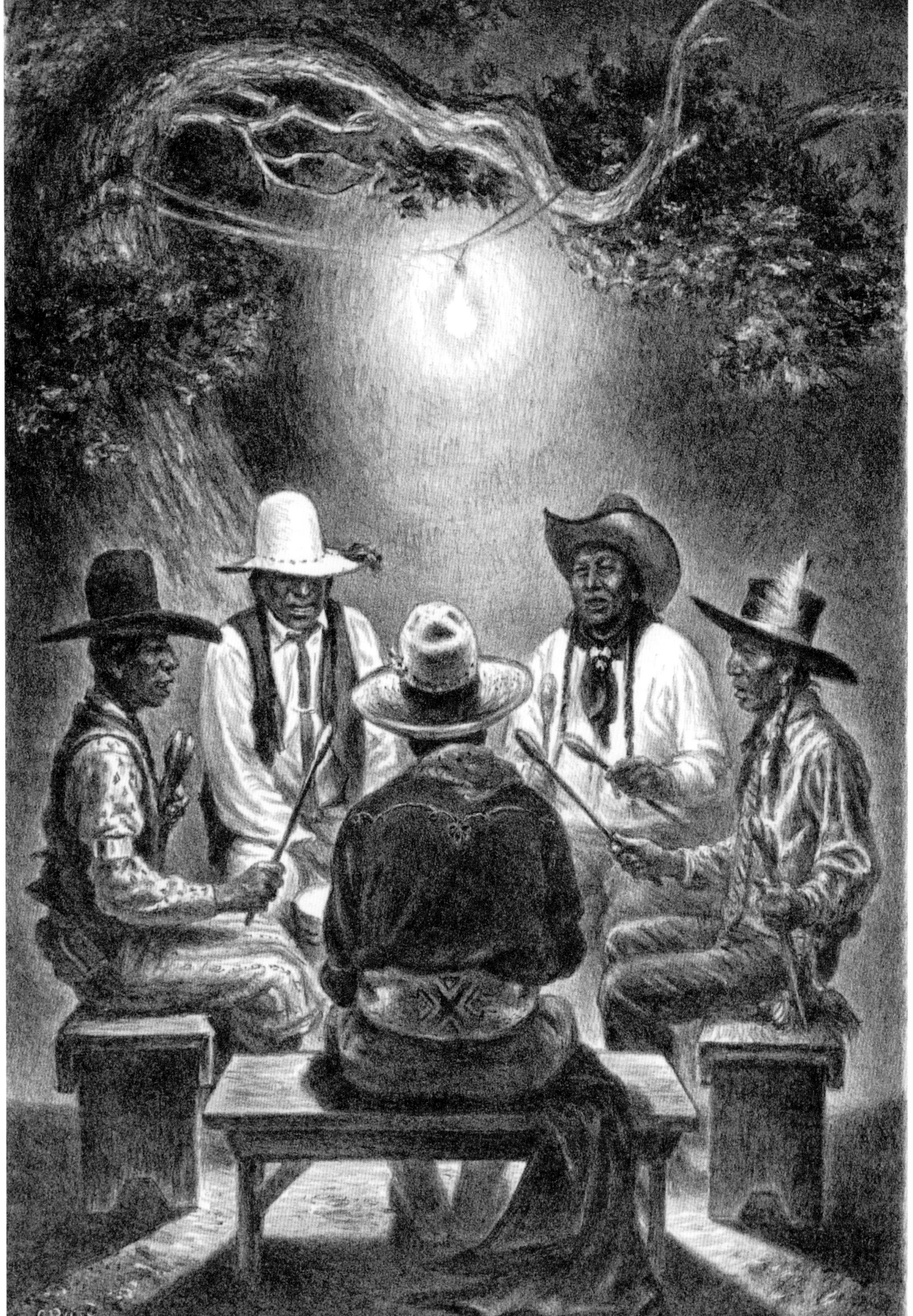

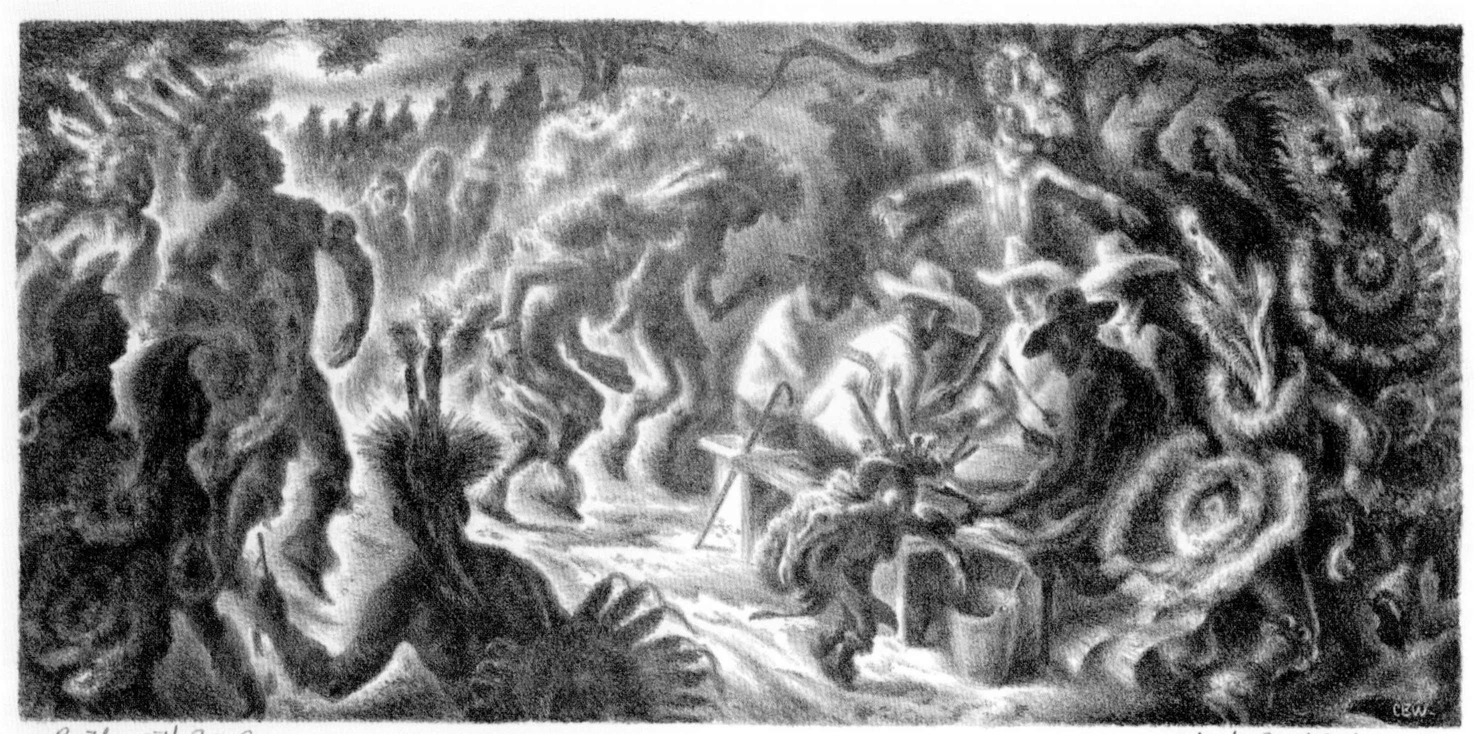

CBW: *Every work of art involves discovery — and is born of desire to know. . .*

RHYTHM OF THE WAR DANCE, 1963. 13 X 20, LITHOGRAPH/PAPER, 1427.732

AFTERNOON DANCE, 1939. 12.5 X 19, LITHOGRAPH/PAPER, 1427.733

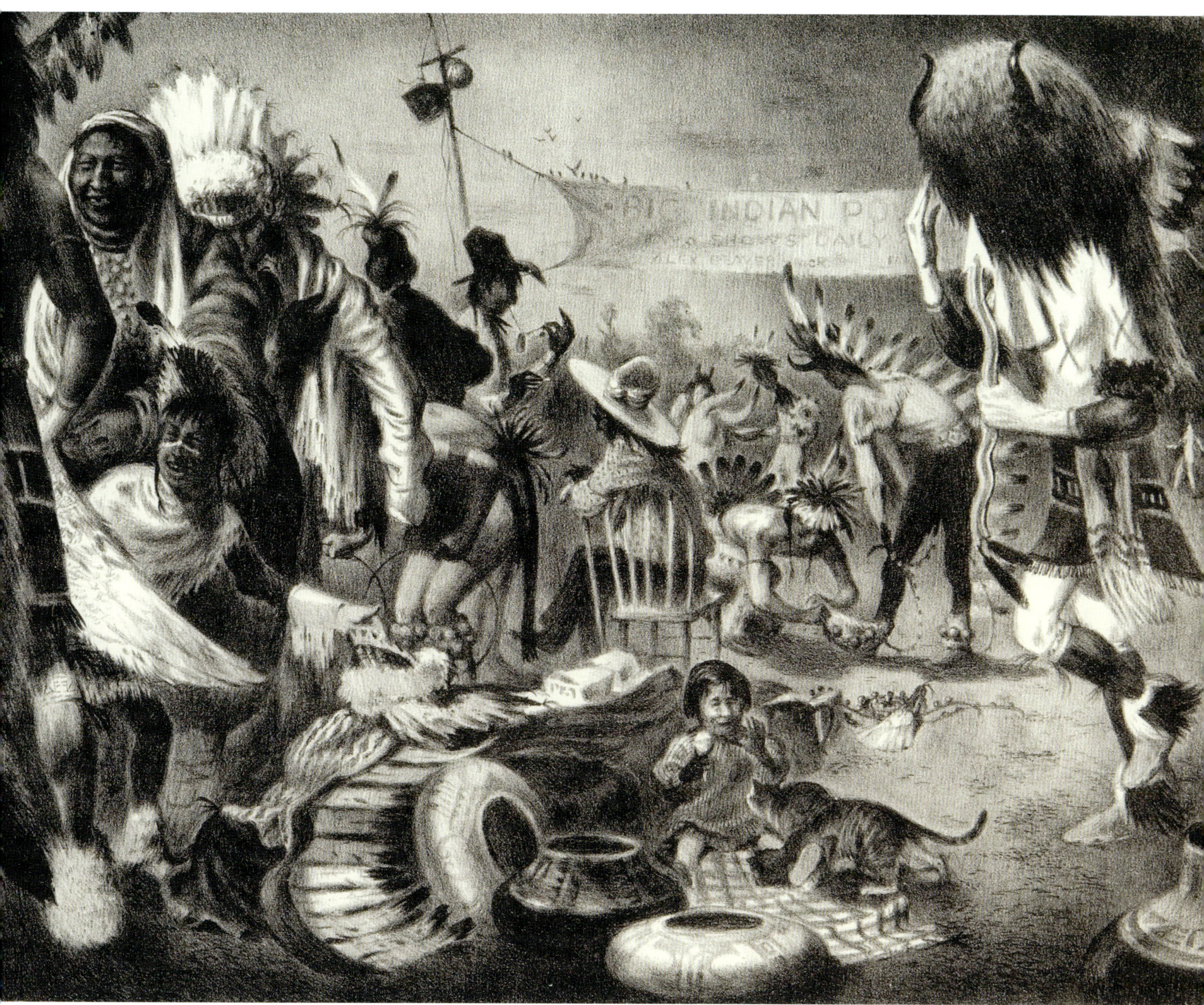

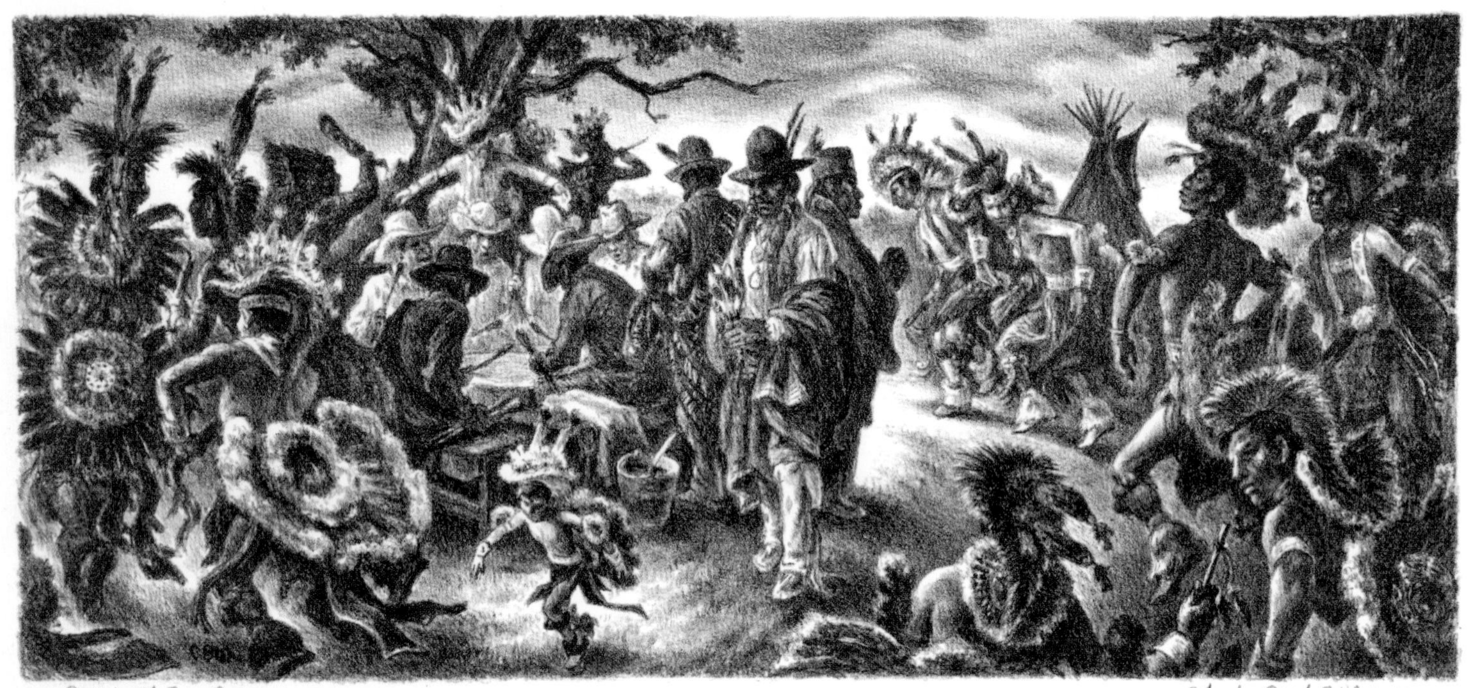

JUDGING THE WAR DANCE, 1993.
9.75 X 19,
LITHOGRAPH/PAPER,
1427.734

OKLAHOMA POWWOW, DETAIL,
1939. 11.5 X 17.5, LITHOGRAPH/
PAPER, 1427.735

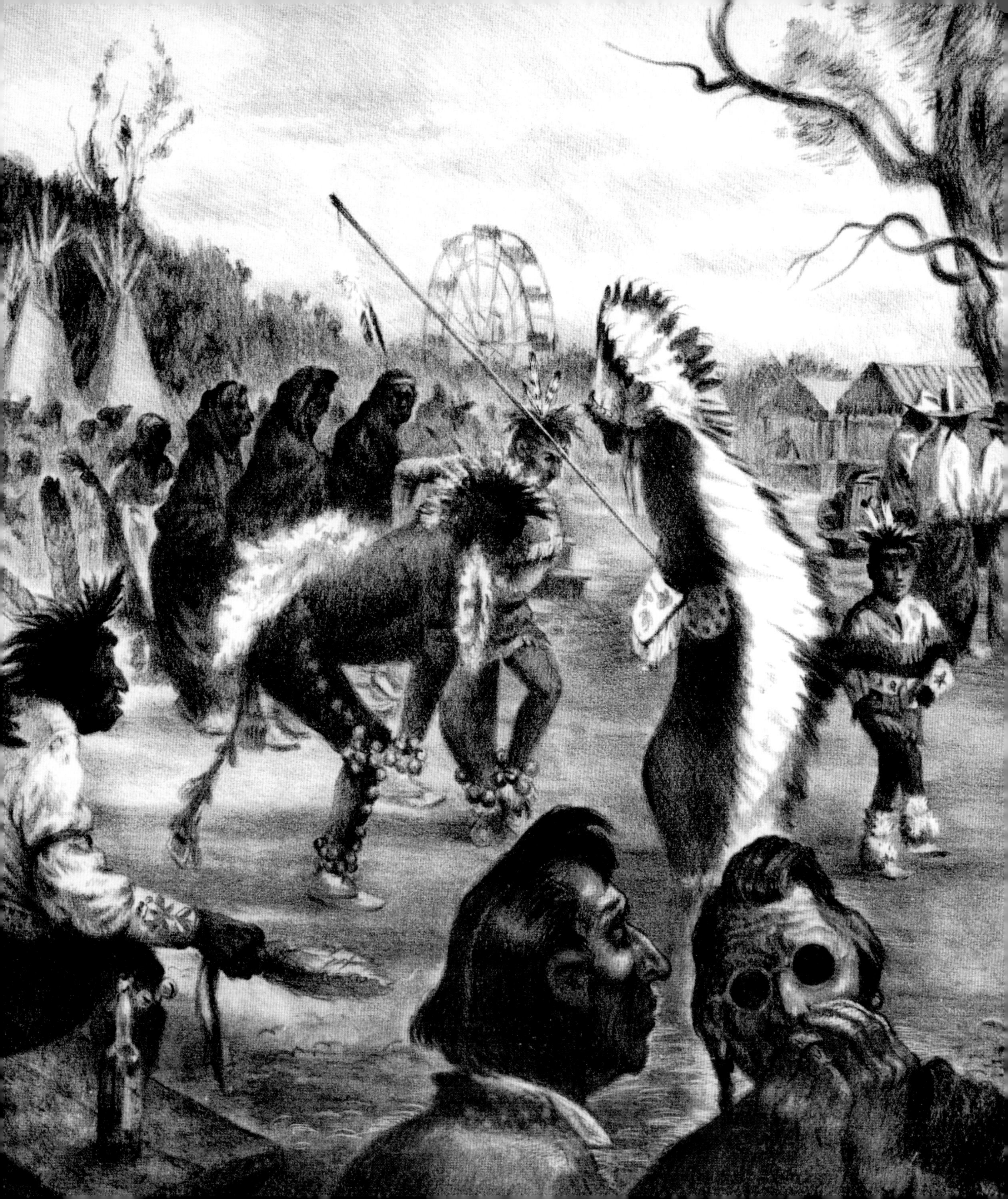

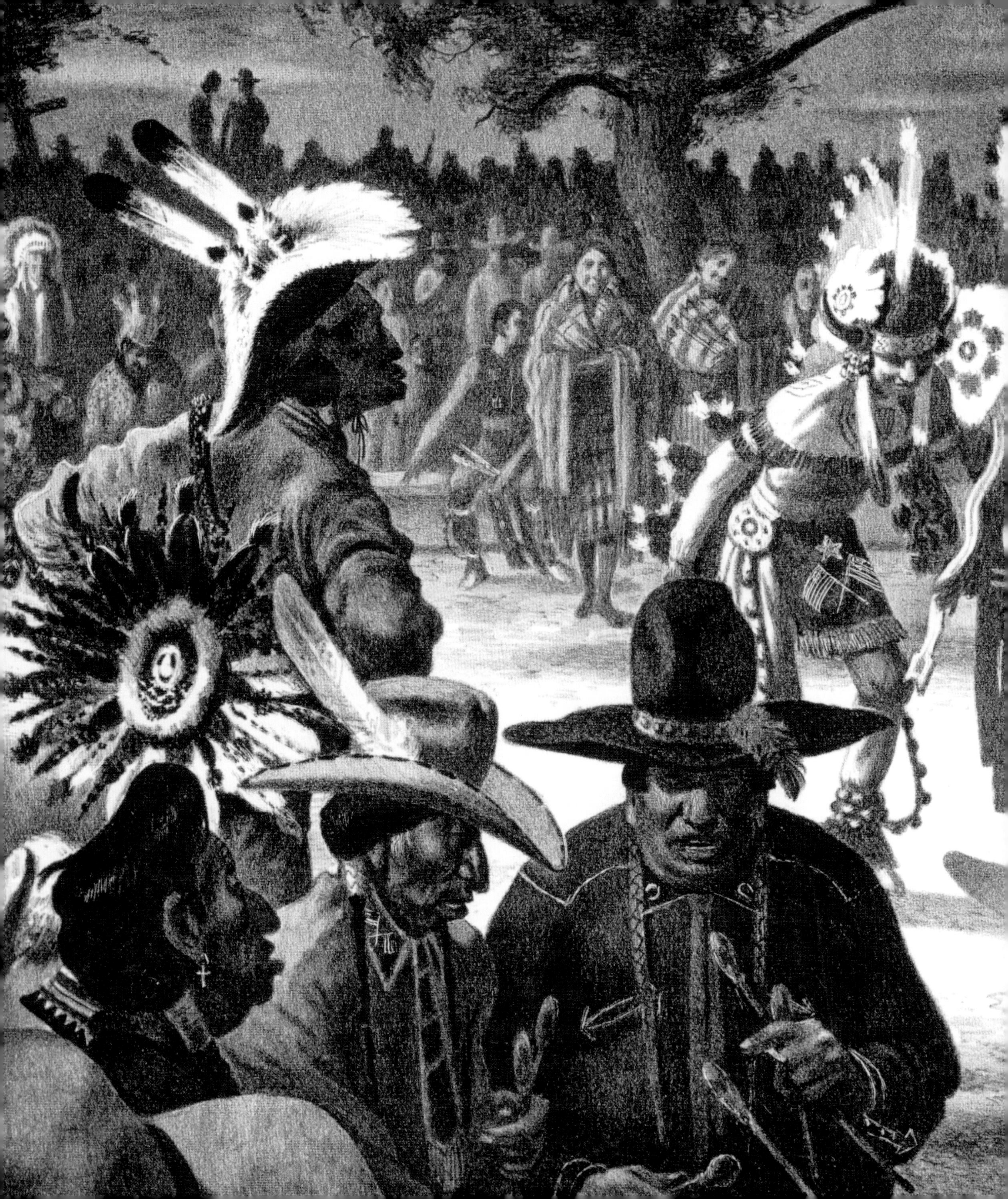

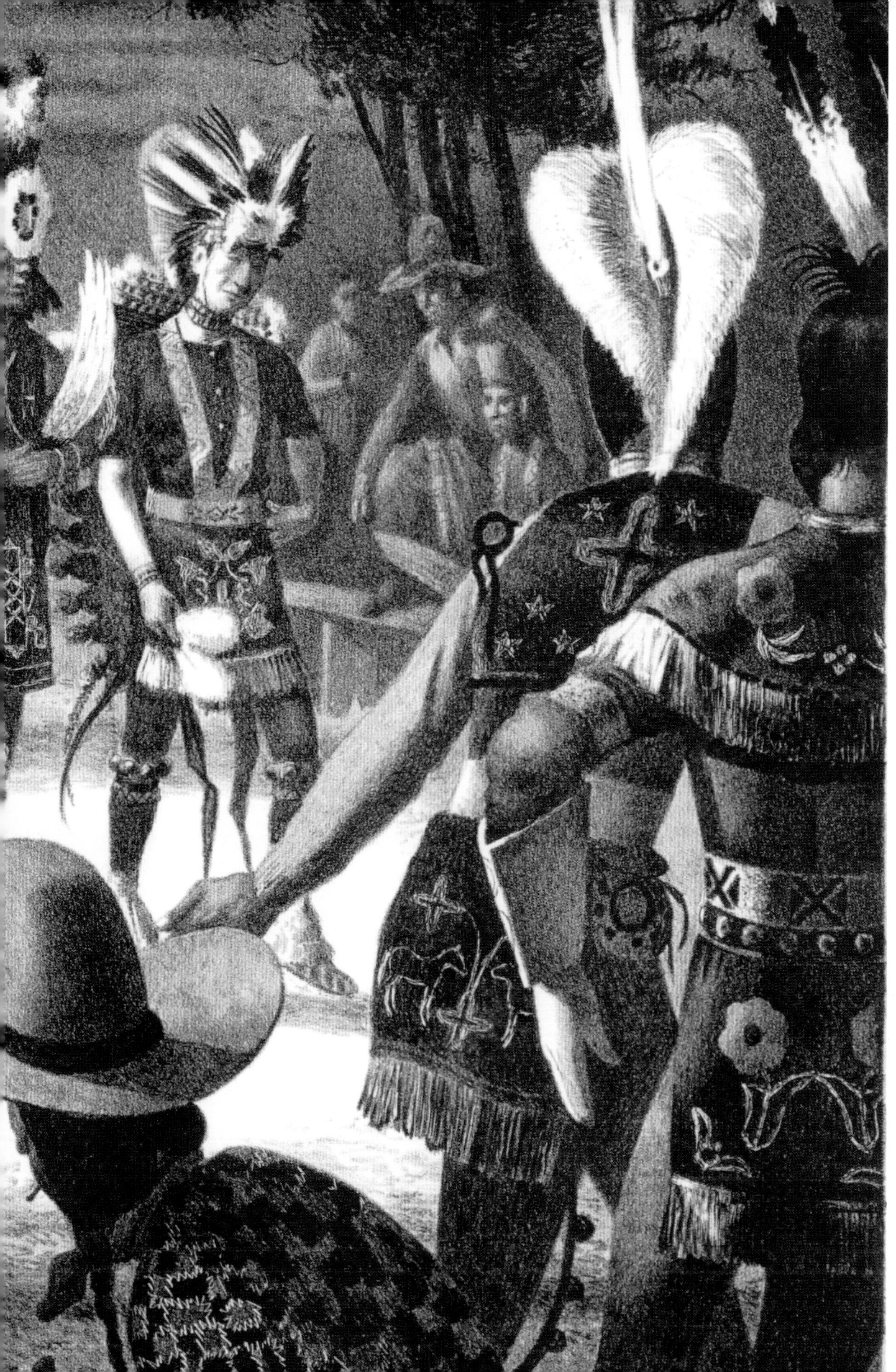

QUAPAW POW WOW,
1941. 11.5 X 17.5,
LITHOGRAPH/PAPER,
1427.736

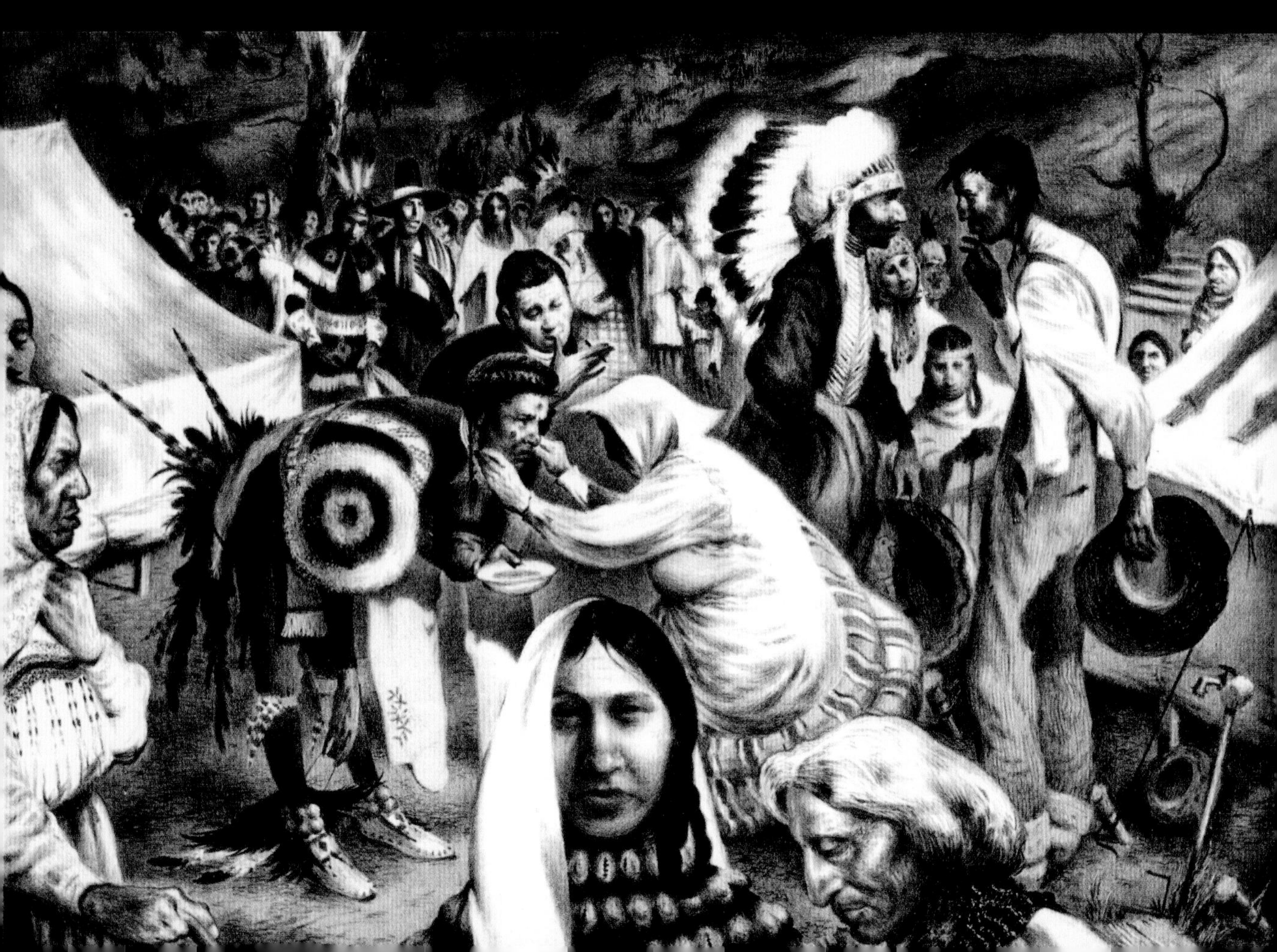

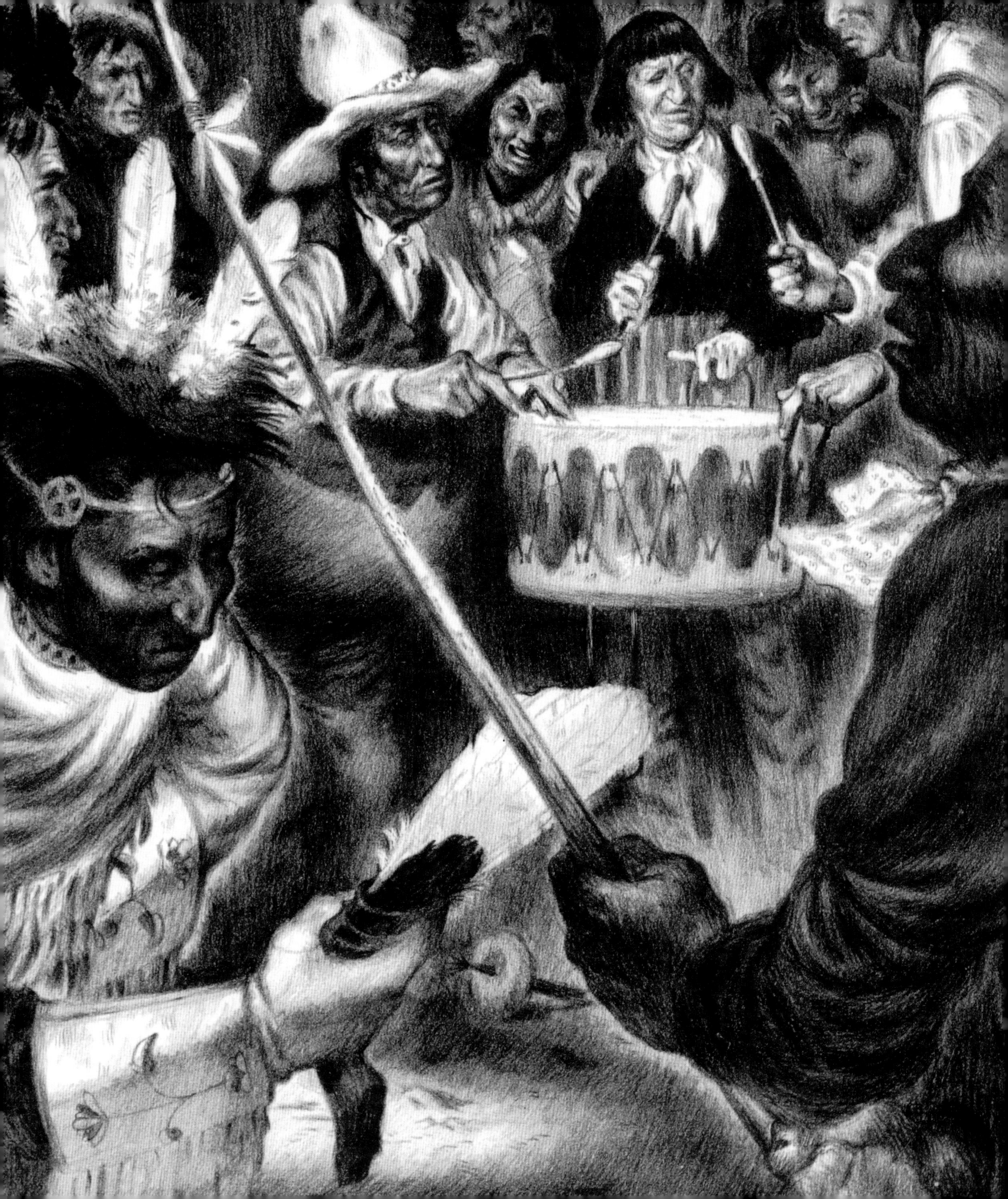

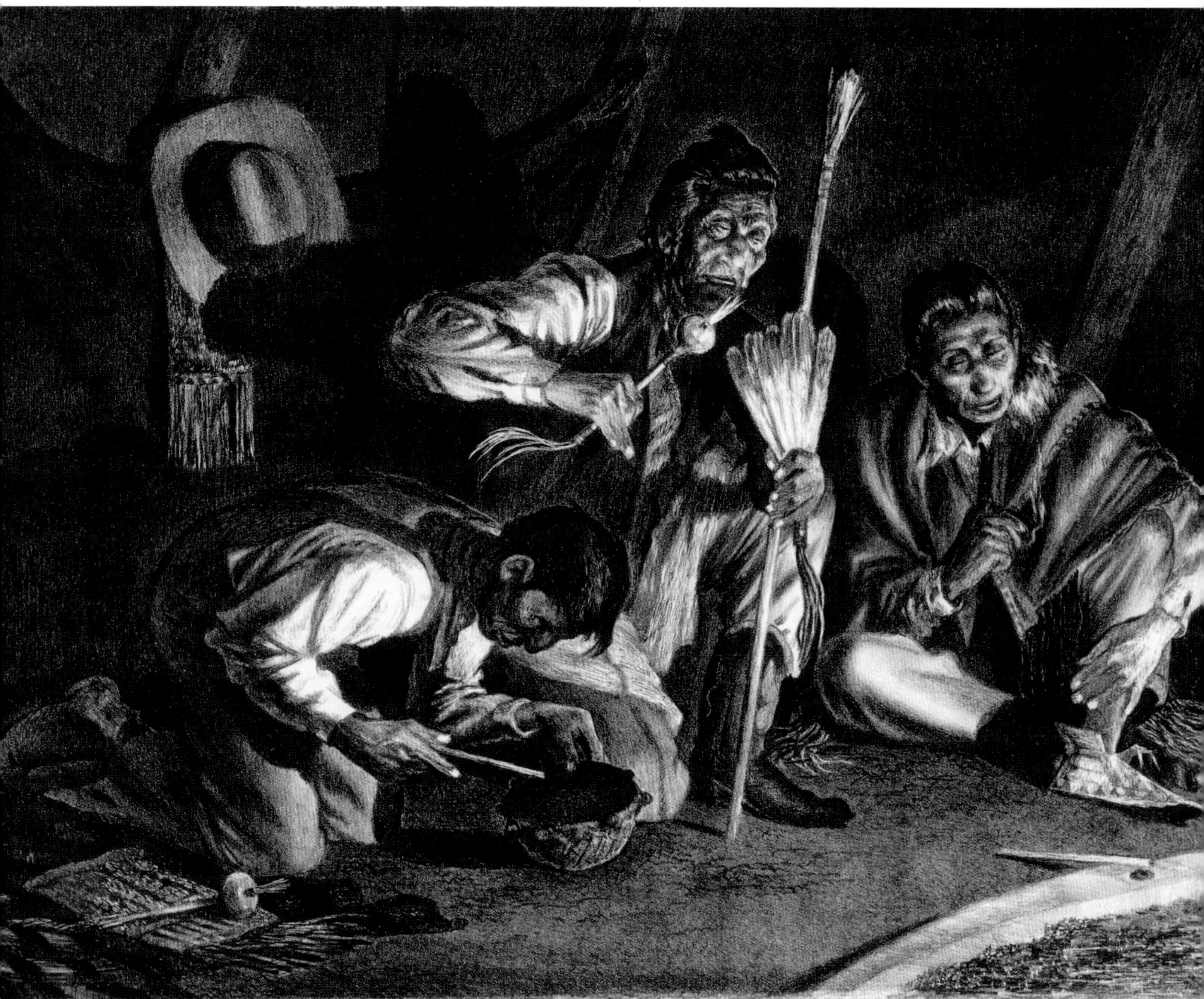

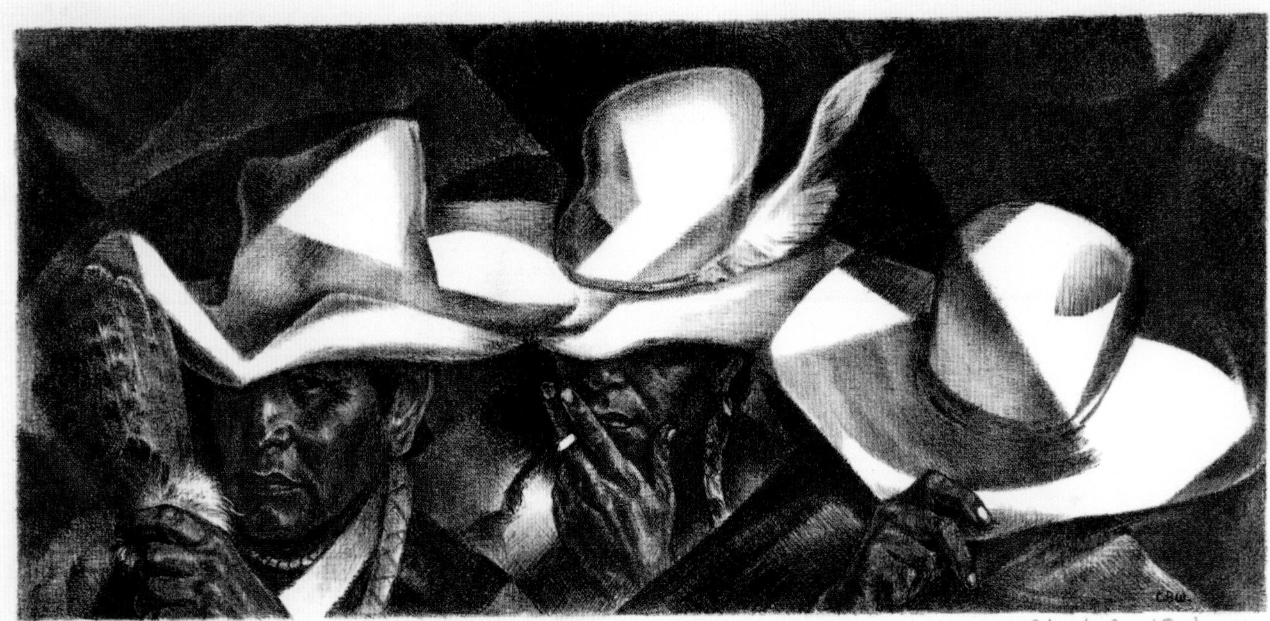

INDIAN PEYOTE MUSIC, 1941.

12.25 X 18.5,

LITHOGRAPH/PAPER,

1427.760

WHITE HATS, 1978.

11.563 X 17,

LITHOGRAPH/PAPER,

1427.757

SHAWNEE RIBBON BETS, 1947.

12.5 X 16.75, LITHOGRAPH/PAPER,

1427.762

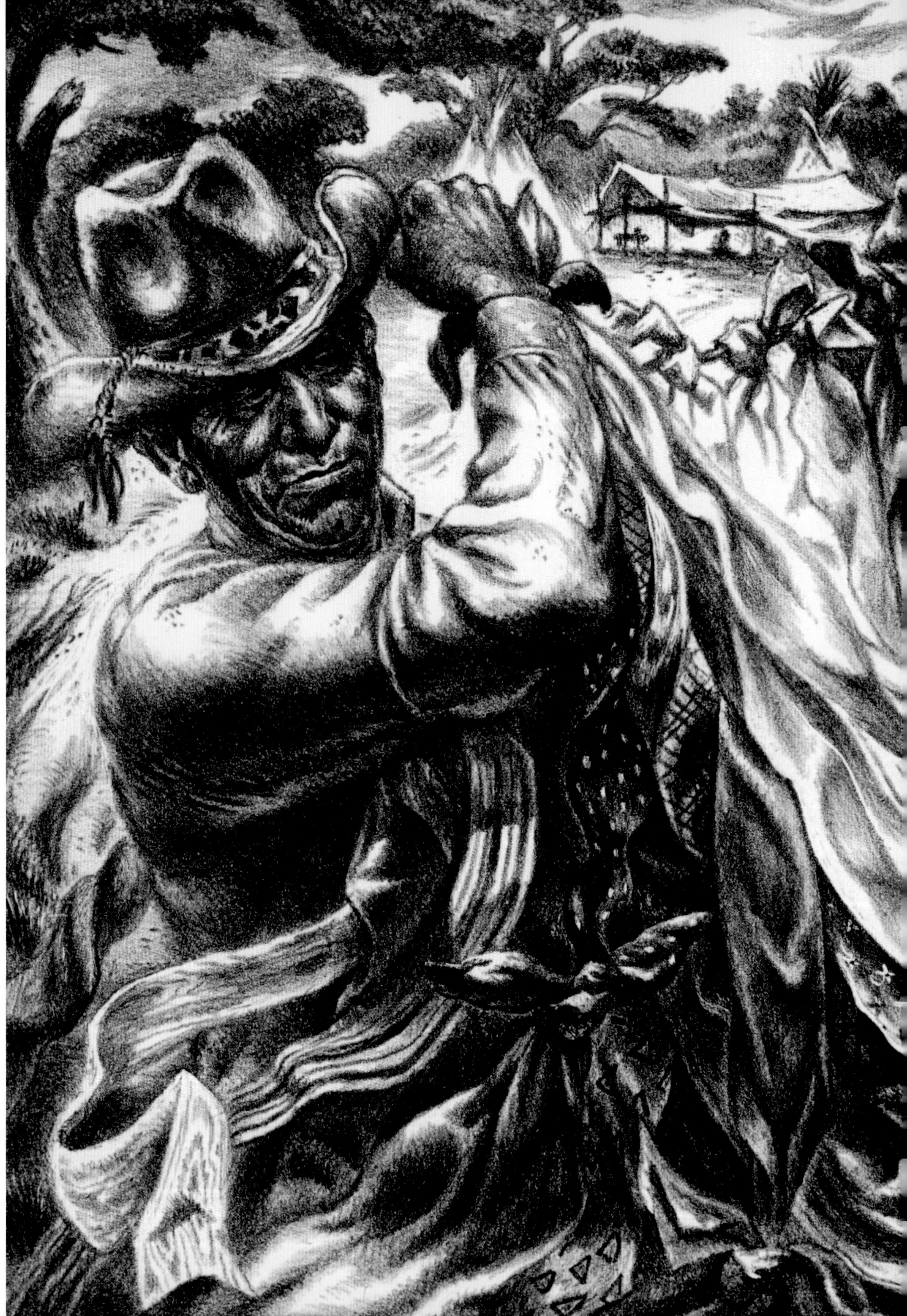

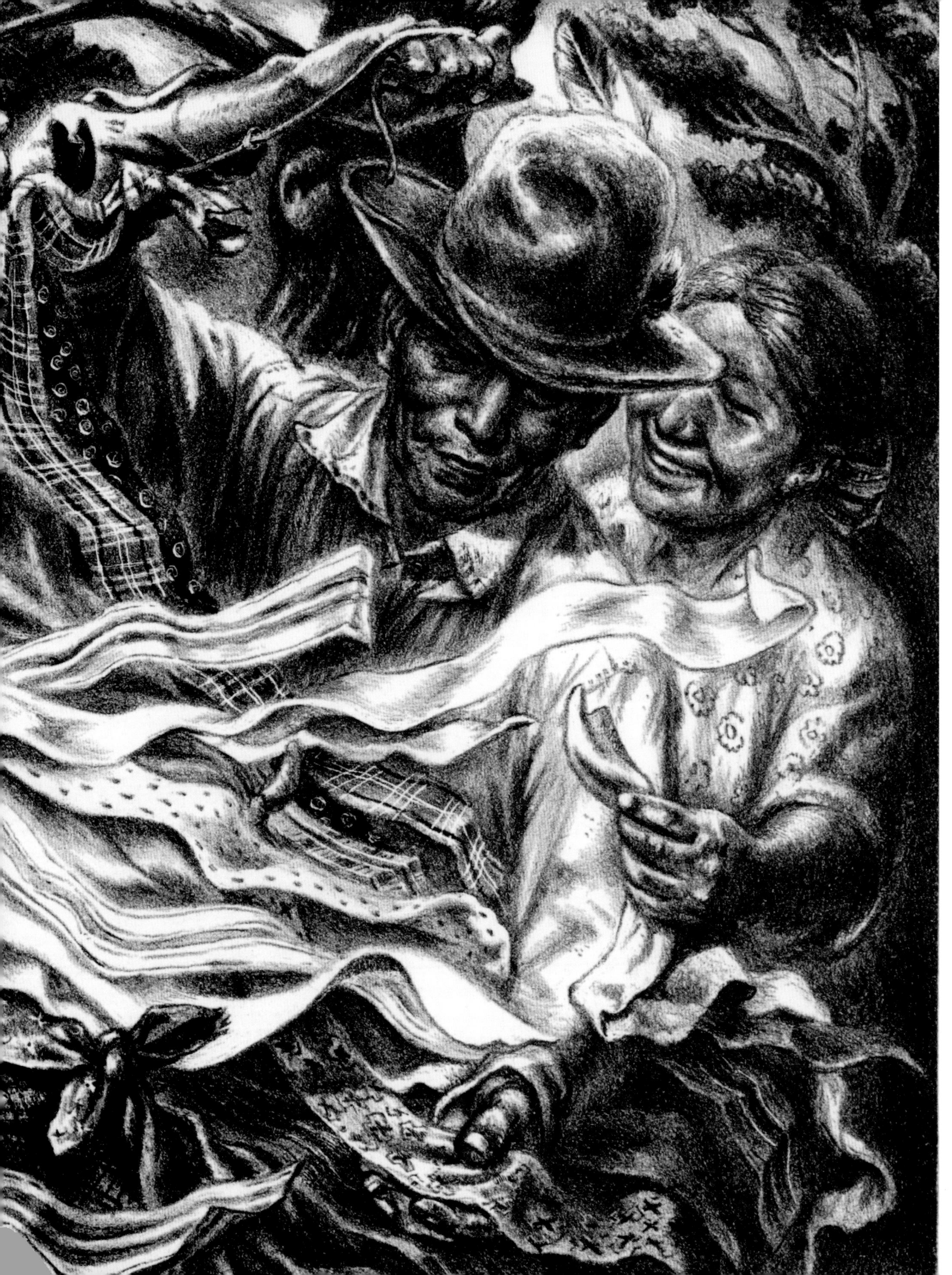

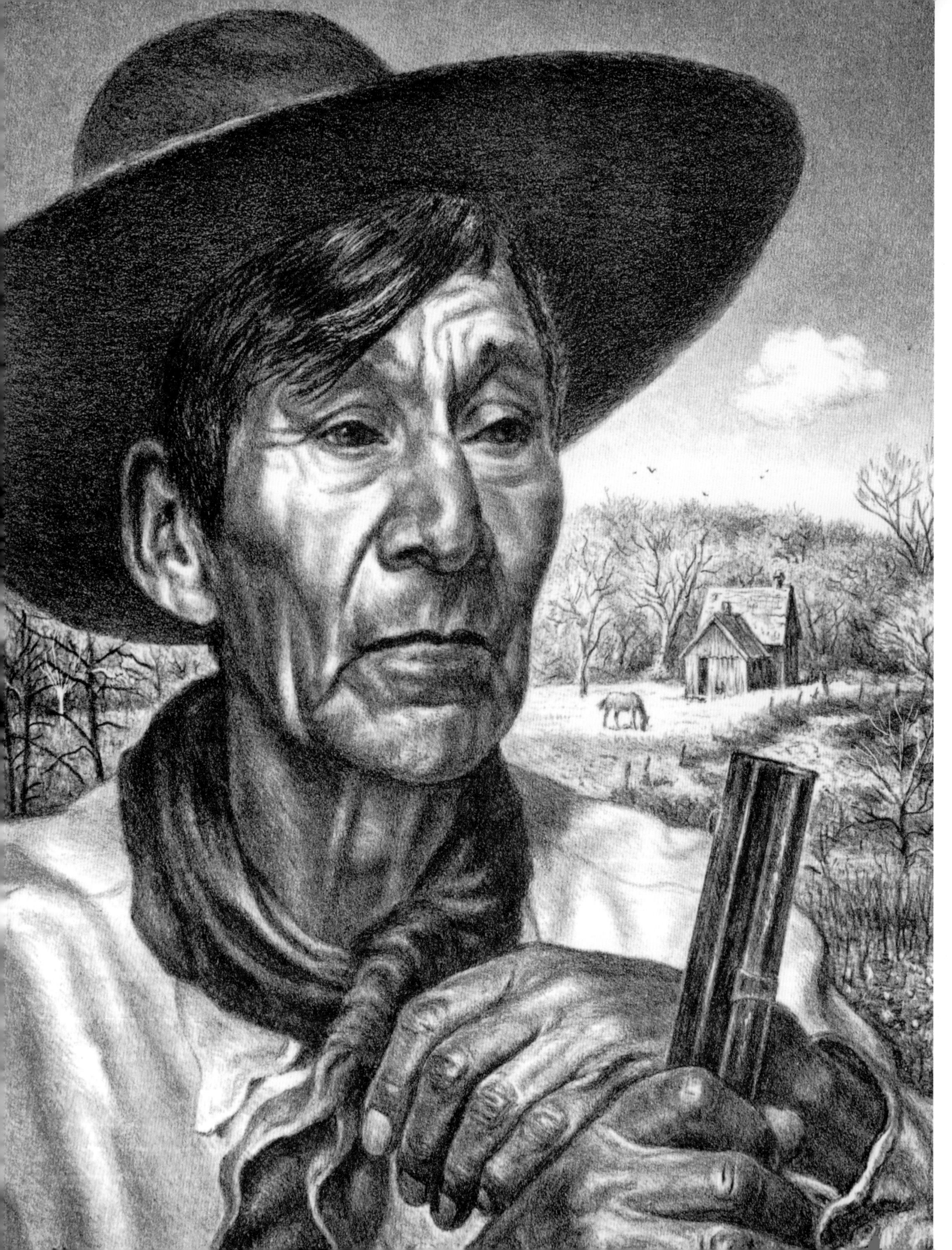

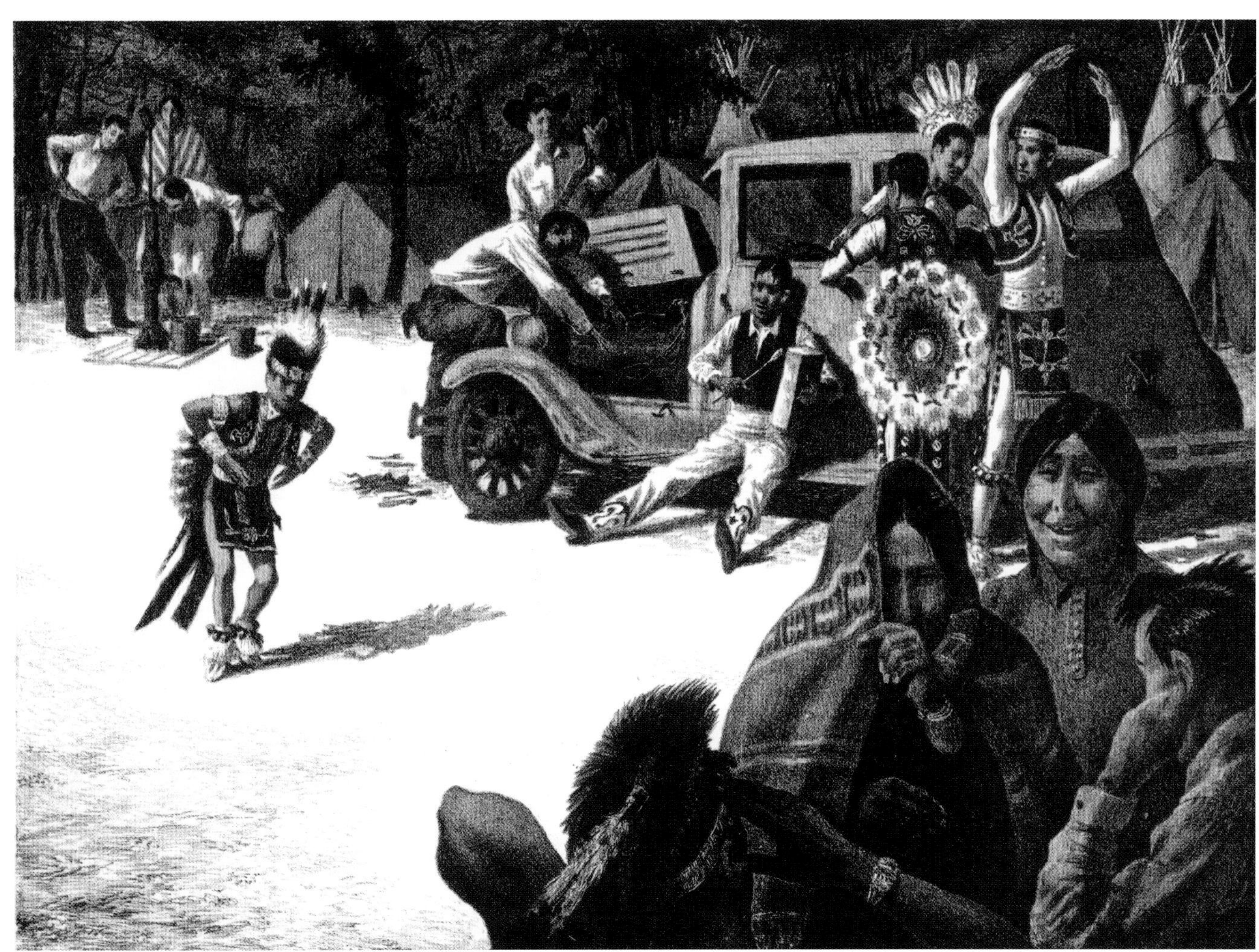

HENRY TURKEYFOOT,
1981. 17 X 14,
LITHOGRAPH/PAPER,
1427.712

VISITING INDIANS,
1941. 12.25 X 18.5
LITHOGRAPH/PAPER,
1427.761

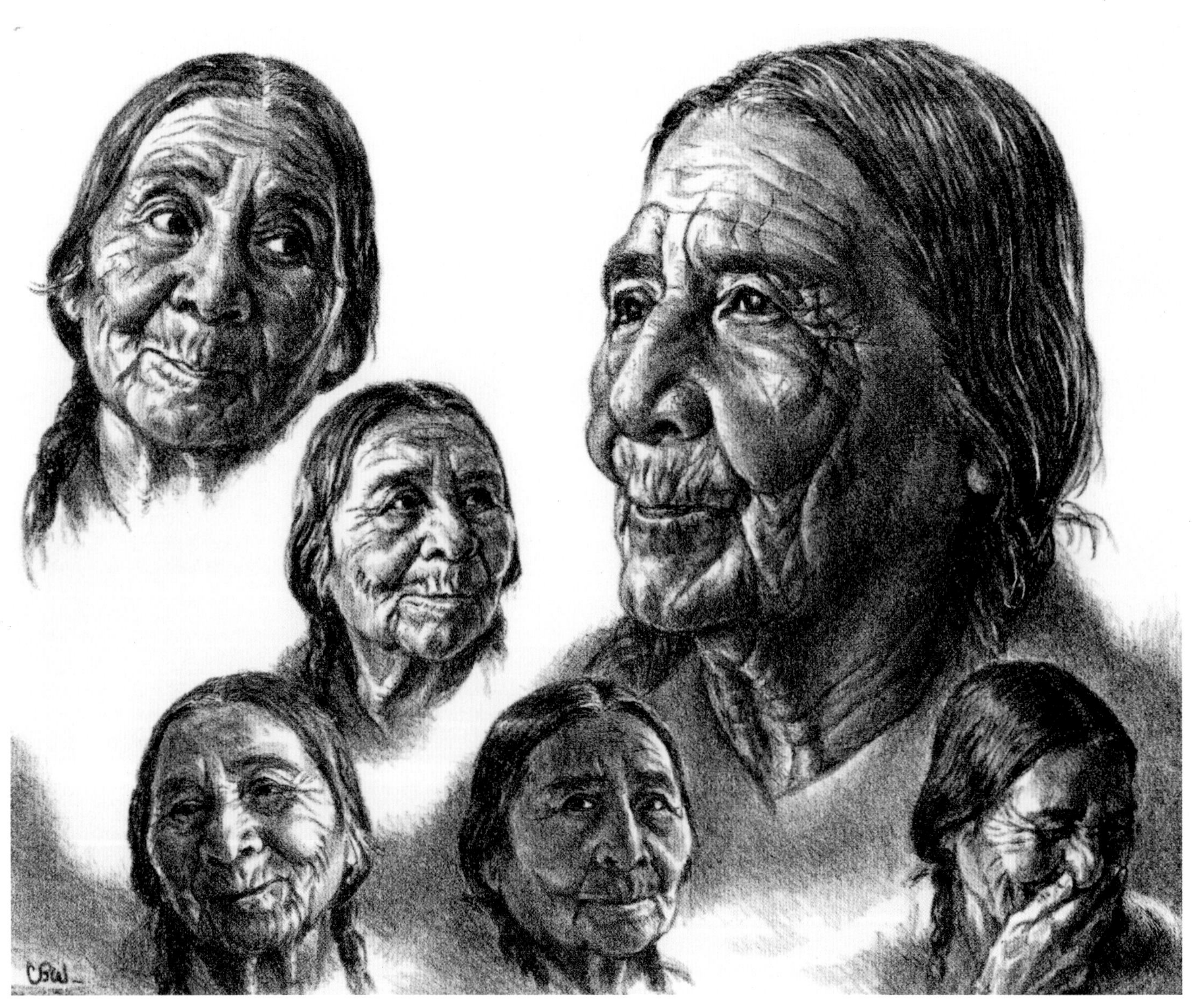

SKETCHES OF EVA, 1995.
12 X 14, LITHOGRAPH/
PAPER, 1400.862

CHEYENNE EARTH
MOTHER, 1980.
10.5 X 10,
LITHOGRAPH/PAPER,
1427.673B

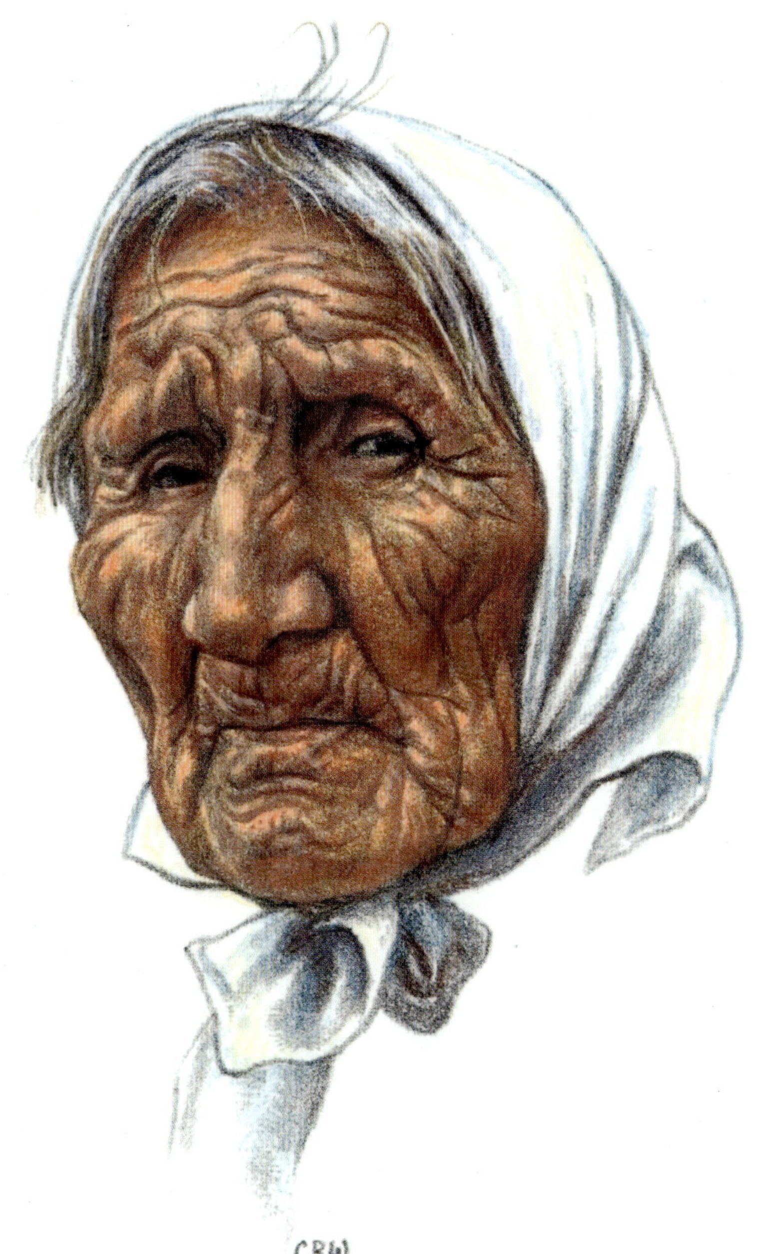

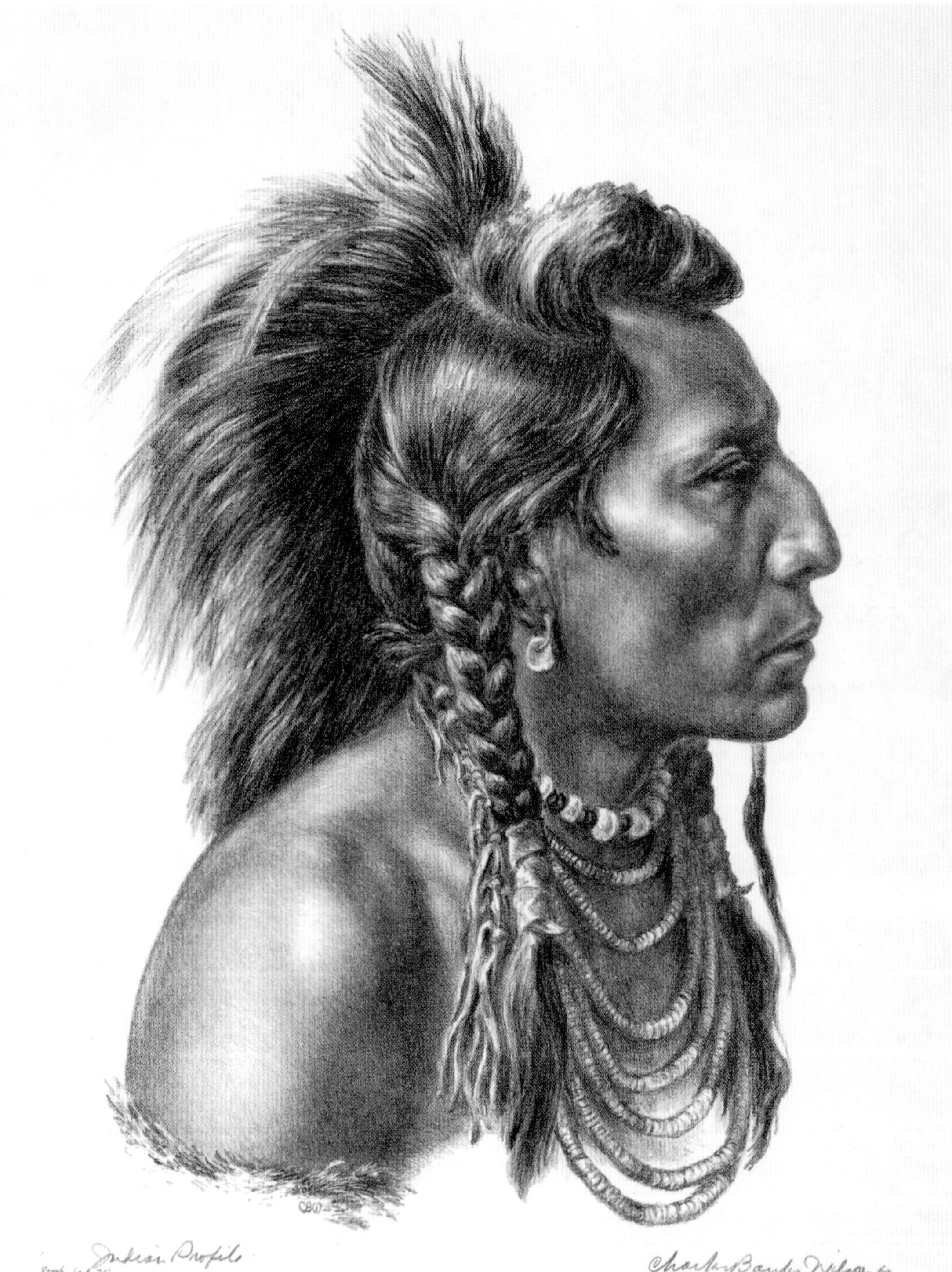

INDIAN PROFILE,
1969. 19 X 13.5,
LITHOGRAPH/
PAPER, 1427.716

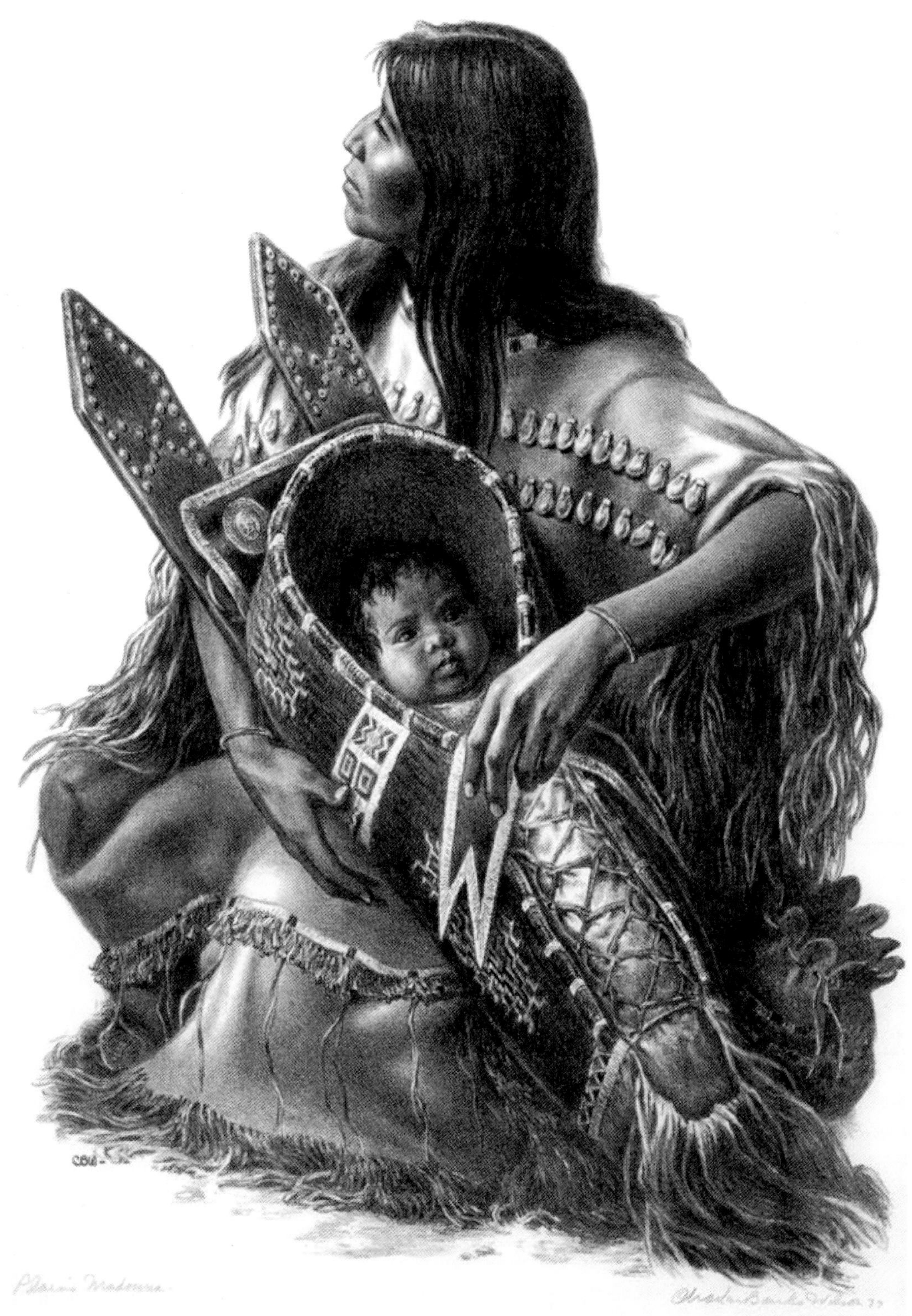

PLAINS MADONNA,
1977.
27.875 X 22,
LITHOGRAPH/
PAPER, 1427.681

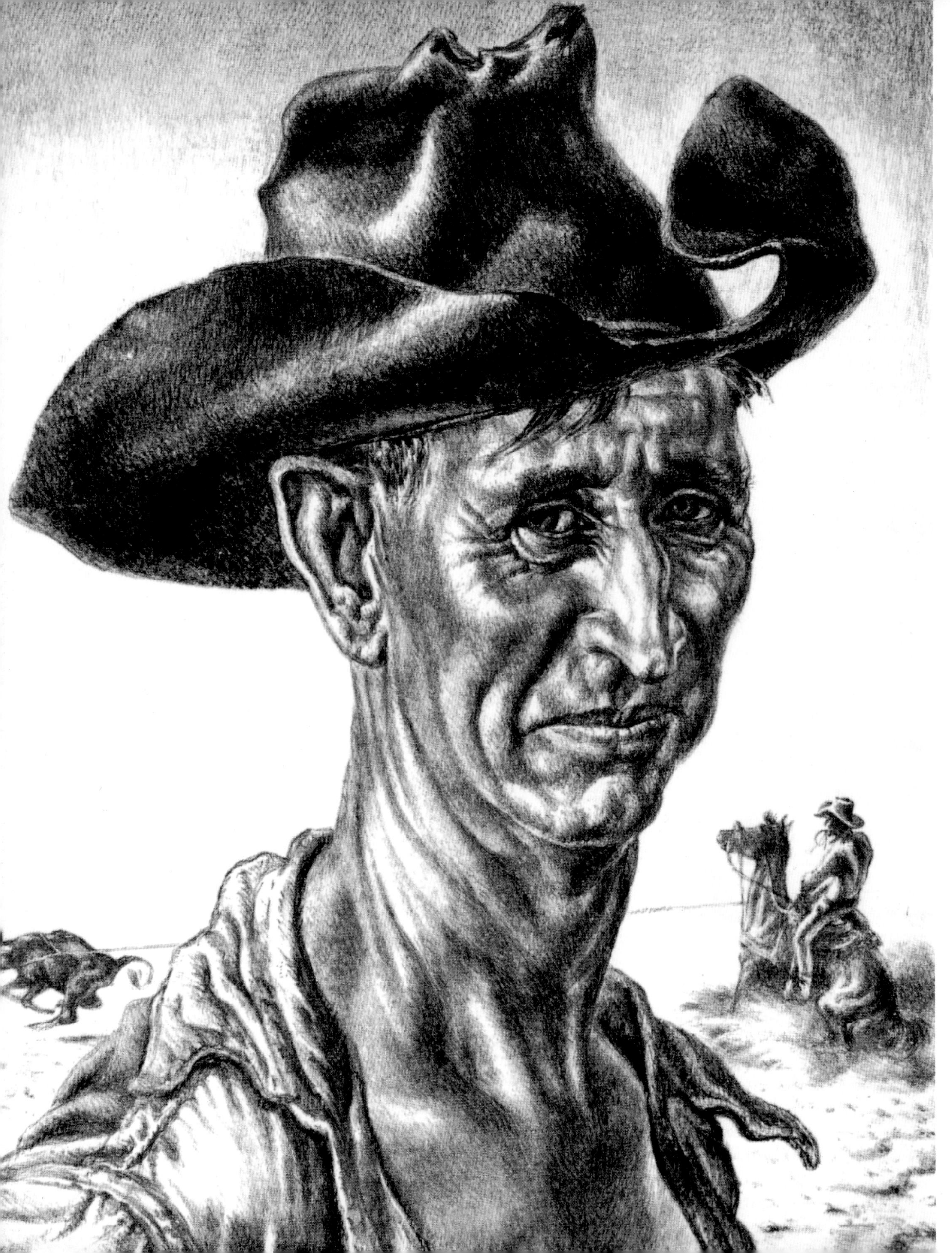

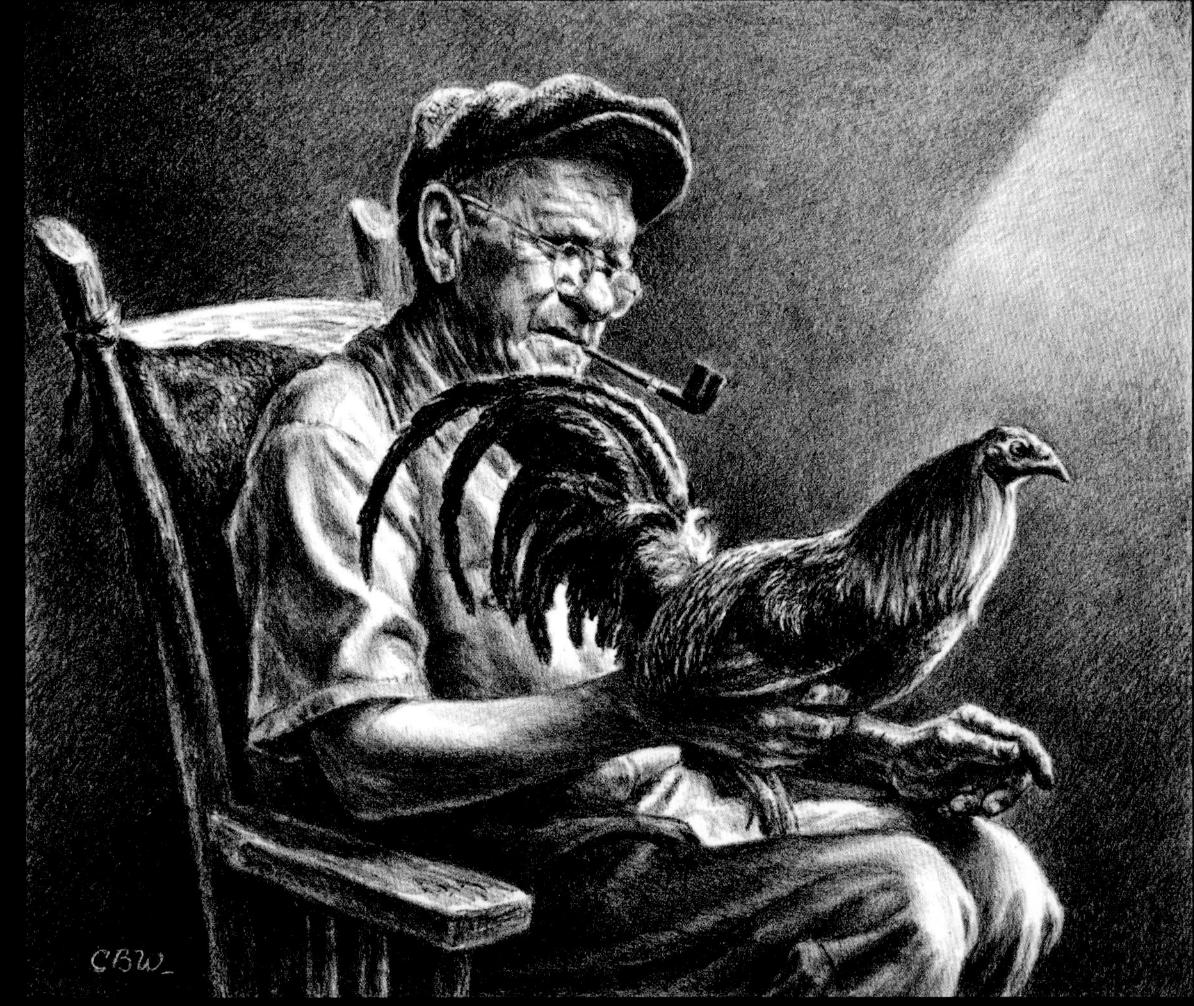

ING COWBOY,

16 X 13.125,

GRAPH/PAPER,

1427.797

WALT'S PRIDE, 1993.

12.5 X 14.5,

LITHOGRAPH/PAPER,

1427.861

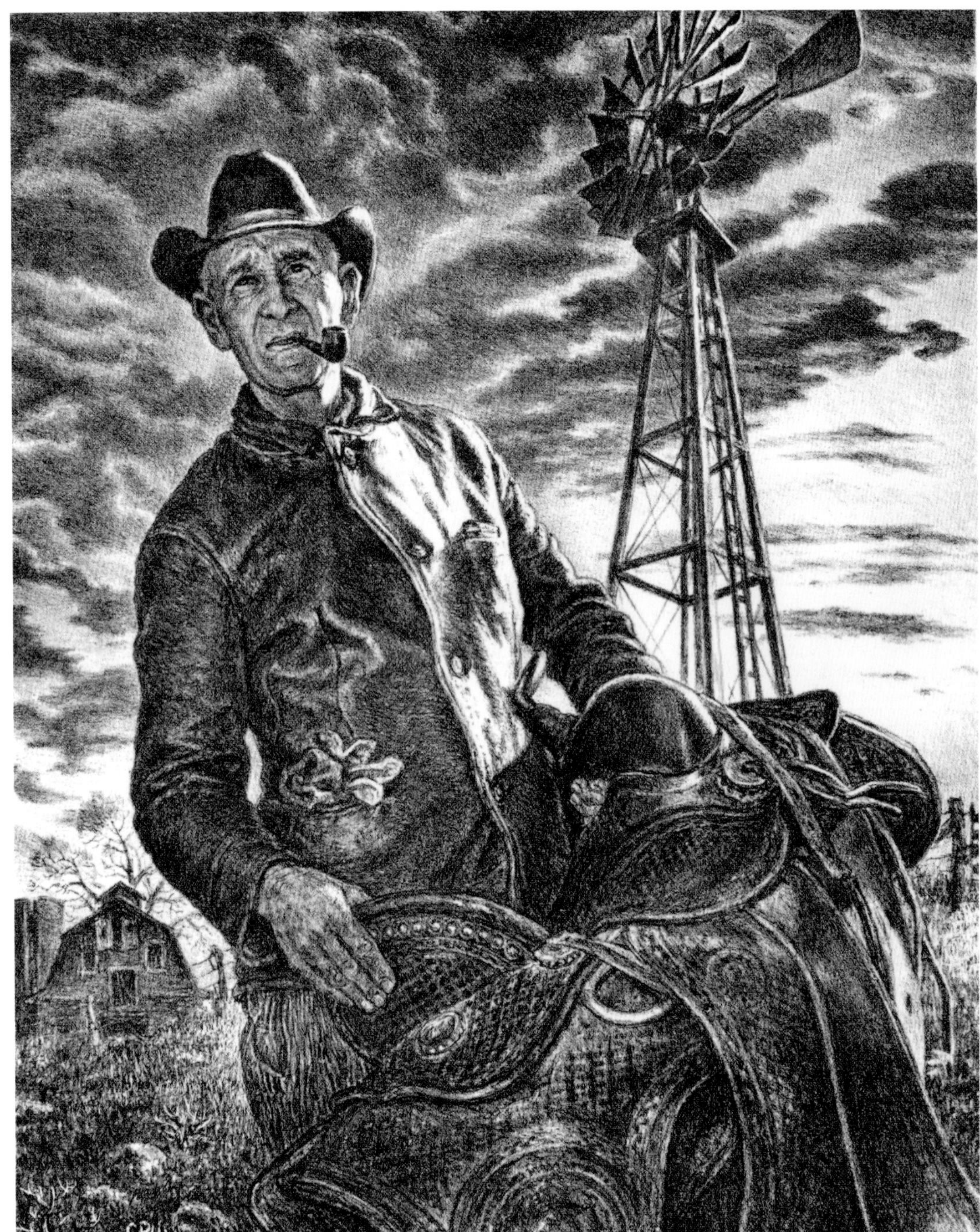

EYE ON
TOMORROW, 1990.
20 X 14.875,
LITHOGRAPH/
PAPER, 1427.793

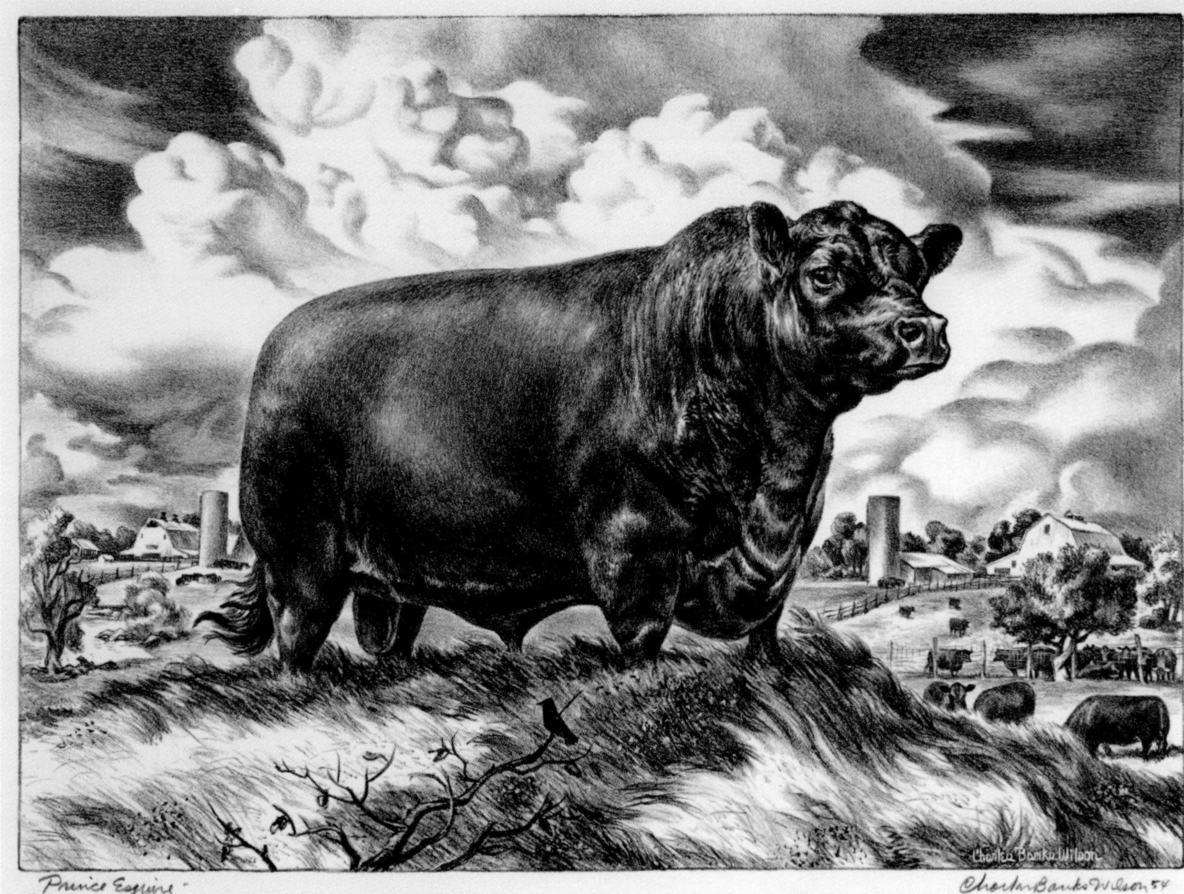

PRINCE
ESQUIRE,
1954.
13 X 17.5,
LITHOGRAPH/
PAPER,
1427.803

A HUMAN
FACE IS
THE ONE
UNIVERSAL
LANGUAGE

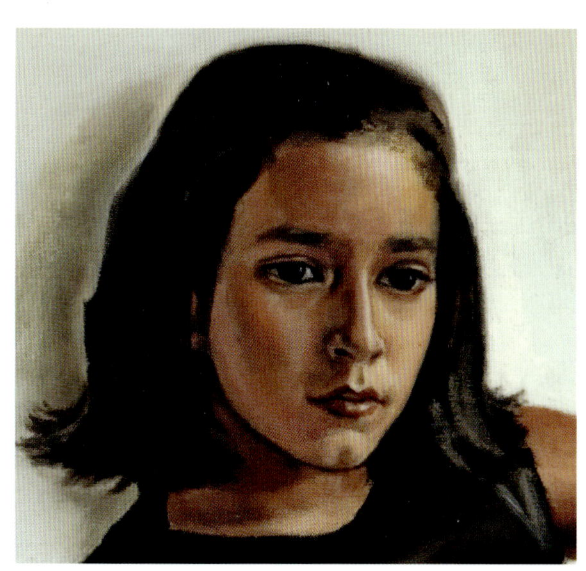

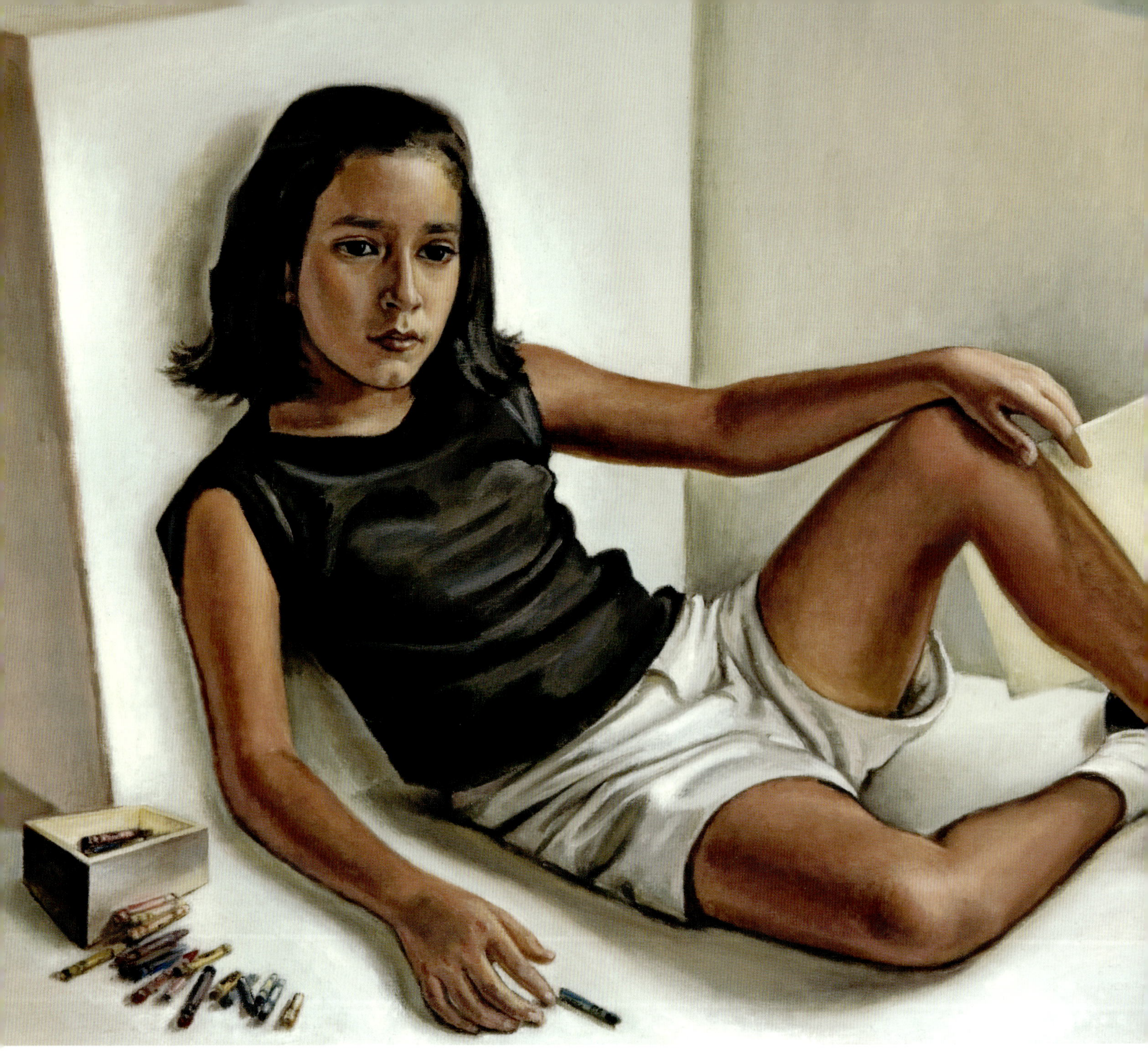

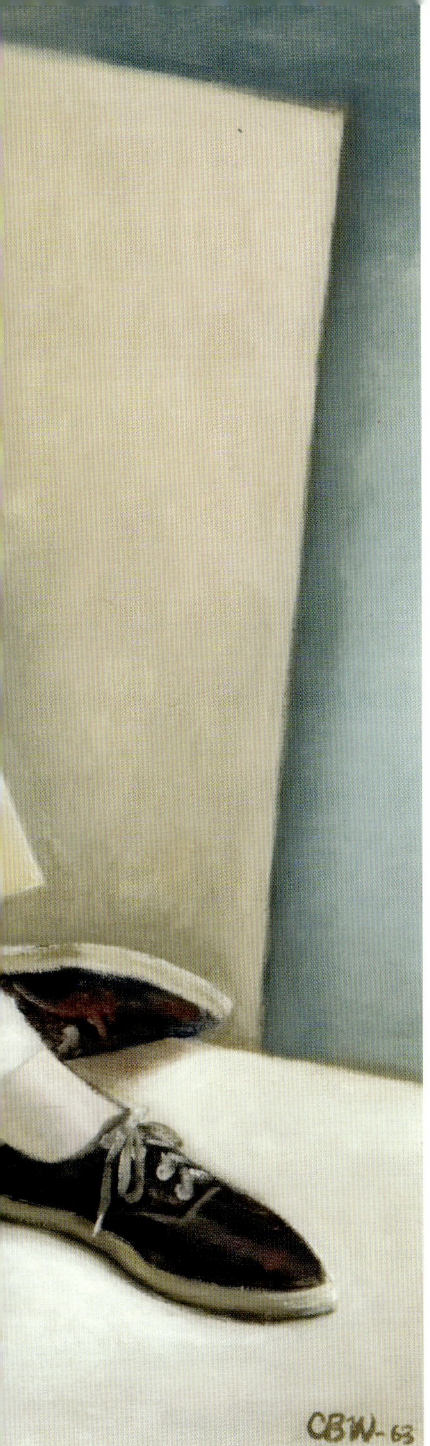

CARRIE, 1963. 23.5 X 35.5,
OIL/CANVAS, COLLECTION
OF THE ARTIST

"A portrait … is evidence of many assembled moments in the life of the subject.

It constitutes a totality of experience rather than a photographic fragment."

In the early 1960s, Charles Banks Wilson accepted a commission from the Oklahoma legislature to paint lifesize portraits of famous Oklahomans. His subjects were without question the most notable and influential individuals of their time: humorist Will Rogers, Cherokee educator Sequoyah, Senator Robert S. Kerr, and athlete Jim Thorpe. The portraits were to be hung on permanent display in the rotunda of the state capitol. "I fully believed I was committing suicide," says Wilson about the commission. Except for Sequoyah, the subjects were very well known and "still vivid in the memories of families and friends." He was not so much concerned about what others would think of his effort, however. Wilson knew what he had to do. His single challenge was to satisfy his own exacting demand to "get it right."

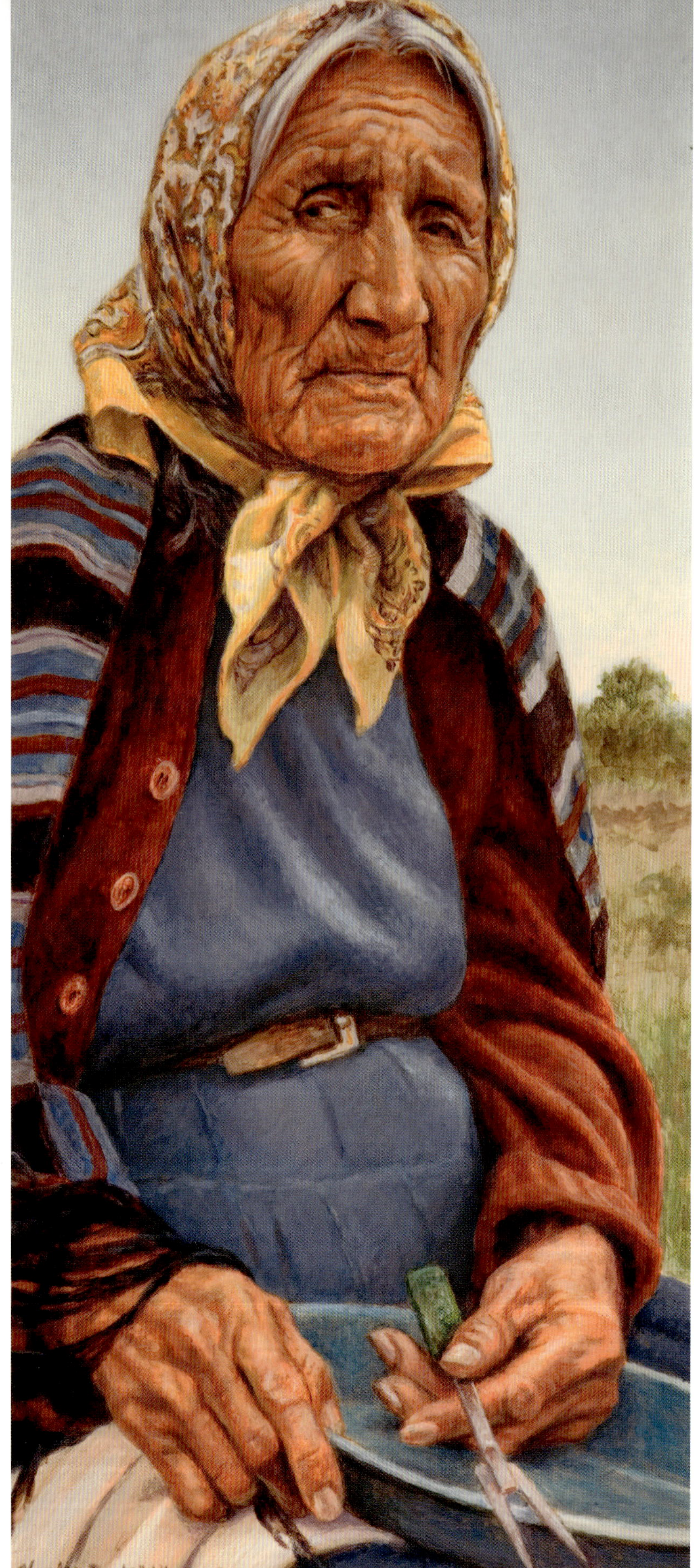

CHEYENNE
MATRIARCH, 1991.
23.625 X 14.875,
OIL/CANVAS,
0137.2464

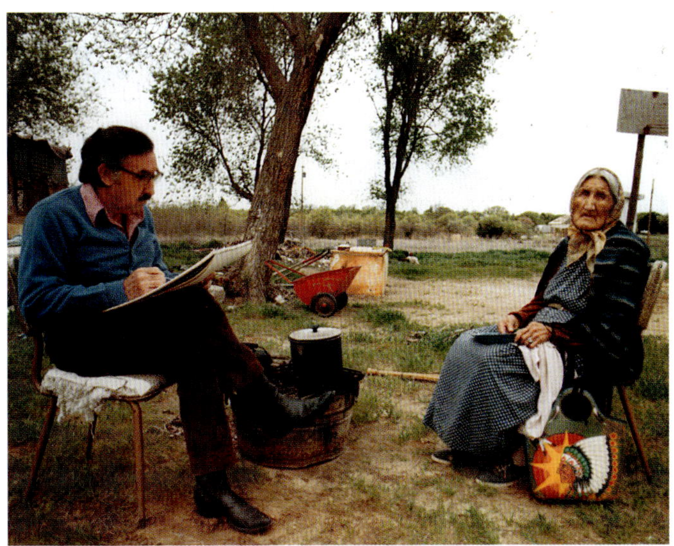

Wilson in 1980, making the original sketch that became the basis for the oil at left, *Cheyenne Matriarch.* CBW: *Composition requires all the cunning of the preparation of a crime. . . . A line — or an area of tone — is not really important because it records what you have seen but because of what it will lead you to see.*

"An artist must inhabit his subject as an actor inhabits his part," Wilson says—and he would spend over four years inhabiting his subjects for the capitol commission. He would draw, make studies, and form intricate clay models before ever picking up a brush. He would devote months to researching and critically thinking about his subjects. "A human face is the one universal language. A portrait is more than the reproduction of a face. An artist must inscribe the character of the subject, not just the features." To inscribe the character of the people he was painting, Wilson would have to understand them as individuals rather than as historical figures. "A man's character is the sum of his interests. It is something that enters into his person." To get it right on the canvas surface, he would have to start from within.

The subject most familiar to Wilson was Will Rogers. He had painted Rogers from life some thirty years before, and the rope-twirling humorist and social observer was still one of Wilson's heros. "Will Rogers saw no difference between the king and the common working man—the things of life are the same to both." Wilson wanted above all to capture the "easy dignity" of Rogers. He discussed his work shortly after completion in an essay in *Oklahoma Today:*

> In the portrait, Rogers stands on a pasture plane-landing strip, a man on the go, coat over his arm, hat in hand. I drew the hands of five men before I found the hand which looked correct. Roger's hands were strong hands, always busy, and to me the wrong hand looked as out of place as would the wrong head. Throughout this commission I felt a very real obligation to each man portrayed.

> For each of the portraits, Wilson employed human models to make the works as accurate and as lifelike as possible. He would use the legs of one model, the ears of another, piecing it all together to represent one unique form. ". . . I found Jim Thorpe's forearm on a man whose work is lifting bricks, and a Thorpe-like deltoid on a young farm worker." The paintings were also intended to be biographical. Each portrait contains not only the public elements of lifetime achievement but also small details that only those intimate with the subject would notice. Regarding Senator Kerr, "Many old friends smile when they notice his tie is uneven."

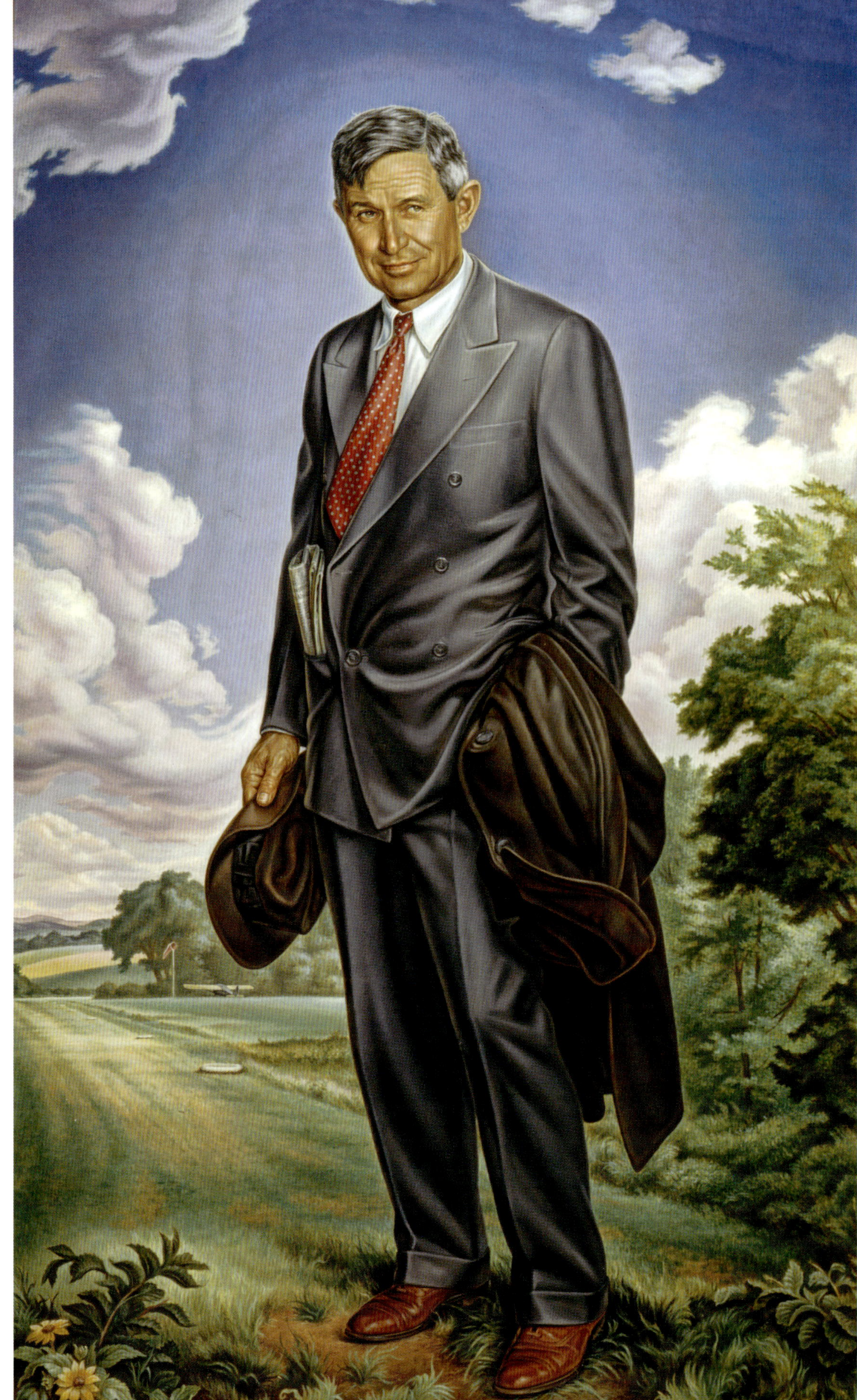

WILL ROGERS,
OIL/CANVAS,
OKLAHOMA
STATE CAPITOL
COLLECTION

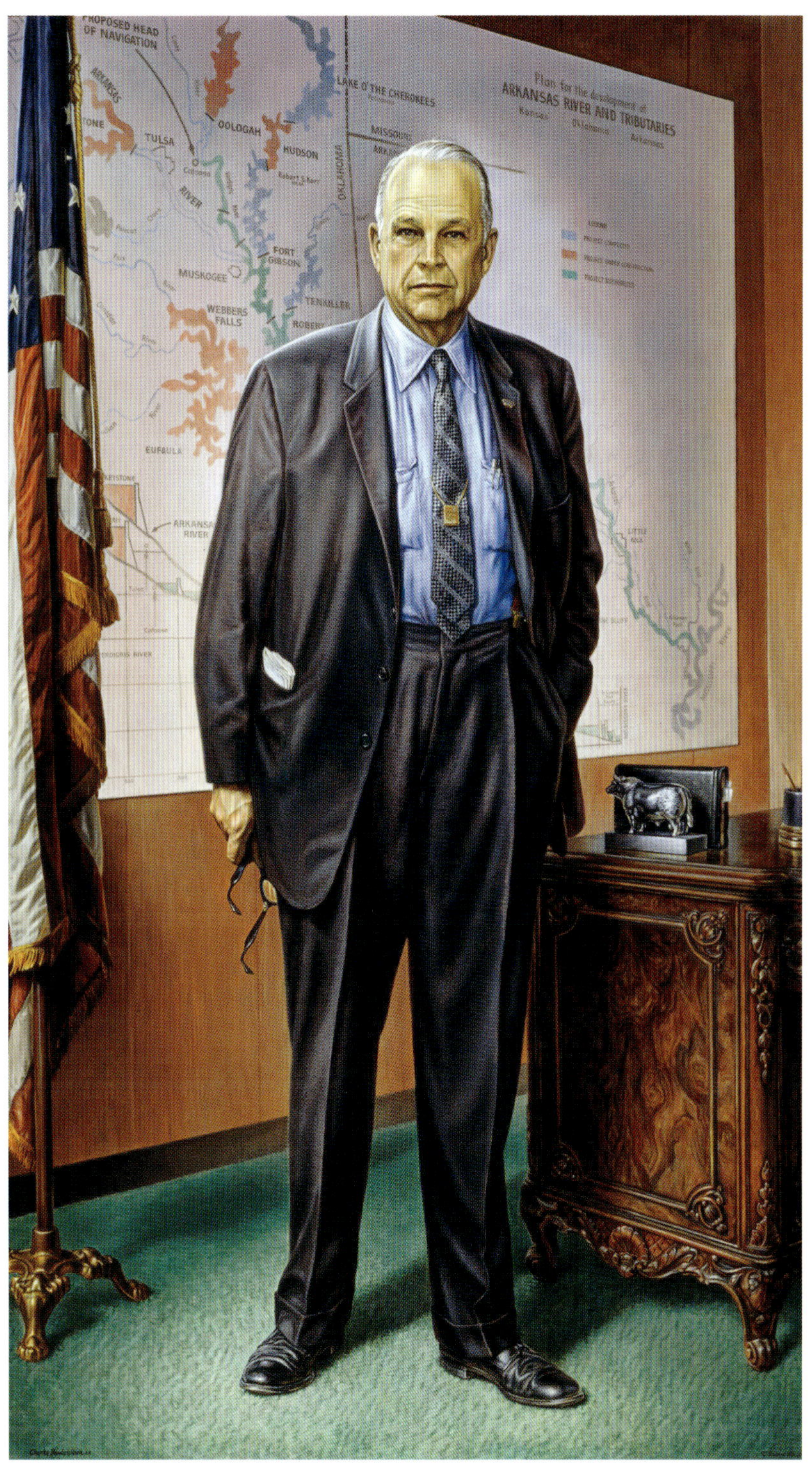

SENATOR ROBERT S.
KERR, OIL/CANVAS,
OKLAHOMA
STATE CAPITOL
COLLECTION

The portrait of Sequoyah brought special challenges for Wilson. All four subjects were deceased, but images of the other three were available in various forms; no images of the Cherokee educator and inventor of the Cherokee syllabary existed except an early 19th-century sketch done for a portrait by Charles Bird King. The portrait itself had been destroyed in a fire at the Smithsonian Institution. Wilson's search for the real Sequoyah would take him deep into brittle archives and library back rooms. "In a lifetime of historical research, I had never found a subject to excite me as much as did this man. His life and accomplishments were a legend to me when I started. When I finished he had become very much a real person."

Wilson's search would also take him down the backroads of Cherokee County, Oklahoma, to look for models. "I was directed to many people, some short and heavy, some tall and lean. In these dissimilar physical types, I found facial features, body figures, and countenances that became part of my Sequoyah. Six men and one woman modeled for parts of the final portrait."

In 1984, Wilson was again commissioned by the Oklahoma legislature to paint a portrait for the state capitol. This time his subject was historian Angie Debo. Well into her nineties at the time, Debo was a woman of rare stature. The daughter of pioneers, she had gone on to earn a doctorate. A gifted historian, writer, and teacher, she ultimately became one of the state's most beloved figures. In the dining room of Debo's home in Marshall, Oklahoma, Wilson sketched and painted "Miss Angie" as she posed in a favorite armchair. "We seemed to hit it right off. I felt that her integrity and great accomplishments deserved the best painting I could do." Debo was not satisfied with Wilson's early efforts. "When a portrait is unsatisfactorily portrayed it is often because the artist has not 'become' his subject. Nothing could be more true for a painter—you cannot paint a tree without in some way becoming a tree." Wilson was determined to capture her character. As the two talked quietly, he studied her aged but noble features—the light inside her that had yet to be extinguished. In the end she was quite pleased. "Few portraits contain the welcome she expresses," Wilson says about the final portrait. "Few contain the generosity she extends to us." Debo later wrote to Wilson about his effort:

> I am so very grateful to you for the genuine plus integrity that went into the painting of that portrait. It is not beautiful—I have never been beautiful—it does not conceal my age. . . . but it shows the characteristic that I now know dominated my life. I don't know how you discovered it, for I did not tell you. I did not even realize its importance but it was always there . . . it was drive. It carried me through a whole lifetime.

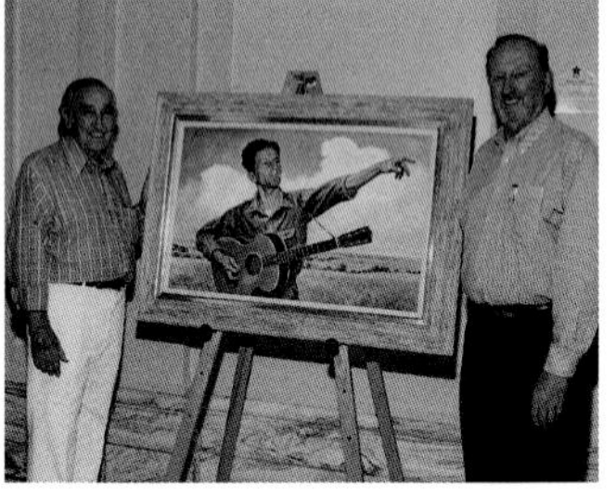

Charles Banks Wilson, left, with Senator Charles Ford at the unveiling of the Woody Guthrie portrait commissioned for the Oklahoma State Capitol in 2004.

WOODY GUTHRIE,

OIL/CANVAS,

OKLAHOMA

STATE CAPITOL

COLLECTION

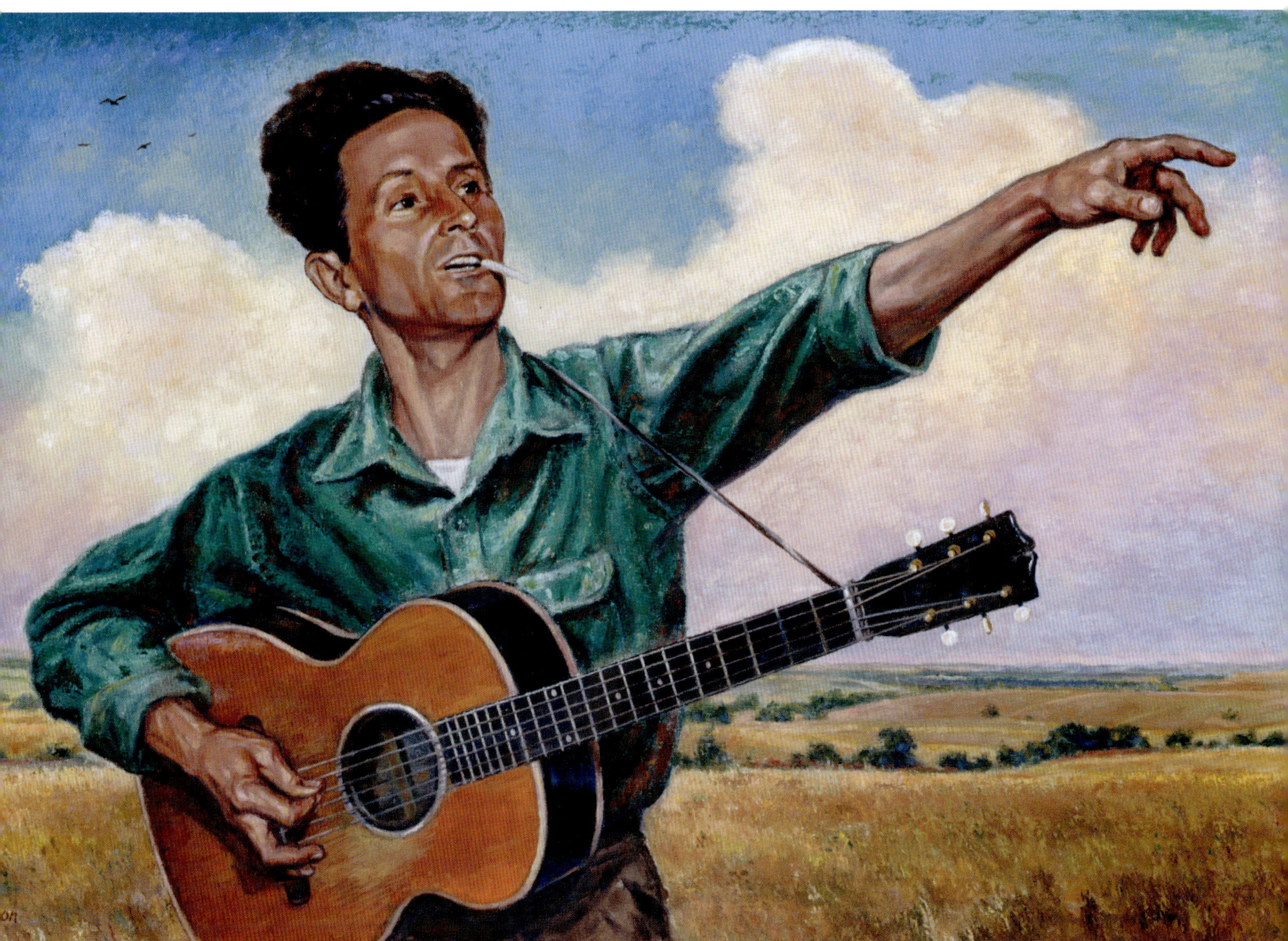

Wilson's most recent commission from the Oklahoma legislature occurred in 2001 when he was approached to paint a portrait of another notable Oklahoman. "I really did not want to do another," he recalled. "They eventually said I could pick any subject I wanted. Of course, I could not turn that down. I knew immediately what I wanted to do." Wilson's subject was songwriter-activist Woody Guthrie, considered by some to be too politically charged a choice. It was no matter to Wilson who had known Guthrie during his days in New York as a young man. "He was as down to earth as they come," says Wilson. "I recall watching him perform in a ritzy hotel club in Manhattan. He was wearing a tuxedo and was just getting ready to play when he looked out at all of the quality people in the audience. Woody shrugged, slung his guitar over his shoulder walked over to me. He shook his head and said, 'What am I doing here?' Then he just walked out." In 2002, Guthrie's portrait was unveiled at the state capitol and was well received. "One fact about art is that all people bring their own experience to it. To me, the Guthrie portrait is a religious painting. It pictures a human being with outstretched arms—receiving anointment from God—no different than the way the Michelangelo portrays man on the Vatican ceiling."

Other Wilson portraits include two of former Speaker of the House Carl Albert, one at the Oklahoma State Capitol and a second in the U.S. House of Representatives. Wilson also painted Thomas Gilcrease, founder of the Gilcrease Institute, Rodeo champions Freckles Brown and Jim Shoulders, and dozens of American Indians. His portrait of his daughter Carrie was considered by artist Alexander Hogue to be among his best.

In 1962, he painted Thomas Hart Benton, the only portrait done from life other than by Benton himself. "He complained a lot," Wilson says about the sitting. "I told him he was being paid back for all the misery he had put his subjects through." The two had become friends after Wilson helped Benton locate American Indian models for a mural at the Harry S. Truman library. The portrait is prominently displayed in Wilson's home. "Not a day goes by that I don't look at it and wonder what he's thinking," says Wilson. "Sometimes I have to say to him, Tom, mind your own business!" —RANDY RAMER

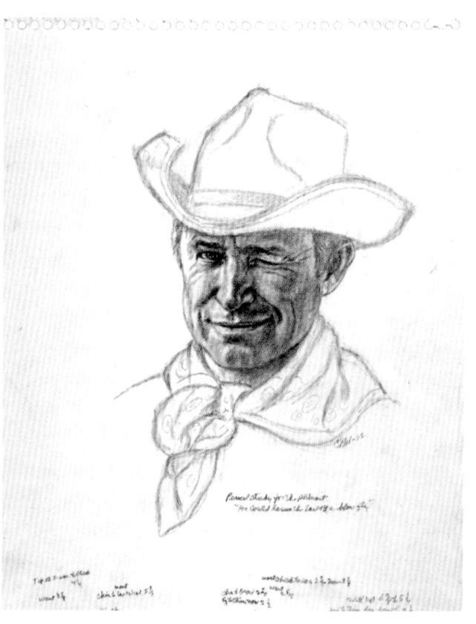

WILL ROGERS, 2002.
14 X 11, GRAPHITE/PAPER,
1327.3878

CBW: *I admire the cunning strokes of Benton's pencil. . .*

THOMAS HART
BENTON, 1961.
33.5 X 25,
EGG TEMPERA,
COLLECTION OF
THE ARTIST

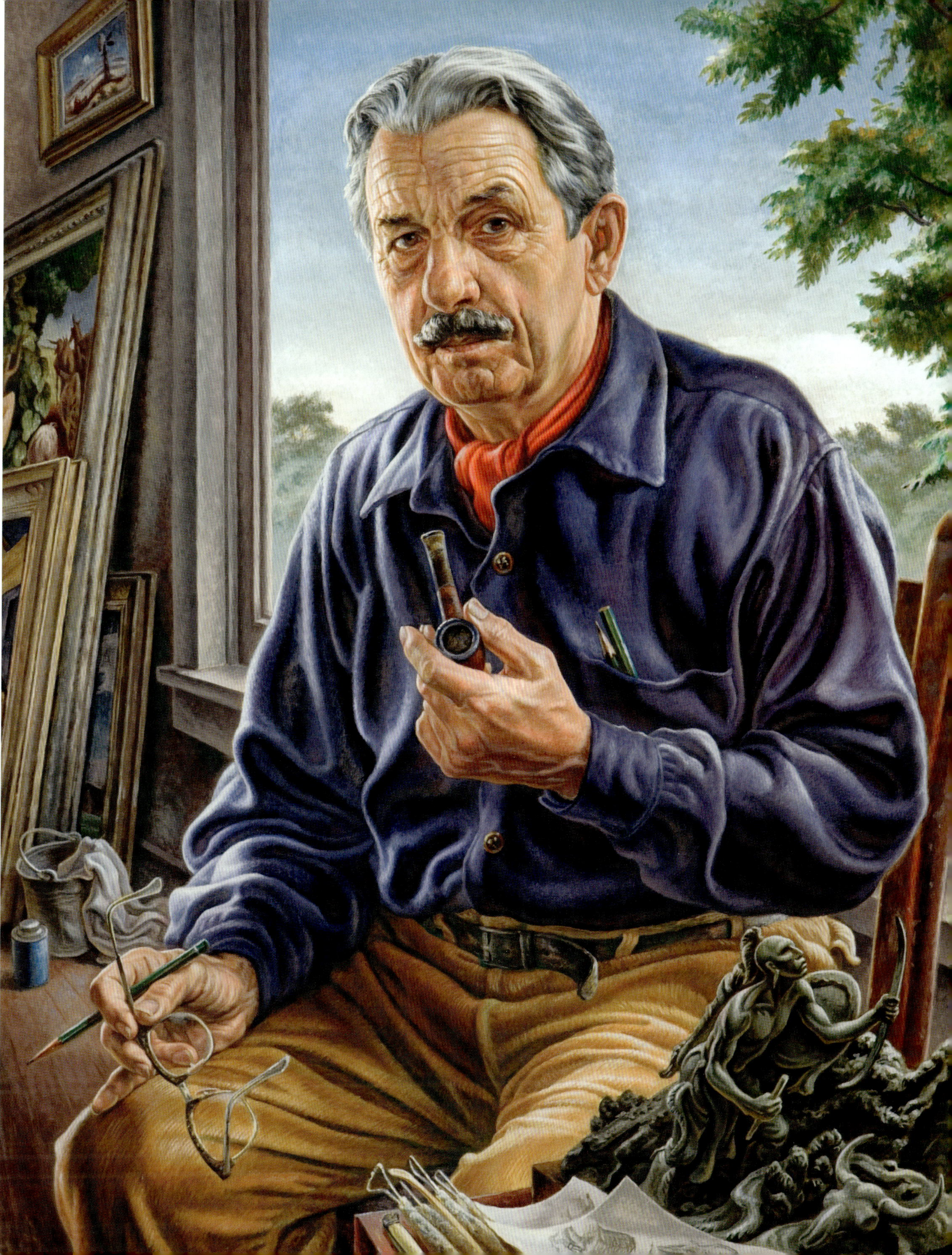

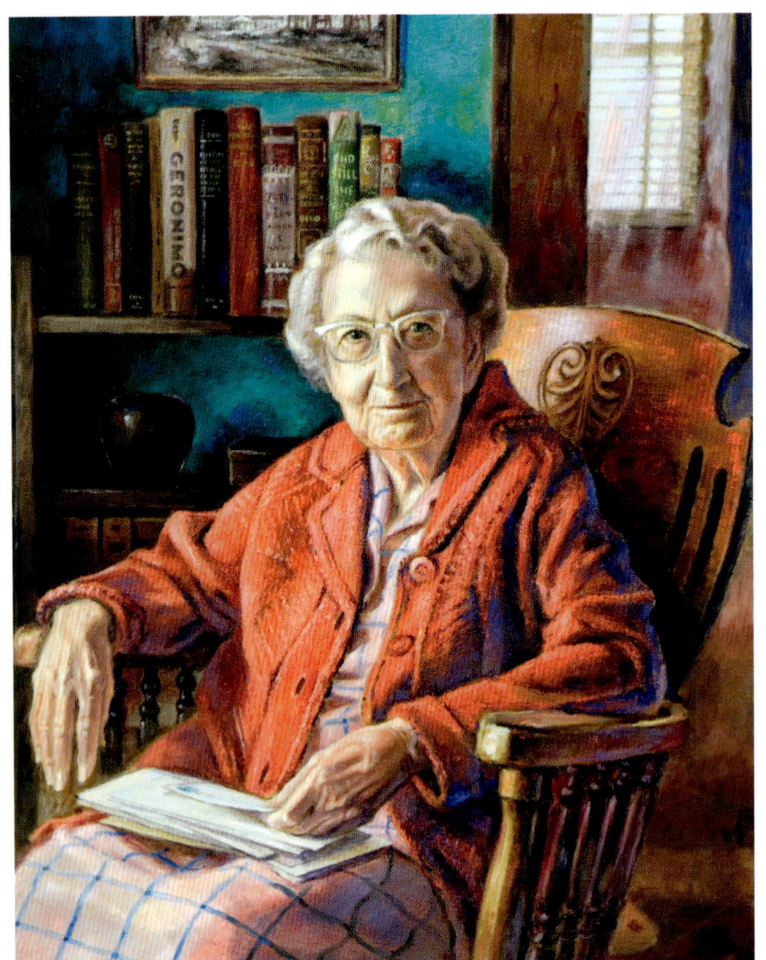

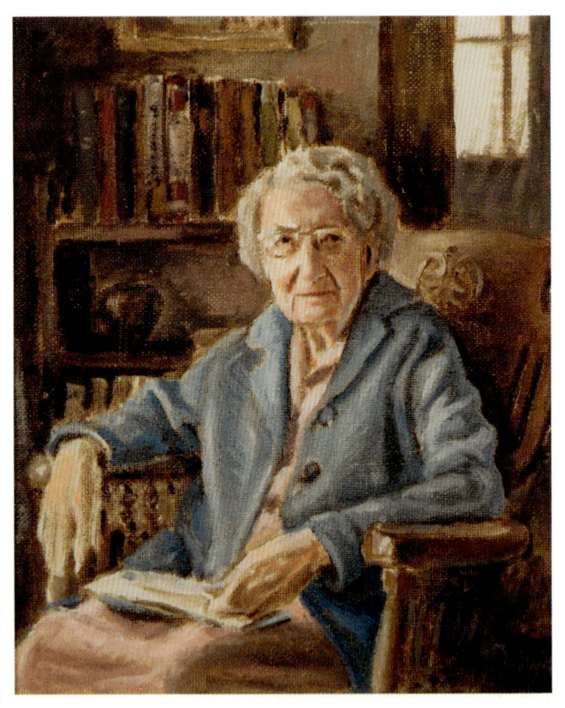

FROM TOP LEFT: ANGIE DEBO,
26.5 X 21.75, OIL/CANVAS,
COLLECTION OF THE ARTIST;
ANGIE DEBO, 14.375 X 12.125,
OIL/CANVAS. 0137.2462;
ANGIE DEBO, 1984. 14 X 11,
GRAPHITE/PAPER, 1327.2075

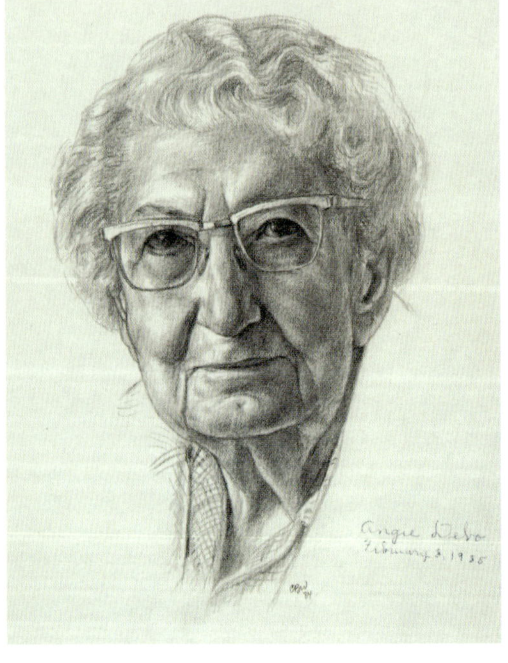

ANGIE DEBO,
OIL/CANVAS,
OKLAHOMA
STATE CAPITOL
COLLECTION

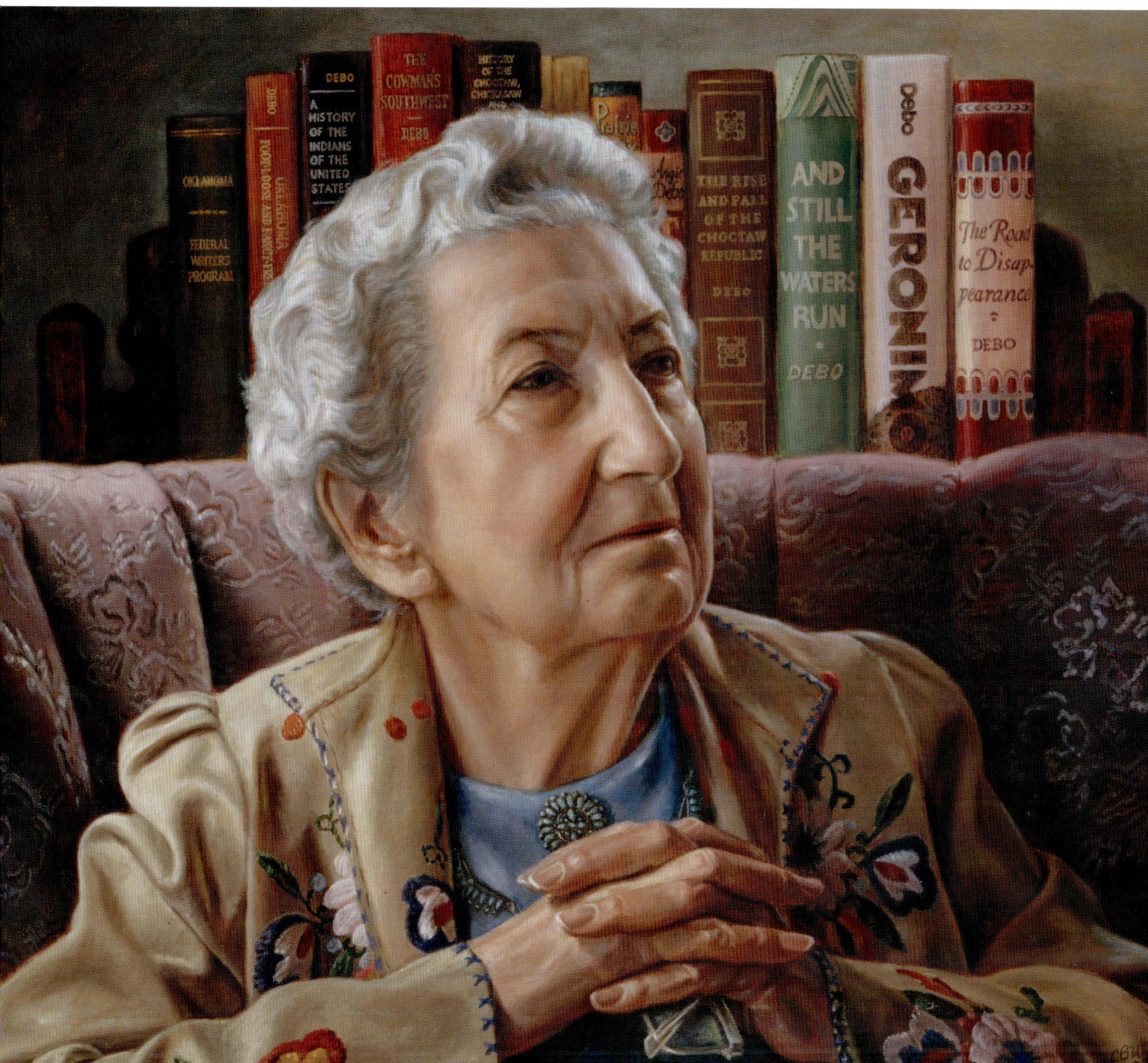

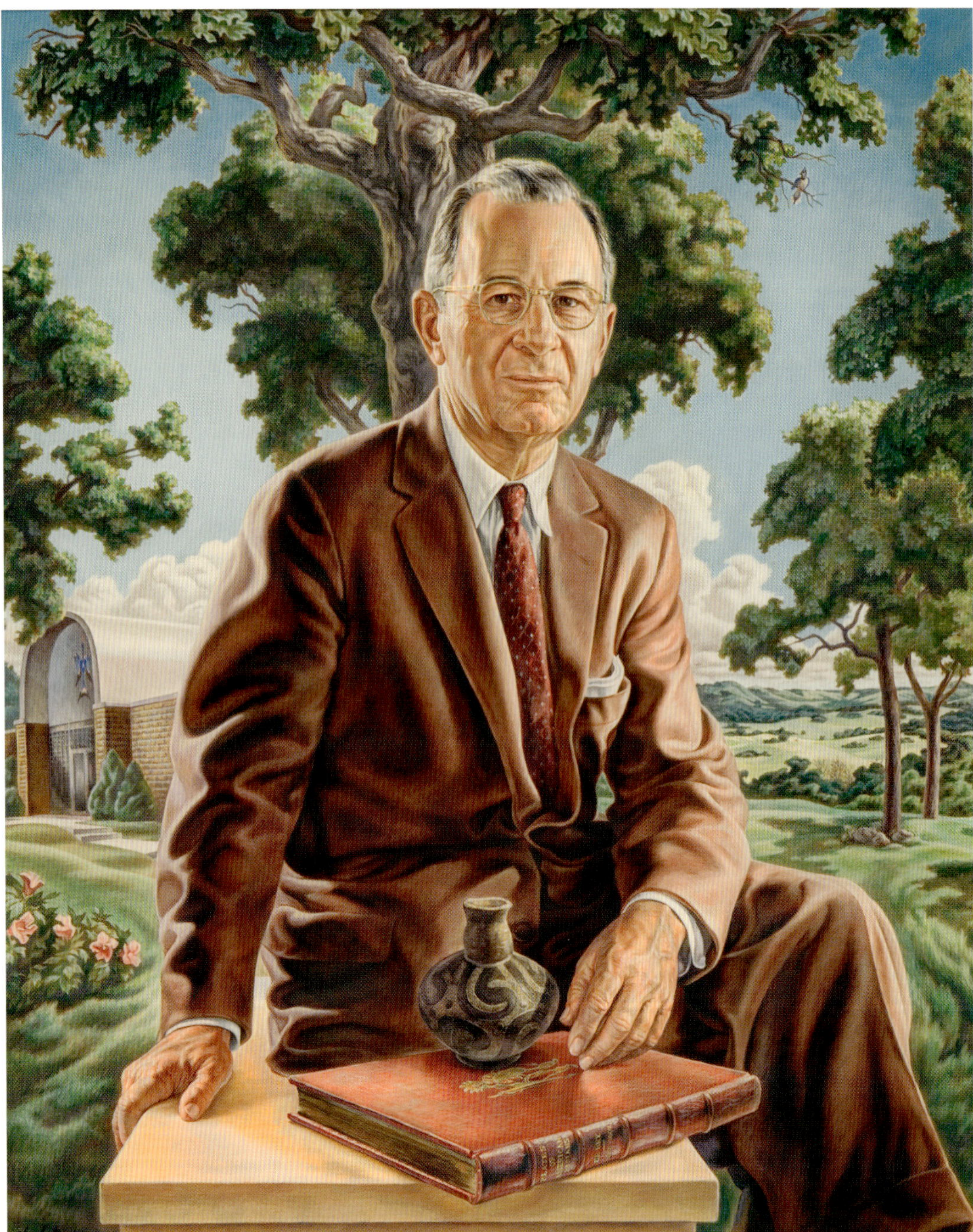

THOMAS
GILCREASE, 1958.
40 X 32, EGG
TEMPERA,
0127.2300

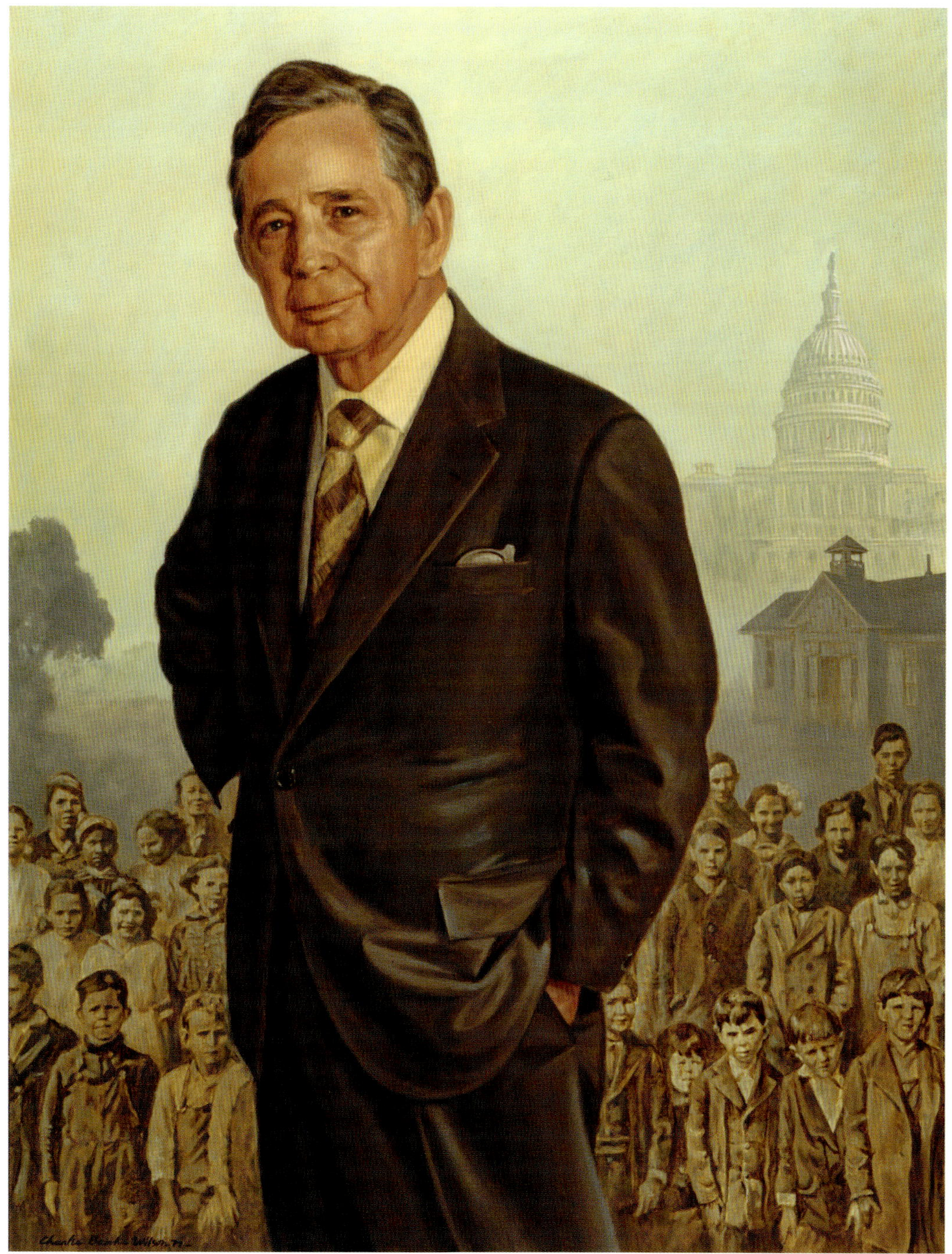

CARL ALBERT,
OIL/CANVAS,
OKLAHOMA
STATE CAPITOL
COLLECTION

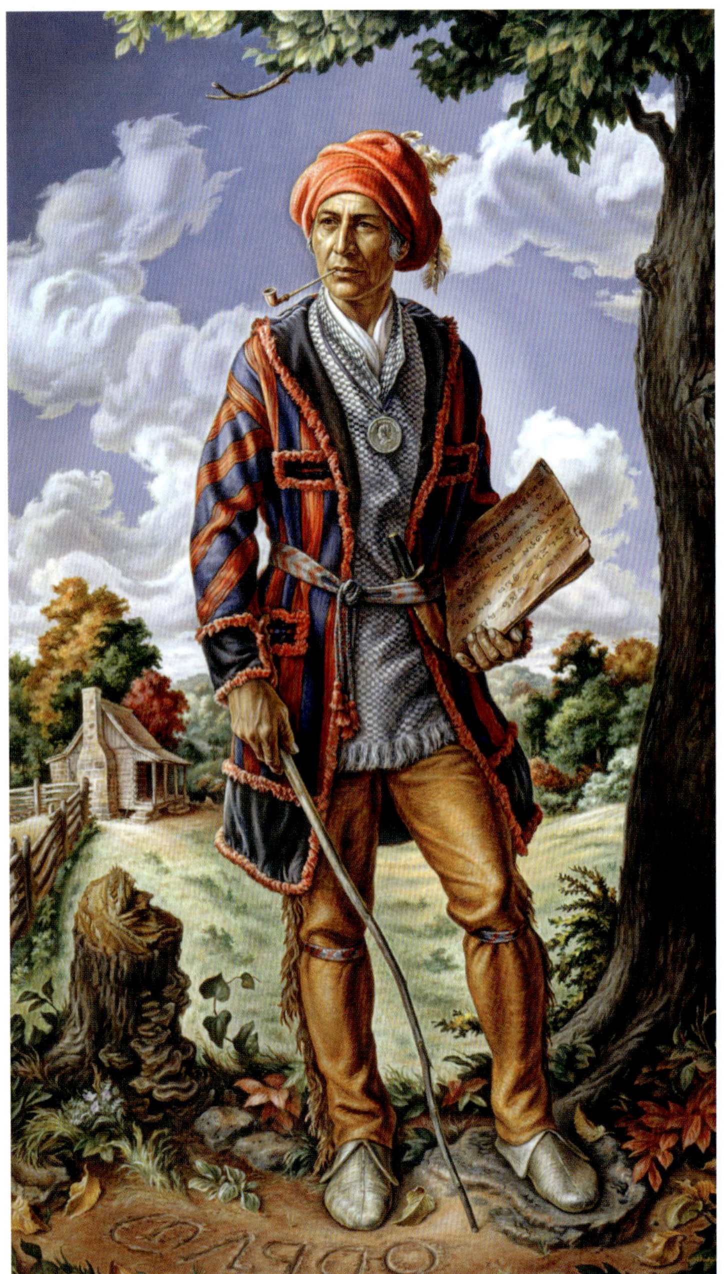

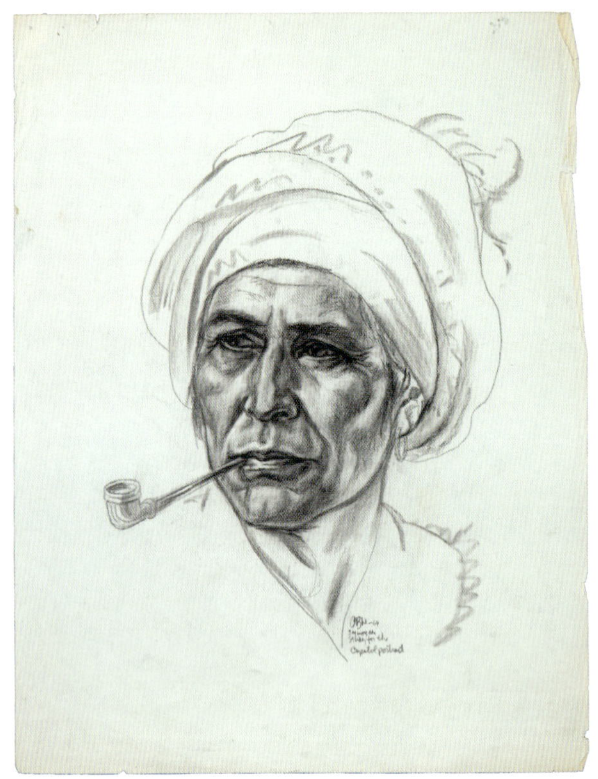

CBW: *The mind constructs and painting reflects.*

SEQUOYAH, OIL/CANVAS, OKLAHOMA STATE CAPITOL COLLECTION

SEQUOYAH, 1964. 22 X 17, GRAPHITE/PAPER, 1427.679

SEQUOYAH THE GREAT CHEROKEE, 1981. 23.625 X 19.75, LITHOGRAPH/PAPER, 1427.704

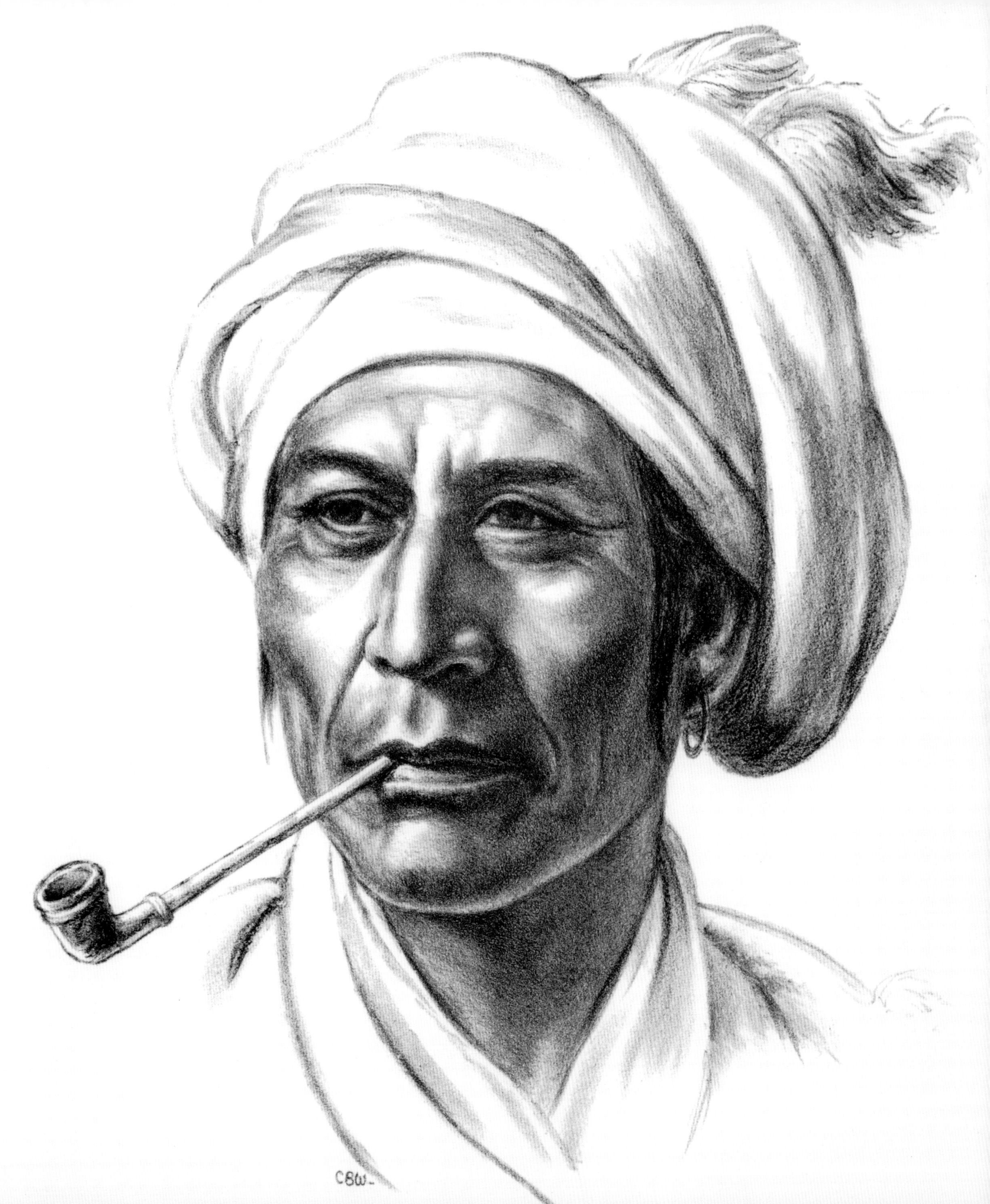

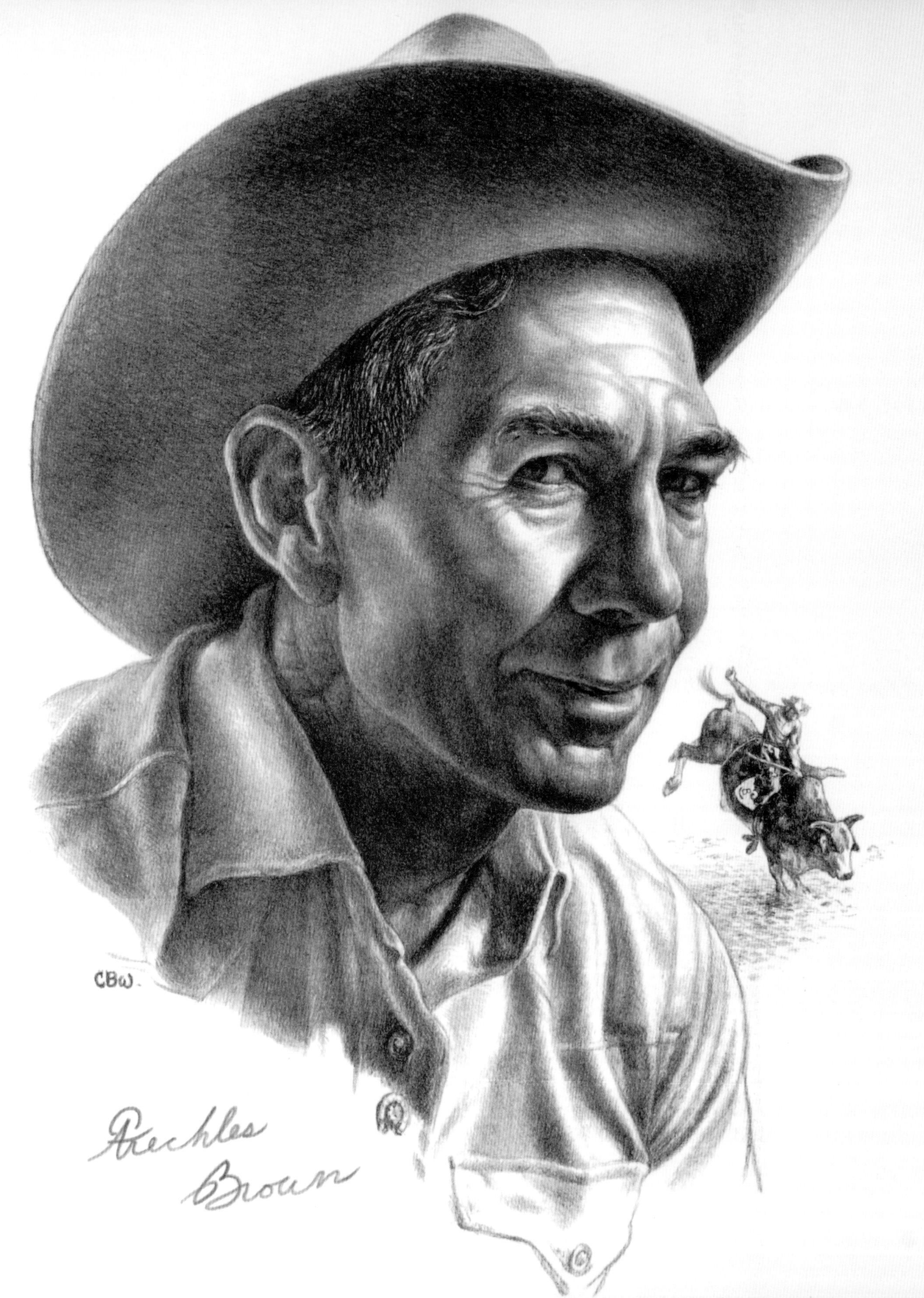

CBW.
Reckless
Brown

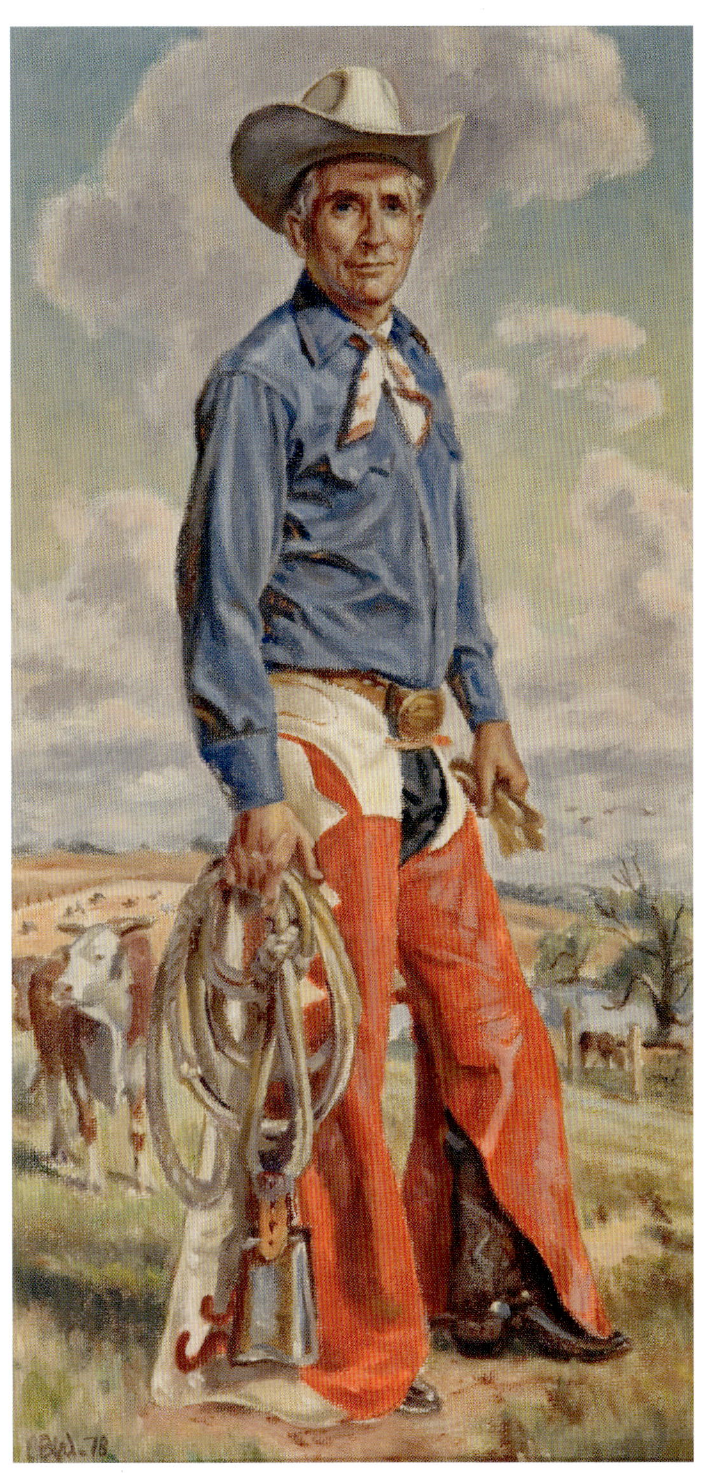

BULLRIDER, 1976, 21.5 X 16.5, LITHOGRAPH/PAPER, 1427.708

JIM SHOULDERS, STUDY, 1978. 20.25 X 16.5, OIL/CANVAS, 0137.2461

ART LARGE
AS LIFE

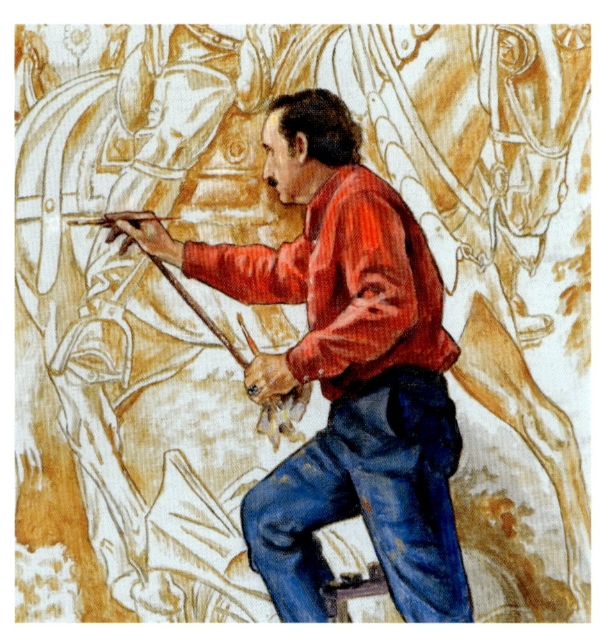

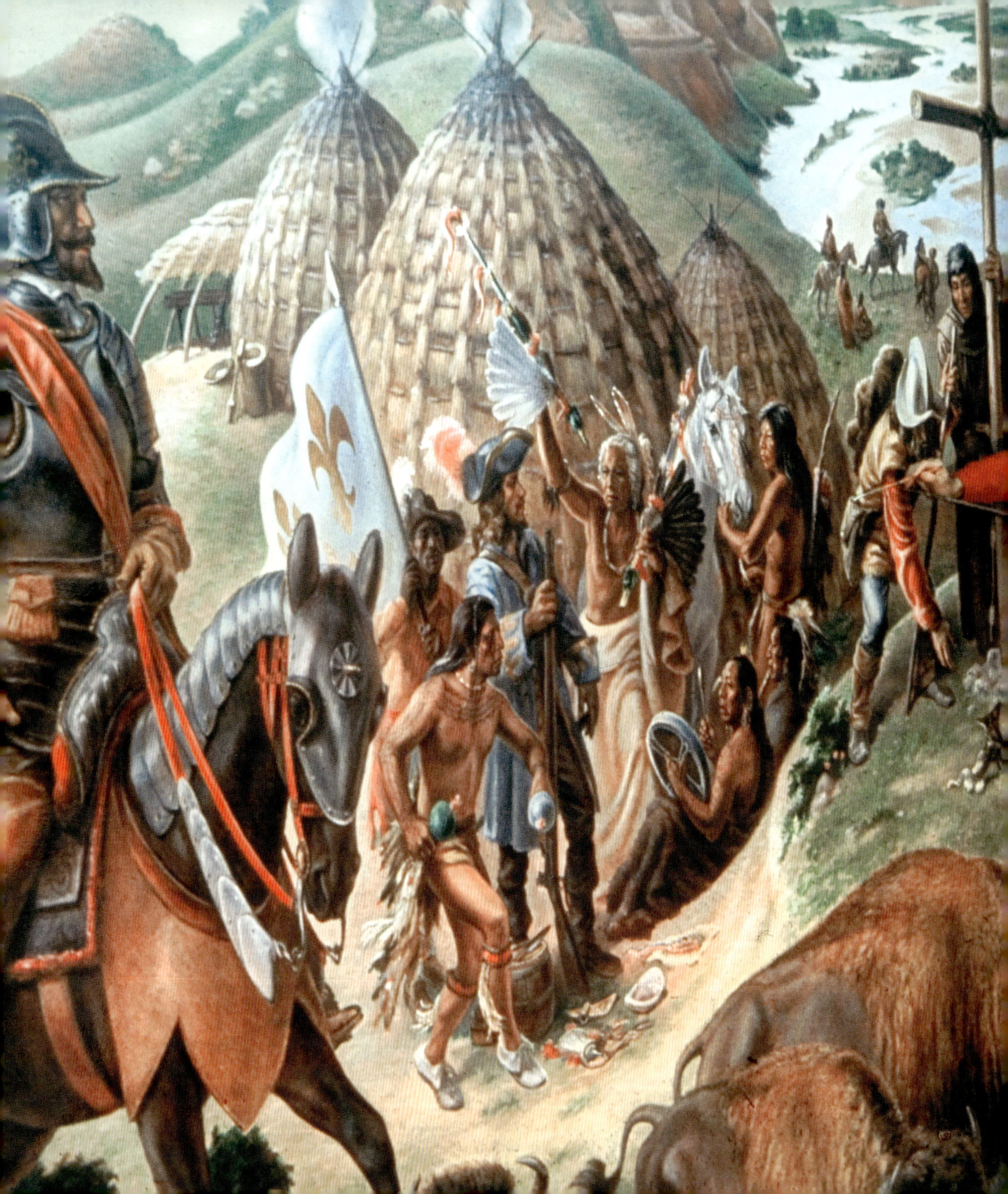

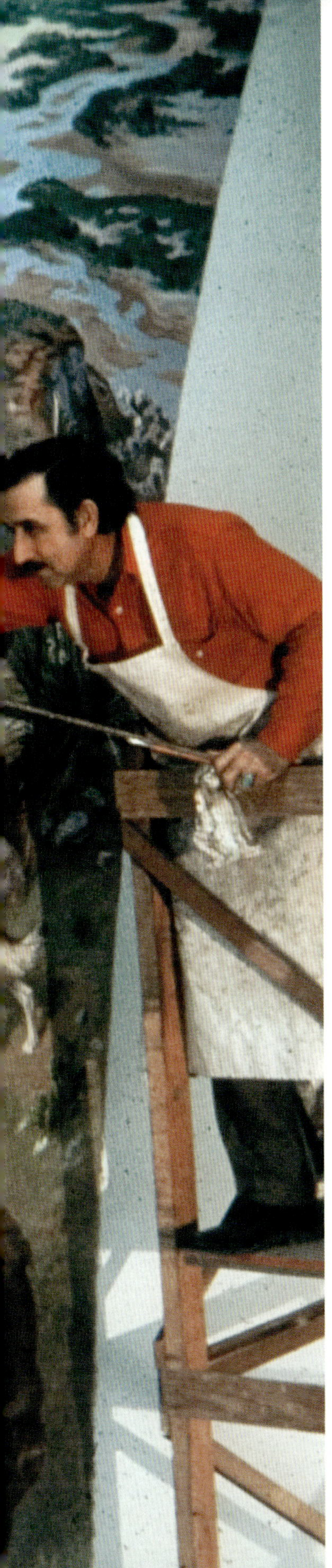

At the opening of the Harry S. Truman library in Independence, Missouri, Thomas Hart Benton introduced Charles Banks Wilson to the former president as "America's finest artist-historian." The description was apt. In 1970, Wilson was again asked by the Oklahoma legislature to depict subjects central to the history of the state and ultimately to the history of the nation.

The work would represent the culmination of all Wilson's efforts and experiences from earliest youth to that very moment, and would forever seal his reputation as Oklahoma's most celebrated and accomplished artist. His charge was straightforward—depict the history of the state from the time of European contact through statehood on four distinct murals in the vaulted heights of the capitol building rotunda—but the challenge was estimable. The murals were planned on a grand scale, some twenty-six feet wide and thirteen feet in height. Wilson would need to summon all his skills and abilities, not just as an artist, but as a researcher and interpreter of collective memory.

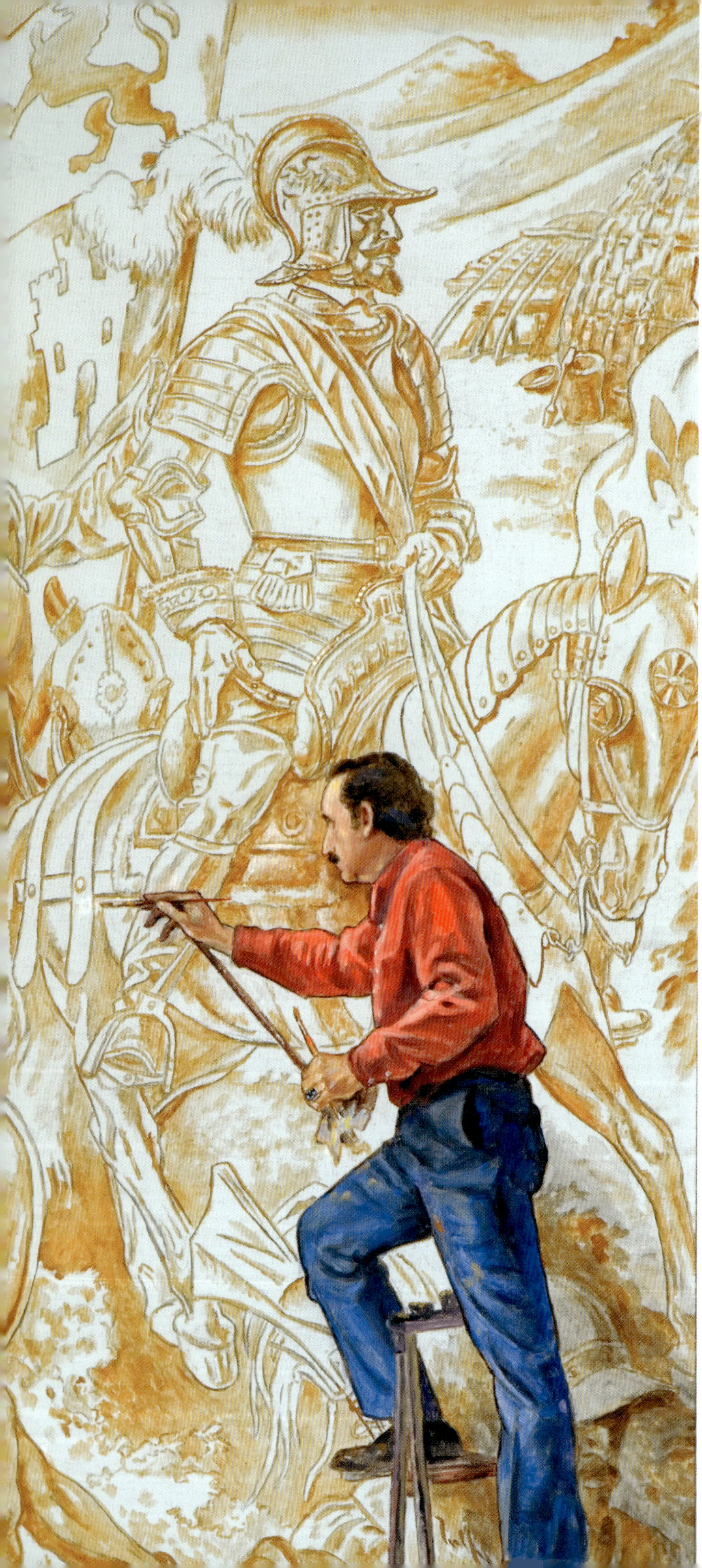

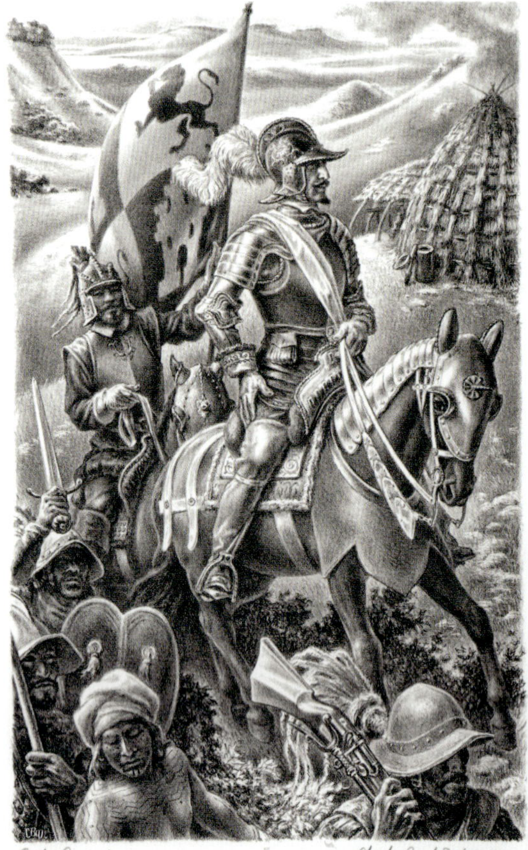

LEFT: Wilson recorded himself painting
one of the Capitol murals in a self-portrait
in the collection of the artist. FACING:
Looking in the mirror. Wilson's rendering
of Spanish explorer Francisco Vasquez de
Coronado was based on his own likeness.
CBW: *A painting should not only appeal, but
should also "mean." . . . Painting is a form of
poetry made to be seen.*

TOP:
ENTER CORONADO, 1976.
27.5 X 20.5, LITHOGRAPH/
PAPER, 1427.680

OVERLEAF:
MURAL: DISCOVERY
AND EXPLORATION

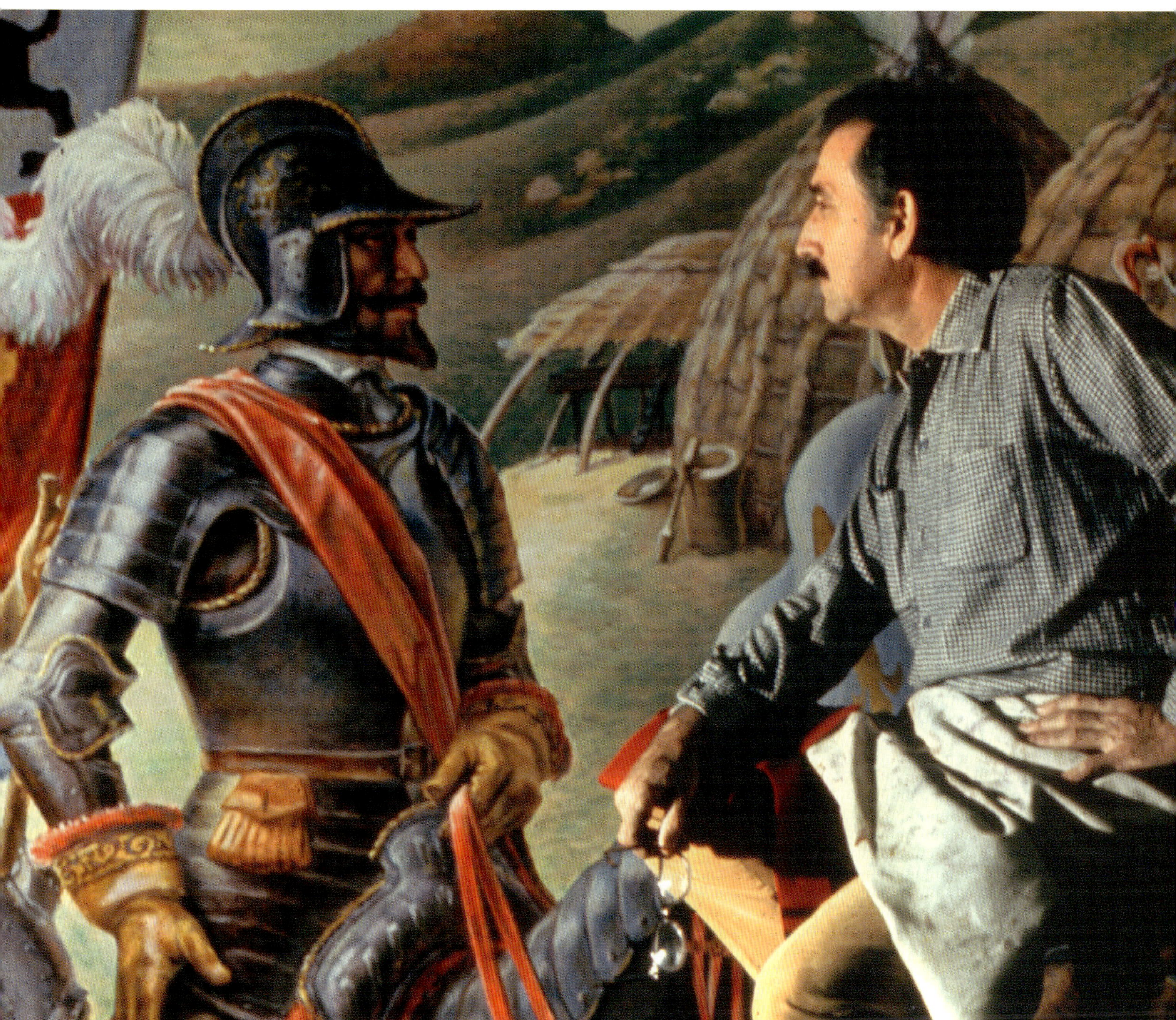

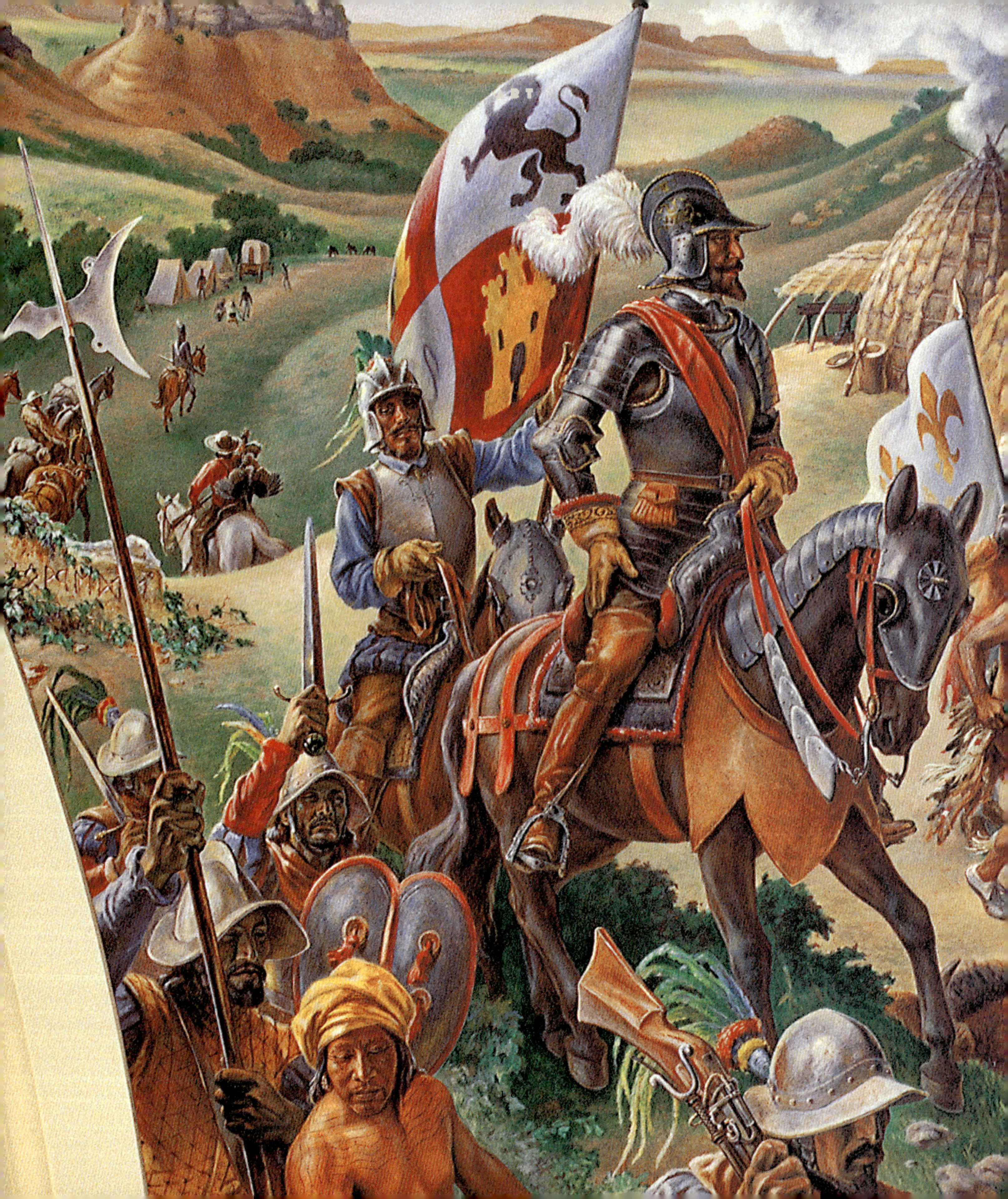

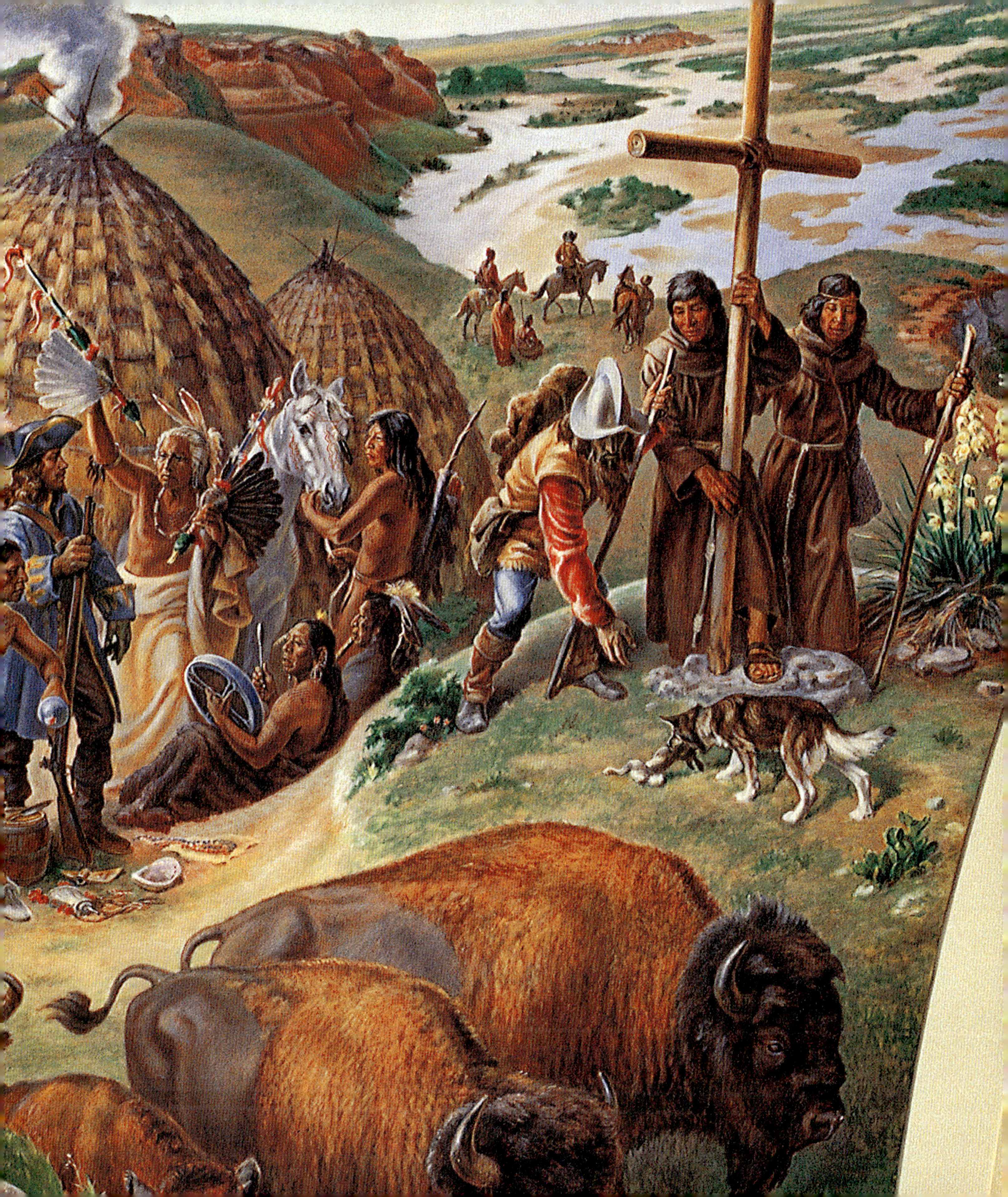

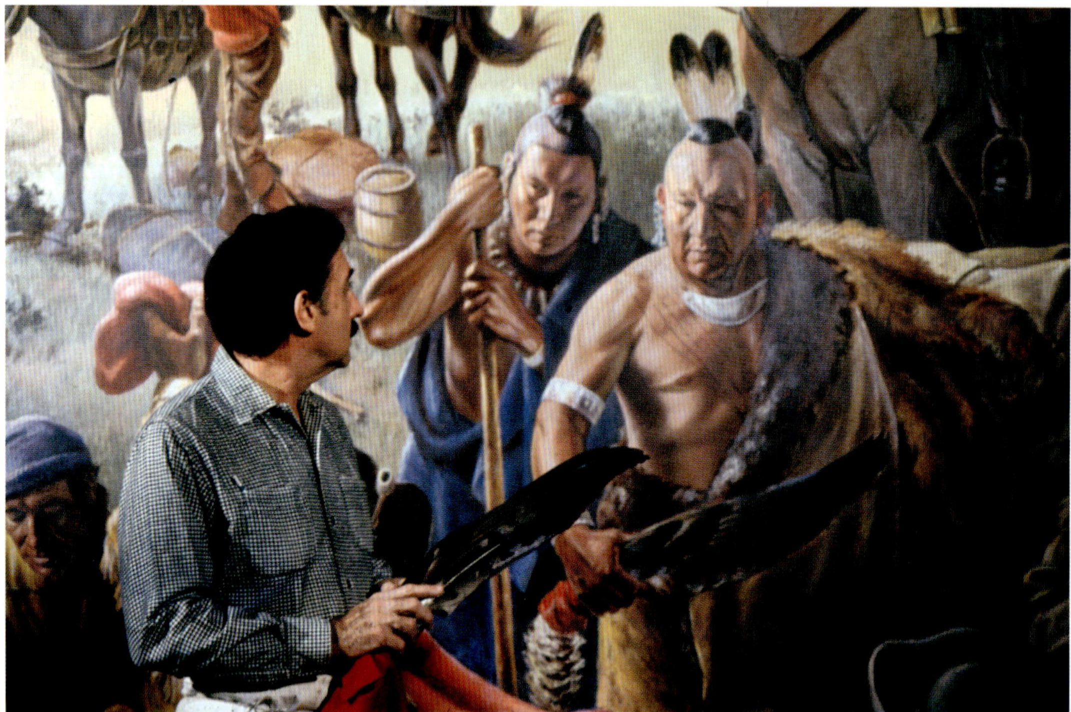

"Oklahoma is wider than our view of it," says Wilson. In preparation for the project, he set out to give his fellow citizens "an awareness of their intensely individual past." To do so, he would spend countless hours in planning and experimenting with ways of demonstrating that past. "A picture renders experience visible." The experience Wilson was commissioned to render was fundamental to the lives of his neighbors, kinsmen, and friends—to all contemporary Oklahomans. It was a story that had long informed his notions regarding his place in the world, his "struggle to give meaning to experience." Wilson's truth was in no small measure the truth of those around him. His many years of work depicting the deep truth of ordinary people would now support this struggle.

A fisherman once said to Wilson, "Sometimes you are at the right place at the right time, but the fish isn't ready." With regard to the capitol murals, the fish was more than ready. Indeed, no other artist living or past was capable of the task. Wilson's abilities had been honed at Indian powwows and gatherings, in the homes and workplaces of regular folks, and the rural landscapes around him. They had been formed from earnest effort, and a genuine interest in and appreciation of his subject matter. They had been formed from his exacting standards regarding authenticity, his desire to "picture the truth" about the world around him.

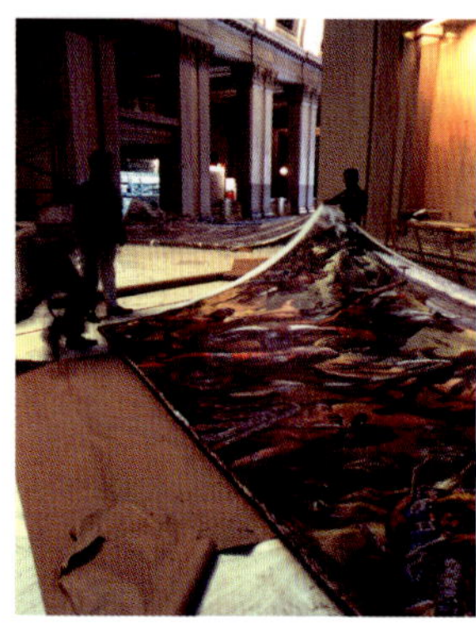

Wilson holds a feather fan he observed in attaining an accurate representation for his mural. Preparing to install the canvases was a technically challenging process.

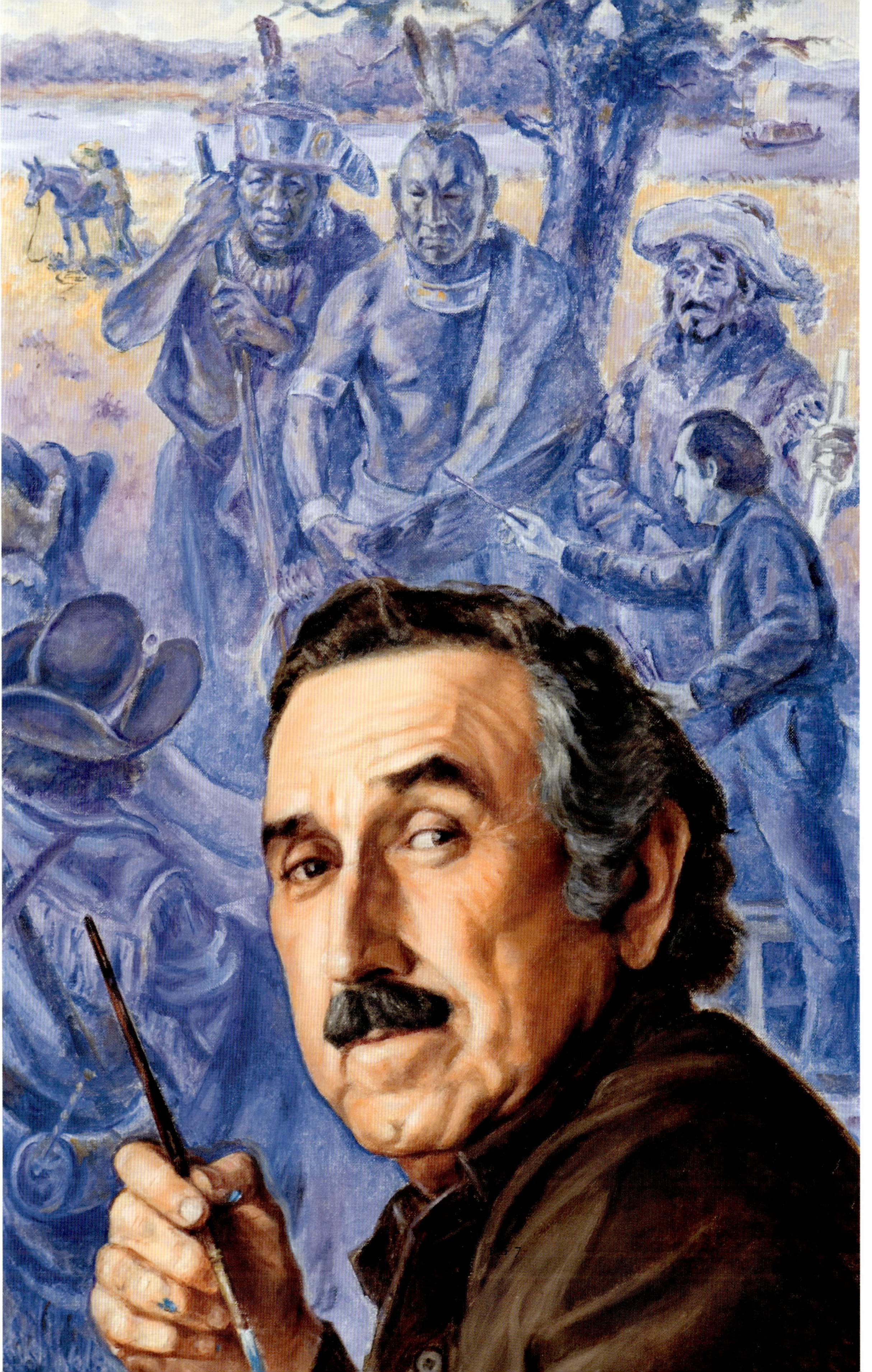

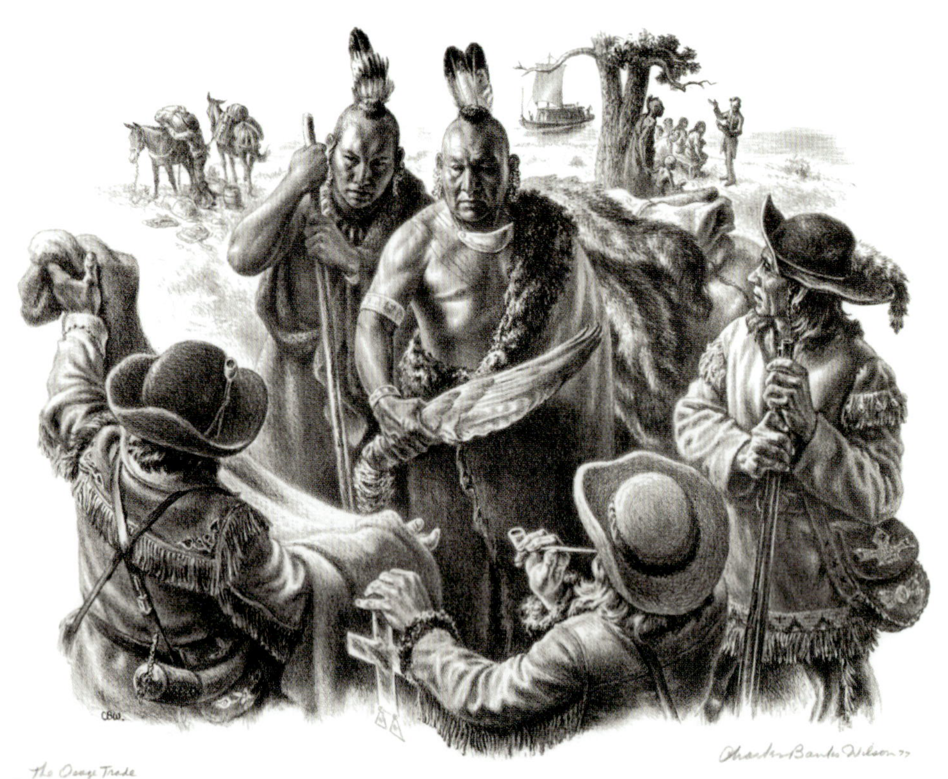

THE OSAGE TRADE,
1977. 22.75 X 26.875,
LITHOGRAPH/PAPER,
1427.678

STUDY OF OSAGE
MAN FROM INDIAN
IMMIGRATION MURAL,
GRAPHITE/PAPER,
1327.2706

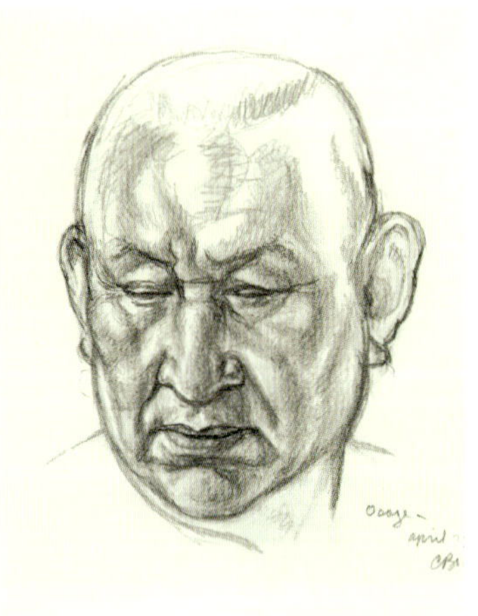

MURAL:

FRONTIER TRADE

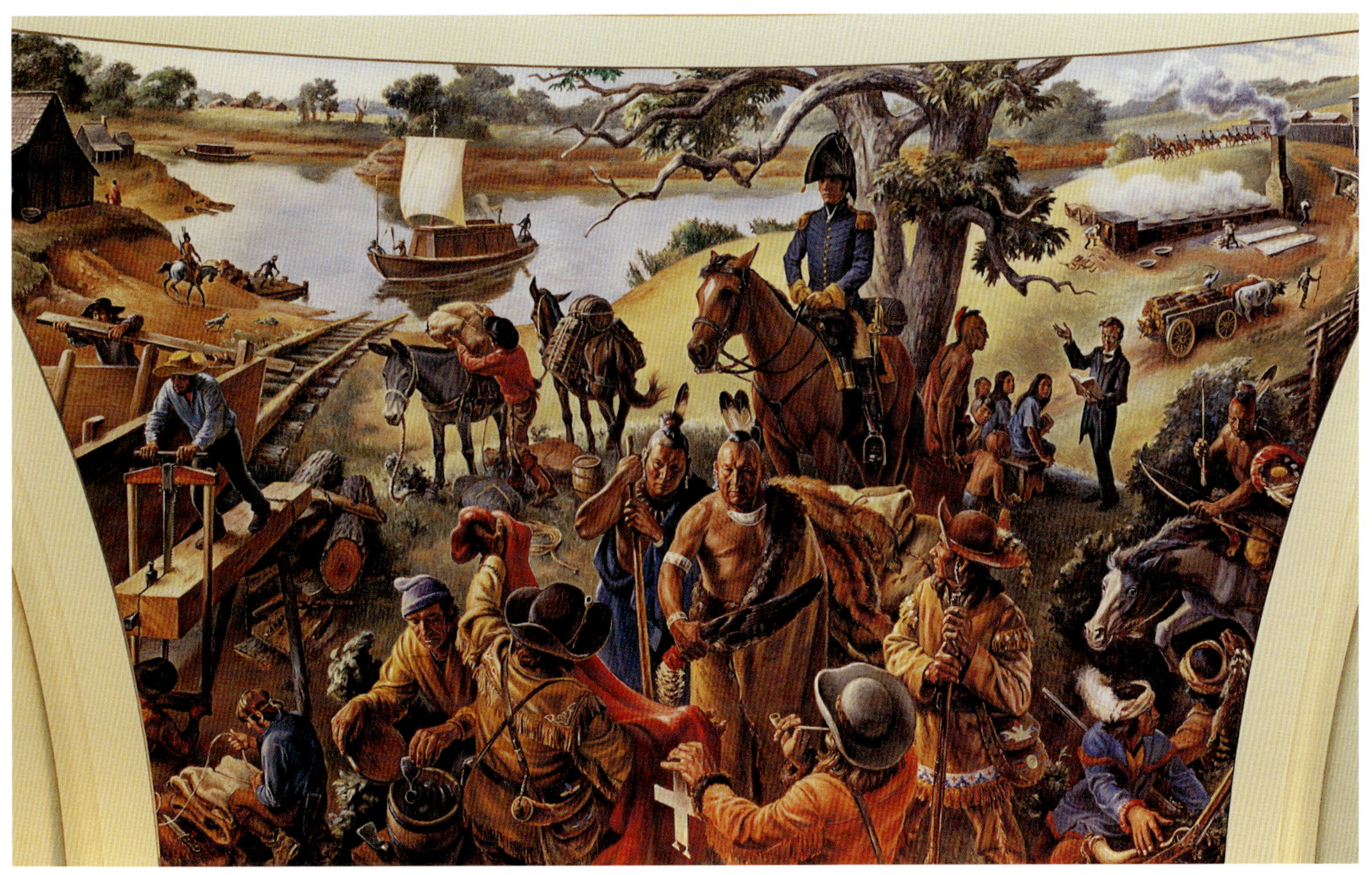

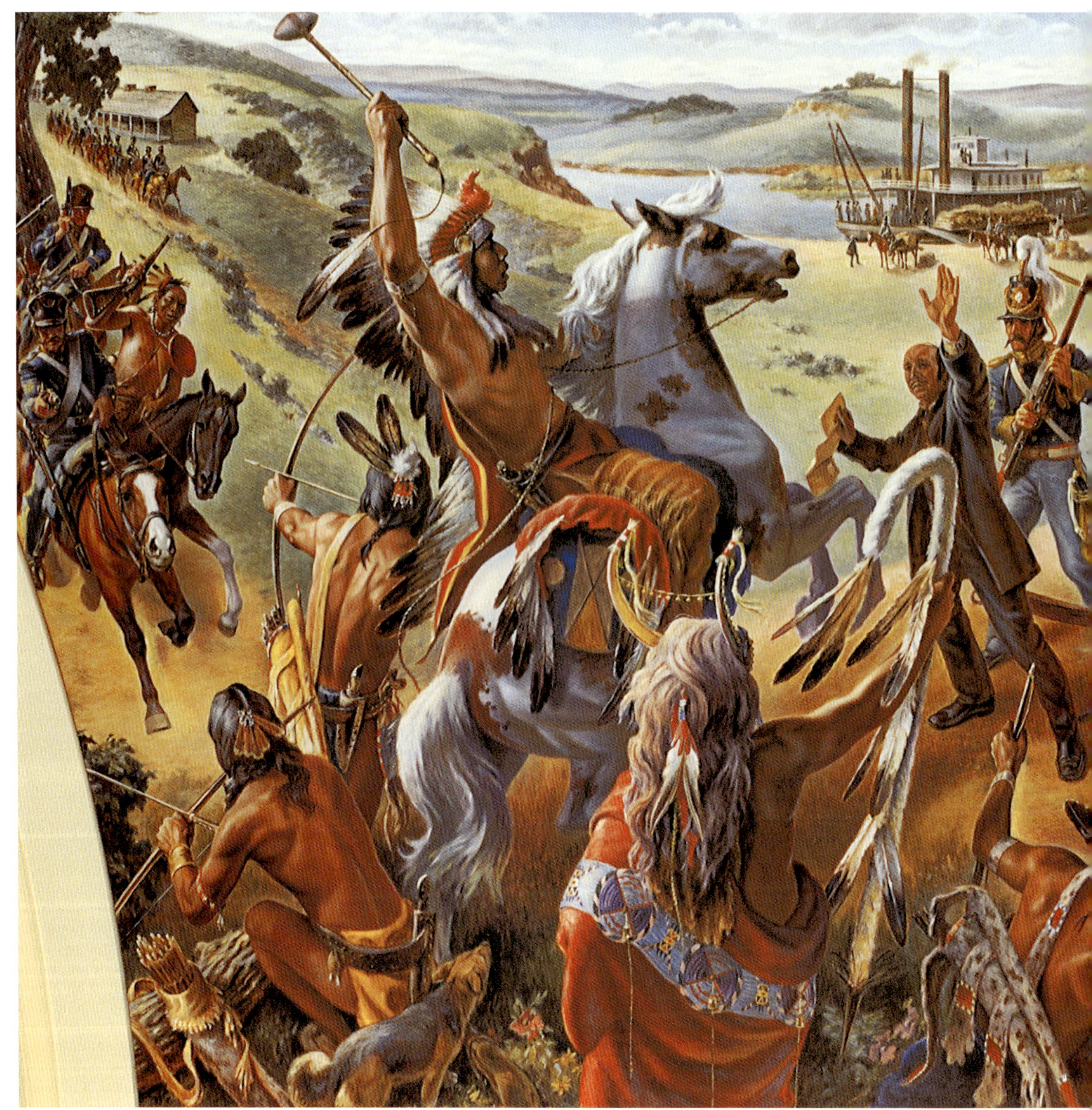

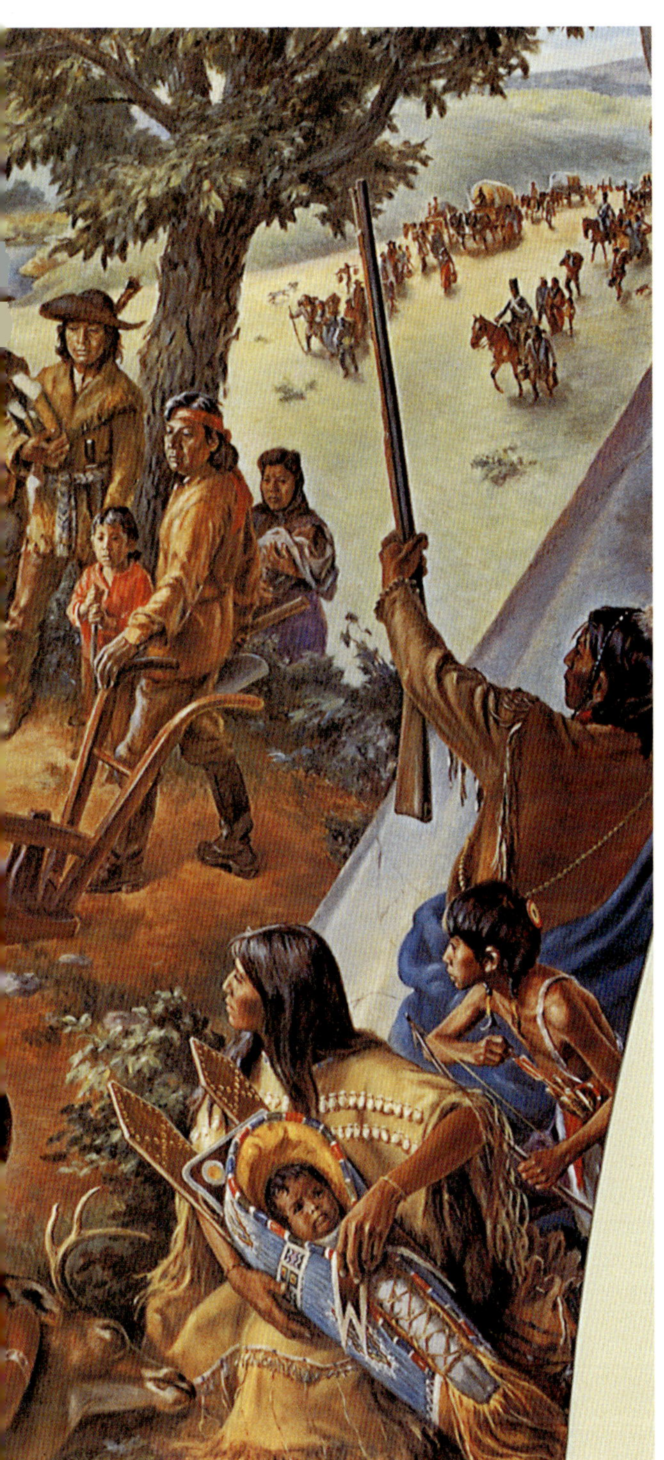

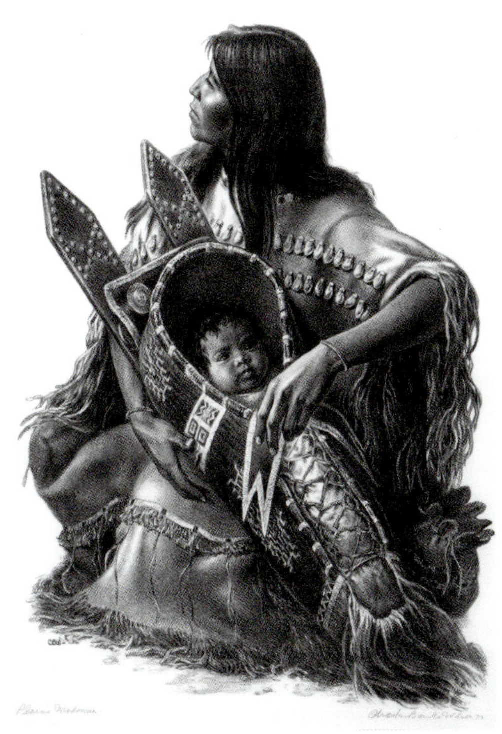

MURAL:

INDIAN

IMMIGRATION

PLAINS

MADONNA, 1977.

27.875 X 22,

LITHOGRAPH/

PAPER, 1427.681

From his studio across from the small town bus station to the resources of libraries, archives, and museums around the world, Wilson's skills as an artist-historian were unparalleled. "A painting should not only appeal but should also mean," he says. His life had been spent in the collection of information, images, and ideas. Combined, these elements would form the foundation of a meaning that no other individual could express. His ability as an artist and his comprehensive knowledge of history would come together in a way he had never imagined. Wilson's time and place was at hand.

"The success of the artist-historian comes from mastering the art of communication," says Wilson. He first had to consider what he wanted to communicate. The four-year project began with simple sketches. He organized the murals into segments chosen to best illustrate the distinct shifts in the history of the region. The first, called *Discovery and Exploration,* would depict images from the period 1541 to 1820. The remaining murals were developed around similar themes: Frontier Trade, Indian Immigration, Non-Indian Settlement. Both thematically and in execution, the murals would focus on movement. "A good form appeals pleasantly to the eyes long before there is any notice of the subject," Wilson says. He wanted the murals to possess an animation that would communicate both the sweep of time and the human drama of change. He wanted the scenes to flow seamlessly from one to another and back again.

And so he set to work. Each vignette was drawn from life and required that Wilson spend countless hours in the field to find just the right subjects. He sketched people's faces and important landmarks. He drew real animals on real prairies. Every artifact and implement was meticulously researched. Again, Wilson developed intricate clay models, not only to assist in the execution of his ideas but also to spur and organize the ideas themselves. Above all, he wanted the murals to be comprehensive. He would leave nothing out in an effort to tell the true story of his state and his people. Through his murals, the Oklahoma character in all its diversity is revealed.

"There is no way we can guarantee success—but we can deserve it," says Wilson. The artist's success with the Oklahoma murals can only be credited to something deeply rooted in Wilson's character. His attention to detail, his need to "get it right," was fundamental. "Unusual opportunities mean unusual obligations," he says. His need has never been to merely satisfy himself with a given work. His obligation has been to his subjects and to the viewer.

"My art has been about people," he says. "Every man belongs to an age. In 1945, I came back from a life in Chicago and New York—opened my eyes and took a look —and did what I was called to do. I accepted my world and found it."

—RANDY RAMER

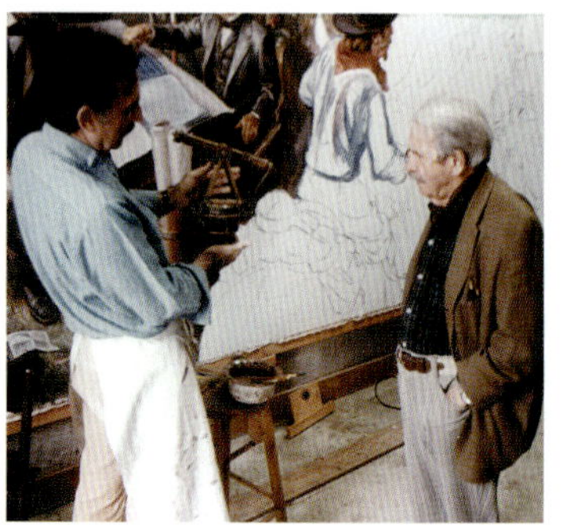

Wilson with Thomas Hart Benton in the early 1970s. Wilson was an unabashed admirer of Benton. CBW: *Tom Benton's concern was structure — his painting is characterized by structured design. . . . Benton was a genius.*

STUDY OF A MAN FOR THE MURAL NON-INDIAN SETTLEMENT, 11 X 8, GRAPHITE/PAPER, 1327.2693

SKETCHES FOR MURALS, 17 X 11, GRAPHITE/PAPER, 1327.2748

OVERLEAF: MURAL: NON-INDIAN SETTLEMENT

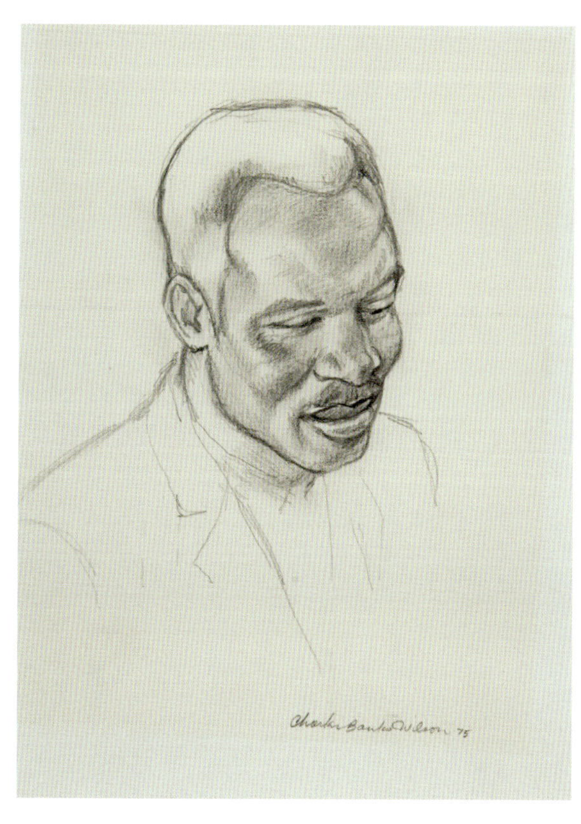

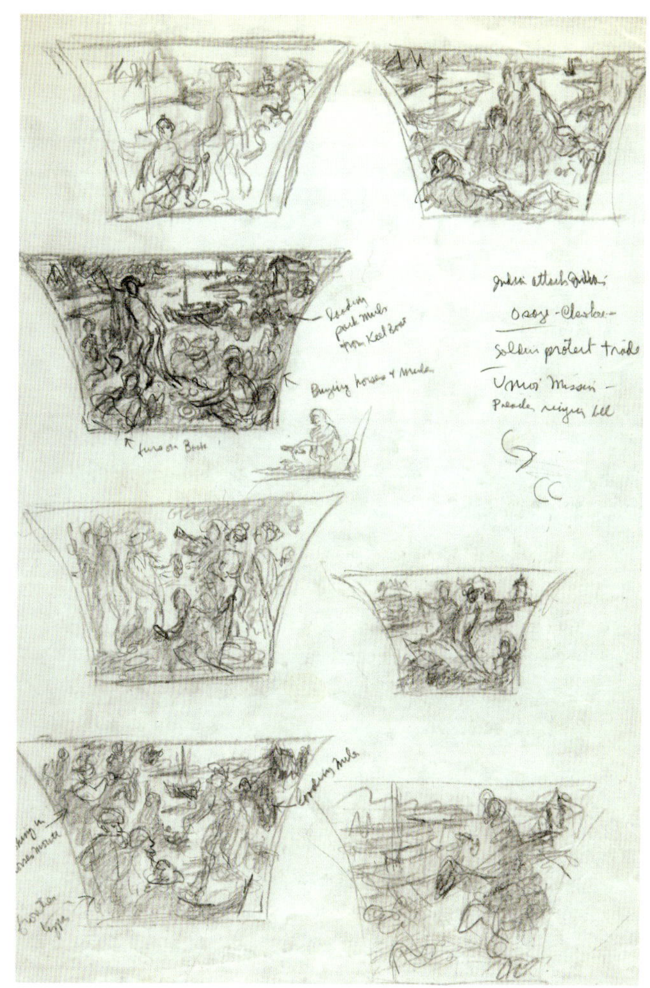

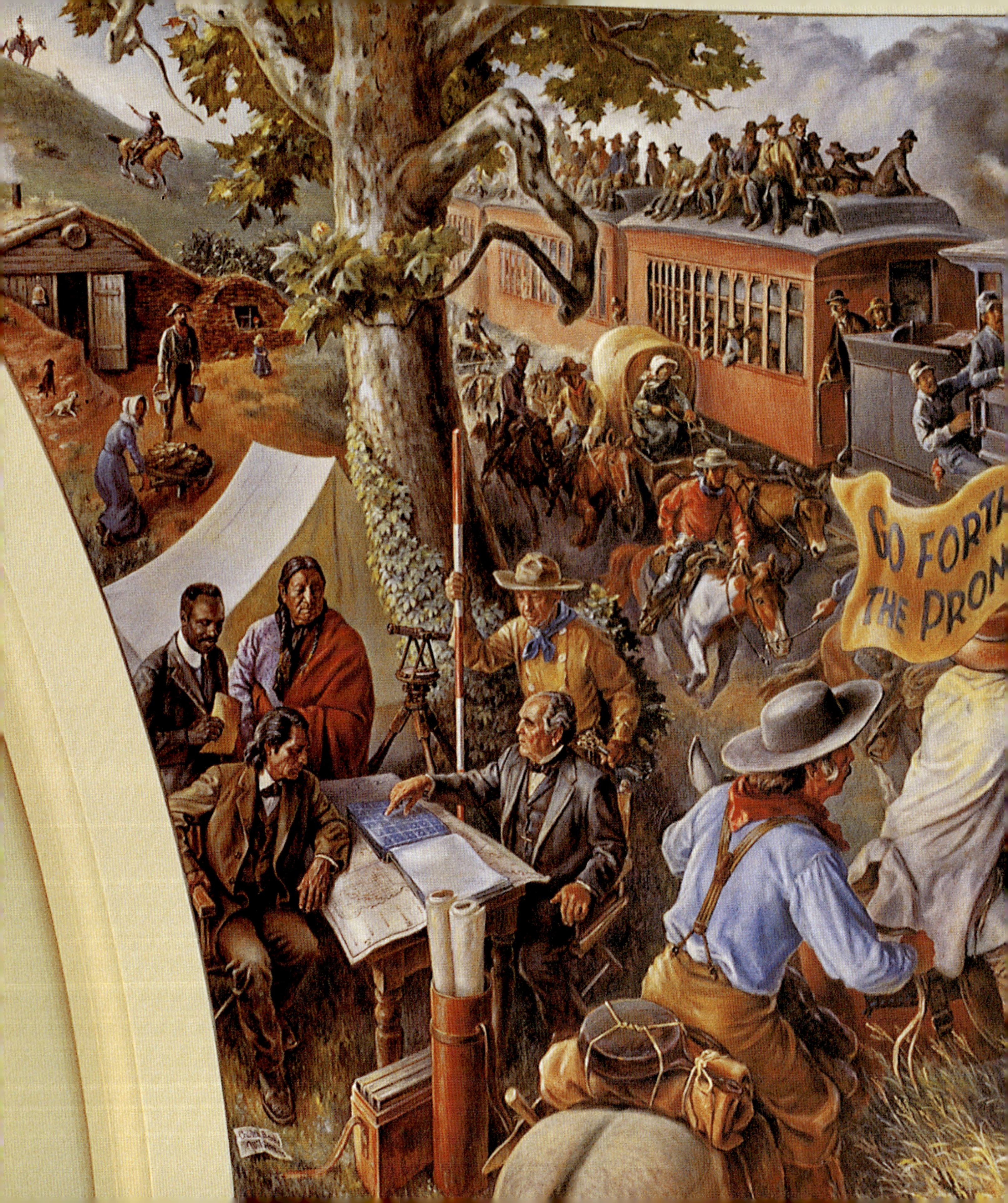

GO FORTH
THE PRON

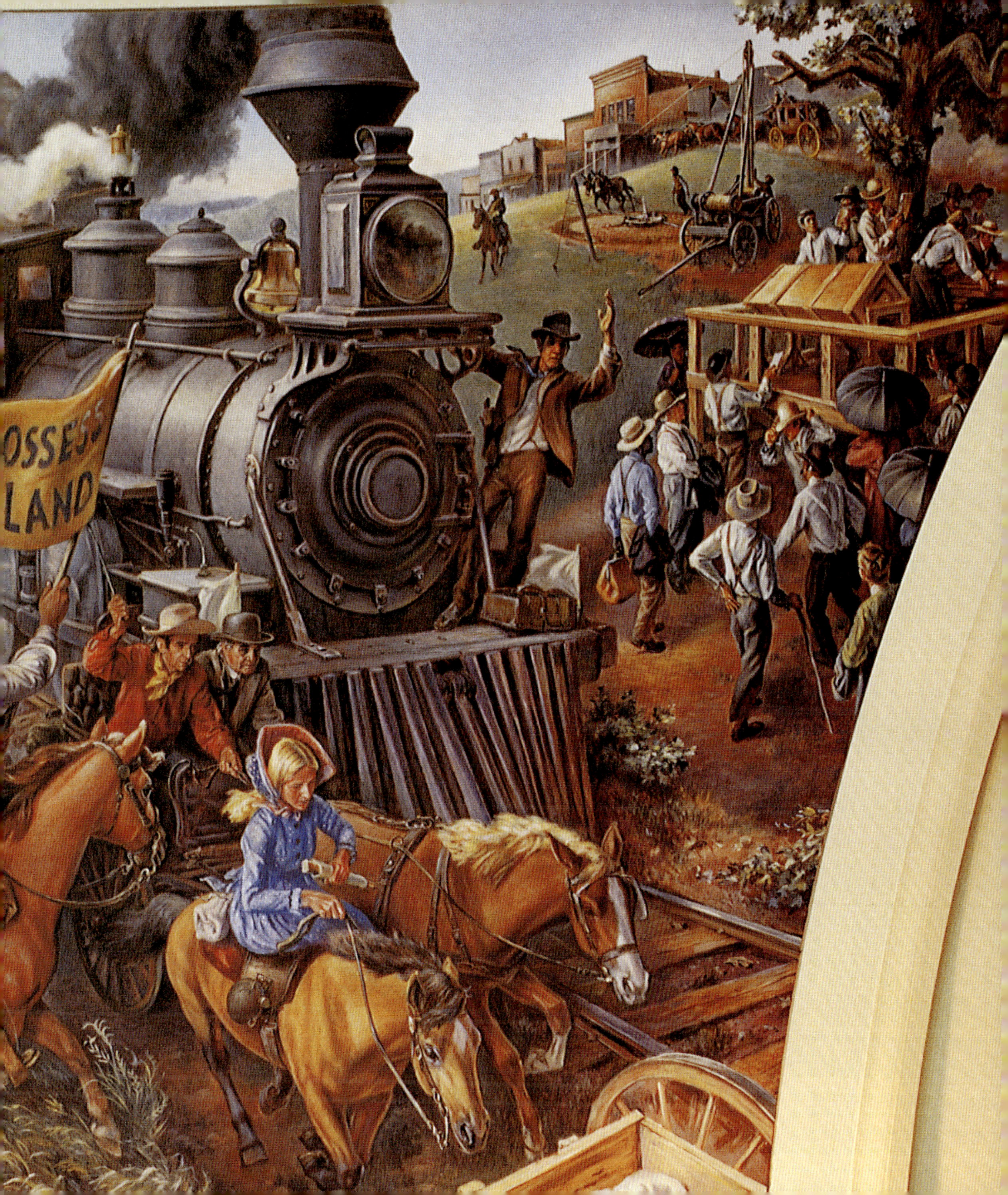

OSSESS
LAND

1918	Born August 6, 1918 in Springdale, Arkansas
1936	Entered the Chicago Art Institute; made first lithographs
1937	Began what would later be known as the Purebloods series
1938	Started entering work in regional shows
1939	Participated in the U.S. Office of Education Fine Arts National Student Show, Washington, D.C.
	Received Purchase Award from Chicago Society of Lithographers and Etchers
	Set up studio in Miami, Oklahoma
1940	Examples of work added to the Chicago Art institute collection
1941	Moved to New York City
	Won first place award in Brooklyn Art Museum's annual regional exhibition
1942	Exhibited at National Academy of Design, New York City
	Participated in the Metropolitan Museum of Art's Artists for Victory exhibition
1943	Exhibited at the Library of Congress, Washington, D.C.
1944	*Ozark Summer,* a lithograph, purchased by the Metropolitan Museum of Art
	Represented in the National Print Annual
1945	Moved back to Miami, Oklahoma
	Won first place award at Oklahoma Artists Annual Exhibition, Philbrook Art Center, Tulsa
1946	Exhibited at the Smithsonian Institution, Washington D.C.
	Began teaching at Northeastern State University
1952	Set up lithography press and began making his own prints
1955	Completed forty illustrations for a new Oklahoma history textbook for the public school system
1956	Commissioned by John D. Rockefeller Jr. to paint a mural, *The Trapper's Bride*
1957	Produced *Ten Little Indians*
	Commissioned to paint portrait of Thomas Gilcrease
1961	Included in an international exhibit sponsored by the U.S. State Department
1962	Elected a fellow of the International Institute of Arts and Letters, Geneva, Switzerland
	Portrait of Thomas Hart Benton unveiled by Harry S. Truman
1963	Commissioned by the Oklahoma State Legislature to paint three lifesize portraits: Governor Robert S. Kerr, Will Rogers, and Sequoyah. A fourth portrait of Jim Thorpe was later commissioned.
1969	Commissioned by the Oklahoma State Legislature to paint four murals for the Oklahoma state capitol building
1970	An article in *Oklahoma's Orbit* revealed the principal themes selected for the proposed murals: discovery and exploration; frontier trade; Indian immigration; and settlement
1971	Accepted invitation to England to assist in designs for First Americans, a medallion series issued by the Wedgwood pottery
1976	Accepted the first Governor's Art Award
	Oklahoma state capitol rotunda containing Wilson murals dedicated on November 16
1979	Received a Western Heritage Award from the National Cowboy Hall of Fame (now National Cowboy Hall of Fame and Western Heritage Museum)
	Subject of a documentary, *Roots of Oklahoma,* produced by the National Endowment for the Arts
1981	Exhibition of Wilson portraits sponsored by the Oklahoma State Society in Washington, D.C.
1984	Commissioned to paint portrait of Angie Debo
1983	*Search for the Purebloods* published
1988	*The Lithographs of Charles Banks Wilson* published
2001	Named an Oklahoma Cultural Treasure by the Oklahoma Arts Council